First World War
and Army of Occupation
War Diary
France, Belgium and Germany

38 DIVISION
Headquarters, Branches and Services
General Staff
1 July 1917 - 20 February 1919

WO95/2540/2

The Naval & Military Press Ltd
www.nmarchive.com
Published in association with The National Archives

Published by

The Naval & Military Press Ltd

Unit 10 Ridgewood Industrial Park,

Uckfield, East Sussex,

TN22 5QE England

Tel: +44 (0) 1825 749494

www.naval-military-press.com

www.nmarchive.com

This diary has been reprinted in facsimile from the original. Any imperfections are inevitably reproduced and the quality may fall short of modern type and cartographic standards.

© Crown Copyright
Images reproduced by permission of The National Archives, London, England, 2015.

Contents

Document type	Place/Title	Date From	Date To
War Diary	Norrent Fontes.	01/07/1917	19/07/1917
War Diary	Proven	19/07/1917	20/07/1917
War Diary	Rear H.Q. Dragon Camp.	21/07/1917	21/07/1917
War Diary	Advanced HQ Elverdinghe Chateau	22/07/1917	29/07/1917
War Diary	Rear H.Q. Dragon Camp.	30/07/1917	30/07/1917
War Diary	Adv. H.Q. Elverdinghe Chateau.	30/07/1917	30/07/1917
Miscellaneous	38th Division No. I.G./1026 A.G. Base.	06/10/1917	06/10/1917
War Diary	Elverdinghe Chateau.	31/07/1917	31/07/1917
War Diary	Elverdinghe	31/07/1917	01/08/1917
Miscellaneous	38th (Welsh) Division Operation Orders For Working On Generally Throughout The Training In July 1917	02/07/1917	02/07/1917
Map	Artillery Creeping Barrage Map.		
Operation(al) Order(s)	38th (Welsh) Division Order No. 105	10/07/1917	10/07/1917
Miscellaneous	March Table (To Accompany 38th Division Order No. 105)	10/07/1917	10/07/1917
Operation(al) Order(s)	Amendment To 38th Division Order No. 105	11/07/1917	11/07/1917
Operation(al) Order(s)	38th (Welsh) Division Order No. 106	11/07/1917	11/07/1917
Miscellaneous	March Table (To Accompany 38th (Welsh) Division Order No. 106)	11/07/1917	11/07/1917
Operation(al) Order(s)	38th Division No. G.S.6649	15/07/1917	15/07/1917
Miscellaneous	38th (Welsh) Division Operations. Division Order No. 107. Addendum No. 2. Issues of Maps.	16/07/1917	16/07/1917
Operation(al) Order(s)	38th (Welsh) Division Order No. 107	16/07/1917	16/07/1917
Operation(al) Order(s)	Distribution of Division Order No. 107		
Operation(al) Order(s)	Addenda To 38th (Welsh) Division Order No. 106	17/07/1917	17/07/1917
Miscellaneous	38th Division No. G.S.S. 58/22. 38th (Welsh) Division Operations. Division Order No. 107	17/07/1917	17/07/1917
Operation(al) Order(s)	38th (Welsh) Division Order No. 108	17/07/1917	17/07/1917
Operation(al) Order(s)	Move Table (To Accompany 38th Divn. Order No. 108)	17/07/1917	17/07/1917
Miscellaneous	A Form. Messages And Signals.		
Miscellaneous	38th Division No. G.S.6677	18/07/1917	18/07/1917
Miscellaneous	38th Div. No. G.S. 6695 Addendum No. 2 To 38th Division Order No. 108	19/07/1917	19/07/1917
Miscellaneous	38th Division No. G.S. 6698 Addendum No. 3 To 38th Division Order No. 108	20/07/1917	20/07/1917
Operation(al) Order(s)	38th Division No. G.S.S.58/25. 38th (Welsh) Division Order No. 107	23/07/1917	23/07/1917
Operation(al) Order(s)	38th Division No. G.S.S.70/1	22/07/1917	22/07/1917
Operation(al) Order(s)	38th (Welsh) Division Order No. 111	24/07/1917	24/07/1917
Miscellaneous	38th Division No. G.S.S. 58/32. 38th (Welsh) Division Operations. Division Order No. 112. Addendum No. 1	25/07/1917	25/07/1917
Operation(al) Order(s)	38th Division No. G.S.S. 58/29. 38th (Welsh) Division Operations. Division Order No. 107. Addendum No. 5	28/07/1917	28/07/1917
Operation(al) Order(s)	38th (Welsh) Division Order No. 112	25/07/1917	25/07/1917
Miscellaneous	C Form Messages And Signals.		
Operation(al) Order(s)	38th (Welsh) Division Order No. 114	25/07/1917	25/07/1917
Miscellaneous	Move Table (To Accompany 38th D.O. No. 114)	25/07/1917	25/07/1917
Operation(al) Order(s)	38th (Welsh) Division Order No. 116	27/07/1917	27/07/1917
Miscellaneous	38th Division No. G.S.6815	27/07/1917	27/07/1917

Type	Description	Date From	Date To
Operation(al) Order(s)	38th (Welsh) Division Order No. 113	25/07/1917	25/07/1917
Miscellaneous	38th Division No. G.S.6815	27/07/1917	27/07/1917
Operation(al) Order(s)	38th (Welsh) Division Order No. 115	27/07/1917	27/07/1917
Operation(al) Order(s)	38th (Welsh) Division Order No. 117	28/07/1917	28/07/1917
Miscellaneous	Operation Orders By Lieut Col, B.S. Phillpotts. D.S.O. Commanding Royal Engineers, 38th Division. Order No. 27	29/07/1917	29/07/1917
Operation(al) Order(s)	38th Division No. G.S.S. 58/44 38th Division Order No. 107 Addendum No. 7	30/07/1917	30/07/1917
War Diary	Elverdinghe Chateau.	01/08/1917	01/08/1917
Miscellaneous			
War Diary	Elverdinghe Chateau.	01/08/1917	01/08/1917
War Diary	Dragon Camp.	02/08/1917	05/08/1917
War Diary	Proven.	06/08/1917	16/08/1917
War Diary	Elverdinghe Chateau	01/08/1917	02/08/1917
War Diary	Elverdinghe	02/08/1917	02/08/1917
War Diary	Dragon Camp	03/08/1917	05/08/1917
War Diary	Proven	06/08/1917	18/08/1917
War Diary	Elverdinghe Chateau.	19/08/1917	31/08/1917
Miscellaneous	Action To Be taken In the Event Of SOS or enemy counter attack.		
Miscellaneous	38th Division No. G.S.6989. O.B./188 Fifth Army G.A. 213/6 XIV Corps No. G. 76/3	20/08/1917	20/08/1917
Miscellaneous	Ref Attached BM. 4142 No1 Included	20/08/1917	20/08/1917
Heading	On His Majesty's Service. Hurry 11 BM 4142 4145 4146		
Miscellaneous	38th Division No. G.S.S. 87/1	22/08/1917	22/08/1917
Miscellaneous	38th Division No. G.S. 7038 To Be Burnt After Being Read 113th Brigade.	23/08/1917	23/08/1917
Miscellaneous	Fifth Army No. G.A. 837/1 G.H.Q. No. G.A. 70. XIV Corps No G. 154/4 38th Division No. G.S. 7049	24/08/1917	24/08/1917
Miscellaneous	38th Division No. G.S.7136. 113th Brigade.	31/08/1917	31/08/1917
Miscellaneous	38th Division No. G.S. 6981 113th Brigade.	19/08/1917	19/08/1917
War Diary	Elverdinghe Chateau.	01/09/1917	11/09/1917
War Diary	Proven.	11/09/1917	12/09/1917
War Diary	La Gorgue.	13/09/1917	16/09/1917
War Diary	Croix Du Bac.	17/09/1917	30/09/1917
Operation(al) Order(s)	38th (Welsh) Division Order No. 128	02/09/1917	02/09/1917
Miscellaneous	38th Division No. G.S.7197 XIV Corps No. G. 55/2. 38th Division.	03/09/1917	03/09/1917
Miscellaneous	38th Division No. G.S.7197. XIVth Corps No. G. 55/2. 115th Bde. B.M.	03/09/1917	03/09/1917
Miscellaneous	Fifth Army. S.G.571/26	02/09/1917	02/09/1917
Miscellaneous	Fifth Army. S.G.671/26	02/09/1917	02/09/1917
War Diary	Croix Du Bac	01/10/1917	31/10/1917
Heading	General Staff. 38th Division November 1917 Vol 24		
Miscellaneous	File No. G.12. Minor Operation Proposed Raid by 11 N. Lanc. R. 120th Bde. 40th Div.		
War Diary	Croix Du Bac.	01/11/1917	30/11/1917
Miscellaneous	38th Division No. S.S.111/5	12/11/1917	12/11/1917
Miscellaneous	Narrative Of The Attack Of The Pilckem Ridge By The 38th (Welsh) Division.		
War Diary	Fifth Army G.A. 790/4 XIV Corps No. G. 44/3. 38th Division No. G.S. 6858. XIV Corps.		
Miscellaneous	H.Q., XIV Corps.	04/08/1917	04/08/1917
Miscellaneous	Fifth Army G.A. 657/275		

Miscellaneous	38th Division No. G.S.7197. XIVth Corps No. G. 55/2. 115th Bde. B.M.	04/09/1917	04/09/1917
Miscellaneous	38th Division No. G.S.6864. 113th Brigade.	04/08/1917	04/08/1917
Miscellaneous	XI Corps No. A.128/466 The G.O.C. 38th Division	12/08/1917	12/08/1917
Miscellaneous	Fifth Army No. G.A.837/1 G.H.Q. No. G.A. 70. XIV Corps No G. 154/4 38th Division No. G.S. 7049	24/08/1917	24/08/1917
Operation(al) Order(s)	38th (Welsh) Division Order No. 109		
Heading	General Staff. 38th Division. December 1917. Vol 25		
Heading	Cover for Documents. Nature of Enclosures. 113th, 114th, 115th Infantry Bde Orders		
War Diary	Croix Du Bac.	01/12/1917	30/12/1917
Heading	General Staff 38th Division January 1918 Vol 26		
Heading	Cover for Documents. Nature of Enclosures. 38th Div. Orders Instructions etc.16.8.18		
War Diary	Croix Du Bac.	01/01/1918	14/01/1918
War Diary	Merville.	15/01/1918	31/01/1918
Heading	General Staff. 38th Division February 1918. Vol.27		
Heading	Cover for Documents. Nature of Enclosures. 38 Div Arty Order V		
War Diary	Merville.	01/02/1918	15/02/1918
War Diary	Steenwerck.	16/02/1918	28/02/1918
Map	Map A.		
Map	Square T.		
Miscellaneous	Glossary		
Miscellaneous	Trench Map St. Julien. 28 N.W.2. Edition 5A		
Heading	General Staff. 38th Division March 1918. Vol.28		
Heading	Cover for Documents. Nature of Enclosures. CRE Orders etc		
War Diary	Steenwerck.	01/03/1918	30/03/1918
War Diary	Merville.	31/03/1918	31/03/1918
Heading	General Staff 38th (Welch) Division April 1918 Report On Operations 19th To 25th April 1918. Operation Orders.		
War Diary	Merville.	01/04/1918	01/04/1918
War Diary	Toutencourt.	01/04/1918	11/04/1918
War Diary	Contay.	12/04/1918	30/04/1918
Operation(al) Order(s)	38th (Welsh) Division Order No. 168 Appendix 1	02/04/1918	02/04/1918
Miscellaneous	Messages And Signals. Appendix 2		
Miscellaneous	Messages And Signals. 113th Brigade. Appendix 3		
Miscellaneous	Messages And Signals. 113th Brigade. Appendix 4		
Miscellaneous	Messages And Signals. 113th Bde. Appendix 5		
Operation(al) Order(s)	38th (Welsh) Division Order No. 169 Appendix 6	10/04/1918	10/04/1918
Miscellaneous	Table Of Reliefs And Moves To Accompany 38th Div Order No 169	10/04/1918	10/04/1918
Miscellaneous	Messages And Signals 113th Brigade. Appendix 7		
Miscellaneous	38th (Welsh) Division Order No. 170 Appendix 8	18/04/1918	18/04/1918
Operation(al) Order(s)	Amendment No. 1 To 38th Division Order No. 171 Appendix 9	20/04/1918	20/04/1918
Operation(al) Order(s)	38th (Welsh) Division Order No. 171	20/04/1918	20/04/1918
Miscellaneous	Table Of Machine Gun Action. (38th Divn. Order. No. 171.)	20/04/1918	20/04/1918
Operation(al) Order(s)	Amendment No. 2 to Divisional Order No. 171	21/04/1918	21/04/1918
Miscellaneous	Messages And Signals. Appendix 10		
Operation(al) Order(s)	38th (Welsh) Division Order No. 172	23/04/1918	23/04/1918
Miscellaneous	Relief Table Issued With 38th Division Order No. 172	23/04/1918	23/04/1918
Operation(al) Order(s)	38th (Welsh) Division Order No. 172	23/04/1918	23/04/1918

Miscellaneous	Relief Table Issued With 38th Division Order No. 172	23/04/1918	23/04/1918
Miscellaneous	C Form. Messages And Signals.		
Miscellaneous	Report On Operations, 38th (Welsh) Division Period 19th April-25th April (Both Inclusive).	26/04/1918	26/04/1918
Operation(al) Order(s)	38th (Welsh) Division Order No. 173. Appendix 11	25/04/1918	25/04/1918
Operation(al) Order(s)	38th (Welsh) Division Order No. 174. Appendix 12	26/04/1918	26/04/1918
Miscellaneous	Relief Table Issued With 38th Division Order No. 174		
Miscellaneous	38th Division No. GSS 10/63/1. 113th Brigade. Warning Order For Relief Of 35th Division. Appendix 13		
Operation(al) Order(s)	38th Division No. GSS. 10/63 Amendment No. 1 To 38th (Welsh) Division Order No. 175. Appendix 14	29/04/1918	29/04/1918
Operation(al) Order(s)	38th (Welsh) Division Order No. 175	29/04/1918	29/04/1918
Miscellaneous	Relief Table To Accompany 38th Division Order No. 175	29/04/1918	29/04/1918
Miscellaneous	Central Registry. Subject and Office of Origin.		
Miscellaneous			
Miscellaneous	Not To Be Written On.		
Miscellaneous	C Form. Messages And Signals.		
Miscellaneous	4th Corps. G.B 268		
Heading	Cover for Documents. Nature of Enclosures. 113 Inf Bde Orders		
Heading	General Staff. 38th Division May 1918 Vol.30		
War Diary	Contay.	01/05/1918	06/05/1918
War Diary	Toutencourt	06/05/1918	19/05/1918
War Diary	Herissart.	20/05/1918	31/05/1918
Miscellaneous	Statement By Liaison Officer, 157 Bde. R.F.A.	10/05/1918	10/05/1918
Miscellaneous	38th Div. G. Report On Operation By 114th Infantry Brigade 10th May 1918	10/05/1918	10/05/1918
Miscellaneous	V Corps Report On Operations For Week Ending 16/5/1918 Appendix V.	16/05/1918	16/05/1918
Heading	114 Inf Bde Orders		
Heading	General Staff. 38th Division June 1918 Vol.31		
War Diary	Herissart.	01/06/1918	05/06/1918
War Diary	Lealvillers.	05/06/1918	30/06/1918
Miscellaneous	38th Division No. GSS. 2/33 V Corps Report On Operations For Week Ending 13/6/1918	13/06/1918	13/06/1918
Miscellaneous	38th Division No. GSS. 2/33. V Corps Report On Operations For Week Ending 20/6/18	20/06/1918	20/06/1918
Miscellaneous	38th Division No. GSS. 2/33. V Corps Report On Operations For Week Ending 26/6/18	26/06/1918	26/06/1918
Heading	General Staff. 38th Division July 1918 Vol.32		
Heading	Cover for Documents. Nature of Enclosures. 115 Inf Bde Orders		
War Diary	Lealvillers.	01/07/1918	31/07/1918
Miscellaneous	Weekly Report On Operations Week Ending 10th July 1918	10/07/1918	10/07/1918
Operation(al) Order(s)	Operation Order No. 171 2nd Battalion Royal Welsh Fusiliers.	10/07/1918	10/07/1918
Miscellaneous	Report On Raid Carried Out By 24 R.W.F. On Night Of 11-12 July 1918	11/07/1918	11/07/1918
Miscellaneous	Adjt. Dosa. Report on Raid "B" Co.	13/07/1918	13/07/1918
Miscellaneous	Adjt. Dosa		
Miscellaneous	Report on Raid From C Company Right Assaulting Company.	11/07/1918	11/07/1918
Miscellaneous	To Adj Dosa Report on Raid.	12/07/1918	12/07/1918

Miscellaneous	Adjt. Dosa Report on Raid "A" Coy.	13/07/1918	13/07/1918
Miscellaneous	Report On Raid Of Hamel Village By 2nd. Bn. Royal Welsh Fusiliers On Night 11th/12th July.	11/07/1918	11/07/1918
Miscellaneous	Notes & Lessons.	14/07/1918	14/07/1918
Map	Map. "B". Appendix C		
Miscellaneous	Raid By 2nd. R.W.F.		
Map	Hamel Section-Sheet 57D S.E		
Miscellaneous	115th Infty. Bde. B.M. 9206. 38th Division.	14/07/1918	14/07/1918
Miscellaneous	Report On Raid Of Hamel Village By 2nd. Bn. Royal Welsh Fusiliers On Night 11th/12th July.	11/07/1918	11/07/1918
Miscellaneous	Notes & Lessons.	14/07/1918	14/07/1918
Miscellaneous	Our Artillery. Appendix A		
Map	Enlarged from Sheet 57D S.E.		
Miscellaneous	Weekly Report On Operations Week Ending 17th July 1918	17/07/1918	17/07/1918
Miscellaneous	Headquarters 38th. (Welsh) Division.	23/06/1918	23/06/1918
Heading	HQ GS38D Dupl Aug 18		
Heading	D.A.G. G.H.Q 3rd Echelon		
War Diary	Lealvillers.	01/08/1918	24/08/1918
War Diary	Hedauville.	24/08/1918	25/08/1918
War Diary	Usna Redoubt.	25/08/1918	26/08/1918
War Diary	Contalmaison.	26/08/1918	31/08/1918
War Diary	West Of High Wood.	31/08/1918	31/08/1918
Map	Map X		
Operation(al) Order(s)	38th Divisional Artillery O.O. No. 72	14/08/1918	14/08/1918
Operation(al) Order(s)	38th (Welsh) Division Order No. 201	15/08/1918	15/08/1918
Miscellaneous	Amendment No. 1 to D.O.201	15/08/1918	15/08/1918
Miscellaneous	38th Division No. GSS. 1/18/2. 113th Brigade.	16/08/1918	16/08/1918
Operation(al) Order(s)	38th Division Royal Engineers Operation Order No 66	15/08/1918	15/08/1918
Operation(al) Order(s)	38th (Welsh) Division Order No. 205	20/08/1918	20/08/1918
Operation(al) Order(s)	38th (Welsh) Division Order No. 206	20/08/1918	20/08/1918
Map	Tracing To Accompany 38th Div. O.206		
Operation(al) Order(s)	38th (Welsh) Division Order No. 206	20/08/1918	20/08/1918
Operation(al) Order(s)	38th Divisional Artillery Operation Order No. 77	21/08/1918	21/08/1918
Operation(al) Order(s)	38th (Welsh) Division Order No. 209	21/08/1918	21/08/1918
Operation(al) Order(s)	38th (Welsh) Division Order No. 208	21/08/1918	21/08/1918
Operation(al) Order(s)	38th (Welsh) Division Order No. 207	21/08/1918	21/08/1918
Miscellaneous	Appendix 8 Headquarters.	20/08/1918	20/08/1918
Miscellaneous	Appendix 7		
Miscellaneous	Appendix 6. Prisoners Of War And Battle Straggler Posts		
Miscellaneous	Appendix 4		
Miscellaneous	Appendix 3		
Operation(al) Order(s)	115th Brigade Order No. 258	22/08/1918	22/08/1918
Operation(al) Order(s)	38th Divisional Artillery Operation Order No. 79	22/08/1918	22/08/1918
Miscellaneous			
Miscellaneous	38th (Welsh) Division Order No. 210	22/08/1918	22/08/1918
Operation(al) Order(s)	38th (Welsh) Division Order No. 212	22/08/1918	22/08/1918
Diagram etc	Map "A"		
Miscellaneous	Table "A"		
Miscellaneous			
Miscellaneous	38th Divisional Artillery Operation Order No. 78	22/08/1918	22/08/1918
Miscellaneous			
Operation(al) Order(s)	114th Infantry Brigade Order No. 197	22/08/1918	22/08/1918
Operation(al) Order(s)	38th (Welsh) Division Order No. 211	22/08/1918	22/08/1918
Miscellaneous	38th (Welsh) Division Order No. 211	22/08/1918	22/08/1918

Type	Description	Date From	Date To
Operation(al) Order(s)	38th (Welsh) Division Order No. 211	22/08/1918	22/08/1918
Map	Map "A"		
Miscellaneous	Table "A".		
Miscellaneous	38th Division Royal Engineers C.R.E's Operation Order No. 67	23/08/1918	23/08/1918
Operation(al) Order(s)	38th Divisional Artillery Operation Order No. 81	23/08/1918	23/08/1918
Operation(al) Order(s)	38th (Welsh) Division Order No. 213	23/08/1918	23/08/1918
Miscellaneous	38th (Welsh) Division. Tactical Instructions In Connection With D.O.213		
Miscellaneous	38th Division No. GSS 1/13 38th (Welsh) Division. Warning Order.	28/08/1918	28/08/1918
Operation(al) Order(s)	38th. Divisional Artillery Operation Order No. 80	23/08/1918	23/08/1918
Miscellaneous	HQ GS 38 D Vol 33 Sep 18		
Miscellaneous	DAG 3rd Echelon		
War Diary	West Of High Wood.	01/09/1918	03/09/1918
War Diary	Les Boeufs.	04/09/1918	11/09/1918
War Diary	Etricourt.	12/09/1918	21/09/1918
War Diary	Lechelle.	22/09/1918	29/09/1918
War Diary	V.18.c.1.9. 57 C.	29/09/1918	30/09/1918
Operation(al) Order(s)	38th (Welsh) Division Order No. 228	11/09/1918	11/09/1918
Miscellaneous	3rd New Zealand (Rifle) Order, No. 180	11/09/1918	11/09/1918
Operation(al) Order(s)	Appendix No. I To 3rd N.Z. (Rifle) Bde.		
Operation(al) Order(s)	38th (Welsh) Division Order No. 229	13/09/1918	13/09/1918
Operation(al) Order(s)	38th (Welsh) Division Order No. 230	15/09/1918	15/09/1918
Operation(al) Order(s)	Addendum No. 1 To 38th (Welsh) Division Order No. 230	15/09/1918	15/09/1918
Miscellaneous	Messages And Signals.		
Miscellaneous	C Form. Messages And Signals.		
Miscellaneous	A Form Messages And Signals.		
Map	France Map To Accompany 38th Div. O. No. 231		
Miscellaneous	BM 1120 16/9/18 B.G.C. R.M.	16/09/1918	16/09/1918
Miscellaneous	115th Infantry Brigade. B.M. 1088. 38th Division. Notes On Recent Fighting.	26/09/1918	26/09/1918
Operation(al) Order(s)	38th (Welsh) Division Order No. 231	15/09/1918	15/09/1918
Operation(al) Order(s)	GSS. 1/22/A. Amendment No. 1 To 38th (Welsh) Division Order No. 231	16/09/1918	16/09/1918
Operation(al) Order(s)	GSS. 1/22/A. Amendment No. 2 To 38th (Welsh) Division Order No. 231	16/09/1918	16/09/1918
Miscellaneous	B.M. 1176	17/09/1918	17/09/1918
Miscellaneous	Ref: Vth Corps Letter No. G.X.4223 Of 30.8.18	30/08/1918	30/08/1918
Miscellaneous	38th Division No. GSS. 1/22	17/09/1918	17/09/1918
Miscellaneous	B.M. 1167	17/09/1918	17/09/1918
Miscellaneous	38th Division No. GSS. 1/22/A. 113th Brigade.	17/09/1918	17/09/1918
Miscellaneous Diagram etc	Instructions For Signal Communications.		
Miscellaneous	Instructions For Signal Communications.	15/09/1918	15/09/1918
Operation(al) Order(s)	Reference 38th Division Order No. 231. Medical Arrangements.	16/09/1918	16/09/1918
Miscellaneous	BM 1123 16-9-18	16/09/1918	16/09/1918
Miscellaneous	38th Division No. 2/54. 113th Brigade.	21/09/1918	21/09/1918
Miscellaneous	H.Q. 115 Bde Ref. Your B.M. No 1088 of 12/9/18	12/09/1918	12/09/1918
Heading	S.S.143/I 2nd American Corps Orders & Instrns.		
Map	France		
Heading	S.S.143/I 2nd American Corps Orders & Instrns.		

Operation(al) Order(s)	2nd Corps Memorandum G-3 No. 1. 2nd American Corps France, 28th Sept. 18 Instructions For Operations Section No. 14	29/09/1918	29/09/1918
Heading	War Diary. G.S. 38th Division. October 1918		
Miscellaneous	Subject.		
Heading	Volume IV Comments On Chapter V		
Heading	HQ GS 38 D Vol 34 V Corps October 1918		
War Diary		01/10/1918	04/10/1918
War Diary	Epehy.	04/10/1918	07/10/1918
War Diary	Hindenburg Line.	08/10/1918	10/10/1918
War Diary	Villers Outreaux.	10/10/1918	10/10/1918
War Diary	Clary.	11/10/1918	11/10/1918
War Diary	Bertry.	11/10/1918	23/10/1918
War Diary	Dugouts on S. Side of Inchy Le Cateau Road.	23/10/1918	24/10/1918
War Diary	Montay.	24/10/1918	25/10/1918
War Diary	Richemont.	25/10/1918	31/10/1918
Miscellaneous	38th Division No. GSS. 2/33. Summary Of Operations, October 5th To 11th Inclusive.	05/10/1918	05/10/1918
Heading	Cover for Documents. Nature of Enclosures. H.145 Gas Operation 14/15 Octr		
Miscellaneous	C Form. Messages And Signals.		
Miscellaneous	33rd Division "G" Reference Operation GN/18	13/10/1918	13/10/1918
Miscellaneous	Precautions To Be Taken During Projector Gas Attack		
Map	33rd Division Sheet 57B (Part Of) K Scale 1/10,000		
Miscellaneous	38th Division "G" Reference Operation GN/18	13/10/1918	13/10/1918
Miscellaneous	Precautions To Be Taken During Projector Gas Attack.		
Map	V Corps 38th Division Sheet 57B (Part Of) K Scale 1/10,000		
Miscellaneous	38th Division No. S.S.145. 115th Brigade.	13/10/1918	13/10/1918
Miscellaneous	C Form Messages And Signals		
Miscellaneous	A Form Messages And Signals.		
Miscellaneous	R.A., 38th. Div. No. G.S.309/28	14/10/1918	14/10/1918
Miscellaneous	A Form Messages And Signals.		
Miscellaneous	38th Division	13/10/1918	13/10/1918
Miscellaneous	Messages & Signals. To 115th Brigade.		
Miscellaneous	Special Companies, R.E., Third Army.	18/10/1918	18/10/1918
Miscellaneous	C Form (Original) Messages And Signals.		
Miscellaneous	A Form Messages And Signals.		
Miscellaneous	38th Division GSS. 2/23/1. Appendix To Report On Operations 23/10/18 To 30/10/18	23/10/1918	23/10/1918
Miscellaneous	38th Division No. GSS. 2/23/1. V Corps. Report On Operations 23/10/18 To 30/10/18	23/10/1918	23/10/1918
Map	Map Showing Information From Photos Taken 14-10-18		
Map	Corps Topo. Section Reference. Parts Of 57c & 62c		
Heading	The D.A.G. 3rd Echelon B.E. Force.		
Heading	General Staff. 38th Division November 1918 Vol.36		
Heading	Cover for Documents. Nature of Enclosures. GSC 1/22/J 38 Bn M.G.C. Orders		
War Diary	Richemont.	01/11/1918	04/11/1918
War Diary	Englefontaine.	05/11/1918	05/11/1918
War Diary	Locquignol.	05/11/1918	19/11/1918
War Diary	Aulnoye.	20/11/1918	30/11/1918
Heading	General Staff. 38th Division December 1918 Vol 37		
Heading	Registered The Officer To A.G's Office The Base ?		
Miscellaneous			

War Diary	Aulnoye.	01/12/1918	30/12/1918
War Diary	Inchy.	30/12/1918	30/12/1918
War Diary	Glissy.	31/12/1918	31/12/1918
War Diary		01/01/1919	20/02/1919

ORIGINAL

WAR DIARY of GENERAL STAFF 38TH (WELSH) DIVISION   Army Form C. 2118.

or

INTELLIGENCE SUMMARY.   VOLUME XX.

(Erase heading not required.)

Instructions regarding War Diaries and Intelligence Summaries are contained in F.S. Regs., Part II. and the Staff Manual respectively. Title pages will be prepared in manuscript.

Place	Date	Hour	Summary of Events and Information	Remarks and references to Appendices
NORRENT FONTES.	JULY. 1917.			
	1st.		General Staff and C. R. E. laid out replica of trenches on training ground. Company and Platoon Training.	
	2nd.		Battalion Training. Field Company R. E. continued preparation of training area.	
	3rd.		Battalions digging trenches on training area. Musketry. Field Company completed the marking out of the ground.	
	4th.		General Staff visited Gas and Projector demonstration at ELNAUT. Corps Commander visited Brigades at training.	
	5th.		Conference of Divisional Commanders at Corps Headquarters. Brigade Training.	
	6th.		G.O.C. visited Brigades practising on replica of trenches. Hostile aeroplane raid on AIRE and ISBERQUES. Conference of Brigadiers at Divisional Headquarters.	
	7th.		G.O.C. visited brigades at training. Demonstration on Training Area of different types of Aeroplanes.	
	8th.		Brigades did 2 hours drill in Billeting Area. Rest of day Brigade and Battalion Sports.	
	9th.		113th Infantry Brigade practised attack over replica of trenches between 9.a.m. and 1.p.m. 114th Infantry Brigade ditto from 1.p.m. to 5.p.m. 115th Infantry Brigade Musketry and drill.	
	10th.		Brigade Training over replica of trenches. (Move of Division to PROVEN AREA. O.O.106 issued.	Copy
	11th.		176th Machine Gun Company gave demonstration of barrage fire on Training Area. Brigade training.	
	12th.		At 9.a.m. attack over replica of trenches. 113th Infantry Brigade on the Left, 114th Infantry Brigade on the Right, with 115th Infantry Brigade in Reserve, 1 Field Company and R.A.M.C. took part.	
	13th.		114th Infantry Brigade Sports, etc. 113th Infantry Brigade attack by Companies over replica trenches. 115th Infantry Brigade attack over replica.	
	14th.		115th Infantry Brigade field firing. 113th Infantry Brigade rest. 114th Infantry Brigade training.	
	15th.		Half 113th Infantry Brigade and 114th Infantry Brigade move by bus to HAZEBROUCK AREA. (See O.O.106).	
	16th.		Half 113th Infantry Brigade and 114th Infantry Brigade move by road. (See O.O.106). Operation Orders issued for the attack of the 38th (Welsh) Division on the PILCKEM RIDGE. O.O.107.	Copy
	17th.		Brigades on the move towards PROVEN, except Half 113th and 114th Infantry Brigades.	
	18th.		"B" Group of Brigades and 115th Infantry Brigade on the move to the PROVEN AREA.	
	19th.		113th Infantry Brigade move to Corps Staging Area.	
PROVEN.			Divisional Headquarters move to PROVEN. See (O.O.106). Divisional Commander and G. S. O. 1. attended Corps Conference.	/20th.

Army Form C. 2118.

WAR DIARY
or
INTELLIGENCE SUMMARY.

(Erase heading not required.)

Page 2.

Place	Date	Hour	Summary of Events and Information	Remarks and references to Appendices
PROVEN.– Rear H.Q. DRAGON CAMP.	JULY 1917. 20th 21st.		Divisional Headquarters move from PROVEN to DRAGON CAMP. (O.O.108). 113th and 114th Infantry Brigades take over the ZWAANHOF SECTOR from 29th Division. (O.O.108). Our bombardment continued. At 6.p.m. our artillery put up a 15 minutes barrage. Practically no bombardment. Enemy engaged CANAL BANK and back areas during the night.20/21st.	App 3.
Advanced HQ ELVERDINGHE CHATEAU	22nd.		During the night 21/22nd July enemy engaged back areas, especially Track 10. A deserter of the 392 I.R. came over to our lines at 6.30.a.m. Guards Division (on our left) carried out a bombardment at 3.30.p.m. Hostile artillery less active during the day.	App 4.
	23rd.		Hostile artillery continued active at nights on roads and tracks. Our battery positions being engaged with gas shells. Our bombardment continues. Our raiding party found enemy holding shell holes in front of front line trench.	
	24th.		Our bombardment continues satisfactorily. Corps Commanders Conference with Divisional Commander, Brigadiers, and Company Commanders regarding holding the line. G.O.C., 20th Division and G.S.O.3. 38th Division went up to SIGNAL COT.	App 5.
	25th.		38th Division attempted a daylight raid on the hostile trenches, under a barrage. No enemy were found in the front line trenches, but the party was fired at from shell holes between front and support line. (O.O. 110 issued).24th.	App 6.
	26th.		Bombardment continued steadily. At 12 midnight 26/27th we attempted to raid the enemy's trenches under a barrage, but were met with strong opposition. Orders issued to Battalion Reliefs. (O.O. 114).	App 7.
	27th.		Air reconnaissance reported no enemy within 1200 yards of our trenches. Orders issued to send out patrols at 5.p.m. (O.O. 115 issued). Patrols met with strong opposition from shell holes, and had to withdraw: eventually we joined up the left from the north of BAIRD TRENCH in front of FARM 14, linking up with the Guards Division. 113th and 114th Infantry Brigades took over Battle Fronts at 2.p.m.(See O.S. 6815 attached).	
	28th.		O.O. 116 issued regarding practice barrage on whole Army front on 28th July. Intercepted wireless message ordering 2 German harassing fire and bombardment continues. counter attacks on Guards Division front: one battalion was seen advancing through ABRI WOOD and were immediately engaged by our artillery. No counter attack was attempted.	App. 8
	29th.		O.O. 117 issued regarding defensive measures for 38th Division. Our bombardment continues. Very few of the enemy were very little hostile artillery. Our patrols were out all day in the direction of CACTUS JUNCTION. A party of the seen and Germans were seen to enter GRANDE BARRIERE HOUSE and a 15" obtained a direct hit.	App. 9

WAR DIARY
or
INTELLIGENCE SUMMARY.

Page 3.

(Erase heading not required.)

Army Form C. 2118.

Place	Date	Hour	Summary of Events and Information	Remarks and references to Appendices
Rear H.Q. DRAGON CAMP.— Adv.H.Q. ELVERDINGHE CHATEAU.	JULY 1917. 30th.	5.p.m.	Little hostile activity on Divisional front. Occasional shots on east CANAL BANK. Our bombardment increased during the day. Searching and harassing fire during the night. Advanced Divisional Headquarters proceeded from DRAGON CAMP to ELVERDINGHE CHATEAU. Concentration marches completed.	

Wharington Capt.
for Lieut-Colonel,
General Staff 38th (Welsh) Division.

25/9/17.

S E C R E T   38th Division No.I.G.1026

A. G., Base.

       Herewith last 5 pages of War Diary of the GENERAL STAFF 38TH (WELSH) DIVISION, for the month of JULY 1917, which were ommitted from this office No.I.G.971 dated 25/9/17.

6/10/17.
                           Major-General,
              Commanding 38th (Welsh) Division.

Army Form C. 2118.

WAR DIARY
of
INTELLIGENCE SUMMARY.
(Erase heading not required.)

HEADQUARTERS, 38TH (WELSH) DIVISION.

Instructions regarding War Diaries and Intelligence Summaries are contained in F. S. Regs., Part II. and the Staff Manual respectively. Title pages will be prepared in manuscript.

Place	Date	Hour	Summary of Events and Information	Remarks and references to Appendices
ELVERDINGHE CHATEAU.	31st JULY 1917	2-54.a.m.	3 Infantry Brigades report Dispositions complete by 2-54.a.m.	
		3-50.a.m.	Zero hour.	
		4-12.a.m.	Right Group report no shelling on front line. Light barrage on Canal.	
		4-30.a.m.	Left Group report hostile barrage slack. Right Group report hostile rockets sent up from well back.	
		4-40.a.m.	Report from 114th Brigade that Left front Coy. 13th Welsh had reached objective with no opposition. No news from 113th Brigade.	
		4-58.a.m.	Few gas shells heard in direction of FLORENS FARM.	
		5-7.a.m.	114th Brigade report 1st prisoner captured of 392nd Regt.	
		5-10.a.m.	115th Brigade report 11 bridges complete over canal.	
		5-21.a.m.	113th Brigade report 13th R.W.F. captured BLUE LINE and in touch with 16th R.W.F. At 5-22.a.m. capture of BLUE LINE confirmed by F.O.O. Everything going well.	
		5-25.a.m.	F.O.O. AT EOLIAN FARM reports everything up to time. Little hostile fire and practically no resistance. Many prisoners.	
		5-30.a.m.	Two prisoners of 392nd Rgt. and one of 3rd Gds. Res. Div: captured by 114th Brigade.	
		5-35.a.m.	Report from 114th Brigade - 10th Welsh have taken CANDLE TRENCH and re-organisation going on. Prisoners going back in considerable numbers. Casualties moderate. One prisoner of 8th Coy. LEHR REGT. 15th Welsh Regt. consolidating CANDLE TRENCH.	
		5-49.a.m.	113th Brigade reports CANCER TRENCH reached 5-50.a.m. Enemy barrage on New Line and our Support.Line. Prisoners captured belong to Gds.Fus.,3rd Gds.Res.Div: who have been in line two days.	
		5-45.a.m.	10th Welsh (114th Brigade) report to have taken CAESARS SUPPORT and RESERVE and CHEMIN TR. Confusion owing to loss of direction. Attack proceeding successfully on CANDLE. Few casualties. 15th Welsh gone through to CANDLE TRENCH.	
		5-47.a.m.	38th Div: Arty report our Infantry are over CANCER and CANDLE TRENCHES.	

WAR DIARY

HEADQUARTERS, 38TH (WELSH) DIVISION.

Army Form C. 2118.

Page 5

INTELLIGENCE SUMMARY.

(Erase heading not required.)

Place	Date	Hour	Summary of Events and Information	Remarks and references to Appendices
ELVERDINGHE	31st July 1917	5-50.a.m.	113th Brigade report (by phone) 7 prisoners of 392 Regt. and Guards Fusiliers.	
		5-50.a.m.	Aeroplane map received by XIV Corps suggests BLUE LINE captured. Only portion not marked being CARIBOO TRENCH. Capture of CANDLE and CANCER TRENCH confirmed.	
		6-10.a.m.	XIV Corps report uncertain whether CACTUS AVENUE held by us.	
		6-15.a.m.	13th R.W.F. report having seen their troops enter PILCKEM and go over Ridge.	
		6-20.a.m.	113th Brigade also state uncertain that CACTUS AVENUE is held. Told to verify and capture same if necessary (Telephone)	
		6-30.a.m.	113th Brigade report BLUE LINE being consolidated at 6-30.a.m. R.F.Parties gone forward.	
		6-30.a.m.	Int.9th Sqn.R.F.C. report (phone) Our troops near CACTUS AVENUE and CACTUS RESERVE at 5-30.a.m. No enemy seen in CADDIE POINT. (113th Brigade informed 6-51.a.m.) (Phone)	
		6-36.a.m.	113th Brigade report BLACK LINE captured.	
		6-45.a.m.	Colonel RUDKIN (Right Group) reports on phone message from Infantry (visual) BLACK LINE reached 6-40.a.m.	
		6-57.a.m.	F.O.O. at MARSOUIN reports BLACK LINE taken and pretty well dug-in. Not much opposition. Outposts are out.	
		7-50.a.m.	114th Brigade report BLACK LINE captured at 7.a.m.	
		7-45.a.m.	Aeroplane map shows 13th Welsh H.Q. CHEMIN TR., 16th R.W.F. H.Q. at LIEVRE CABT.	
		8-7.a.m.	F.O.O. at PILCKEM MILL at 7-30.a.m. reports Infantry on the way to GREEN LINE. Few casualties and a few prisoners. Same F.O.O. reports at 8.a.m. our Infantry at IRON CROSS.	
		8.a.m.	Tree O.P. reports Infantry pack horses have crossed trench at CORNER HOUSE.	
		8-10.a.m. (Time not certain)	Aeroplane map shows leading Infantry 500 yds. West of IRON CROSS.	
		8-15.a.m.	(Phone) 115th Brigade reports 11th S.W.B. at CADDIE RESERVE at 6-27.a.m. All other units reported at 6-45.a.m. at German front line except 16th Welsh Regt.	
		8-15.a.m.	115th Bde. message reports 17th R.W.F. crossing German Front line at 6-45.a.m. and 10th S.W.B. arrived KIEL COT. at sametime.	
		8-14.a.m.	113th Brigade reports 13th R.W.F. relieved 16th R.W.F. on BLACK LINE and BLUE LINE. Two Companies 16th R.W.F. gone forward in support of 15th R.W.F. and two Coys. 16th R.W.F. in hand near CHIMNEY HOUSE. Germans running before our barrage. 60 Germans sent back prisoners.	
		8-25.a.m.	(Phone) F.O.O. reports from CANDLE SUPPORT,GREEN LINE taken with slight casualties. German resistance feeble. Enemy counter-attacking. Our Cavalry patrols seen going North.	
		8-30.a.m.	Visual message picked up by CANAL BANK O.P.	
		8-35.a.m.	51st Div: Arty phones - Left Inf.Brigade (51st Div) is held up at BLACK LINE.	
		8-35.a.m.	Message from 114th Bde. - 14th Welsh report 7-12.a.m. Bn.H.Q. at C.8.b.5.9. BLACK LINE being consolidated. Two companies ready to move forward under barrage.	

Army Form C. 2118.

Page 6

WAR DIARY
or
INTELLIGENCE SUMMARY

HEADQUARTERS, 38TH (WELSH) DIVISION.

(Erase heading not required.)

Instructions regarding War Diaries and Intelligence Summaries are contained in F. S. Regs., Part II. and the Staff Manual respectively. Title pages will be prepared in manuscript.

Place	Date	Hour	Summary of Events and Information	Remarks and references to Appendices
ELVERDINGHE	31st July.	8-44.a.m.	115th Bde. phone message - Gen. PRICE-DAVIES has gone to VILLA GRETCHEN. Practically certain GREEN LINE taken. Germans running away from our barrage.	
		8-47.a.m.	114th Brigade message - 3 Companies 13th Welsh consolidating CANDLE TR. 1 Coy. being re-organised.	
		9-15.a.m.	Div:Intelligence Officer reports that prisoners of 3rd Bn. Guards Fusiliers taken. They were brought up to hold the CANDLE TRENCH Line. We have broken up the crack Regiment of the German Army, nicknamed the "BERLIN COCKCHAFERS".	
		9-12.a.m.	Report by runner from PERISCOPE HOUSE (sent on by phone) At 8-35.a.m. practically no hostile fire of any kind on our Infantry.	
			38th D.A. telephone message - Canal Bank O.P. reports 8-50.a.m. (delayed) - Hostile fire very light. Hostile artillery spreading their fire promiscuously.	
		9-30.a.m.	115th Bde. asked on phone if troops are moving towards STEENBEEK. (Probably Forward Station)	
		9-35.a.m.	Phone message - 115th Brigade moving up towards 114th Stn. (Probably Forward Station)	
		9-44.a.m.	115th Brigade report. GREEN LINE taken. 115th Brigade have passed through. 77.mm.Bty. and M.G's causing considerable trouble from position 50 from C.2.d.20.95. All the fire seems to be coming from the left front. In touch with troops on Right and Left on GREEN LINE. Casualties not very heavy.	
		10-5.a.m.	Phone message. Germans put down barrage of 4.2 on CADDIE TRENCH. 5 rounds to a minute. (From R.A.)	
		10-20.a.m.	B.M.115th Bde. phones - Div:Liaison Officer from 115th Bde. killed. subsequently found to be wounded.	
		10-25.a.m.	XIX Corps report whole of GREEN LINE captured and in touch with 51st Div; on right and French Corps on Left.	
		10-40.am.	114th Brigade message. - 14th Welsh report enemy shelling heavily in front of STRAY FARM and IRON CROSS. 2 Companies pushing on in front of STRAY FARM.	
		10-55.a.m.	114th Brigade report Advanced Bde.H.Q. established in THE NILE C.13.d.55.70.	
		11-30.am.	(R.A.) phone message) F.O.O. reported at 11-30.a.m. from STRAY FARM that he had been 500 yds. North of THE INGS and close to STEENBEEK. As far as he could see we had affected crossing. Cavalry not up. Our losses slight. Situation comparatively quiet. Most of the shelling coming from U.21. and U.22.	
		11-30.a.m.	Message from 114th Bde. 14th Welsh digging in 50 yds. in front of IRON CROSS with 2 Coys. Remaining 2 Coys sent up to reinforce. Bn.H.Q.C.8.b.3.9. H.Q.15th Welsh at C.8.b.2.4. 15th Welsh have 3 Coys. consolidating BLACK LINE.— CANDLE SUPPORT and CANDLE TRENCH. H.Q.13th Welsh C.8.c.05.60. 10th Welsh assisting 15 Welsh - remainder carrying. Enemy shelling IRON CROSS - CANDLE TRENCH H.Q.10th Welsh CHEMIN TR. Slight confusion reported. Considerable number of enemy dead; several parties of prisoners; one party numbering 100.	

WAR DIARY HEADQUARTERS, 38TH (WELSH) DIVISION.

INTELLIGENCE SUMMARY.

(Erase heading not required.)

Army Form C. 2118.

Page 7.

Place	Date	Hour	Summary of Events and Information	Remarks and references to Appendices
ELVERDINGHE	31st July	11-55.a.m.	113th Brigade report at 10-55.a.m. 15th R.W.F. with 2 Companies on front of GREEN Line and 2 in support. 17th R.W.F. reports hung up by M.G. fire. Tank seen going over IRON CROSS Ridge on Right of Div: 15th R.W.F. consolidating from PERISCOPE HOUSE to about C.5.c.0.8. near CANDLE AVENUE in touch with 14th Welsh. GREEN Line being heavily shelled.	
		12-15.p.m.	(R.A. phones message) F.O.O. near CANAL BANK reports Hostile fire increasing everywhere notably round PILCKEM.	
		12-25.p.m.	19th (Pnr) Bn.Welsh Regt. report ARTILLERY TRACK from HUDDLESTON X RDS. to BOSCHE HO. ready for Field guns at 11-55.a.m.	
		12-24.p.m.	122nd Brigade R.F.A. ordered forward.	
		12-25.p.m.	Corps report capture of Line of STEENBEEK confirmed by Arty. F.O.O.	
		12-28.p.m.	113th Brigade reports 15th R.W.F. consolidating satisfactorily on GREEN Line. Left Coy. just behind Road running through U.27.c and C.3.a. Right Coy. 500 yds. in front of this Rd. En touch with Battns. on either flank. H.Q. 16th R.W.F. at TELEGRAPH HO. Prisoners still coming in.	
		12-30.p.m.	Div:Intelligence Officers reports total prisoners to that time - 6 Officers, 450 Other Ranks. Message from 115th Bde. IRON CROSS reached. Situation not clear as 17th R.W.F. reports at 12-25.p.m. that Battn. is within 300 yds. of objective (GREEN Dotted Line) No report from 11th S.W.B. Heavy shelling in PILCKEM and IRON CROSS. Some enemy M.G. fire over IRON CROSS Ridge. Reported that STEENBEEK has been crossed.	
		12-30.p.m.		
		12-45.p.m.	115th Brigade Advanced H.Q. established at C.3.a.9.5.	
		1.p.m.	114th Bde. message - 14th Welsh established on GREEN Line - 2 Coys in front and 2 in support. Also reported that 11th S.W.B. established on STEENBEEK. 14th Welsh getting in touch with Brigade on the Left.	
		1-30.p.m.	114th Brigade message - 15th Welsh on line Tramway C.4.a.1.2.-C.3.b.7.5.and consolidating.	
		1-55.p.m.	114th Brigade message - 15th Welsh report at 1.p.m. Left front Coy did not proceed with Strong Point at C.2.d.4.2½. Strong Point being made on BLACK Line.	
		2.p.m.	113th Bde. H.Q. ready to move from WELSH HARP to C.2.a.9.5. 15th R.W.F. at BATTERY COPSE.	
			15th R.W.F. CANCER TR. - 16th R.W.F. TELEGRAPH HO.	
		3-20.p.m.	115th Brigade instructed to get in touch with 115th Brigade and inform 115th Brigade to push on with Left front and gain crossings of STEENBEEK.	
		4-15.p.m.	Message from 115th Brigade. Situation on STEENBEEK as follows - Two Battns have consolidated. 17th R.W.B. suffered casualties and have not consolidated the East Bank of STEENBEEK. Colonel TAYLOR wounded. 11th S.W.B. on right have crossed the STEENBEEK with One Coy. and have consolidated according to plan - Battn. suffered some casualties. S.O.S. sent up at 3-30.p.m. rendered necessary owing to the enemy collecting in shell holes West of	

Army Form C. 2118.

Page 8

WAR DIARY
or
INTELLIGENCE SUMMARY.

HEADQUARTERS, 38TH (WELSH) DIVISION.

(Erase heading not required.)

Place	Date	Hour	Summary of Events and Information	Remarks and references to Appendices
ELVERDINGHE	31st July. (Contd)	4-15.p.m.	LANGEMARCK prior to attack and then advancing to counter-attack. Our S.O.S. caused enemy to hurry back into LANGEMARCK. Enemy's Artillery put heavy barrage on STEENBEEK and also PILCKEM RIDGE. Reinforcements brought up from one Coy of each Res: Battn. of 115th Bde. to support 17th R.W.F. and 11th S.W.B. Through communication not established from Brigade to CANAL BANK	
		5-10.p.m.	115th Brigade instructed to get in touch with Guards on Left and capture East Bank of STEENBEEK.	
		5-30.p.m.	11th S.W.B. report to 115th Bde. enemy counter attack unsuccessful. Enemy still holding AU BON GITE and to the East of LANGEMARCK. Reported that enemy retiring in two's and three's. Red and Green Lights being sent up by enemy. On left of 115th Bde. reported that enemy driven off. Left Battalion in touch with neighbouring units in either places.	
		6-50.p.m.	115th Brigade H.Q. moving to PERISCOPE HOUSE.	
		6-40.p.m.	Message from G.O.C. 115th Bde. - 15th R.W.F. consolidating behind IRON CROSS ROAD. 14th R.W.F. being sent forward to consolidate along GREEN Line. 15th R.W.F. takes over BLACK Line - CANCER TRENCH LINE and BLUE Line. 16th R.W.F. goes to HARVEY TRENCH.	
		7-50.p.m.	Line held will be WESTERN BANK of STEENBEEK.	
		9-45.p.m.	115th Bde. H.Q. at WELSH HARP with Adv. H.Q. at PERISCOPE HOUSE.	
		9-55.p.m.	Information from 115th Brigade timed (6.4.p.m.) Guards Brigade left roughly U.27.b.2.2. N.W. to SIGNAL FARM with a post on far side of STEENBEEK about U.27.b.8.7. 17th R.W.F. reinforced by one Coy. 16th Welsh holding on to STEENBEEK but not clear though reported one Post is on far bank. 11th S.W.B. reports holding STEENBEEK except for AU BON GITE. 10th S.W.B. and 16th Welsh in C.5.a. 10th S.W.B. H.Q. C.5.b.2.2. 16th Welsh H.Q. at C.2.b.7.0. 17th R.W.F. report 5.p.m. our line begins U.27.b.2.2. along Railway to West Bank of STEENBEEK U.28.a.5.5. with one Coy. 11th S.W.B. dug in.	
		11.p.m.	115th Brigade instructed to clear situation using Stokes Mortars. AU BON GITE to be cleared.	
		11.p.m.	Information from 115th Brigade (Recd. 9-35.a.m. 1st Aug.) Report at 8-15.p.m. Situation normal. Intermittent shelling on Brigade Area. We hold West Bank of STEENBEEK on whole Brigade front with both flanks in touch.	
ELVERDINGHE	1st August	5-30.a.m.	Situation unchanged.	

6/10/17.

[signature]
Captain,
General Staff 38th (Welsh) Division.

S E C R E T

COPY NO. 22

9.5.6507.

38TH (WELSH) DIVISION
OPERATION ORDERS FOR WORKING ON GENERALLY
THROUGHOUT THE TRAINING IN JULY 1917.

Reference :- Attached Map, 1/10,000   2nd July 1917
THEROUANNE MAP

PLAN   1. (a) The XIV Corps with the ___ Corps on the right, and the ___ Corps on the left will attack the German lines.

(b) The attack will be made in a series of bounds. Each bound is defined by a coloured line on Map 1 attached.

       First Bound   -   BLUE Line
       Second Bound -   BLACK Line
       Third Bound   -   GREEN Line
       Fourth Bound -   RED Line.

(c) 'Z' Day, the date of the attack, will be notified later.

OBJECTIVE OF THE DIVISION   2. The boundaries between which the Division will attack are shown on Map 1 attached.
The objective of the Division on 'Z' Day is the GREEN Line between C.4.a.2.2 and C.27.c.55.60 and the passages of the BECHSTEIN.
When these have been secured Cavalry will be pushed forward to reconnoitre the RED Line. All ground gained by the Cavalry will be taken over by the Reserve Infantry Brigade of the Division.
The ___ th Division will be on the Right, and the ___ th Division on the left of the Division.

DISTRIBUTION FOR THE ATTACK OF INFANTRY, R.E. & PIONEERS   3. The Division will attack with the 114th Infantry Brigade on the Right, and the 113th Infantry Brigade on the Left, with the 115th Infantry Brigade, R.E. and Pioneers in reserve.
Assembly areas and inter-Brigade Boundaries are shown on Map 1 attached.

OUTLINE OF ACTION OF THE INFANTRY   4. The 113th and 114th Infantry Brigades will form up each on a front of two Battalions. The first and second objectives will be taken by the first two Battalions of each attacking Brigade. The third objective will be taken by the third Battalion of each attacking Brigade which will pass through the first two Battalions of each Brigade. The third Battalions will move in time to reach the BLACK Line at Zero plus 3.15, crossing the present British Front Line at not later than Zero plus 1.45.
The fourth Battalions will be in Brigade Reserve. When the advance on the GREEN Line is made each attacking Brigade will hold the BLUE and BLACK Lines with one Battalion, reforming one of the first assaulting Battalions to form a reserve at the disposal of Divisional Headquarters at BOCHE HO.

The

The 115th Infantry Brigade will gradually follow up
the two leading Brigades arriving at the German Front
Line at Zero plus 3 hours, and at the BLACK Line at
Zero plus four hours.
Two Battalions of the 115th Infantry Brigade will sieze
and hold the passages of the BECHSTEIN, passing through
the 113th and 114th Brigades.
These Battalions will move from the GREEN Line at Zero
plus 5.30. They will, unassisted by R.E. and Pioneers,
make Bridgeheads at AU BON GITE, U.28.a.30.55 and
U.28.a.10.80.
The remaining Battalions of the 115th Infantry Brigade
will follow in Reserve.
On the BECHSTEIN being captured, the ____ Squadron
Cavalry will reconnoitre to the RED Line.
G.O.C. 115th Infantry Brigade will arrange to take over
and hold adequately all ground gained by the Cavalry.

CONSOLIDATION AND STRONG POINTS

5. All objectives will be consolidated, special attention being paid to -

    (i) The line JOLIE FARM, CANDLE TRENCH, CANCER TRENCH, TELEGRAPH HOUSE.

    (ii) The GREEN Line.

    (iii) The Eastern Bank of the BECHSTEIN.

    (iv) All ground gained East of the BECHSTEIN.

Consolidation will be carried out on the principle of
first establishing a line of cruciform posts supporting
each other by fire. In the case of the GREEN Line,
when these have been made, a continuous fire trench
and support trench will be added.

Strong Points for which R.E. assistance will be given
will be made as under :-

BLUE LINE :-   By 114th Infantry Brigade
                  Enclosure at C.8.c.0.8
                  GALLWITZ FARM.
            By 113th Infantry Brigade
                  HOUSE 10
                  ZOUAVE HOUSE.

BLACK LINE:- By 114th Infantry Brigade
                  JOLIE FARM
                  Enclosure at CAN of CANDLE TRENCH
            By 113th Infantry Brigade
                  Enclosure near P of PILCKEM
                  TELEGRAPH HOUSE.

GREEN LINE:- By 114th Infantry Brigade
                  Enclosure at C.4.a.0.5.
        (a) Enclosure from C.3.b.45.70 -)
                  U.27.d.25.10 (two Platoons).)
                  About C.3.b.2.3
            By 113th Infantry Brigade
                  U.27.c.5.2.
                  U.27.c.60.65
                  U.27.c.90.20

Garrisons

5. (Contd)

Garrisons for each of the above will be one Platoon, except one marked (a) which will be two Platoons. For each of the above, ½ a Section R.E. ((a) 1 Section) will be detailed to assist the garrison on making the Strong Point, and will assemble with these Garrisons. Garrisons will be sent forward by Brigadiers immediately a line has been captured. When a point has been made the R.E. will proceed to the nearest Brigade Forward Station and report the fact.
The 113th Infantry Brigade will also make Strong Points at CHIMNEY HO. and Gdo. BARRIERE HO., but will not be given R.E. for this purpose.

LINE OF THE BECHSTEIN

The 115th Infantry Brigade (without R.E.) will make Bridgeheads at AU BON GITE, U.28.a.30.55 and U.28.a.10.80 with Garrisons of 1 Company, 2 Platoons and 2 Platoons respectively.

ACTION OF INFANTRY IN CASE OF BEING HELD UP

6. In the event of any Unit on either flank of the Division, or of any Unit in the Division being held up, the Units on the flanks of the Unit held up will on no account check their advance. They will form defensive flanks, assist, by enfilade fire, the troops held up, and press forward so as to envelope the point of resistance which is holding up the attack.
It is of vital importance that the barrage be followed as close as possible by the Infantry, any "nests" of Germans left being treated by reserves.

ARTILLERY

7. The Divisional Artillery will be composed of six R.F.A. Brigades and will support the attack by –

  (i) A Creeping Barrage.
  (ii) A Standing Barrage.

A tracing marked 2, showing the Creeping barrage, is attached.

The main points which affect the Infantry are :-

  (a) Ordinary lifts are made by 100 yards every 4 minutes.
  (b) The barrage will be on the German Front Line for 8 minutes.
  (c) That barrages are piled on to each objective and the German second line system so that the leading lines of Infantry will be able to enter them all together when the barrage lifts.
  (d) That protective barrages are formed 200 yards beyond each objective. These barrages will also sweep and search.

On the GREEN Line being captured i.e. at Zero plus 4.10, two Artillery Brigades will move forward to positions in NILE VALLEY C.13.b., and to B.12.d. respectively to support the advance of the 115th Infantry Brigade beyond the GREEN Line. When these Artillery Brigades are in action, another Artillery Brigade will be immediately pushed up to the PILCKEM RIDGE, being followed by the remaining three Brigades in succession, each moving forward when the preceding one has got into action on the PILCKEM RIDGE.

MACHINE GUNS

8. ~~Machine Guns will be divided into two parts~~ -

    (i) To form Corps and Divisional Barrages.
    (ii) To accompany Infantry Brigades.

The first part will be formed by the 176th Machine Gun Company, another Machine Gun Company to be detailed later, and four guns from each of the 113th, 114th and 115th Machine Gun Companies, making a total of 44 Machine Guns.
These will act under the orders of the D.M.G.O. Captain EVANSON.
The Machine Gun Barrage will be directed so as to fall 500 yards beyond the Artillery Creeping Barrage.
Map 3 showing the Machine Gun Barrages is attached.
The guns will be divided into three main groups, two groups maintaining fire while one group is moving.
They will be so placed that, apart from forming a Creeping Barrage, they will be able to form a S.O.S. Barrage in front of each objective.
The second part i.e. Brigade Machine Gun Companies, less one section each, will remain under command of Brigade Commanders.
They will be utilised to assist in helping forward the advance of their Brigades and when the final objectives of their Brigade are reached will cover consolidation and ward off counter attacks. As far as possible they will be in rear of the lines they are covering.

R.E.
PIONEERS.
ATTACHED
INFANTRY
BATTALION.

9. The following parties will be detailed for work as under :-

R.E.
    123rd Field Company for STRONG POINTS on BLACK and BLUE Lines.
    124th Field Company for STRONG POINTS on GREEN Line.
    1 Section 151st Field Company for erection of CACTUS PONTOON BRIDGE commence work at ZERO plus 2 hours.
    1 Section 151st Field Company on extension of trench tramways. Commence work at Zero plus 3 hours.
    151st Field Company (less 2 Sections) in reserve on West CANAL BANK.

19th (Pioneer) Bn. WELSH REGT.
    1 Company with Corps on 60 c.m. light railway.
    1 Company making C.T. in NO MANS LAND from HUDDERSFIELD to CAESARS LANE, from C.13.3. to CAESARS NOSE and from C.7.5. to FARM 14. Commence at Zero plus 1 hour.
    1 Company making pack mule track from BRIDGE 6.W. to KIEL COT., BILCKEM HILL and IRON CROSS. Commence work at Zero plus 2 hours.
    Headquarters and 1 Company in reserve on West CANAL BANK.

ATTACHED INFANTRY BATTALION.
    2 Companies on Artillery track from MARENGO CAUSEWAY to the NILE. Commence at Zero plus 3 hours.
    Battalion less 2 Coys. on Ammunition wagon tracks from the NILE to CACTUS PONTOON. Commence work at Zero plus 3 hours.

Page 5.

CONTACT AEROPLANES
10. Contact aeroplanes (type R.E.8.) of 9th Squadron, R.F.C. will fly over the line and call for flares from the Leading Troops at the following hours.

BLUE Line	Zero plus 1 hour.
German 2nd Line	Zero plus 1 hour 37 minutes.
BLACK Line	Zero plus 2 hours 30 minutes.
GREEN Line	Zero plus 4 hours 30 minutes.
BECKSTEIN	Zero plus 6 hours 45 minutes.

Special marks for these aeroplanes will be detailed later.

LIAISON.
11. The 114th Infantry Brigade will toll off special parties of 1 officer and 6 other ranks each to get in touch with the .... Division on the right at
5 CHEMINS CROSS ROADS.
MARSOUIN FARM.
JOLIE FARM
N.W. Corner of RUDOLPHE FARM WOOD
CROSS ROADS 150 yds. N.W. of VARNA FARM.

113th Infantry Brigade will toll off parties similarly to get in touch with the Division on the left at
CABLE SUPPORT
CARIBOO TRENCH
CHIMNEY HOUSE
GDE. BARRIERE HOUSE
U.27.c.35.50.

115th Infantry Brigade will act similarly on the right at
THE BECKSTEIN.
CROSS ROADS U.29.c.25.65.
CROSS ROADS U.29.b.05.15.

and on the left at
RAILWAY CROSSING over the BECKSTEIN
Crossing at U.22.c.80.42.
Crossing at U.22.d.40.98.

SYNCHRONISATION OF WATCHES.
12. From the 9th July inclusive watches at Head Quarters of Infantry Brigades and Divisional Artillery will be synchronised daily with a watch which will be sent round from Divisional Headquarters by the 11-30.a.m. D.R.
General Officers Commanding Infantry Brigades and C.R.A. will arrange for a similar daily synchronisation in the evening with the units under their command.

DIVISIONAL REPORT CENTRE.
13. Divisional Report Centre will be at 114th Infantry Brigade Headquarters ESTREE BLANCHE.

ACKNOWLEDGE.

H. E. Pryce
Lieut. Colonel,
General Staff, 38th (Welsh) Divn.

2nd July, 1917.

Copies to :-
113th Brigade (7)
114th Brigade (7)
115th Brigade (7)
C.R.E. (No map)
176th M.G.Coy. "
D.M.G.O. "
38th Div: "Q" "
A.D.M.S. "
A.P.M. "

For information to :-
19th Welsh Regt.
38th Div: Arty.
38th Div: Sniping Coy.

ARTILLERY CREEPING BARRAGE MAP.   MAP 2.   SECRET.

Scale - 1:10,000

COPY NO. 9

S E C R E T

38TH (WELSH) DIVISION ORDER No. 105

Ref:- Sheets 27 & 28 1/40,000   10th July 1917
      Sheet 5A. 1/100,000

1. The 38th Division will march from the ST. HILAIRE AREA to the PESELHOEK AREA in accordance with the attached Table.

2. The completion of each day's march will be reported to Divisional Headquarters by Group Commanders.

3. Up to the CAESTRE AREA a distance of 500 yards will be maintained between each Battalion of Infantry, Field Ambulance and Section of Divisional Supply Column; and, where first line transport is marching separately, between the transport of each Battalion.
   From CAESTRE onwards a distance of 200 yards will be maintained as above.

4. Headquarters Section Sniping Company will rejoin Divisional Headquarters at NORRENT FONTES by 5 p.m. 15th July.

5. Divisional Report Centre will close at NORRENT FONTES at 10 a.m. on the 16th instant and will re-open at the same hour at GODEWAERSVELDE.
   Divisional Report Centre will close at GODEWAERSVELDE at 10 a.m. on the 17th instant and will re-open at the same hour at DRAGON CAMP.

ACKNOWLEDGE

R.S. Follett Maj.
for Lieut. Colonel,
General Staff, 38th (Welsh) Division.

Issued to Signals at :-

Copies to :-

G.O.C.	Train	First Army
G.S.	A.D.M.S.	Second Army
"Q"	S.S.O.	XIV Corps "G"
Signals	D.A.D.O.S.	XIV Corps "Q"
C.R.A.	A.P.M.	D.A.D.P.S. XIV Corps
C.R.E.	Camp. Comdt.	Guards Division.
113th Brigade	Div. Gas Offr.	29th Division
114th Brigade	Sniping Company	51st Division
115th Brigade	176th M.G.Coy.	Adjt. i/c Camps
19th Welsh Regt.	Div. Depot Battn.	R.T.O. POPERINGHE

S E C R E T

MARCH TABLE
(To accompany 38th Division Order No. 105)

Unit	Date	Move From	Move To	Route	Billets From	Under orders of	Remarks
No.1 113th Bde. Bde. H.Q. L.T.M.Bty. M.G.Coy. 2 Battns. Proportion 331 Coy. ASC. 129 Fd.Ambce.	13/7/17	FLECHIN AREA	CAESTRE AREA	By bus Via AIRE and HAZEBROUCK. Mounted portion by march Via same route.	Area Comndt. CAESTRE	G.O.C. 113th Brigade	Busses not to move before 10 a.m. Marching portion to enter AIRE at 9.45 a.m.
No.2 114th Bde. Bde. H.Q. L.T.M.Bty. M.G.Coy. 2 Battns. Proportion 332 Coy. ASC.	13/7/17	ESTREE BLANCHE AREA	CAESTRE AREA	-ditto-	-ditto-	G.O.C. 114th Brigade	Busses not to move before 10 a.m. Marching portion to enter AIRE at 9.15 a.m.
No.3 H.Q. 115th Bde M.G.Coy. L.T.M.Bty. "A" Battn. "B" Battn. 129 Fd.Ambce.	14/7/17 14/7/17 14/7/17 14/7/17 14/7/17 14/7/17	CAESTRE AREA -ditto- -ditto- -ditto- -ditto- -ditto-	"G" Camp -ditto- -ditto- CARDOEN F^m "P" Camp To be arranged by "Q" Branch				Busses not to move before 10 a.m.
Proportion 331 Coy. ASC.	14/7/17	-ditto-	INTERNATIONAL CORNER				

MARCH TABLE (Contd)   Page 2

Unit	Date	Move From	Move To	Route	Billets from	Under orders of	Remarks
No.1 as in 2 H.Q. 114th.Bde. M.G.Coy. L.T.M.Bty. "A" Battn. "B" Battn. Proportion 332 Coy. ASC.	14/7/17 -ditto- -ditto- -ditto- -ditto- -ditto- -ditto-	CAESTRE AREA -ditto- -ditto- -ditto- -ditto- -ditto-	VOX VRIE Fm. -ditto- -ditto- ROUSSEL Fm. "H" Camp INTERNATIONAL CORNER				Busses not to move before 10 a.m.
No.5 2 Battns. 114th Bde. 332 Coy. ASC. 130 Fd.Ambco. 176th M.G.Coy. Mobile Vet.Sec.	14/7/17 -ditto- -ditto- -ditto- -ditto- -ditto-	ESTREE BLANCHE AREA -ditto- -ditto- -ditto- -ditto- -ditto-	TANNAY PLAINE HAUT PLAINE BAS STEENBECQUE HOULERON HOULERON	AIRE - NEUFPRE PECQUEUR.	Mairie STEEN- BECQUE.	An Officer to be detailed by G.O.C. 114th Bde.	To cross line WITTERNESSE - GUARBECQUE at 9.15 a.m. March to be completed by 1 p.m.
No.6 2 Battns. 113th Bde. 121 Fd.Coy. RE 331 Coy. ASC.	14/7/17	FLECHIN AREA	STEENBECQUE LA HAUT LES CISEAUX	Via LINGHEM AIRE and BOESEG- HEM.	Mairie STEEN- BECQUE	An Officer to be detailed by G.O.C. 113th Bde.	To cross line WITTERNESSE - GUARBECQUE at 10.30 a.m. March to be completed by 1 p.m.
No.7 115th Bde. 333 Coy. ASC. 131 Fd.Ambce.	14/7/17	LAIRE AREA	LAMBRES MOLINGHEM to GUARBECQUE ISBERGUES LA ROPIE	Via ST. HILAIRE	Mairie STEEN- BECQUE	Under orders of G.O.C. 115th Bde.	Not to be N. of line WITTERNESSE - GUARBECQUE before 11 a.m. March to be completed by 1 p.m.
No.8 as in 6.	15/7/17	STEENBECQUE AREA.	CAESTRE AREA	By march route Via HAZE- BROUCK	Area Commdt. CAESTRE		To arrive CAESTRE AREA 9 a.m.
No.9 as in No.5	15/7/17	-ditto-	-ditto-	-ditto-	-ditto-		To arrive CAESTRE AREA 9 a.m.

Page 3.

MARCH TABLE (CONTD.)

Unit.	Date	Move From	Move To	Route	Billets from	Under orders of	Remarks.
No. 10. as in No. 7.	15/7/17	STEENBECQUE Area	CAESTRE Area.	By march route via HAZEBROUCK	Area Comdt. CAESTRE		To arrive CAESTRE Area. 10.a.m.
No. 11. as in No. 6.	16/7/17	CAESTRE Area.	EECKE Area	By march route	Area Comdt. EECKE		To arrive EECKE Area. 8.a.m.
No. 12. as in No. 5.	16/7/17	ditto	ditto	ditto	ditto		To arrive EECKE at 8-30.a.m.
No. 13. as in No. 7.	16/7/17	ditto	ditto	ditto	ditto		To arrive EECKE Area 9.a.m.
No. 14. Div: H.Q. H.Q.Secn. Sniping Coy.	16/7/17	NORRENT FONTES.	GODESWAERS-VELDE.	Mounted portion by march route via HAZEBROUCK & CAESTRE. Dismounted portion by bus.		Camp Comdt.	
No. 15. 114th Brigade "C" Battn. "D" Battn. 176th M.G.Coy. Mob:Vet:Secn. 332nd Coy.ASC. 130th Fd.Amb.	17/7/17 " " " " " "	EECKE Area " " " " " "	L.2.Work A.18.a.8.4. A.16.a.9.8. A.9.c.6.6. {INTERNATIONAL CORNER. Tombe arranged by "Q"	ABEELE - POPERINGHE			To pass ABEELE at 8.a.m.
No. 16. 113th Brigade "C" Battn. "D" Battn. 124th Fd.Coy.R.E. 331st Coy. ASC.	17/7/17 " " " "	EECKE Area " " " "	"X" Line. (A.11.central A.17.b.2.8. A.10.c.8.1. INTERNATIONAL CORNER.	ditto			To pass ABEELE at 8-30.a.m.

Page 4.

MARCH TABLE (Contd.)

Unit	Date.	From	To	Route	Remarks.
No. 17. 115th Brigade Bde. H.Q. "A" Battn. "B" Battn. "C" Battn. "D" Battn. 115th M.G.Coy. 115th T.M.Bty. 333 Coy. ASC. 151st Fd.Amb.	17/7/17. " " " " " " " "	EECKE Area. " " " " " " " "	VOV VRIE Fm. "H" Camp. "P" Camp. "G" Camp. A.10.d.6.6. A.16.a.7.8. VOX VRIE Fm. INTERNATION CRNR. Under orders of "Q".	ABEELE - POPERINGHE	To pass ABEELE at 9.a.m.
No. 18. As In E.O. 14.	17/7/17.	GODESWAERS -VELDE.	DRAGON CAMP.	- ditto -	Mounted portion to pass ABEELE at 9-15.a.m.

10th July, 1917.

O.O. SECRET

AMENDMENT TO 38TH DIVISION ORDER NO 105.

1. In March Table, item No. 1 and No. 3 delete 129th Field Ambulance.

2. In march Table, items Nos. 6 and 16, add 129th Field Ambulance.

ACKNOWLEDGE.

R.S. Follett May
for Lieut. Colonel,
18th July, 1917. General Staff, 38th (Welsh) Division.

SECRET

Copy No. 9

38TH (WELSH) DIVISION ORDER NO. 106.

11th July, 1917.

1. The units of the Division in the ST. HILAIRE Area will move to the PROVEN Area in accordance with the attached march table.

2. In case the commencement of operations is deferred, concentration will be correspondingly deferred whether the movement has commenced or not.

3. In view of the large number of movements taking place within the areas of several armies, all units must conform <u>rigidly</u> to all orders as regards times and routes, maintaining at the same time the strictest march discipline.

4. The previous orders issued in 38th (Welsh) Division Order No. 105 regarding Routes, Billets, March Intervals, and O.C. March Unit etc., will hold good as far as CAESTRE and EECKE. Exact hours and routes from CAESTRE and EECKE to PROVEN will be notified later on receipt from XIV Corps.

<u>ACKNOWLEDGE.</u>

H.E. Pryce

Lieut. Colonel,
General Staff, 38th (Welsh) Division.

Issued to Signals at 11-30.p.m.

Copies to :-

G.O.C.	A.D.M.S.	XIV Corps "G"
G.S.	S.S.O.	XIV Corps "Q"
"Q"	D.A.D.O.S.	D.A.D.P.S., XIV Corps
Signals	D.A.D.V.S.	Guards Divn.
C.R.A.	A.P.M.	29th Div
C.R.E.	Camp Comdt.	20th Div:
113th Bde.	Div: Gas Offr.	51st Div:
114th Bde.	Sniping Coy.	Area Comdt. PROVEN.
115th Bde.	176th M.G.Coy.	
19th Welsh Regt.	First Army	
Train.	Second Army	

SECRET

MARCH TABLE (To accompany 38th (Welsh) Division Order No.106)

No.	GROUP Composition	From	13th July To	14th July To	15th July To	16th July To	17th July To	Remarks
1.	113th Inf. Bde. H.Q. 2 Battns. 113th Bde. 113th M.G.Coy. 113th L.T.M.Bty. Proportion 331 Coy. A.S.C.	FLECHIN AREA	(a) CAESTRE AREA	(b) P.1. PROVEN AREA				(a) By 1st Army busses which remain at CAESTRE for next day's move. (b) Report to Area Commandant PROVEN for billets.
2.	114th Inf. Bde. H.Q. 2 Battns. 114th Bde. 114th M.G.Coy. 114th L.T.M.Bty. Proportion 332 Coy. A.S.C.	ESTREE BLANCHE AREA	(a) CAESTRE AREA	(b) P.1. PROVEN AREA				(a) As for (a) above. (b) As for (b) above.
3.	2 Battns. 113th Bde. 331 Coy. A.S.C. 129th Fd. Ambce.	FLECHIN AREA		(c) STEEN-BECQUE AREA	(c) CAESTRE	(d) P.1. PROVEN		(c) By march route. (d) By march route. Packs of Battns. 113th and 114th Bdes. to be carried by busses provided by XIV Corps.
4.	2 Battns 114th Bde. 332nd Coy. A.S.C. 130th Fd. Ambce	ESTREE BLANCHE AREA		(c) STEEN-BECQUE AREA	(c) CAESTRE	(d) P.1. PROVEN		
5.	124th Fd. Coy. R.E. 115th Inf. Bde. 131st Fd. Ambce. 333rd Coy. A.S.C. 176 M.G.Coy. & Mob Vet Sec:	LAIRE AREA		(c) STEEN-BECQUE AREA	(c) CAESTRE	(c) ECKE	(c) P.5. PROVEN	Note:- All billets in B.1 and P.5 PROVEN AREAS will be provided by Area Commandant PROVEN.
6.	Divisional H.Q. H.Q. Secn. Sniping Company.	NORRENT FONTES				(c) GODES-WAERS-VELDE.	(c) P.5. PROVEN.	

11th July 1917.

S E C R E T　　　　　　　　　　　　38th Division No. G.S.6649

Reference 38th Division Order No. 105.

1.　　All troops of the 38th Division marching from CAESTRE AREA on the 18th instant will not use the ST. SYLVESTRE CAPPEL - STEENVOORDE ROAD.

　　　　The BORRE le BREARDE - ST. SYLVESTRE CAPPEL ROAD will not be used by troops of the 38th Division before 7 a.m. on the 18th instant, but may be used after that hour.

2.　　115th Infantry Brigade Group will not enter the EECKE AREA before 8 a.m. on the 18th instant.

ACKNOWLEDGE

　　　　　　　　　　　　　　　　　R.J. Follett Maj.
　　　　　　　　　　　　　　　　　for Lieut. Colonel,
15/7/1917.　　　　　General Staff, 38th (Welsh) Division.

Copies to :- All recipients of 38th Division Order No. 105.

Lieut. Colonel C.C. Norman, D.S.O. 15th R.W.F
　　Commanding B Group 113 Bde
Lieut. Col. J.H. Hayes, D.S.O 14th Welsh Regt
　　Commdg No. 2 Group 114th Bde.

SECRET

38th Division No. G.S.S.58/19.

38TH (WELSH) DIVISION OPERATIONS.

DIVISION ORDER NO. 107.

ADDENDUM NO. 2.

ISSUE OF MAPS.

1. Map I has been distributed to the following :-

    113th Brigade
    114th Brigade
    115th Brigade
    XIV Corps
    Guards Divn.
    51st Divn.

2. Map 2 is issued with the order to :-

38th Div: Arty.	XIV Corps "G"
38th H.Bombt.Group.	Guards Divn.
113th Brigade	20th Divn.
114th Brigade	29th Divn.
115th Brigade	51st Divn.
D.M.G.O.	9th Squadron R.F.C.
176th M.G.Coy.	XIV Corps Cav: Regt.

3. (a) The reference to Maps showing M.G.Barrages in para. 9 of Order No. 107 will be amended to read 3.A and 3.B.
   (b) Maps A and B issued with G.S.S.58/7 Instructions No. 13 - MACHINE GUN BARRAGES - will be re-numbered 3.A and 3.B. respectively.
   These will be used in conjunction with Division Order No. 107.
   (c) Maps 3.A. and 3.B. are issued on the same scale as INSTRUCTIONS NO 13.

H.E. Pryce
Lieut. Colonel,
General Staff, 38th (Welsh) Division.

16th July, 1917.

Copies to all recipients of Division Order No. 107.

SECRET.

Copy No. 11

38TH (WELSH) DIVISION ORDER NO. 107.

Ref:- Maps, 1/10,000 (ST.JULIEN, 28 N.W.2 Edition 5A.
              (BIXSCHOOTE, 20 SW.4 Edition 4A.

16 JUL 1917
~~15th July, 1917.~~

PLAN.
1.(a) The XIV Corps with the XVIII Corps on the Right and the I French Corps on the Left will attack the German lines.

(b) The attack will be made in a series of bounds. Each main bound is defined by a cloured line on Map 1 attached.

  First Bound - BLUE Line.
  Second Bound - BLACK Line.
  Third Bound - GREEN Line.
  Fourth Bound - GREEN Dotted Line.

Subsequent bounds will be made to ground gained by the Cavalry vide Divisional Instructions No. 10. and para. 5 of this order, ending at the RED Line.

(c) 'Z' Day, the date of the attack, and Zero hour will be notified later.

OBJECTIVE OF THE DIVISION
2. The boundaries between which the Division will attack are shown on Map 1 attached.
The objective of the Division on 'Z' Day is the GREEN Line between C.4.a.2.2. and C.27.c.55.60., and the passages of the STEENBEEK.
When these have been secured Cavalry Patrols will be pushed forward to reconnoitre the RED Line. All ground gained by the Cavalry will be taken over by the Reserve Infantry Brigade of the Division.
The 51st Division will be on the Right, and the Guards Division on the left of the Division.

DISTRIBUTION FOR THE ATTACK OF INFANTRY, R.E. & PIONEERS
3. The Division will attack with the 114th Infantry Brigade on the right, and the 113th Infantry Brigade on the Left, with the 115th Infantry Brigade, R.E. and Pioneers in Reserve. Assembly areas and Inter-Brigade Boundaries are shown on Map 1 attached. Details of the Assembly March are given in Instructions No. 11.

OUTLINE OF ACTION OF THE INFANTRY
4. The 113th and 114th Infantry Brigades will form up each on a front of two Battalions. The first objective will be taken by two Battalions of the 114th Infantry Brigade, and two half Battalions of the 113th Infantry Brigade. The BLACK Line will be taken by two half Battalions from the 114th Infantry Brigade and two half Battalions from the 113th Infantry Brigade. The GREEN Line will be taken by two half Battalions of the 114th Infantry Brigade, and one Battalion of the 113th Infantry Brigade. One Battalion of the 113th Infantry Brigade will be in Brigade Reserve. The 114th Infantry Brigade, when the BLACK Line has been captured, will reform both the Battalions (less two Platoons for Strong Points) that captured the BLUE Line, and make them the Brigade Reserve.
/ The 115th

Page 2.

The 115th Infantry Brigade will gradually follow up the two leading Brigades arriving at the German Front Line at Zero plus three hours, and at the BLACK Line at Zero plus four hours.

After the GREEN Line has been captured, two Battalions of the 115th Infantry Brigade will pass through the 113th and 114th Infantry Brigades, leaving the GREEN Line at Zero plus 5 hours, and sieze and hold the passages of the STEENBEEK, i.e. the GREEN Dotted Line.

The remaining Battalions of the 115th Infantry Brigade will remain in Reserve about KIEL COT. in Square C.7.d.

When the line of the STEENBEEK is captured by the 115th Infantry Brigade the following action will be taken.

Under Corps Orders Cavalry will reconnoitre to discover the position and state of the enemy.

For detailed action of the Cavalry see Instructions No. 10.

G.O.C. 115th Brigade will arrange to take over and hold adequately all ground gained by the Cavalry at each bound.

The two Battalions of the 115th Infantry Brigade left about KIEL COT. will be prepared to push forward to support the advance towards LANGEMARCK in the event of the Cavalry finding it unoccupied.

The 113th and 114th Infantry Brigades will each adopt the following dispositions.

Two Battalions will hold the GREEN Line and ground between the BLACK and GREEN Lines. One Battalion will hold the BLACK Line and German 2nd Line system. One Battalion disposed behind CANDLE - CANCER Trench in Brigade Reserve.

CONSOLIDATION AND STRONG POINTS.

5. All objectives will be consolidated, special attention being paid to :-
   (i) The Line JOLIE FARM, CANDLE TRENCH, CANCER TRENCH, TELEGRAPH HOUSE.
   (ii) The GREEN Line.
   (iii) The Eastern Bank of the STEENBEEK.
   (iv) All ground gained East of the STEENBEEK.

Each Line of consolidation when gained will become a line of resistance. Counter-attacks if made will be checked on these lines. An outpost line will be established in front of the Lines of consolidation. Consolidation will be carried out on the principle of first establishing a line of cruciform posts which will support each other by fire. Later on they will be linked up by a continuous trench. In the case of the GREEN Line, when these posts have been made, a continuous fire trench and support trench will be added.

Apart from the above posts, strong points will be made as under :-

BLUE Line :- By 114th Infantry Brigade
                Enclosure at C.8.c.0.8.
                GALLWITZ FARM.
              By 113th Infantry Brigade
                HOUSE 10.
                ZOUAVE HOUSE.

BLACK Line :- By 114th Infantry Brigade
                JOLIE FARM.
                Enclosure, the centre of which is at C.2.d.30.02.
              By 113th Infantry Brigade.
                Enclosure near P of PILCKEM
                TELEGRAPH HOUSE.

GREEN Line :- By 114th Infantry Brigade
           Enclosure at C.4.a.05.45.
     (*) Enclosure from C.3.b.45.70 -)
           U.27.d.25.20. (Two Platoons))
           About C.3.b.25.30.
        By 113th Infantry Brigade
           Enclosure, centre of which is
           U.27.c.50.34.
           U.27.c.65.73
           U.27.c.90.33.

Garrisons for each of the above will be one Platoon, except the one marked (*) which will be two Platoons. For each of the above, ½ Section R.E. ((*) 1 Section) will be detailed to assist the Garrison in making the Strong Point.

These R.E. parties will be kept back near the CANAL BANK till the BLACK Line is reported captured, when they will be sent forward by Brigadiers to join the Garrisons who will have commenced work as soon as a line has been captured. When a point has been made, the R.E. who assisted in making the Point will proceed to the nearest Brigade Forward Station and report the fact to the C.R.E.

The 113th Infantry Brigade will also make Strong Points at CHIMNEY HO. and GDE. BARRIERE HO., but will not be given R.E. for this purpose.

LINE OF THE STEENBEEK

The 115th Infantry Brigade (Without R.E.) will make Bridgeheads at AU BON GITE, U.28.a.30.55 and U.28.a.10.80 with Garrisons of 1 Company, 2 Platoons and 2 Platoons respectively.

BEYOND THE STEENBEEK

As the Cavalry advances and occupies ground it will hand the same over to the 115th Infantry Brigade. The main lines which the 115th Infantry Brigade should be prepared to hold are :-
    (i) Western edge of LANGEMARCK with Strong Points at U.28.b.77.15., U.28.b.30.56 and U.22.c.72.10.
    (ii) About 300 yards N.E. of LANGEMARCK with Strong Points at U.29.b.03.68 - U.23.d.13.22 - U.23.c.45.80 and U.22.b.90.21.
    (iii) The RED Line with Strong Points at U.23.d.97.23 - U.24.c.40.90 - U.23.b.67.17 and U.23.b.06.70.

ACTION OF INFANTRY IN CASE OF BEING HELD UP

6. In the event of any Unit on either flank of the Division, or of any Unit in the Division being held up, the Units on the flanks of the Unit held up will on no account check their advance. They will form defensive flanks, assist by enfilade fire the troops held up and press forward so as to envelope the point of resistance which is holding up the attack.

It is of vital importance that the barrage be followed as close as possible by the Infantry, any "nests" of Germans left being treated by reserves.

/7.

Page 4.

ARTILLERY.

7. The Divisional Artillery will be composed of six R.F.A. Brigades, 6 Batteries 2" T.M's, 3 - 6" Newton T.M's and 2 Batteries 9.45" T.M's.
The R.F.A. Brigades will support the attack by -
    (i) A Creeping Barrage.
    (ii) A Standing Barrage.
A tracing marked 2, showing the Creeping Barrage up the GREEN Line, is attached.
A tracing will be issued later showing the barrage onwards to the GREEN Dotted Line and the RED Line.
The main points which affect the Infantry are :-
    (a) Ordinary lifts are made by 100 yds every four minutes.
    (b) The Barrage will be on the German front line for six minutes.
    (c) Barrages are piled on to each objective and the the German Second Line system so that the leading lines of Infantry will be able to enter them all together when the barrage lifts.
    (d) Protective barrages are formed on all hostile trenches within 400 yards of an objective, otherwise 400 yards beyond each objective. These barrages will also sweep and search. These barrages will become intense 30 seconds before the advance from the BLUE, BLACK and GREEN Lines.

Barrage guns will create smoke barrages as under :-
From Zero plus 50 minutes to plus 1 hour 5 minutes beyond the BLUE Line.
From Zero plus 2 hours 14 minutes to plus 3 hours beyond the BLACK Line.
From Zero plus 4 hours and 21 minutes to 4 hours plus 45 minutes beyond the GREEN Line.

On the GREEN Line being captured i.e. at Zero plus 4 hours 10 minutes, two Artillery Brigades will move forward to positions in NILE VALLEY C.13.b. and CANAL BANK B.18.d. respectively to support the advance of the 115th Infantry Brigade beyond the GREEN Line.
When these Artillery Brigades are in action two more Artillery Brigades will be immediately pushed up to under cover of the PILCKEM Ridge between the BLUE and the BLACK Lines. When in position the remaining two Brigades will move forward to the West Bank of the CANAL.
On 'Z' plus 1 day these last two Brigades will move forward as far as possible to positions previously reconnoitred.
The Divisional Artillery will be assisted by a Heavy Artillery Bombardment Group of 4 - 6" Howitzer Batteries and 2 - 8" Howitzer Batteries.
The following guns will be at the disposal of the G.O.C. Division after Zero if required :-
    2 - 6" Howitzer Batteries.
    2 - 4.5" Howitzer Batteries.
    2 - 18-pr. Batteries drawn from super-imposed batteries.
These batteries will continue their Corps Tasks until required by the G.O.C. Division.

/ 8 OIL DRUMS.

Page 5.

OIL DRUMS.

8. At Zero plus 3 minutes there will be a discharge of oil drums from gas projectors on -
   (a) The German 2nd Line system between CHEMIN DRIVE ~~AVENUE~~ and TELEGRAPH HOUSE
       and
   (b) CANAL DRIVE from CARIBOO TRENCH to near TELEGRAPH HOUSE.

MACHINE GUNS.

9. Machine Guns will be divided into two parts -
   (i) To form Corps and Divisional Barrages.
   (ii) To accompany Infantry Brigades.

The first part will be formed by the 176th Machine Gun Company, two Machine Gun Companies to be detailed later from another Division, and four guns from each of the 113th, 114th and 115th Machine Gun Companies, making a total of 60 Machine Guns.
These will act under the orders of the D.M.G.O. - Major EVANSON.
The Machine Gun Barrages will be directed so as to fall 500 yards beyond the Artillery Creeping Barrage.
Maps 3, 3A and 3B showing the Machine Gun Barrages are attached.
The guns will be divided into three main groups, two groups maintaining fire while one group is moving.
They will be so placed that, apart from forming a Creeping Barrage they will be able to form an S.O.S. Barrage in front of each objective.
The Second part i.e. Brigade Machine Gun Companies, less one section each, will remain under command of Brigade Commanders.
They will be utilised to assist in helping forward the advance of their Brigades and when the final objectives of their Brigades are reached will cover consolidation and ward off counter attacks.
As far as possible they will be in rear of the lines they are covering, and will be disposed in depth.

R.E.,PIONEERS ATTACHED INFANTRY BATTALION.

10. The following parties will be detailed for work as under :-
R.E.
  123rd Field Company for Strong Points on BLACK and BLUE Lines.
  124th Field Company for Strong Points on GREEN Line.
  1 Section 151st Field Company for erection of CACTUS PONTOON Bridge at C.7.c.0.5. commence work at Zero plus 2 hours.
  1 Section 151st Field Company on extension of trench tramways. Commence work at Zero plus 3 hours.
  151st Field Company (less 2 Sections) in reserve on WEST CANAL BANK.

19th (PIONEER) BN. WELSH REGT.
  1 Company with Corps on 60 cm. light railway.
  2 Companies making pack mule track from BRIDGE 6.W. to KIEL COT., PILCKEM MILL and IRON CROSS. Commence work at Zero plus 2 hours.
  Headquarters and 1 Company in reserve on West CANAL BANK.

ATTACHED INFANTRY BATTALION.
  Two Companies on Artillery track from MARENGO CAUSEWAY to the NILE. Commence at Zero plus 3 hours.
  Battalion (less 2 Coys) on Ammunition Wagon tracks from the NILE to CACTUS PONTOON BRIDGE, via HUDDLESTON Road. Commence work at Zero plus 3 hours.

Page 6.

CONTACT AEROPLANES. 11. Contact aeroplanes (Type R.E. 8) of 9th Squadron, R.F.C. will fly over the line and call for ~~green~~ white flares from the leading Troops at the following hours :-

BLUE Line   Zero plus 1 hour.
BLACK Line   Zero plus 2 hours 25 minutes.
GREEN Line   Zero plus 4 hours 20 minutes.
GREEN Dotted   Zero plus 5 hours 40 minutes.
Line (STEENBEEK)
Wherever)   1-30.p.m.
leading   )   4.p.m.
troops are)   8.p.m.

Special marks for these aeroplanes will be as follows :-
Two Black rectangular flags each 2 ft. X 1 ft.3 in., attached to and projecting from the lower planes on each side of the fuselage.
Detailed instructions for intercommunication with aeroplanes are given in INSTRUCTIONS NO. 15.

LIAISON. 12. The 114th Infantry Brigade will toll off special parties of 1 officer and 6 other ranks each to get in touch with the 153rd Infantry Brigade, 51st Division on the Right at :-
　　5 CHEMINS CROSS ROADS.
　　MARSOUIN FARM
　　JOLIE FARM
　　N.W.Corner of RUDOLPHE FARM WOOD
　　VARNA FARM.
113th Infantry Brigade will tell off parties similarly to get in touch with the 2nd Guards Brigade, Guards Division on the left at :-
　　CABLE SUPPORT
　　CARIBOO TRENCH
　　CHIMNEY HOUSE
　　GDE. BARRIERE HOUSE
　　U.27.c.35.63.
115th Infantry Brigade will act similarly on the right with the 154th Infantry Brigade at
　　THE STEENBEEK.
　　CROSS ROADS U.29.c.27.77.
　　CROSS ROADS U.29.b.05.15.
and on the left with the 1st Guards Brigade at
　　RAILWAY CROSSING over the STEENBEEK.
　　RAILWAY CROSSING at U.22.c.80.42.
　　RAILWAY CROSSING at U.22.d.40.98.

S.O.S. SIGNAL 13. The S.O.S. SIGNAL to show that the enemy's Infantry are counter-attacking will be a coloured Rifle Grenade bursting into two red and two green Lights.

SYNCHRONISATION OF WATCHES. 14. From 'W' Day inclusive watches at Headquarters of Infantry Brigades and Divisional Artillery will be synchronised daily with a watch which will be sent round from Divisional Headquarters by a Staff Officer.
On 'Y' Day the watches will be synchronised twice.
General Officers Commanding Infantry Brigades and C.R.A. will arrange for a similar daily synchronisation in the evening with the units under their command.

DIVISIONAL REPORT CENTRE 15. Divisional Report Centre will be at ELVERDINGHE CHATEAU from 10.p.m. on the night 'Y'/'Z'.

　　ACKNOWLEDGE.

H. E. Pryce
Lieut. Col.,
General Staff, 38th (Welsh) Divn.

Issued to Signals at 6pm
Copies to (See overleaf)

Page 7.

Distribution of Division Order No. 107.

G.O.C.
G.S.O.1.
G.S.
"Q" (To inform Administrative
    Units of Extracts
    affecting them)
Signals
38th Div: Arty.
C. R. E.
38th Heavy Bombardment Group
113th Brigade
114th Brigade
115th Brigade
19th Welsh Regt.
176th M.G.Coy.
A.D.M.S.
D.M.G.O.

XIV Corps "G"
XIV Corps "Q"
Guards Divn.
20th Divn.
29th Divn.
51st Divn.
9th Squadron R.F.C.
"Q" Special Coy. R.E.
XIV Corps Cavalry Regt.

SECRET

ADDENDA TO 38TH (WELSH) DIVISION ORDER NO. 106.

17th July 1917.

MOVES 18TH & 19TH JULY 1917.

1. 18th July
   Units.   Move from   Move to

   "C" Bn. 113th Bde.   )
   "D" Bn. 113th Bde.   )   CAESTRE Area.   P.5. PROVEN.
   331st Coy. A.S.C.   )
   129th Fd. Amb.   )

   Route - GODEWAERVELDE - WATOU.
           To be North of POPERINGHE - WATOU - HOUTKERQUE Road
           by 9-30.a.m.

2. 18th July
   Units.   Move from   Move to

   "C" Bn. 114th Bde.   )
   "D" Bn. 114th Bde.   )   CAESTRE Area.   P.5. PROVEN.
   332nd Coy. A.S.C.   )
   130th Fd. Amb.   )

   Route - GODEWAERVELDE - WATOU.
           To be North of POPERINGHE - HOUTKERQUE Road by 10.a.m.

3. 19th July
   Units.   Move from   Move to

   115th Inf. Bde.   )
   333rd Coy. A.S.C.   )   EECKE Area.   P.5. PROVEN.
   131st Fd. Amb.   )

   Route - STEENVOORDE - Road Junction K.32.d.4.0. - K.17.c.0.8. -
           WATOU.
           Column to be North of POPERINGHE - WATOU - HOUTKERQUE Rd.
           by 10.a.m.

4. All the above Groups report to Area Commandant PROVEN regarding
   P.5. Area.

5. A distance of 500 yards will be maintained between Battalions,
   Companies A.S.C. and Field Ambulances from CAESTRE onwards.

P.T.O.

Page 2.

6. Para. 5 of 38th Division No. 105 is cancelled.

The Divisional Report Centre will close at NORRENT FONTES at 11.a.m. on the 19th instant, and will re-open at the same hour at PROVEN.

Mounted portion of Divisional Headquarters will march as in Serial 6 of 38th Division Order No. 106.

ACKNOWLEDGE.

R.S Follett Maj
for Lieut. Colonel,
General Staff, 38th (Welsh) Division.

Issued to Signals at 6.a.m.

Copies to all recipients of 38th Div: Order No. 106.
and to :-
Lt.Col. C.C.NORMAN,D.S.O. 15th R.W.F.
Commanding "B" Group 113th Brigade
Lt.Col. J.H.HAYES,D.S.O. 14th Welsh Regt.
Commanding No. 2 Group 114th Brigade.

S E C R E T.
--*-*-*-*-*-*
38th Division No. G.S.S.58/22.

38TH (WELSH) DIVISION OPERATIONS.
DIVISION ORDER NO. 107.

ADDENDUM NO. 3.

1. Para.5. - BLUE Line.
   For enclosure at C.8.c.0.8. road C.8.d.0.8.

2. Para. 7., Line 8.
   After "GREEN" insert "dotted".
   Erase lines 9 and 10.

3. Para. 6. Line 23.
   After "otherwise" read "200" instead of "400".

4. Para. 7. Lines 37 and 38.
   For C.13.b. and B.12.d. read C.13.d. and B.18.b. respectively.

5. Para. 8 (a).
   For "CHEMIN AVENUE" read "CHEMIN DRIVE".

H. E. Pryce
Lieut. Colonel,
17th July, 1917.   General Staff, 38th (Welsh) Division.

SECRET

COPY NO. 9

38TH (WELSH) DIVISION ORDER NO. 108.

Ref:- Maps 1/40,000 Sheets 27 & 28.   17th July 1917.

1. The 38th Division will relieve the 29th Division in the ZWAANHOF SECTOR on the 19th/20th and 21st July in accordance with the attached Table.

2. 113th and 114th Infantry Brigades will each detail 50 men to relieve 100 men of the 29th Division attached to the 173rd Tunnelling Company R.E. in CANAL BANK on 20th/21st.

3. Until 10 a.m. 21st July troops of the 38th Division will come under orders of 29th Division on passing East of the ELVERDINGHE - BRIELEN ROAD.

4. The 113th Brigade Headquarters will relieve the 86th Brigade Headquarters on the night of the 20th/21st July.
   G.O.C. 114th Infantry Brigade will remain at Headquarters 86th Brigade until the relief is complete on the night of the 20th/21st July, when he will move into his own Headquarters on the East CANAL BANK at C.19.a.25.95.

5. All details of 38th Division not going into the trenches, other than first line transport, will be accommodated in P.2 (87th Brigade Area) from 18th instant onwards. Exact Camp will be wired later.

6. East of POPERINGHE - PROVEN Road a distance of 200 yards will be maintained between Companies.

7. All details of relief to be arranged between Brigadiers concerned.

8. Completion of reliefs and moves will be wired to Divisional Head-Quarters in Code.

9. G.O.C. 38th Division will assume command of ZWAANHOF SECTOR at 10 a.m. on 21st instant.

ACKNOWLEDGE

B.S. Follett Maj.
for Lieut. Colonel,
General Staff 38th (Welsh) Division.

Issued to Signals at 6 a m

Copies to :-

G.O.C.	A.D.M.S.	XIV Corps "G"
G.S.	S.S.O.	XIV Corps "Q"
"Q"	D.A.D.O.S.	D.A.D.P.S., XIV Corps
Signals	D.A.D.V.S.	Guards Divn.
C.R.A.	A.P.M.	29th Division
C.R.E.	Camp Comdt.	20th Division
113th Bde.	Div. Gas Offr.	51st Division
114th Bde.	Sniping Coy.	Area Comdt. PROVEN
115th Bde.	176th M.G.Coy.	R.T.O. POPERINGHE
19th Welsh Regt.	Adjt i/c Camps.	Div. Depot Battn.
Train.	D.M.G.O.	

S E C R E T

MOVE TABLE (To accompany 38th Divn. Order No. 108)

Date	Unit	From	To	Relieving	Remarks
19th July	"C" Bn. 113th Bde. "D" Bn. 113th Bde. "C" Bn. 114th Bde. "D" Bn. 114th Bde.	P.5.	Corps Staging Areas F.5.b. F.11.a. & b. F.6.a.		Marching by Track 9. Battn. not to cross ELVERDINGHE - BRIELEN RD. before 10 p.m. Halting at "G" Camp for dinners and rest.
Night 19/20th July	"A" Bn. 114th Bde.	P.1.	L.2.	2nd R.Fus., 86th Bde.	Marching by Track 10. Bn. not to cross ELVERDINGHE - BRIELEN RD. before 10 p.m. Halting at "H" Camp for dinners and rest.
	"A" Bn. 113th Bde.	P.1.	CANAL BANK	1st. R.Dublin Fus. 86th Brigade	Marching by Track 10. Bn. not to cross ELVERDINGHE - BRIELEN RD. before 10 p.m. Halting at "H" Camp for dinners and rest.
	19th (Pioneer) Bn. Welsh Regt. (less 1 Coy.)	PROVEN	CANAL BANK & RIVOLI FM.	1/2 Mon. Regt., who will have left beforehand, but will arrange for an Officer to hand over	Marching by Track 10. Not to cross ELVERDINGHE, BRIELEN RD. before 11 p.m. Halting at "H" Camp for dinners and rest.
20th July.	2 Secs. 114 M.G.Coy. 1 Secn. 114 M.G.Coy. ½ T.M.Bty. 114th Bde.	P.1. P.1. P.1.	Right Sub-Sector L.2.)Right Bn.)86th Bde.	Sub-sector 8 guns Right Bn./86 Bde 4 guns 83 Bde in L.2. Relieving ½ 86th T.M. Bty.	Marching by Track 9 --ditto-- --ditto--
	2 secs. 113 M.G.Coy.	P.1.	Left Sub-Sector	)8 guns Left Bn. Sub-)sector 86th Bde.	Marching by Track 10.
	1 Sec. 113 M.G.Coy	P.1.	"X" Line	4 guns 86 Bde. in "X" Line.	Marching by Track 10.
	½ T.M.Bty. 113 Bde.	P.1.	Left Battn. 86th Bde.	relieving ½ 86th T.M.Bty.	Marching by Track 10.
					Whole of above to move in small parties at big intervals after crossing DROMORE CORNER - VLAMERTINGHE ROAD.

Page 2.

MARCH TABLE (Continued)

Date.	Unit.	From	To	Relieving	Remarks.
20th July.	"C" Bn. 114th Bde.	Corps Staging Area.	VOX VRIE.	—	Move to be completed by noon. "Q" will provide tents and shelters.
	"C" Bn. 113th Bde.	-ditto-	DUBLIN CAMP A.10.d.9.6.	1 Bn. S.W.B.	Move to be completed by noon. To provide 450 men for work under G.O.C.,R.A. XIV Corps on dugouts, tramlines &c. on 21st. July.
	1 Sec. 114 M.G.Coy. ½ Sec. 114 T.M.Bty. 1 Sec. 113 M.G.Coy. ½ Sec. 113 T.M.Bty.	P.1.	Corps Staging Area. F.11. a. & b. F.5.b. and F.6.a.	—	Move to be completed by noon.
	176th M.G.Coy.	P.5.	A.16.a.8.8.	4 A.A.guns of 29/ Div. at DRAGON CAMP	
Night 20/21st July.	"A" Bn. 114th Bde.	L.2.	Right Sub-Sector.	1/Lan:Fus: 86 Bde.	
	"A" Bn. 113th Bde.	CANAL BANK.	Left Sub-sector.	16/Middlesex Regt. 86th Bde.	
(*)	"B" Bn. 114th Bde.	P.1.	L.2.	"A" Bn. 114th Bde.	To leave P.1. by 10.a.m. Marching by Track 9. Halting at G Camp for dinners and rest.
(*)	"B" Bn. 113th Bde.	P.1.	CANAL BANK	"A" Bn. 113th Brigade.	To leave P.1. by 10.a.m. Marching by Track 10. Halting for dinners and rest,at "H" Camp. (*)"B" Bns. 113 & 114 Bdes not to cross ELVERDINGHE - BRIELEN RD. before 10.p.m.
	124th Fd.Coy.R.E.	Corps Staging Areas.	CANAL BANK.	Kent Fd.Coy.R.E. in CANAL BANK.	Marching by Track 10. NOT to cross ELVERDINGHE - BRIELEN RD. before midnight. Halting at "H" Camp for dinners and rest.
	113th Bde. H.Q.	-ditto-	CANAL BANK.	86th Bde. H.Q. in CANAL BANK.	
	114th Bde. H.Q.	-ditto-	CANAL BANK. C.19.a.25.95.	—	

Page 3.

MARCH TABLE (Continued)

Date.	Unit.	From	To	Relieving	Remarks.
21st July	38th Div: H.Q.	PROVEN.	DRAGON CAMP.		These to be completed by noon.
	"D" Bn. 114th Bde.	Corps Staging Area.	"G" Camp and HOURSLOW CAMP (A.11.c.6.5.)		—do.—
	"D" Bn. 115th Bde.	—ditto—	"H" Camp.		
	1 Sec: 114 L.G.Coy.	—ditto—	"G" Camp		
	½ Sec: 114 T.M.Bty.		"G" Camp		
	1 Sec: 113 L.G.Coy.		"H" Camp.		
	½ Sec: 113 T.M.Bty.		"H" Camp.		
	115th Brigade.	P.5.	Corps Staging Areas.F.11.a. & b, F.5.b. and F.6.a.		Move to be completed by noon.

B S Follett ?

Lieut. Colonel,
General Staff, 38th (Welsh) Division.

17th July, 1917.

"A" Form.
MESSAGES AND SIGNALS.

Army Form C.2121 (in pads of 100).

SECRET

TO — 113th Brigade
~~114th Brigade~~
115th Brigade

38th Divn Q

Sender's Number.	Day of Month	In reply to Number.	AAA
G.S. 6678	18th		

Bde H.Q. of P1 are at F.15 central.
Bde H.Q. of P5 are at E.17.b.0.9
Bde H.Q. of Corps staging area are not yet fixed

From 38th Divn

P.S. Follow msg for General Col.

S E C R E T   38th Division No. G.S.6677

18th July 1917

Trains having now been allotted for the relief, the following alterations and additions to 38th Division Order No. 108 are issued :-

1. Para. 5
   Site for Details Camp is X.27.a.2.3 Sheet 19.

2. Addition to MOVE TABLE on night 19/20th
   "A" Bn. 114th Brigade) 200 all ranks of each Battn.
   "A" Bn. 113th Brigade) entrain PROVEN 9 p.m. and arrive ELVERDINGHE 9.35 p.m.

3. Alteration to MOVE TABLE on night 19/20th
   19th Welsh Regt.) Entrain PROVEN 11.50 p.m. and arrive
   (less 1 Coy.) ELVERDINGHE 12.25 a.m.

4. Alteration to move Table on 20th

   2 Secs. 114th M.G.Coy.)   Entrain PROVEN 11.50 p.m. 19th
   1 Secn. 114th M.G.Coy.)   and arrive ELVERDINGHE 12.25 a.m.
   ½ T.M.Bty. 114th Bde.)   20th.

   2 Secs. 113th M.G.Coy.)   NOTE :- Total accommodation for
   1 Secn. 113th M.G.Coy.)   Units (other than 19th
   ½ T.M.Bty. 113th Bde.)   Welsh Regt. already
                                        provided for) 800 O.R's.

5. Alteration to MOVE TABLE night 20th/21st.

   "B" Bn. 114th Bde.) Leave P.1 by 10 a.m. and march to
   "B" Bn. 113th Bde.) Corps Staging Area No. 2. Entrain 800 all ranks of each Battn. at INTERNATIONAL CORNER 10 p.m. and arrive ELVERDINGHE 10.35 p.m.

   124th Fd. Coy. R.E. move from P.5 and not from Corps Staging Area. Entrain PROVEN 11.50 p.m. and arrive ELVERDINGHE 12.25 a.m.

   NOTE :- Total accommodation for Units (other than 124th Field Coy. R.E. already provided for) 300 Other Ranks. Will stop at INTERNATIONAL CORNER if required.

   H.Q. 113th Bde.) Move from P.1 and not from Corps Staging
   H.Q. 114th Bde.) Area - by one of above trains, if G.O's.C. wish.

ACKNOWLEDGE

R. S. Follett May
Lieut. Colonel,
General Staff, 38th (Welsh) Divn.

Copies to :- All recipients of D.O. 108

SECRET

38th Div: No. G.S. 6695.

ADDENDUM NO. 2 to 38TH DIVISION ORDER NO. 108.

1. Two Battalions of 115th Infantry Brigade will move on afternoon of 20th July from P.5.Area to Corps Staging Area No. 2 -(F.11.a. and b - F.5.b. and F.6.a.)

2. 38th Div: "Q" will allot billeting area.

3. Route from P.5. will be in accordance with Fifth Army Traffic Map

4. Para. 5. of 38th Div: Order No. 108 is cancelled and the following will be substituted :-

   5. All details of 38th Division, not going into the trenches, will remain in their First Line Transport Lines, *until further orders.*

ACKNOWLEDGE.

19th July, 1917.

R.S. Follett
Maj.=for Lieut. Colonel,
General Staff, 38th (Welsh) Divn.

S E C R E T   38th Division No. G.S. 6698

ADDENDUM NO. 3 to 38TH DIVISION ORDER NO. 108.

Reference Para. 4 of Divisional Order No. 108.

G.O.C. 114th Brigade will not take over the command of Right Battalion front of ZWAANHOF SECTOR on night 20th/21st July. G.O.C. 113th Brigade will command the whole front of the ZWAANHOF SECTOR from the time of completion of relief.

The following moves will take place :-

1. **20th July**

   Headquarters 114th Brigade from P.1 to "H" Camp.

2. **21st July**

   (a) 38th Divisional Sniping Company from PROVEN to "H" Camp.

   (b) 38th Divisional Gas School from PROVEN to "H" Camp.

   (c) Salvage Company from PROVEN to 28/A.16.a.8.5.

3. Traffic routes Fifth Army will be strictly adhered to.

ACKNOWLEDGE

20th July 1917.   Lieut. Colonel,
                                   General Staff, 38th (Welsh) Division.

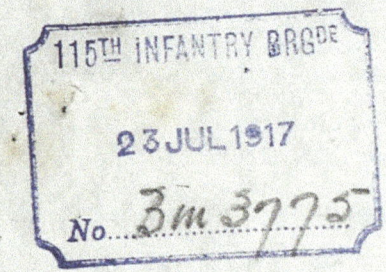

SECRET

38th Division No. G.S.S.58/25.

38TH (WELSH) DIVISION ORDER NO.107.
ADDENDUM NO. 4.

Paragraph 7.

After "Barrage guns will create smoke barrages as under" insert -

"Unless the Wind is East of S.E. or N.W." when the Corps may order the barrage not to be formed, but the smoke barrage will be made unless Corps Orders to the contrary are received.

Paragraph 11, 2nd Line.

For "GREEN" road "WHITE".

ACKNOWLEDGE.

H.E. Pryce Lieut. Colonel,
General Staff, 38th (Welsh) Divn.

22nd July, 1917.

Copies to all recipients of Division Order No. 107.

? look up

S E C R E T   38th Division No. G.S.S.70/1

Reference 38th Division Order No. 109.

This Gas was discharged on the night 20th/21st instant.

                                             R.S. Follett May
                                         Lieut. Colonel,
22/7/1917.   General Staff, 38th (Welsh) Divn.

Copies to all recipients of 38th D.O. 109

S E C R E T   COPY NO. 9

38TH (WELSH) DIVISION ORDER NO. 111

Ref :- Sheet 28 N.W. 1/20,000   July 24th 1917.

1. G.O.C. 114th Infantry Brigade will assume Command of the front of the ZWAANHOF SECTOR at 12 noon to-morrow the 25th instant.
   G.O.C. 113th Infantry Brigade will move to "H" Camp on relief.

2. G.O.C. 114th Infantry Brigade will continue to occupy the present Headquarters on the WEST CANAL BANK until such time as his new Headquarters on the EAST CANAL BANK are completed.
   Completion of relief will be wired to D.H.Q. in Code.

   ACKNOWLEDGE

                                           H.E. Pryce
                                                   Lieut. Colonel,
                              General Staff, 38th (Welsh) Division.

Issued to Signals at 3 p.m.
Copies to :-

G.O.C.	A.D.M.S.	XIV Corps "G"
G.S.	S.S.O.	XIV Corps "Q"
"Q"	D.A.D.O.S.	D.A.D.P.S. XIV Corps.
Signals	D.A.D.V.S.	Guards Division
C.R.A.	A.P.M.	29th Division
C.R.E.	Camp Commdt.	20th Division
113th Brigade	Div. Gas Offr.	51st Division
114th Brigade	Sniping Coy.	Area Commdt. "G" Camp
115th Brigade	176th M.G.Coy.	Div. Depot Battn.
19th Welsh Regt.	Adjt. i/c Camps	
38th Heavy Bombt. Group		
Train	D.M.G.O.	

SECRET

38th Division No. G.S.S.58/32.

38TH (WELSH) DIVISION OPERATIONS.

DIVISION ORDER NO. 112.

ADDENDUM NO.1.

In third line for "both" substitute "Guards and 38th"

H.E. Pryce
Lieut. Colonel,
General Staff, 38th (Welsh) Division.

25th July, 1917.

As per D.O. 112.

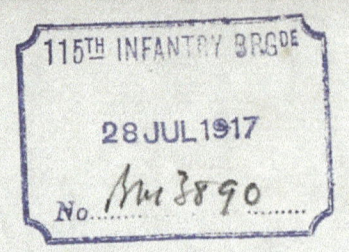

SECRET

38th Division No. G.S.S.58/29.

38TH (WELSH) DIVISION OPERATIONS.
DIVISION ORDER NO. 107.
ADDENDUM NO. 5.

Artillery will cease fire on "Z" day in accordance with the following orders :-

At Zero plus 5 hours 50 minutes all Field Artillery fire will cease, and will not re-open except on an "S.O.S" call from the ground, or "LL" call from the air. "G.F." calls will not be answered until definite information has been received by Divisions to the exact location of all patrols on their respective fronts.

Heavy Artillery will not fire after Zero plus 5 hours 50 minutes S.W. of a line U.9.d.2.4. - U.18.c.0.0. - V.25.c.0.0. without orders from Corps Headquarters, except in the case of an "S.O.S" or "LL" call.

ACKNOWLEDGE.

H. E. Payne
Lieut. Colonel,
25th July, 1917.   General Staff, 38th (Welsh) Division.

Copies to :-

G.O.C.
G.S.O.1
G.S.
"Q"
Signals
38th Div: Arty.
38th H.Bombt.Group.
C.R.E.
113th Brigade
114th Brigade
115th Brigade
19th Welsh Regt.
176th M.G.Coy.
D.M.G.O.
A.D.M.S.

XIV Corps "G"
XIV Corps "Q"
Guards Div:
20th Div:
29th Div:
51st Div:
9th Squadron R.F.C.
"Q" Special Coy. R.E.
XIV Corps Cavalry Regt.
59th M.G.Coy.
217th M.G.Coy.

SECRET

Copy No. 10

38TH (WELSH) DIVISION ORDER NO. 112.

25th July, 1917.

Reference 1/10,000 Trench Map
and No. 106 Barrage Map.

On the afternoon of "Y" day from 3 to 5.p.m. there will be a concentrated bombardment of the MOUND by all available 2" Trench Mortars of ~~both~~ Guards and 38 Divisions. From 5.p.m. "Y" day to Zero hour, C.R.A's of Divisions are responsible that a box barrage of Field Artillery is kept on the line C.7.c.28.96. - C.7.a.33.32. - B.12.b.88.40. This barrage must be of sufficient intensity to prevent any of the enemy returning to the MOUND after the bombardment ceases.

ACKNOWLEDGE ✓

H.E. Pryce
Lieut. Colonel,
General Staff, 38th (Welsh) Division.

Issued to Signals at 4.30 p.m.

Copies to :-
G.O.C.
G.S.O.1.
G.S.
"Q"
Signals
38th Div: Arty.
38th H.Bombt.Group.
113th Brigade
114th Brigade
115th Brigade

19th Welsh Regt.
C. R. E.
176th M.G.Coy.
59th M.G.Coy.
217th M.G.Coy.
D.M.G.O.
A.D.M.S.
XIV Corps "G"
Guards Div:
20th Div:
29th Div:
51st Div:

Cancelled

S636

"C" Form
MESSAGES AND SIGNALS.   Army Form C. 2123.

Prefix ...... Code AD. Words 12
From YCA
By Roddy

Service Instructions: 1 of 4 adds.
Handed in at YCA.   Office 1.20 p.m.   Received 1.31 p.m.

TO 115 Bde.

Sender's Number: M636
Day of Month: 29

Div order 112 is cancelled

FROM 38th Div
PLACE & TIME 1.5 pm

S E C R E T

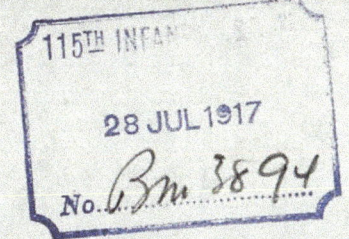

COPY NO. 9

38TH (WELSH) DIVISION ORDER NO. 114

Ref :- Sheet 28 N.W. 1/20,000   25th July 1917

1. On 26th July 1917 the 10th Battalion King's Royal Rifles and the 10th Rifle Brigade will relieve the 15th Battn. Welsh Regiment in L.2 and the 15th Battalion Royal Welsh Fusiliers in the CANAL BANK respectively.

2. Moves will be carried out in accordance with the attached March Table.

3. The 10th Battalion King's Royal Rifles and the 10th Battn. Rifle Brigade will come under the orders of the General Officer Commanding 113th Infantry Brigade when East of the ELVERDINGHE - BRIELEN ROAD.

4. Further arrangements will be made between Brigadiers concerned.

5. Transport of both the 10th Battalion King's Royal Rifles and 10th Rifle Brigade will be located at A.11.c.1.7. One hut will be available for 80 men at A.11.c.1.3.

6. Box respirators will be worn in the 'Alert' position at all times East of the DAWSON'S CORNER - ELVERDINGHE - WOESTEN ROAD whatever the direction of the Wind.

7. G.O.C. ZWAANHOF Front will arrange that sufficient guides meet each of these Battalions on the ELVERDINGHE - BRIELEN ROAD.

8. Completion of relief will be wired to Divisional H.Q. in Code.

ACKNOWLEDGE. ✓

R.S. Follett Maj.
for Lieut. Colonel,
General Staff, 38th (Welsh) Division.

Issued to Signals at 7.15 p.m.

Copies to :-

G.O.C.	A.D.M.S.	D.A.D.P.S. XIV Corps
G.S.	S.S.O.	Guards Division
"Q"	D.A.D.O.S.	29th Division
Signals	D.A.D.V.S.	20th Division
C.R.A.	A.P.M.	51st Division
C.R.E.	Camp Commdt.	59th Inf. Bde.
113th Brigade	Div. Gas Offr.	Area Commdt. "G" Camp
114th Brigade	Sniping Coy.	Div. Depot. Battn.
115th Brigade	176th M.G.Coy.	
19th Welsh Regt.	Adj. i/c Camps	
38th Heavy Bombt.)	D.M.G.O.	
Group)	XIV Corps "G"	
38th Div. Train	XIV Corps "Q"	

SECRET   MOVE TABLE (To accompany 38th D.O. No. 114)

Unit	Place	To	Starting Point	Time of passing S.P.	Route	Remarks
2 Coys. 10th K.R.R.	"H" Camp (A.10.c.1.9)	L.2.	CORNISH CROSS (A.16.a.1.0)	6 p.m.	Track 9	100 yards distance to be maintained between Platoons.
2 Coys. 10th K.R.R.	HOUNSLOW CAMP (A.11.c.6.5)	L.2.	Junction of POPERINGHE - WOESTEN RD. & Track 10. (A.16.b.5.8)	7 p.m.	To A.17.a. 2.2 - Track 9.	-ditto-
10th R.B.	A.10.c.5.6.	WEST CANAL BANK	Junction of POPERINGHE - WOESTEN RD. & Track 10 (A.16.b.5.8)	8.15 p.m.	Track 10	-ditto-
"A" Battn. 114th Brigade	L.2	2 Coys "H" Camp 2 Coys. HOUNSLOW CAMP.	L.2.	10 p.m.	Track 9	-ditto-
"A" Battn. 113th Brigade	WEST CANAL BANK	A.10.c. 5.6.	WEST CANAL BANK	10 p.m.	Track 10	-ditto-

25/7/1917.

S E C R E T

115TH INFANTRY BRGDE
27 JUL 1917
No. Bm 3867   Copy No. 5

38TH (WELSH) DIVISION ORDER NO. 116.

27th July 1917.

1. At 5.15 a.m. tomorrow a practice barrage will be carried out on the whole Army front.

2. The barrage will be as laid down for "Z" Day with the exception of any necessary modifications for raids and that forward guns, 12-inch Howitzers, etc., will not open fire.

3. The barrage will cease at 5.45 a.m. when the normal days programme will be resumed.

4. Under cover of the above barrage one Company of the 15th Welsh will carry out a Raid on CAESAR'S RESERVE. Any special artillery arrangements required by G.O.C. 114th Infantry Brigade will be made in direct communication with O.C. Right Group, Artillery.

5. Artillery and Infantry Brigades will make special arrangements to note time, locality duration and intensity of any hostile barrages put down.

6. Trenches will be lightly held during this practice barrage.

7. Machine Gun barrages will be carried out as for "Z" Day with such Machine Guns as are now in the line.
   No thermite or oil will be fired.

8. R.F.C. will detail machines exactly as for "Z" Day, so that all hostile batteries firing may be located and engaged for destruction.

9. Batteries in rest need not be brought back into the line for the practice barrage.

ACKNOWLEDGE

H.E. Pryce
Lieut. Colonel,
General Staff, 38th, (Welsh) Division.

Issued to Signals at 4 p.m.

Copies to :-

G.O.C.   A.D.M.S.
38th Div. Arty.   "Q"
113th Brigade   29th Division
114th Brigade   20th Division
115th Brigade   Guards Division
19th Welsh Regt.   51st Division
C.R.E.   XIV Corps
Signals   9th Sqdn. R.F.C.
176th M.G.Coy.   XIV Corps Cav. Regt.
D.M.G.O.
8th H.A.G.

S E C R E T
No. Bm 3868
38th Division No. G.S.6815

115TH INFANTRY BRGDE
27 JUL 1917

1. 38th Division Order No. 113 is cancelled.

2. The G.O.C. 113th Inf. Brigade and G.O.C. 114th Inf. Brigade took over their Battle Fronts at 2 p.m. to-day.

3. The dividing line between Brigades will be as shown on Map 1 referred to in Para. 3 of 38th Division Order No. 107.

ACKNOWLEDGE.

27/7/1917.
Lieut. Colonel,
General Staff, 38th (Welsh) Divn.

Copies to all recipients of 38th D.O. 113.

SECRET

38TH (WELSH) DIVISION ORDER NO. 113.   Copy No. 10

25th July, 1917.

General Officer Commanding 114th Infantry Brigade will relieve the General Officer Commanding 113th Infantry Brigade in command of the ZWAANHOF SECTOR, at 2.p.m. 27th instant.

General Officer Commanding 113th Infantry Brigade will move to "H" Camp.

ACKNOWLEDGE:

H.E. Pryce
Lieut. Colonel,
General Staff, 38th (Welsh) Division.

Issued to Sigs :- 8. p.m.

Copies to :-

G.O.C.	113th Bde.	S.S.O.	176th M.G.Coy.
G.S.	114th Bde.	D.A.D.O.S.	Adjt. i/c Camps
"Q"	115th Bde.	D.A.D.V.S.	D.M.G.O.
Signals	19th Welsh.	A.P.M.	XIV Corps "G" & "Q"
C.R.A.	Train.	C.C.	D.A.D.P.S.
C.R.E.	A.D.M.S.	D.Gas O.	Guards, 20th, 29th and
38th H.B.Group.		Sniping Coy.	51st Divisions.
		Area Comdt, "G" Camp.	Div: Depot Battn.

SECRET   38th Division No. G.S.6815

1. 38th Division Order No. 113 is cancelled.

2. The G.O.C. 113th Inf. Brigade and G.O.C. 114th Inf. Brigade took over their Battle Fronts at 2 p.m. to-day.

3. The dividing line between Brigades will be as shown on Map 1 referred to in Para. 3 of 38th Division Order No. 107.

<u>ACKNOWLEDGE.</u>

27/7/1917.   Lieut. Colonel,
           General Staff, 38th (Welsh) Divn.

Copies to all recipients of 38th D.O. 113.

S E C R E T   COPY NO 5

38TH (WELSH) DIVISION ORDER NO. 115

Ref:- Sheet 28 N.W.2 ST. JULIEN   27th July 1917.

1. An air reconnaissance over the Corps Front between 5.40 a.m. and 8.25 a.m. 27/7/17 carried out by machines flying at 1000 feet as far back as ENGLISH FARM, ABRI FARM, STEENBEEK is as follows :-

    "No hostile Machine gun fire or rifle fire and no enemy seen in trenches. A.A. fire very slight and probably from Field Guns. Did not follow our machines behind front line trenches".

2. Patrols, each one Platoon strong, will be sent out on the Divisional Front at 5 p.m. 27th instant as follows :-

    <u>113th Brigade</u> :- One patrol to CACTUS JUNCTION whence they will gain touch with patrols of the Guards Division at C.1.c.55.00. One patrol to CACTUS POINT.

    <u>114th Brigade</u> :- One patrol to GALLWITZ. FM One patrol to CHEMIN TRENCH.

3. As soon as patrols have seized this line, outposts will be established along the line supported by other troops of the 113th and 114th Brigades in the old German front system.

4. Once the outpost line has been established patrols will be pushed forward to discover whether the line TELEGRAPH HOUSE - CANCER TRENCH - CANDLE TRENCH is held by the enemy. The Artillery will be prepared to cover the movement of these patrols. No patrols will move beyond this line without Corps Orders.

5. 114th Inf. Brigade will be prepared to form a defensive flank along CAESAR'S LANE.

6. The 38th Div. Arty. will be prepared to put down the BLUE LINE protective barrage from 5 p.m. onwards.

7. The 38th Div. Arty. will arrange for the necessary Liaison Officers to work with the leading Battalions of the 113th and 114th Brigades.

8. Strong Points will be made on the BLUE LINE as in the original scheme.

9. The 10th Battalion King's Royal Rifles attached 114th Brigade and 10th Battn. Rifle Brigade attached 113th Brigade will take over our present front line as the present front Battalions go forward.

10. The S.O.S. Signal will be a succession of Rifle Rockets each bursting into two red and two green lights simultaneously until the Artillery reply.

11. The above are Divisional Orders for the first bound, but Units must be prepared to make another bound to the CANDLE - CANCER TRENCH Line.

12. No heavy Artillery will fire West of the line JOLIE FARM - PILCKEM MILL - TELEGRAPH HOUSE - GENERAL FARM - WOOD 15 after 5 p.m., or West of the Line IRON CROSS - COLONEL's FARM after 5.45 p.m. till receipt of further orders, or on receipt of an S.O.S. or L.L. call.

13. A contact aeroplane will follow the movements of the patrols, who will show flares when called on.

14. Headquarters 113th Inf. Brigade will be at FUSILIER HOUSE C.13.c.10.15.
    Headquarters 114th Inf. Brigade will be at C.19.c.4.2.

15. Divisional Headquarters remain at DRAGON CAMP.

ACKNOWLEDGE by wire.

Harington Capt.
for
Lieut. Colonel,
General Staff, 38th (Welsh) Divn.

Issued to Signals at 2 p.m.

Copies to :-

G.O.C.
38th Div. Arty.
113th Brigade
114th Brigade
115th Brigade
19th Welsh Regt.
C. R. E.
Signals
173th M.G.Coy.
D.M.G.O.
8th H.A.G.
A.D.M.S.
"Q"

29th Divn.
20th Division
Guards Division
51st Division.
XIV Corps.
9th Sqdn R.F.C.
XIV Corps Cav: Regt.

D. Orders

115TH INFANTRY BRIGADE
28 JUL 1917
No. Bm 3907

SECRET
-*-*-*-*-*-

Copy No. 11

38TH (WELSH) DIVISION ORDER NO 117.

Ref: Trench Maps 1/10,000.   28th July, 1917.

1. During the course of yesterday's reconnaissance the British Line has been advanced from HARVEY TRENCH at Junction C.7.7. to C.7.8. to FARM 14 - CANAL AVENUE - S.W. Corner ARTILLERY WOOD - BOIS FARM.

2. Opposite the Division are the 100th R.I.R., 23rd Reserve (Saxon) Division. The 49th R.Division is opposite the Guards. An intercepted wireless message states that the 49th R.Division must regain the CANAL BANK and that the 100th R.I.R. will co-operate in the direction CACTUS JUNCTION - CABLE SUPPORT.

3. The following defensive measures will be taken :-
113th Infantry Brigade will consolidate new line from Junction HARVEY TRENCH and BAIRD AVENUE, East end of CABLE TRENCH, FARM 14 to C.7.a.20.22., and will have arrangements ready for an immediate counter-attack.
113th and 114th Infantry Brigades will arrange to put sentry posts beyond our front line to give warning of enemy's approach and to send patrols up to our protective barrage line.
Both Brigades will also arrange for bringing heavy Lewis Gun and Machine Gun fire on their front East of the line A in CACTUS TRENCH and Cross Roads at C.1.c.80.15. when required, special attention being paid to bringing enfilade fire on to the enemy's line of advance, and that no fire falls within the Guards Area.
Divisional Machine Gun barrage party will be ready to put down the BLUE Line protective barrage when required.
Artillery will arrange a protective barrage on German Front line to FORTIN 17, Western boundary of same to protect Guards right flank being C.7.d.0.7. - C.7.a.7.3. - C.7.a.5.7. - C.7.a.50.95.

4. **OFFENSIVE MEASURES.**
Divisional Artillery throughout the day will rake intermittently the ground for 200 yards on each side of CACTUS AVENUE, CACTUS RESERVE, CADDIE RESERVE, CAESAR RESERVE in concentrated 3 minute bursts at selected spots.
Artillery Bombardment will be carried out according to programme.

ACKNOWLEDGE.   ✓ *sent*

H. E. Pryce
Lieut. Colonel,
General Staff, 38th (Welsh) Division.

Issued to Signals at 2.20. p.m.

Copies to :-

G.O.C.	176th M.G.Coy.
G.S.O.1	59th M.G.Coy.
G.S.	217th M.G.Coy.
"Q"	A.D.M.S.
Signals	D. M. G. O.
38th Div:Arty.	XIV Corps "G"
C.R.E.	XIV Corps "Q"
8th H.A.G.	Guards Divn.
113th Brigade	20th Div:
114th Brigade	29th Div:
115th Brigade	51st Div:
19th Welsh Regt.	9th Squadron R.F.C.
	XIV Corps Cav: Rgt.

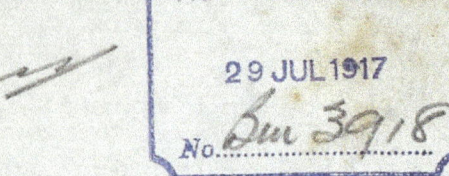

Order 107 File

SECRET.   Copy No. 11

Operation Orders by Lieut Col. B.S.Phillpotts, D.S.O.

Commanding Royal Engineers, 38th Division.

Order No. 27.

Ref. Map; 28. N.W.   29th July,
                                                     1917.

These orders are supplementary to G.S. Division Order
No. 107, and Instructions No. 22. G.S.S. 58/37 of
28.7.17.

1.   Existing bridges and Causeways will be maintained
by the 151st Field Co. R.E from 8.p.m. on 30th July,1917.

2.   As soon as darkness on the evening of the 30th
renders observation impossible, 151st Field Co. R.E will
construct Bridges over the Canal in accordance with
G.S.S. No. 58/15, with the exception that two or three of
the Bridges should lie between 6D and 7Y.
        The material for the 6A Pontoon Bridge will be
taken up to Canal Bank on the evening of 29th inst,
leaving "G" Camp at 9.pm, and unloaded and camouflaged
under arrangements to be made by 151st Field Co. R.E.

3.   At Zero plus 2 hours, two Sections of the 151st
Field Co. R.E will construct CACTUS Pontoon Bridge at
C.7.c.0.5. The bridging equipment will be brought up
under arrangements to be made by the 151st Field Co. R.E,
leaving Bridge Junction at Zero. (See para 11 of these
orders)
        Work on this Bridge will not be continued if
subjected to accurate destructive fire.

4.   The 124th Field Co. R.E will work on Strong Points,
(these Strong Points may have been commenced by Infantry)
advancing from CANAL BANK as soon as it has been
ascertained from 113th and 114th Inf. Brigades that the
fighting line is firmly established on the GREEN line.

5.   The 123rd Field Co. R.E will work on Strong Points
11,12, 13, 14, 15, 16, and 17. A whole Section will be
employed on No. 14.
        The Company will advance from CANAL BANK as soon
as it has been ascertained from 113th and 114th Infantry
Brigades that the fighting line is firmly established on
the line of the STEENBEEK.
        The Company will march from "G" Camp at Zero plus
. O.C. 123rd Field Co. R.E will make his own
arrangements for dinners in some convenient place.

6. The 124th Field Co. R.E. will send an Officer and an orderly at Zero plus one hour to keep in contact with the 113th and 114th Inf. Brigades, so as to obtain the earliest information as to the progress of the advance.
The 123rd Field will similarly send an Officer and an Orderly at Zero plus 4 hours.

7. 2 Coys., 19th Welsh Regt, will make a track for Field Guns from Huddleston Cross Roads (B.7.d.2.4) to the neighbourhood of Boche House (C.8.a.0.9). This track will then be extended towards IRON CROSS.
These Companies will leave the CANAL BANK when the BLACK Line has been captured.
Officers will proceed to 113th and 114th Infantry Brigades 1 hour after Zero to obtain earliest information of the capture of the BLACK Line.

8. R.E's and Pioneers will put in 8 hours work on the site and then return to CANAL BANK, but parties working on Strong Points will not leave their Strong Points if the enemy Infantry are engaging our Troops.

9. Companies will send the following messages by D.R.L.S :-

   (1) Reporting departure for work.
   (2) Progress report after 3 hours work with any information which may be of tactical or engineering utility.
   (3) Progress Report on return from work with information which may be of tactical or engineering utility.

10. One Company of Pioneers will be in Divisional Reserve on the West Canal Bank.

11. The 11th Battn. K. R. R. will detail 1 Company, less 2 Platoons, to accompany the Pontoons of the 151st Field Co. R.E, starting from the advanced R.E. Transport Lines (B.20.a.5.3) at Zero.
The 151st Field Coys pontoons will carry tools for this Company of K. R. R., who will assist in carrying and in making the track.

12. 2 Companies, 11th K. R. R, will march off from Bridge Junction at Zero plus ¼ hour, to work on Field Artillery tracks forward from Marongo Causeway.
Lieut A.H.Soutar, R.E. will accompany this party.

11th Battn. K.R.R. less 2 Coys and 2 Platoons, will march off from Bridge Junction at Zero plus 1¾ hours to Marongo Causeway.
Lieut A.H.Soutar, R.E. will stack tools for this Battn. at Marongo Causeway.
At Zero plus 4 hours R.F.A go to the Nile over Marongo Track.
At Zero plus 5 hours R.F.A pass Huddleston Cross Roads, via Marongo Track.

3.

13. Headquarters, 38th Divisional R.E will proceed from DRAGON CAMP to ELVERDINGHE CHATEAU, opening at ELVERDINGHE CHATEAU at 6.pm on 29th inst.

14. Acknowledge.

Issued at 1.30.am.

Capt. R.E. for.
C.R.E. 38th Division.

Copies to:-

O.C. 123rd Field Co. R.E.
O.C. 124th Field Co. R.E.
O.C. 151st Field Co. R.E.
O.C. 19th Welsh Regt.
O.C. 11th Battn. K.R.R.
Lieut A.H.Soutar. R.E.

G.S. 38th Division.
"Q" 38th Division.
113th Inf. Brigade.
114th Brigade.
115th Inf. Brigade.   } For information.
R.A. 38th Division.
A.D.M.S.
Chief Engineer. XIVth Corps.

S E C R E T

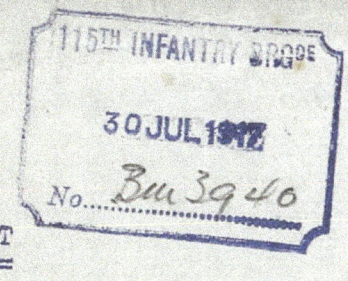

38th Division No. G.S.S. 58/44

38TH DIVISION ORDER NO. 107
ADDENDUM NO. 7

1.   Reference Para. 15 of 38th Division Order No. 107, and Addendum No. 6 (G.S.S.58/40) thereto.

2.   38th Division Report Centre will be at ELVERDINGHE CHATEAU from 10 p.m. to-night 30th July 1917.

ACKNOWLEDGE

30/7/1917.

R.J. Follett *for*
Lieut. Colonel,
General Staff, 38th (Welsh) Division.

Copies to all recipients of 38th D.O. No. 107

Cancelled

WAR DIARY HEADQUARTERS, 38TH (WELSH) DIVISION.
or
INTELLIGENCE SUMMARY.

(Erase heading not required.)

ORIGINAL.

Army Form C. 2118.

Page 1.

Instructions regarding War Diaries and Intelligence Summaries are contained in F.S. Regs, Part II. and the Staff Manual respectively. Title pages will be prepared in manuscript.

Place	Date	Hour	Summary of Events and Information	Remarks and references to Appendices
ELVERDINGHE CHATEAU.	1st August 1917.	5-30.a.m.	Situation unchanged. ~~12th Infantry Brigade took over front held on line of the GREEN BEEK from 11th Infantry Brigade who proceeded to CANAL BANK. At 8-a.m. Supports were and one and Sups and Bdagks placed.~~	
		9-4.a.m.	PILCKEM ROAD running North from CHEMIN CROSS ROADS in C.14.a. reported by 114th Brigade in good condition except for one or two places.	
		11-30.a.m.	113th Brigade report dispositions as follows :- 14th R.W.F. holding GREEN Line with 2 strong Points at U.27.d.2½.2. and U.17.c.9.3½. and linked up with Troops on Right and Left by series of small posts. H.Q.14th R.W.F. at NORMAN JUNCTION C.3.a.7.8. 15th R.W.F. holding line of Road through U.27.c. and C.3.a. H.Q. 15th R.W.F. BATTERY COPSE C.2.b.9.9. 13th R.W.F. holding BLACK Line and CANDLE TRENCH Line with Battalion H.Q. at PERISCOPE HOUSE. 16th R.W.F. in HARVEY and ESSEX TRENCHES with Battn. H.Q. at YORKSHIRE TRENCH. 113th M.G.Coy. and 113th T.M.Bty. at VILLA GRETCHEN. 113th Bde. H.Q. at WELSH HARP with Adv. Bde.H.Q. at PERISCOPE HOUSE.	
		12-59.p.m.	Report from 115th Brigade(timed 6-15.a.m.) - Bridgeheads of STEENBEEK 9* on left of Bde. front seized and 17th R.W.F. consolidating 100 yards beyond East Bank of STEENBEEK and in touch with Guards on the Left on West Bank of STEENBEEK. 11th S.W.B. on Right reported to have seized Bridgeheads with Patrols. (This report was queried)	
		2-40.p.m.	17th R.W.F. reported enemy massing on his front, and putting 4.2" barrage on STEENBEEK.	
		2-40.p.m.	113th Brigade report quiet on both sides. Occasional hostile shelling around PILCKEM CROSS ROADS. 114th Brigade report hostile artillery active.	
		4-20.p.m.	115th Brigade report hostile artillery & fire most severe. No sign of enemy advancing. Withdrawal of our troops on GREEN Line checked. 3 Coys of 16th Welsh sent forward to restore situation.	
		4-30.p.m.	115th Brigade report situation now normal, and our troops returning to STEENBEEK.	
		5.p.m.	(Message timed 3.p.m. only received 9-59.p.m.) From 115th Brigade. Bde.Major who visited Right front reports front in a disorganised state. Enemy snipers very active.	
		5.#.p.m.	Phone message from R.A. reports all quietening down again.	
		5.5.p.m.	Message from 115th Bde. (Recd. 9-25.p.m.) Very heavy enemy shelling on front line West of STEENBEEK temporarily breaking front held. Situation being restored.	
		5-52.p.m.	Message from 115th Bde. (reqd. 8-50.p.m.) 17th R.W.F. holding line West of STEENBEEK very lightly. 10th S.W.B. sending one Coy. to reinforce 11th S.W.B. on right. 115th Bde.	
		6-30.p.m.	(Phone) Liaison Officer Right Arty Group reports that at 5-30.p.m. situation on our front now quiet.	

4 Units   Sigs ✓
M.O. ✗   Staff Cpts ✗
T.M. ✓   3 T O ✗

copy to 113 ✗
        114 ✗
        38 DIV ✗

Original

WAR DIARY

GENERAL STAFF 38TH (WELSH) DIVISION Army Form C. 2118.

INTELLIGENCE SUMMARY.

VOLUME XXI.

(Erase heading not required.)

Instructions regarding War Diaries and Intelligence Summaries are contained in F. S. Regs., Part II and the Staff Manual respectively. Title pages will be prepared in manuscript.

Place	Date	Hour	Summary of Events and Information	Remarks and references to Appendices
ELVERDINGHE CHATEAU.	AUGUST.1917. 1st.		During the day enemy made several counter-attacks. O.O.119 issued regarding further developement of attack in YPRES SALIANT. G.S.S.59/51 issued. Advanced Divisional Headquarters close at ELVERDINGHE CHATEAU and open at DRAGON CAMP at same hour, on August 2nd.	App.1.
DRAGON CAMP.	2nd.		Thunderstorm and rain all day. A fairly quiet day; occasional burst of fire on batteries below the PILCKEM RIDGE.	
	3rd. 4th.		A very quiet day. Heavy rain continued. Enemy put up a barrage on PILCKEM VILLAGE and also on front line trenches during the afternoon, but no attack developed. Hostile aeroplanes active during the afternoon.	App.
	5th.		O.O.121 issued, regarding relief of 38th Division by 20th(Light) Division on 4th August 1917. Patrol reports a footbridge 75 yards north of the DAVIES STREET BRIDGE over the STEENBEEK to be still intact and no enemy seen west of the river. Much hostile aerial activity during the afternoon. A misty morning, but became quite clear and fine in the afternoon. Our own and hostile machines were active. Hostile activity increased. Divisional Headquarters move to PROVEN AREA being relieved by 20th (Light) Division.	
PROVEN.	6th.		Conference of Brigadiers at PROVEN at 10.a.m.	
	5th. 8th.		Divisional Commander visited C.G.S. Divisional rest and cleaning and equipping men. Holiday for all troops. Army Commander visited Brigadiers. G.S.O.3. went on leave. Training commenced.	
	9th.		Quiet day.	
	10th. 11th.		Nothing to report. 38th Division Instructions No.1. issued(G.S.S.33/1) regarding the further attack to be carried out by 20th (Light) Division on the Right and the 29th Division on the left, with the 38th Division and Guards Division in Reserve.	App.3
	11th.		Nothing to report.	
	13th.		Nothing to report.	
	13th. 14th. 15th.		LIEUT-GENERAL HUNTER WESTON visited D.H.Q. Nothing to report. 114th Infantry Brigade move to forward area in Local Reserve 20th Division. G.S.O.3. returned from 7 days leave.	App
	16th.		Amendment to 38th Division Order 122 (G.S.6944) issued regarding cross-country tracks. 20th(Light) Division attacked and gained all objectives including LANGEMARCK. One Battalion 114th Infantry Brigade loaned to 20th Division for"carrying". All Brigade under orders of 20th Division from 6.15.p.m. G.S.6956 warning order possibility of this Division having to relieve 20th Division by to-morrow night.	App

A5834 Wt. W4973/M68- 750,000 8/16 D. D. & L. Ltd. Forms/C.2118/13.

WAR DIARY or INTELLIGENCE SUMMARY

HEADQUARTERS, 38TH (WELSH) DIVISION. Army Form C. 2118.

(Erase heading not required.)

Instructions regarding War Diaries and Intelligence Summaries are contained in F. S. Regs., Part II. and the Staff Manual respectively. Title pages will be prepared in manuscript.

Place	Date	Hour	Summary of Events and Information	Remarks and references to Appendices
ELVERDINGHE CHATEAU	1st August 1917.	7.p.m.	113th Bde. H.Q. moving from WELSH HARP to C.3.b.15.10.	
		7-25.p.m.	Pigeon message from 115th Brigade - "S.O.S."	
		7-30.p.m.	(Phone) Div:Arty report from F.O.O. that S.O.S. has gone up on the Right front and that the Germans are across the STEENBEEK. Right Group barraging line of STEENBEEK.	
		7-33.p.m.	Similar report from Colonel Rudkin (Comdg. Right Group) through a F.O.O. A Major of 60th Rifles (probably Liaison Officer 20th Divn.) reports that S.O.S. gone up on the IRON CROSS Ridge.	
		7-55.p.m.	Message from 15th Welsh that 11th S.W.B. have fallen back. All alright on the GREEN Line.	
		10-6.p.m.	15th Welsh report situation quiet.	
		10-16.p.m.	Orders issued to the three Infantry Brigades that WEST Bank of the STEENBEEK must be held at all costs.	
		10-25.p.m.	Phone message - Some troops holding Gun pits West of the STEENBEEK.	
		10-35.p.m.	Col. RUDKIN reports that his Staff Officer came back having left front line at 6-30.p.m. Apparently our troops have been knocked about and a good number of casualties. 51st Division left Brigade 17th R.W.F. only 140 strong commanded by wounded Captain. 11th and 10th S.W.B. have one Coy. of each Battn. on Right holding road behind STEENBEEK. reported muddled up. (NOTE:- Officer receiving message notes that information is rather doubtful.)	
		10-50.p.m.	General Marden reports by phone. Two Battalions 115th Brigade many casualties. 114th Bde to leave one Battalion in BLUE Line. Men's feet bad owing to extremely wet weather.	
			On night 1st/2nd August 113th Brigade took over front line of the STEENBEEK From 115th Brigade who proceeded to CANAL BANK area and CANDLE - CANCER Line and BLUE and BLACK Lines. 114th Brigade withdrawn to L.2. Area West of the CANAL. Relief complete 2-36.a.m. on 2nd August.	
	2nd August.	7-55.a.m.	115th Brigade H.Q. at WELSH HARP.	
		10-40.am.	113th Brigade reports situation at present as follows:- 10th S.W.B. hold along hedge from Div:Boundary U.28.d.1.2. to Road about U.28.c.8.7. Remainder near VARNA FARM and GAIETY FARM. 11th S.W.B. still holding portion of hedge from CHIEN FM to Left. 16th R.W.F. hold posts at C.4.a.2.3. and C.4.a.6.4. 14th Welsh hold posts at U.28.c.0.25. and U.28.c.0.7. Remainder these Battns along Road between GAIETY FATM and IRON CROSS and between C.3.b.9½.3. and C.3.b.4.7. 13th R.W.F. on line U.27.d.6.9. to U 3.6. 14th R.W.F. thence to Railway. 13th R.W.F. have one Coy. in support just in front of Tramline. 15th R.W.F. hold from IRON CROSS to Railway in rear of Road with posts along GREEN Line. Bn.H.Q. as follows - 13th R.W.F. U.27.c.6.3. 14th R.W.F. NORMAN JUNCTION 15th R.W.F. GDE. BARRIER HOUSE.	

WAR DIARY or INTELLIGENCE SUMMARY

HEADQUARTERS, 38TH (WELSH) DIVISION. Army Form C. 2118.

(Erase heading not required.)

Place	Date	Hour	Summary of Events and Information	Remarks and references to Appendices
ELVERDINGHE	2nd August.		(Continued) H.Q. 15th R.W.F. at GDE. BARRIERE HOUSE. 16th R.W.F. and 14th Welsh Regt. STRAY FARM. 10th S.W.B. RUDOLPHE FARM. 11th S.W.B. West of IRON CROSS.	
		5-55.p.m.	Instructions issued to 3 Brigades. Battalions of 114th and 115th Brigade to be withdrawn from Front Line night 2nd/3rd August.	
		6-30.pm.	Orders issued to 113th Brigade to push out patrols to ascertain positions of enemy.	
		10-20.p.m.	113th Brigade report S.O.S. Signal sent up from Front Line at 10.p.m.	
		12 noon.	Thunderstorm and rain all day. Fairly quiet. Enemy shelled batteries West of PILCKEM RIDGE. Advanced Divisional Headquarters closed at ELVERDINGHE CHATEAU and re-opened at DRAGON CAMP.	
DRAGON CAMP	3rd August 1917.	11.a.m.	38th Div: Sniping Coy. who have proceed to line as a Company report observation impossible.	
		11.a.m.	115th Brigade report 16th Welsh established an BLACK Line. 10th S.W.B.established on CANDLE - CANCER Line. 11th S.W.B. moving to East CANAL BANK. 17th R.W.F. on West CANAL BANK.	
		4-55.p.m.	Situation quiet. Little promiscuous shelling. Slight enemy barrage on PILCKEM Ridge brought on by our bombardment. Heavy rain continued. Fairly quiet day.	
	4th August 1917.		Enemy put up a barrage on PILCKEM VILLAGE and also on Front Line trenches during the afternoon, but no attack developed. Hostile planes active during the afternoon. 114th Brigade relieved 113th Brigade during day and night 4th/5th August.	
	5th.		Patrol reports a footbridge 75 yds. North of the DAVIES STREET Bridge over the STEENBEEK to be still intact and no enemy seen West of the River. Much hostile aerial activity during the afternoon. A misty morning but became quite clear and fine in the afternoon. Our own and hostile machines were active. Enemy showed increased activity.	
PROVEN	6th.		Relief of 38th (Welsh) Division by 20th (Light) Division complete. Div: H.Q. moved to PROVEN. Conference of Brigadiers at PROVEN at 10.am. Div: Commander visited C.C.S.	
	7th.		Holiday for all Troops who have been in the Line. Rest and cleaning and equipping.	
	8th.		Training commenced.	

Army Form C. 2118.

WAR DIARY
or
INTELLIGENCE SUMMARY

(Erase heading not required.)

PAGE 2.

Place	Date	Hour	Summary of Events and Information	Remarks and references to Appendices
PROVEN.	AUGUST 1917. 17th.		Relief of 20th Division by this Division commenced. 114th Infantry Brigade move up into line. G.S.O.3. reconnoitred the STEENBEEK with a view to building more bridges. O.O.123 issued regarding relief of 20th Division.	Opp 6
	18th.		Hostile artillery active, chiefly on back areas. Some hostile aerial activity during the night 17/18th. 114th Infantry Brigade repeated relief complete at 11.p.m. Addendum to O.O.123 issued. Divisional Headquarters closing at PROVEN and opening at ELVERDINGHE CHATEAU.	
ELVERDINGHE CHATEAU.	19th.		Divisional Headquarters move to ELVERDINGHE CHATEAU. G.O.C. 38th Division took over command of LANGEMARCK SECTOR from G.O.C. 20th (Light) Division at 10.a.m. Hostile activity increased about 6.p.m. when battery positions below the PILCKEM RIDGE were heavily engaged. 3 reconnoitring patrols sent out by 114th Infantry Brigade. Our artillery displayed their usual activity. Intermittent shelling of STEENBEEK, DAVIES STREET and PILCKEM RIDGE.	Opp 7
	20th.		Hostile aeroplanes active both by day and night and many bombs were dropped on back areas in the C.C.S.	
	21st.		On the night of the 20/21st we advanced the left of our line. Our heavies were active during the day. Hostile artillery displayed normal activity. Enemy aeroplanes dropped bombs on back areas during the evening. O.O.124 issued stating 115th Infantry Brigade will relieve 114th Infantry Brigade nights 22/23rd and 23/24th.	Opp 8
	22nd.		Our heavies carried an organised bombardment. Hostile artillery active during the morning on forward areas during which CAPTAIN A.SMITH, M.C., C.S.O.2., XIV Corps was badly wounded in HANEBEEK. 11th Division on our right advanced and so straightened out the line. Hostile aeroplanes dropped bombs during the afternoon and again at night.	
	23rd.		O.O.125 issued that on 26th inst 115th Infantry Brigade will attack EAGLE TRENCH. Our bombardment continued. In the evening 2 Germans belonging to the 2nd Battalion 119 I.R. 26th Division lost their way and were captured. They stated that they were being relieved by 204 Division and as a result all our batteries opened fire on roads and tracks. Patrols report EAGLE TRENCH held by the enemy. Our artillery continued bombardment.	Opp 9
	24th.		Situation generally quiet during the day. Intermittent shelling of STEENBEEK.	
	25th.		Our artillery bombarded enemy's trenches according to programme. Hostile artillery less active. Some shelling of back areas with L.v.V. gun. 2 prisoners 125 I.R. captured at 9.30. Hostile aircraft active.	

/26th.

Army Form C. 2118.

WAR DIARY
INTELLIGENCE SUMMARY.
PAGE 3.

(Erase heading not required.)

Instructions regarding War, Diaries and Intelligence Summaries are contained in F.S. Regs., Part II. and the Staff Manual respectively. Title pages will be prepared in manuscript.

Place	Date	Hour	Summary of Events and Information	Remarks and references to Appendices
ELVERDINGHE CHATEAU.	AUGUST 1917. 26th.		Hostile artillery slightly below normal. ..eavy barrage at U.23.c. at 4.a.m. Our bombardment continued during the day and harassing fire by night.	
	27th.		An attempt was made at 1.55.p.m. to capture EAGLE TRENCH but owing to bad weather our troops were unable to keep up with the barrage, and the attack was stopped by machine gun fire from the CEMETERY and PHEASANT FARM. 2 prisoners 185 I.R. 26th Division were taken at U.17.c.	
	28th.		A very quiet day. Very little hostile fire. Our bombardment of EAGLE TRENCH continued. Our patrols were active during the night.	
	29th.		A wounded prisoner of 2nd Battalion 119 Grenadier Regiment was taken at U.23.d.23.86. Hostile artillery fire normal. Our bombardment of EAGLE TRENCH continued. Our patrols were active during the night, but encountered no enemy. O.O.126 issued regarding relief of 115th Infantry Brigade by 113th Infantry Brigade on the Divisional ront. O.O.127 issued regarding relief of 115th Infantry Brigade by 114th Infantry Brigade in support. 38th Division Operations Instructions No.2. issued regarding bombardment of EAGLE TRENCH and the CEMETERY to be continued during 30th and 31st August.	
	30th.		Hostile artillery was fairly quiet. During the day the Divisional Headquarters ELVERDINGHE CHATEAU was lightly shelled with a n.v. gun. WHITE HOUSE entered by our patrols. D.A.A.G. granted 10 days leave to ENGLAND.	
	31st.		Divisional Headquarters was shelled at intervals during the day. Hostile aeroplanes dropped bombs on Corps Headquarters; STRAY FARM (Bde. Headquarters) and IRON CROSS, about 6.p.m. Hostile artillery less active; our bombardment continued with satisfactory results.	

[signature]
Captain,
General Staff 38th (Welsh) Division.

6/10/17.

Secret.   Action to be taken in the
           event of SOS or enemy counter attack.

1) SOS signal: Troops of the leading brigade will

   a) Stand to & those units detailed for counter
      attack will move to position previously
      selected.

   b) The leading Battalion of the support Brigade
      (10 SWB)
      (HUSS) will stand to.

2) Counter Attack.

   a) The red line East of LANGEMARCK is to be
      held at all costs.

   b) The leading Bn will act in accordance with
      the situation.

   c) Adv. HUSS 115 HQ will move up to STRAY FARM

   d) On receipt of the message "COUNTER MOVE"
                                                    an area
      The 10 SW Bn will move up to & occupy at
      about G 3 central, about
      Div front of a line 50 yards in rear of
      road   running SE & NW through IRON CROSS
      The 11 SW Bn will move to an area about G 3 central
                                             V 27 c 3. 1
      The 16 Welch   —   —   C 2 B 8 6
      The 17 RWF & 115 FM Coy —   C 2 B 8 6
      Arrival at the above areas will be reported to adv

      On arrival at position of assembly each unit
      will send two runners to report to HQ 115 Inf Bde HQ
                        STRAY FARM - to await orders - these

Units

The 11th sub Bn. the watch & 19th R.W.F "T.M.B^y" will
as for a possible reman in artillery
formation; & a should be prepared on
receipt of orders to move forward to counter
-attack :~

2) The reserve B^n will move up to reoccupy the
area occupied by the 115 B^n

f) Working Parties will report to & come under orders of nearest
B^n H.Q.

3) Commanding Officers & Coy Commanders will
immediately
reconnoitre their
positions & locate their B^n & Coy H.Q.
advising
selected location of B^n H.Q. by 12 noon 19/2 and
Coy H.Q. by 5 p.m.

4) Units will ensure that their runners
are familiar with the route from the
selected H.Q to STRAY FARM.

B^n Signal officers will similarly ensure
that B^n Runners are familiar with
route from STRAY FARM to selected
B^n H.Q.

f) Working Parties will report to & come under orders
of nearest B^n H.Q
5) acknowledge

BM4142
Operations

38th Division No. G.S.6989.

O.B./188

Fifth Army G.A. 213/6

XIV Corps No. G. 76/3

Fifth Army

With reference to S.S.127, 534 and 535, it has been found that with the strap worn at the back of the head, the Steel Helmet will not remain in place during vigorous action, such as Bayonet Fighting, Bombing, jumping over trenches, and that as a result the men are frequently without any head protection at the very moment when it is most urgently needed.

In future, therefore, the strap will be worn on the point of the chin at all times when on duty, special stress being laid on the word point. If it is behind the point of the chin and round the gullet, the strap has to be so tight in order to retain the helmet during vigorous action as almost to cause strangulation, whereas on the point of the chin a grip can be taken of it by a natural movement of the jaw.

Instructions for drill with the Small Box Respirator, Practice B.1. in S.S.127 and Page 35, S.S.534 should be amended as follows :-

After "Nose Clip" add "At the same time knock off the Steel Helmet from behind with the left hand".

It has been proved by experience that no delay worth considering in the matter of adjusting the Respirator is imposed by this change.

Adv. General Headquarters, (sd) R.BUTLER, M.G.
17th August 1917. for Lieut. General,
  C.G.S.

(2)

113th Brigade	176th M.G.Coy.	38th Div. Depot Bn.
114th Brigade	D.M.G.O.	38th Sniping Coy.
115th Brigade	Div. Gas Offr.	D.A.D.O.S.
38th Div. Arty.	A.P.M.	
C.R.E.	D.A.D.V.S.	
38th Div. Train	Camp Commandant	
A.D.M.S.	38th Signals	
19th Welsh Regt.	38th Div. "Q"	

Forwarded for information and necessary action.

R.S. Follett Maj
for Lieut. Colonel,
General Staff, 38th (Welsh) Division.

20/8/1917.

Ref attached

Brit. 4142 not
included

ON HIS MAJESTY'S SERVICE.

SECRET

38th Division No. G.S.S. 87/1.

~~113th Brigade~~
~~114th Brigade~~
115th Brigade
~~38th Divl. Arty.~~
~~C. R. E.~~
19th Welsh Regt.

In all future operations, unless orders are issued to the contrary, the following instructions will hold good.

"In the event of our Infantry being seriously held up in the advance, the Creeping Barrage will be stopped and ordered to recommence by the C. R. A. concerned, under orders from his Divisional Commander.

Every 18-pr. Creeping Barrage which is stopped and brought back will invariably fire 4 rounds per gun per minute for the 4 minutes immediately prior to the recommencement of the creep forward. This will give the Infantry the necessary warning that the advance is to be resumed.

When a barrage is stopped, the Division on either side must immediately be informed.

When a barrage starts again after being brought back, there will be no fire within 150 yards of the flank of the advance of any Infantry who have got forward."

H. E. Pryce
Lieut. Colonel,
General Staff, 38th (Welsh) Division.

22nd August, 1917.

S E C R E T

38th Division No. G.S.7038

Operations

[Stamp: 115th INFANTRY BRGDE
23 AUG 1917
No. BM/4194]

TO BE BURNT AFTER BEING READ

113th Brigade
114th Brigade
115th Brigade
19th Welsh Regt.
_____

1. During the course of the recent operations there have been four cases in which our line has been slightly altered, and no report of the same has been received by Divisional H.Q.

2. The General Officer Commanding desires to impress on all Battalion, Company, and Platoon Commanders who may be in the front line of the <u>absolute necessity</u> when any change takes place of locating their position accurately on the map, and <u>reporting the same immediately</u> for transmission to Divl. H.Q. through the usual channel.
   Unless this is done, the Artillery and Machine Gun S.O.S. Barrage lines cannot be put down with accuracy, and this may lead to unfortunate results.

3. Battalion and Brigade Commanders will forward all reports of changes in the line by PRIORITY messages, and Signals will see that they are despatched by PRIORITY, and if necessary, in duplicate by different routes or methods to ensure early arrival.

H.E. Pryce Lieut. Colonel,
General Staff, 38th (Welsh) Division.

23/8/1917.

Sufficient Copies for issue to Company Commanders –

TO BE READ OUT TO ALL PLATOON AND SECTION
COMMANDERS AND THEN BURNT.

Copy to :-

   38th Div. Arty.
   C.R.E.
   Signals
   D.M.G.O.

115th Bde Distribution:-
17 R.W.F.   6
10 S.W.B.   6
  S.W.B.   6
16 W.R.   6
Signal Off   1

CONFIDENTIAL.

Fifth Army No. G.A. 837/1

G.H.Q. No. O.A. 70.

XIV Corps No. G.154/4

Fifth Army

38th Division No. G.S.7049

Captured documents detailing the results of the investigation of British prisoners disclose the fact that in many cases individuals have been given information prior to operations which it is unnecessary and very dangerous for them to know.

Although it is essential for everyone taking part in an attack to know everything necessary to enable him to carry out his task, and to co-operate with the action of his neighbours, it is equally essential to ensure that no one knows more of the general plan and objectives of the operation than is absolutely necessary.

It is impossible to lay down definite rules as to the amount of information which should be imparted to the various individuals, units, and formations, in an Army, but the Field-Marshall Commanding-in-Chief looks to Army Commanders to impress on the Commanders and Staffs of all formations the necessity, whenever an order or instruction in connection with forthcoming operations is written or circulated, to limit the information concerning the plan to what is absolutely necessary for the recipient to know for the efficient execution of his duties.

Subordinates should only be made acquainted with such necessary information at the latest possible moment with due regard to the efficient performance of their duties, thus avoiding the dangers inherent to the premature knowledge of secret information.

Adv. G.H.Q.
20th August 1917.

(sd) L.E.KIGGELL, Lieut.-Genl.
C.G.S.

(2)
113th Brigade   19th Welsh Regt.
114th Brigade   C.R.E.
115th Brigade   176th M.G.Coy.

Forwarded for your information.

In this connection please see the attached copy of G.H.Q. letter No. O.B./2015 of 5th April 1917.

The attention of all ranks should be drawn to "Extracts from General Routine Orders" page 70, para. 11. Arrangements must be made for its communication to all reinforcements on arrival

This paragraph should be read to the men periodically.

Sufficient copies are enclosed for issue down to Coys.

24/8/1917.

R.S. Follett May
for
Lieut. Colonel,
General Staff, 38th (Welsh) Division.

CONFIDENTIAL.

Fifth Army No. G.A. 837/1

G.H.Q. No. O.A. 70.

XIV Corps No. G.154/4

38th Division No. G.S.7049

Fifth Army

Captured documents detailing the results of the investigation of British prisoners disclose the fact that in many cases individuals have been given information prior to operations which it is unnecessary and very dangerous for them to know.

Although it is essential for everyone taking part in an attack to know everything necessary to enable him to carry out his task, and to co-operate with the action of his neighbours, it is equally essential to ensure that no one knows more of the general plan and objectives of the operation than is absolutely necessary.

It is impossible to lay down definite rules as to the amount of information which should be imparted to the various individuals, units, and formations, in an Army, but the Field-Marshall Commanding-in-Chief looks to Army Commanders to impress on the Commanders and Staffs of all formations the necessity, whenever an order or instruction in connection with forthcoming operations is written or circulated, to limit the information concerning the plan to what is absolutely necessary for the recipient to know for the efficient execution of his duties.

Subordinates should only be made acquainted with such necessary information at the latest possible moment with due regard to the efficient performance of their duties, thus avoiding the dangers inherent to the premature knowledge of secret information.

Adv. G.H.Q.
20th August 1917.

(sd) L.E.KIGGELL, Lieut.-Genl.
C.G.S.

(2)

113th Brigade   19th Welsh Regt.
114th Brigade   C.R.E.
115th Brigade   176th M.G.Coy.

Forwarded for your information.

In this connection please see the attached copy of G.H.Q. letter No. O.B./2015 of 5th April 1917.

The attention of all ranks should be drawn to "Extracts from General Routine Orders" page 70, para. 11. Arrangements must be made for its communication to all reinforcements on arrival

This paragraph should be read to the men periodically.

Sufficient copies are enclosed for issue down to Coys.

Lieut. Colonel,
General Staff, 38th (Welsh) Division.

24/8/1917.

BM 4285
Operations

38th Division No. G.S.7136.

113th Brigade
114th Brigade
115th Brigade
19th Welsh Regt

The Germans have been noticed lately using stretchers in the day time; on one occasion under cover of a white flag.

It should be remembered that as the Germans often shift Machine Guns on stretchers under pretence of shifting wounded, that such parties are to be fired on.

In the case of a white flag, one warning shot near the party may be first fired, after that the party will be fired at.

H.E. Pryce
Lieut. Colonel,
General Staff, 38th (Welsh) Divn.

31/8/1917.

circulated
1/9/17

S E C R E T 38th Division No. G.S. _____

113th Brigade
114th Brigade
115th Brigade
38th.Div. Arty.
C. R. E.

ACTION TO BE TAKEN BY THE INFANTRY IN THE EVENT OF THE S.O.S. SIGNAL BEING SENT UP OR OF A COUNTER ATTACK TAKING PLACE.

S.O.S. SIGNAL
Troops of the leading Brigade will stand to and those Units detailed for counter attack will move to positions which will have been marked out previously as being the best from which to counter attack.
The leading Battalion of the Support Brigade will stand to.

COUNTER ATTACK
The leading Brigade will act in accordance with the situation. The RED Line is to be held at all costs. Leading Brigade will immediately inform the Support Brigade who will move into a preparatory position in the neighbourhood of the IRON CROSS, from which it can, if necessary move forward to Counter attack.
The Reserve Brigade will move forward and take over the Support Brigade's area, i.e.
    1 Battalion in CANDLE – CANCER trench.
    1 " in old British Front Line.
    2 Battalions in CANAL BANK.
Support Brigade Advanced Headquarters will move up to STRAY FARM so as to be in touch with the Situation.
Brigades will make the necessary reconnaisance forthwith and submit their detailed places to-morrow evening.
Permanent garrisons of 1 Platoon each will be detailed to Strong Points as under:-
By leading Brigade.
    U.29.a.85.30.
    U.29.a.90.85.
    U.23.c.55.65.
    U.22.b.80.30.
    U.22.c.95.15.

Pending further reconnaisances and the laying out of a definite plan the leading Brigade will arrange temporarily for holding AU BON GITE and neighbourhood and U.28.b.55.15. with two Platoons.

H.E. Pryce

Lieut. Colonel,
General Staff, 38th (Welsh) Division.

19/8/1917.

ORIGINAL.

Army Form C. 2118.

WAR DIARY GENERAL STAFF 38TH (WELSH) DIVISION.

INTELLIGENCE SUMMARY.

VOLUME XXII

(Erase heading not required.)

Instructions regarding War Diaries and Intelligence Summaries are contained in F.S. Regs. Part II and the Staff Manual respectively. Title pages will be prepared in manuscript.

Place	Date	Hour	Summary of Events and Information	Remarks and references to Appendices
ELVERDINGHE CHATEAU.	SEPTEMBER.1917.			
	1st.		Corps Operation Order received regarding relief of 38th Division by 20th Division commencing on 9th instant. Hostile artillery active on forward areas during the morning. Our artillery carried out shoots according to programme. A box barrage was put kept up by day and night round CEMETERY (U.24.c.): shell hole shoot at 5.30.a.m: harassing fire by night.	Appx 1
	2nd.		A prisoner of M.G.Coy. 3rd Battalion 119th Grenadier Regiment 28th Division wandered into our lines at 2.30.a.m.Very Heavy hostile artillery fire on Batteries around PILCKEM. Hostile aeroplanes dropped a number of bombs on back areas about 11.p.m.	Appx 2
	3rd.		O.O.128 issued regarding hostile relief. (119th Grenadiers) in EAGLE TRENCH on the 3rd inst. Hostile artillery shelled ANGEMARCK during the morning. Our artillery carried out bombardment according to programme. H.V. guns shelled ELVERDINGHE intermittently by day and night. Great aerial activity by day and night, in the latter case, bombs were dropped on back areas.	
	4th.		O.O.129 issued regarding relief of 113th Infantry Brigade by 114th Infantry Brigade on the Divisional front. Hostile artillery activity was above normal: the battery positions in C.8.a. again received a heavy barrage. Hostile aircraft was very active by day and night. Our artillery carried out searching fire and a shell hole shoot according to programme. Great aerial activity on both sides; one of our machines crashed near HIGHLAND FARM, but both observer and pilot escaped with bruises. About midnight several bombs were dropped round the Divisional Headquarters at ELVERDINGHE CHATEAU, killing one signaller and wounding about 10 of the Headquarters party.	
	5th.		Our artillery bombarded enemy's defences and billets according to programme.	
	6th.		Our artillery carried out irregular bursts of fire round the CEMETERY (U.23.b. and U.22.a.): harassing fire and shell shoot. — ANGEMARCK, PILCKEM RIDGE and the STEENBEEK were shelled during the afternoon. One of our aeroplanes fell in flames near BOESINGHE.	Appx 3
	7th.		O.O.130. issued regarding bombardment of PHEASANT FARM and EAGLE TRENCH vicinity. Our artillery carried out an organised shoot according to programme, but owing to mist, observation was difficult.	Appx 4
	/8th.		O.O.131 issued regarding relief of 38th Division by 20th Division. About midnight bombs were dropped on back areas, a few falling in the vicinity of Divisional Headquarters at ELVERDINGHE. O.O.132. issued regarding bombardment of LOUIS FARM, WHITE HOUSE and PHEASANT FARM by Heavy Artillery.	Appx 5

Army Form C. 2118.

WAR DIARY
or
INTELLIGENCE SUMMARY.
(Erase heading not required.)

PAGE 2.

Place	Date	Hour	Summary of Events and Information	Remarks and references to Appendices
ELVERDINGHE CHATEAU.	SEPTEMBER.1917. 8th.		O.O.134 issued regarding bombardment of EAGLE TRENCH by heavy Artillery. LANGEMARCK received a heavy barrage. 2 prisoners of the 185th I.R., 208th Division were rounded up. Our artillery carried out harassing fire, and co-operated with heavy Artillery shoots. Our patrols active.	O.pp 6
	9th.		At 1.a.m. our artillery carried out a programme of harassing fire against a suspected trench relief. Hostile artillery active against our battery positions in C.7.b. and d. and MARSOUIN. 3 Germans belonging to 1st Battalion, 185th I.R. 208th Division lost their way and were caught by a patrol near U.23.d.90.45. about midnight.	
	10th.		LANGEMARCK, the STEENBEEK and ELVERDINGHE CHATEAU grounds were heavily engaged during the early morning. O.O.133 issued regarding transfer of 38th Division from Fifth Army (XIV Corps) to First Army (XI Corps). O.O.135 issued regarding relief of 57th Division by 38th Division.	O.pp 7 O.pp 8
	11th.		38th Division relieved by 20th Division in the Line. G.O.C., 20th Division takes over command at 10.a.m. 3.p.m. Conference at Divisional Headquarters at PROVEN of Brigadiers. 9.p.m. Hostile aerial activity over PROVEN.	
PROVEN.	12th.		The Prince of Wales came to bid Divisional Headquarters Au Revoir on leaving XIV Corps. 115th Infantry Brigade arrive in EEKE AREA.	
LA GORGUE.	13th.		Divisional Headquarters closed at PROVEN at 10.a.m. and opened at LA GORGUE at 1.p.m. 115th Infantry Brigade move to MORBECQUE; 114th Infantry Brigade to EECKE.	O.pp 9
	14th.		113th Brigade move to EECKE AREA. 114th " " " MORBECQUE AREA. 115th " " " ESTAIRES.	
	15th.		XI Corps Commander visited Divisional Headquarters. O.O.136 issued regarding relief of 57th Divisional Artillery by the 38th Divisional Artillery. 113th Infantry Brigade move to MORBECQUE AREA. 114th Infantry Brigade " " ESTAIRES AREA. 115th Infantry Brigade " " NIEPPE AREA.	O.pp 10
	16th.		O.O.137 issued regarding bombardments of FRELINGHIEN by all guns and howitzers of the 38th Divn. *113th Infantry Brigade arrive at ESTAIRES. 114th Infantry Brigade take over FLEURBAIX SECTION. 115th Infantry Brigade ARMENTIERES SECTION.	
CROIX DU BAC.	17th.		Divisional Headquarters took over new sector at CROIX DU BAC relieving 57th Division. Hostile artillery very quiet. Our aircraft active.	/18th.

Army Form C. 2118.

WAR DIARY
or
INTELLIGENCE SUMMARY.

(Erase heading not required.)

PAGE 3.

Place	Date	Hour	Summary of Events and Information	Remarks and references to Appendices
CROIX DU BAC.	SEPTEMBER 1917.			
	18th.		Our Machine Guns were active in the Left sub-sector during the night. 2 escaped Russian prisoners entered our trenches at I.26.5. They were employed near DON on trenches along the Canal East of the village.	
	19th.		Hostile aeroplanes active during the day. Enemy attempted to raid our trenches under cover of a heavy artillery and Trench Mortar barrage in the ARMENTIERES SECTION. They were driven off by the 115th Infantry Brigade leaving one dead in our hands. None of our men were missing. At 4.a.m. a German patrol made a second attempt to gain identification: one member deserted and remained in our lines.	
	20th.		Some hostile machine gun fire during the night. About midnight 2 escaped German prisoners were captured in our support line. They had walked from ST OMER. O.O.139 re hostile relief.	Opp 11. Opp. 12.
	21st.		O.O.158. issued regarding attachment of 2 Battalions of the C.E.P. to the 114th Infantry Brigade. Our patrols were active in the ARMENTIERES SECTION but no enemy were seen. Hostile machine guns showed some activity during the night in the BOIS GRENIER SECTION.	
	22nd.		Hostile artillery showed more activity. Hostile artillery hostile trench mortars showed some activity in the FLEURBAIX SECTION. displayed some slight activity on ARMENTIERES. Our artillery fired in punishment.	
	23rd.		Hostile aeroplanes active along the whole Divisional front and in the vicinity of CROIX DU BAC. Hostile artillery quiet, except in the vicinity of HOUPLINES which received a few rounds. FLEURBAIX was	
	24th.		Battalion of Portuguese attached to 114th Infantry Brigade for instruction. engaged during the afternoon and also a battery position in the vicinity.	
	25th.		Corps Conference. Our artillery carried out registration on FROMELLES and targets in 0.13.b. and 0.3.c. Hostile artillery showed normal activity. HOUPLINES and ARMENTIERES were shelled intermittently during the day.	
	26th.		Our artillery engaged active French Mortars in the FLEURBAIX SECTION, FRELINGHIEN was registered on during the day. Hostile artillery engaged our trenches in the ARMENTIERES SECTION intermittently during the day.	
	27th.		O.O.140. issued regarding attachment of Companies of the 4th and 17th Battalions, 5th Provisional Brigade, 2nd Division C.E.P. CHAPELLE D'ARMENTIERES was engaged during the morning with 10.5.c.m. Hows. Our artillery engaged FRELINGHIEN during the night. Hostile aircraft were active by day and night. During the night our machines successfully bombed railways and towns in the rear of the enemy's lines. Prisoners captured at YPRES state that the 4th Bavarian Division was relieved by 2nd Guard Reserve Division.	Opp p. 13.
	28th.			

Army Form C. 2118.

WAR DIARY
or
INTELLIGENCE SUMMARY.
(Erase heading not required.)

Page 4.

Instructions regarding War Diaries and Intelligence Summaries are contained in F. S. Regs., Part II. and the Staff Manual respectively. Title pages will be prepared in manuscript.

Place	Date	Hour	Summary of Events and Information	Remarks and references to Appendices
CROIX DU BAC.	SEPTEMBER. 1917.			
	28th.		Some hostile artillery activity in the ARMENTIERES SECTION. During the night lachrymatory gas T.M. shells were fired onto our line in I.10.d.	
	29th.		Hostile aeroplanes and our own dropped bombs. Hostile artillery showed normal activity in the ARMENTIERES SECTION. Our artillery fired in registration and punishment for hostile activity. Hostile aerial activity was above normal by day, and at night hostile planes flying low fired their machine guns down the roads.	
	30th.		Hostile artillery was more active in the FLEURBAIX and BOIS GRENIER SECTIONS, and normal in the ARMENTIERES SECTION. Our artillery fired in punishment for hostile activity. Hostile aircraft were very active throughout the day and from 9.p.m. to midnight.	

15/10/17.

[signature]
Captain,
General Staff 38th (Welsh) Division.

SECRET

Copy No. 11

38TH (WELSH) DIVISION ORDER NO. 128.

Ref:- 1/10,000 Maps.   2nd September 1917.

1. It is probable that the front line Battalion of the 119th Grenadiers will be relieved in EAGLE TRENCH and neighbourhood between midnight and 4.a.m. on the 3rd instant. Action will be taken as under tonight 2nd/3rd September.

2. Divisional Artillery will put heavy bursts of fire on to the ground in rear of EAGLE TRENCH, the ground between EAGLE TRENCH and the CEMETERY and the shell hole areas in the neighbourhood of EAGLE TRENCH from 12 midnight to 4.a.m., during which hours also certain guns will sweep the LANGEMARCK - POELCAPPELLE Road.

3. XIV Corps Heavy Artillery will fire on shelters V.15.c.99.60. to V.21.a.99.01. (exact location to be obtained from XIV Corps Intelligence) from 4-30.a.m. to 5-30.a.m., the time at which relieved Battalion should be arriving there. Corps Heavy Artillery will also fire on Battalion Head Quarters V.16.c.65.30. from 10.p.m to 11.p.m. and from 4-30.a.m. to 5-30.a.m.

   Right Bombardment Group will at frequent intervals search Roads as follows :-
   (a) POELCAPPELLE - STADENREEF 10.p.m. to midnight.
       (especially road junction V.14.c.99.60.)
   (b) POELCAPPELLE - LANGEMARCK Road (as far West as U.24.a.20.05)
       10.p.m.to 4.a.m.
   (c) POELCAPPELLE - SPRIET ROAD - 1.a.m. to 4.a.m.

4. 30,000 rounds will be fired on the LANGEMARCK - POELCAPPELLE Road from machine guns between 12 midnight and 4.a.m. under orders of the D.M.G.O.

5. G.O.C. 113th Infantry Brigade will arrange for Lewis Guns sweeping all shell hole areas between 12 midnight and 4.a.m.

6. All working parties will be West of the STEENBEEK by 12.m.n. by which hour all carrying parties should have finished their work.

ACKNOWLEDGE.

R.S. Follett May
for Lieut. Colonel,
General Staff, 38th (Welsh) Division.

Issued to Signals at 3-20.p.m.

Copies to :-
G.O.C.	113th Brigade	XIV Corps G
G.S.O.1	114th Brigade	Guards Divn.
G.S.	115th Brigade	51st Divn.
"Q"	19th Welsh Regt.	20th Divn.
Signals	176th M.G.Coy.	XIV Corps H.A.
38th Div: Arty.	D.M.G.O.	
Right Bombt. Group	Sniping Coy.	
C.R.E.		

SECRET

38th Division No. G.S. 7197

XIV Corps No. G.55./2.

38th Division
----

1. Herewith 18 copies of Figth Army letter S.G. 671/26 for distribution down to Battalion Commanders.

2. This stirring paper can be summed up in the two following simple priciples -

    (a) If leading troops are seen to be retiring, it is the duty of the nearest Battalion in support to go forward at once without waiting for orders from the Brigade.

    (b) On reaching objective, every man not detailed for consolidation will shoot at every German he sees.

3. Training on these lines will be initiated at once.

                                (sd) E. SEYMOUR. Captain for Brigadier General,
3rd September 1917.   General Staff, XIV Corps.

(2)

113th Brigade
114th Brigade
115th Brigade

    In forwarding these points made by the Army Commander the Major General directs that all training must be devoted to instilling an Offensive Spirit in Officers, N.C.O's and Men.

    They must be taught how to meet an enemy counter attack by advancing with the bayonet and when the enemy turn and run our troops must at once lie down and open rapid fire.

    Special attention is directed to paragraph 13 of the Army Commander's letter.

                                            R.S. Follett May
                                               for Lieut. Colonel,
4th September 1917.   General Staff, 38th (Welsh) Division.

SECRET.

38th Division No.G.S.7197.
XIVth Corps No. G.55/2.
115th Bde., B.M.

38th Division.

1. Herewith 18 copies of Fifth Army letter S.G.671/26 for distribution down to Battalion Commanders.

2. This stirring paper can be summed up in the two following simple principles –

   (a) If leading troops are seen to be retiring, it is the duty of the nearest Battalion in support to go forward at once without waiting for orders from the Brigade.

   (b) On reaching objective, every man not detailed for consolidation will shoot at every German he sees.

3. Training on these lines will be initiated at once.

                                      (sd.) E. SEYMOUR, Captain for
                                                    Brigadier General,
3rd September, 1917.   General Staff, XIV Corps.

(2).

115th Brigade.

In forwarding these points made by the Army Commander the Major General directs that all training must be devoted to instilling an Offensive Spirit in Officers, N.C.O's. and men.

They must be taught how to meet an enemy counter attack by advancing with the bayonet and when the enemy turn and run our troops must at once lie down and open rapid fire.

Special attention is directed to paragraph 13 of the Army Commander's letter.

                                      (Sd.) R.S.Follett, Major,
                                            for Lieut. Colonel,
4th September, 1917.   General Staff, 38th (Welsh) Division.

SECRET.

38th Division No.G.S.7197.
XIVth Corps No. G.55/2.
115th Bde., B.M.

38th Division.

1. Herewith 18 copies of Fifth Army letter S.G.671/25 for distribution down to Battalion Commanders.

2. This stirring paper can be summed up in the two following simple principles -

    (a) If leading troops are seen to be retiring, it is the duty of the nearest Battalion in support to go <u>forward at once</u> without waiting for orders from the Brigade.

    (b) On reaching objective, every man not detailed for consolidation will shoot at every German he sees.

3. Training on these lines will be initiated <u>at once.</u>

                                         (sd.) E.SEYMOUR, Captain for
                                                    Brigadier General,
3rd September, 1917.   General Staff, XIV Corps.

(2).

115th Brigade.

In forwarding these points made by the Army Commander the Major General directs that all training must be devoted to instilling an Offensive Spirit in Officers, N.C.O's. and men.

They must be taught how to meet an enemy counter attack by advancing with the bayonet and when the enemy turn and run our troops must at once lie down and open rapid fire.

Special attention is directed to paragraph 15 of the Army Commander's letter.

                                           (Sd.) R.S.Follett, Major,
                                               for Lieut. Colonel,
4th September, 1917.   General Staff, 38th (Welsh) Division.

SECRET.

Fifth Army.
S.G.671/26.

2nd September, 1917.

1. The evidence of recent operations points, in many cases, to the regrettable fact that our troops, even after a most successful attack have, on occasion, given up all the ground gained in the face of a German counter-attack. This has even occurred as soon as a counter-attack, although only in small force, has been seen advancing, and men have begun to retire without attempting to repel or even to fire at the attacking troops. I am fully aware that there are many units and formations in the Army to whom these remarks do not apply, but I regard this tendency as so dangerous that I wish to let everyone know my views.

2. Unfortunately, it is not only our leading troops who have been involved; but it seems also that supporting bodies of our troops in rear, who may have been consolidating strong points or localities or moving up to the support of the attacking waves, have immediately commenced to withdraw as soon as our leading lines have been seen retiring.

3. Nothing could be worse. If such action becomes general throughout an Army that Army will never achieve success and will lose a great deal. Troops who retire not only cause unnecessary losses to their comrades and their Country but bring dishonour to their arms and their nation, and victory is indefinitely delayed.

4. I am convinced, from what I know of the gallant courage, self-sacrifice, cheerful endurance and fine discipline of our troops, that this action is not due to any lack of fighting spirit. It is due, to my mind, to lack of training, and the failure to realize that the counter-attack is inevitable, that it has to be met and that it can be defeated by rifle fire provided that Officers, N.C.O's. and men show a bold and resolute bearing, such as British troops have always shown during a thousand years of fighting.

5. This resolute spirit and this use of the rifle must be most strongly impressed on the men, as well as on the Officers and N.C.O's.; for the men will often have neither Officer nor N.C.O. within their reach in this "shell hole" fighting.

6. All ranks must realize that their honour is involved in holding on to what they have gained, and the great capacity for resistance that they possess, especially against the indifferent Bosch Infantry.

They must remember how constantly a few resolute men, who use their weapons energetically, can hold up a whole line of attack. Particularly is this so when opposing German Infantry. They will never come on unless our men first commence to retire.

7. The duty of holding on, of "sticking it out" and the energetic use of rifles and Lewis guns, must be firmly fixed in the minds of all those who consolidate supporting points in rear, as well as those actually in the front line. They are there solely to support their comrades in front and to prevent the line from being forced further back.

In too many cases troops detailed for the important duties of holding these supporting points have commenced to retire the moment they have seen their leading waves coming back. This is a most serious failure in their duties as soldiers, and is a disgrace not only to the uniform they wear but to the British nation.

I am, however, confident, as I have previously stated, that this has been due not to lack of courage but to faulty training, and a failure to realise in what direction duty lies.

8. Supporting troops on the move have failed in exactly the same way, and have been known to fall back directly they have seen troops in front of them retire. It would almost seem as though they had imagined their duty to consist in keeping the proper distance between lines. Far from that being so, their duty lies in deploying, and advancing to the attack the moment the leading line is seen to be wavering or falling back. This duty must be clear to them and they must be firmly determined to fulfil it.

By immediately moving to the attack they carry with them all the air of courage, resolution and the offensive spirit which cannot fail to affect the spirits of their comrades in front who are being forced back, and will also have a corresponding influence upon the resolution of the enemy's threatened advance.

It is therefore this moral as well as physical support which will stay the retreat of our men and even carry them forward again, and will instil hesitation and fear into the enemy's mind and cause him certainly to retreat in his turn or at least to stay his further advance.

9. The first and clearest duty of all those in command of troops in support and reserve is to push on within supporting distance of the troops in front and, on the slightest sign of wavering or retreat in the leading waves, to at once, deploy and advance all or part of their force.

10. The above points must be made clear to all; and their duty to their comrades, to the uniform they have the honour to wear, and to their great and beloved Country, must be impressed upon all our young Officers and N.C.O's. by lectures, and on all possible occasions.

The great moral superiority of the British over the Bosch must never be forgotten. No Bosch will come on if our troops show a firm front and make energetic use of their rifles, and the Bosch cannot stop the British soldier if the latter means to advance.

11. In all training schemes the men must be habitually exercised in meeting a sudden counter-attack by steady fire. Two men advancing with flags will be sufficient to represent the counter-attack.

In Company, Battalion or Brigade attacks, the supports and reserve must also be frequently practised in meeting counter-attacks by deploying and advancing through the waves in front of them.

12. Officers in charge of these exercises will occasiona[lly] test the training of support and reserve troops by suddenl[y] ordering the leading waves of the attack to halt and comme[nce] falling back. The supporting troops on seeing the check in front will at once deploy and advance with a cheer, car[ry]ing with them the retiring men who will turn and commence [to] advance again when these supporting troops reach them.

Whenever this is done those troops which are ordered to fall back must understand that they do so only in order that the supports and reserves may receive proper training. They must on no account be allowed to think that their retirement is justifiable.

13. I direct that a copy of this paper be given to every Commanding Officer, and that every Brigadier will first rea[d] it to his Commanding Officers and impress upon them most ca[re]fully the points referred to.

These will afterwards assemble their Officers and read the paper to them, and impress upon them the far-reaching consequences of these matters to the whole Army.

(Sd.) H.P.GOUGH,
General,
Commanding Fifth Army.

SECRET.

Fifth Army.
S.G.671/26.

2nd September, 1917.

1. The evidence of recent operations points, in many cases, to the regrettable fact that our troops, even after a most successful attack have, on occasion, given up all the ground gained in the face of a German counter-attack. This has even occurred as soon as a counter-attack, although only in small force, has been seen advancing, and men have begun to retire without attempting to repel or even to fire at the attacking troops. I am fully aware that there are many units and formations in the Army to whom these remarks do not apply, but I regard this tendency as so dangerous that I wish to let everyone know my views.

2. Unfortunately, it is not only our leading troops who have been involved; but it seems also that supporting bodies of our troops in rear, who may have been consolidating strong points or localities or moving up to the support of the attacking waves, have immediately commenced to withdraw as soon as our leading lines have been seen retiring.

3. Nothing could be worse. If such action becomes general throughout an Army that Army will never achieve success and will lose a great deal. Troops who retire not only cause unnecessary losses to their comrades and their Country but bring dishonour to their arms and their nation, and victory is indefinitely delayed.

4. I am convinced, from what I know of the gallant courage, self-sacrifice, cheerful endurance and fine discipline of our troops, that this action is not due to any lack of fighting spirit. It is due, to my mind, to lack of training, and the failure to realize that the counter-attack is inevitable, that it has to be met and that it can be defeated by rifle fire provided that Officers, N.C.O's. and men show a bold and resolute bearing, such as British troops have always shown during a thousand years of fighting.

5. This resolute spirit and this use of the rifle must be most strongly impressed on the men, as well as on the Officers and N.C.O's.; for the men will often have neither Officer nor N.C.O. within their reach in this "shell hole" fighting.

6. All ranks must realize that their honour is involved in holding on to what they have gained, and the great capacity for resistance that they possess, especially against the indifferent Bosch Infantry.

They must remember how constantly a few resolute men, who use their weapons energetically, can hold up a whole line of attack. Particularly is this so when opposing German Infantry. They will never come on unless our men first commence to retire.

7. The duty of holding on, of "sticking it out" and the energetic use of rifles and Lewis guns, must be firmly fixed in the minds of all those who consolidate supporting points in rear, as well as those actually in the front line. They are there solely to support their comrades in front and to prevent the line from being forced further back.

2.

In too many cases troops detailed for the important duties of holding these supporting points have commenced to retire the moment they have seen their leading waves coming back. This is a most serious failure in their duties as soldiers, and is a disgrace not only to the uniform they wear but to the British nation.

I am, however, confident, as I have previously stated, that this has been due not to lack of courage but to faulty training, and a failure to realise in what direction duty lies.

8. Supporting troops on the move have failed in exactly the same way, and have been known to fall back directly they have seen troops in front of them retire. It would almost seem as though they had imagined their duty to consist in keeping the proper distance between lines. Far from that being so, their duty lies in deploying, and advancing to the attack the moment the leading line is seen to be wavering or falling back. This duty must be clear to them and they must be firmly determined to fulfil it.

By immediately moving to the attack they carry with them all the air of courage, resolution and the offensive spirit which cannot fail to affect the spirits of their comrades in front who are being forced back, and will also have a corresponding influence upon the resolution of the enmy's threatened advance.

It is ~~therefore~~ this moral as well as physical support which will stay the retreat of our men and even carry them forward again, and will instil hesitation and fear into the enemy's mind and cause him certainly to retreat in his turn or at least to stay his further advance.

9. The first and clearest duty of all those in command of troops in support and reserve is to push on within supporting distance of the troops in front and, on the slightest sign of wavering or retreat in the leading waves, to at once, deploy and advance all or part of their force.

10. The above points must be made clear to all; and their duty to their comrades, to the uniform they have the honour to wear, and to their great and beloved Country, must be impressed upon all our young Officers and N.C.O's. by lectures, and on all possible occasions.

The great moral superiority of the British over the Bosch must never be forgotten. No Bosch will come on if our troops show a firm front and make energetic use of their rifles, and the Bosch cannot stop the British soldier if the latter means to advance.

11. In all training schemes the men must be habitually exercised in meeting a sudden counter-attack by steady fire. Two men advancing with flags will be sufficient to represent the counter-attack.

In Company, Battalion or Brigade attacks, the supports and reserve must also be frequently practised in meeting counter-attacks by deploying and advancing through the waves in front of them.

12. Officers in charge of these exercises will occasionally test the training of support and reserve troops by suddenly ordering the leading waves of the attack to halt and commence falling back. The supporting troops on seeing the check in front will at once deploy and advance with a cheer, carrying with them the retiring men who will turn and commence to advance again when these supporting troops reach them.

Whenever this is done those troops which are ordered to fall back must understand that they do so only in order that the supports and reserves may receive proper training. They must on no account be allowed to think that their retirement is justifiable.

13. I direct that a copy of this paper be given to every Commanding Officer, and that every Brigadier will first read it to his Commanding Officers and impress upon them most carefully the points referred to.

These will afterwards assemble their Officers and read the paper to them, and impress upon them the far-reaching consequences of these matters to the whole Army.

(Sd.) H.P.GOUGH,
General,
Commanding Fifth Army.

SECRET.

Fifth Army.
S.G.671/26.

2nd September, 1917.

1. The evidence of recent operations points, in many cases, to the regrettable fact that our troops, even after a most successful attack have, on occasion, given up all the ground gained in the face of a German counter-attack. This has even occurred as soon as a counter-attack, although only in small force, has been seen advancing, and men have begun to retire without attempting to repel or even to fire at the attacking troops. I am fully aware that there are many units and formations in the Army to whom these remarks do not apply, but I regard this tendency as so dangerous that I wish to let everyone know my views.

2. Unfortunately, it is not only our leading troops who have been involved; but it seems also that supporting bodies of our troops in rear, who may have been consolidating strong points or localities or moving up to the support of the attacking waves, have immediately commenced to withdraw as soon as our leading lines have been seen retiring.

3. Nothing could be worse. If such action becomes general throughout an Army that Army will never achieve success and will lose a great deal. Troops who retire not only cause unnecessary losses to their comrades and their Country but bring dishonour to their arms and their nation, and victory is indefinitely delayed.

4. I am convinced, from what I know of the gallant courage, self-sacrifice, cheerful endurance and fine discipline of our troops, that this action is not due to any lack of fighting spirit. It is due, to my mind, to lack of training, and the failure to realize that the counter-attack is inevitable, that it has to be met and that it can be defeated by rifle fire provided that Officers, N.C.O's. and men show a bold and resolute bearing, such as British troops have always shown during a thousand years of fighting.

5. This resolute spirit and this use of the rifle must be most strongly impressed on the men, as well as on the Officers and N.C.O's.; for the men will often have neither Officer nor N.C.O. within their reach in this "shell hole" fighting.

6. All ranks must realise that their honour is involved in holding on to what they have gained, and the great capacity for resistance that they possess, especially against the indifferent Bosch Infantry.

They must remember how constantly a few resolute men, who use their weapons energetically, can hold up a whole line of attack. Particularly is this so when opposing German Infantry. They will never come on unless our men first commence to retire.

7. The duty of holding on, of "sticking it out" and the energetic use of rifles and Lewis guns, must be firmly fixed in the minds of all those who consolidate supporting points in rear, as well as those actually in the front line. They are there solely to support their comrades in front and to prevent the line from being forced further back.

2.

In too many cases troops detailed for the important duties of holding these supporting points have commenced to retire the moment they have seen their leading waves coming back. This is a most serious failure in their duties as soldiers, and is a disgrace not only to the uniform they wear but to the British nation.

I am, however, confident, as I have previously stated, that this has been due not to lack of courage but to faulty training, and a failure to realise in what direction duty lies.

8. Supporting troops on the move have failed in exactly the same way, and have been known to fall back directly they have seen troops in front of them retire. It would almost seem as though they had imagined their duty to consist in keeping the proper distance between lines. Far from that being so, their duty lies in deploying, and advancing to the attack the moment the leading line is seen to be wavering or falling back. This duty must be clear to them and they must be firmly determined to fulfil it.

By immediately moving to the attack they carry with them all the air of courage, resolution and the offensive spirit which cannot fail to affect the spirits of their comrades in front who are being forced back, and will also have a corresponding influence upon the resolution of the enemy's threatened advance.

It is therefore this moral as well as physical support which will stay the retreat of our men and even carry them forward again, and will instil hesitation and fear into the enemy's mind and cause him certainly to retreat in his turn or at least to stay his further advance.

9. The first and clearest duty of all those in command of troops in support and reserve is to push on within supporting distance of the troops in front and, on the slightest sign of wavering or retreat in the leading waves, to at once, deploy and advance all or part of their force.

10. The above points must be made clear to all; and their duty to their comrades, to the uniform they have the honour to wear, and to their great and beloved Country, must be impressed upon all our young Officers and N.C.O's. by lectures, and on all possible occasions.

The great moral superiority of the British over the Bosch must never be forgotten. No Bosch will come on if our troops show a firm front and make energetic use of their rifles, and the Bosch cannot stop the British soldier if the latter means to advance.

11. In all training schemes the men must be habitually exercised in meeting a sudden counter-attack by steady fire. Two men advancing with flags will be sufficient to represent the counter-attack.

In Company, Battalion or Brigade attacks, the supports and reserve must also be frequently practised in meeting counter-attacks by deploying and advancing through the waves in front of them.

3.

12.   Officers in charge of these exercises will occasionally test the training of support and reserve troops by suddenly ordering the leading waves of the attack to halt and commence falling back. The supporting troops on seeing the check in front will at once deploy and advance with a cheer, carrying with them the retiring men who will turn and commence to advance again when these supporting troops reach them.

    Whenever this is done those troops which are ordered to fall back must understand that they do so only in order that the supports and reserves may receive proper training. They must on no account be allowed to think that their retirement is justifiable.

13.   I direct that a copy of this paper be given to every Commanding Officer, and that every Brigadier will first read it to his Commanding Officers and impress upon them most carefully the points referred to.

    These will afterwards assemble their Officers and read the paper to them, and impress upon them the far-reaching consequences of these matters to the whole Army.

                        (Sd.)   H.P.GOUGH,
                                                     General,
                      Commanding Fifth Army.

S E C R E T.

Fifth Army.
S.G.671/26.

2nd September, 1917.

1. The evidence of recent operations points, in many cases, to the regrettable fact that our troops, even after a most successful attack have, on occasion, given up all the ground gained in the face of a German counter-attack. This has even occurred as soon as a counter-attack, although only in small force, has been seen advancing, and men have begun to retire without attempting to repel or even to fire at the attacking troops. I am fully aware that there are many units and formations in the Army to whom these remarks do not apply, but I regard this tendency as so dangerous that I wish to let everyone know my views.

2. Unfortunately, it is not only our leading troops who have been involved; but it seems also that supporting bodies of our troops in rear, who may have been consolidating strong points or localities or moving up to the support of the attacking waves, have immediately commenced to withdraw as soon as our leading lines have been seen retiring.

3. Nothing could be worse. If such action becomes general throughout an Army that Army will never achieve success and will lose a great deal. Troops who retire not only cause unnecessary losses to their comrades and their Country but bring dishonour to their arms and their nation, and victory is indefinitely delayed.

4. I am convinced, from what I know of the gallant courage self-sacrifice, cheerful endurance and fine discipline of our troops, that this action is not due to any lack of fighting spirit. It is due, to my mind, to lack of training, and the failure to realise that the counter-attack is inevitable, that it has to be met and that it can be defeated by rifle fire provided that Officers, N.C.O's and men show a bold and resolute bearing, such as British troops have always shown during a thousand years of fighting.

5. This resolute spirit and this use of the rifle must be most strongly impressed on the men, as well as on the Officers and N.C.O's; for the men will often have neither Officer nor N.C.O. within their reach in this "shell hole" fighting.

6. All ranks must realise that their honour is involved in holding on to what they have gained, and the great capacity for resistance that they possess, especially against the indifferent Bosch Infantry.

They must remember how constantly a few resolute men, who use their weapons energetically, can hold up a whole line of attack. Particularly is this so when opposing German Infantry They will never come on unless our men first commence to retire.

7. The duty of holding on, of "sticking it out" and the energetic use of rifles and Lewis guns, must be firmly fixed in the minds of all those who consolidate supporting points in rear, as well as those actually in the front line. They are there solely to support their comrades in front and to prevent the line from being forced further back.

In too many cases troops detailed for the important duties of holding these supporting points have commenced to retire the moment they have seen their leading waves coming back. This is a most serious failure in their duties as soldiers, and is a disgrace not only to the uniform they wear but to the British nation.

I am, however, confident, as I have previously stated, that this has been due not to lack of courage but to faulty training, and a failure to realise in what direction duty lies.

8. Supporting troops on the move have failed in exactly the same way, and have been known to fall back directly they have seen troops in front of them retire. It would almost seem as though they had imagined their duty to consist in keeping the proper distance between lines. Far from that being so, their duty lies in deploying, and advancing to the attack the moment the leading line is seen to be wavering or falling back. This duty must be clear to them and they must be firmly determined to fulfil it.

By immediately moving to the attack they carry with them all the air of courage, resolution and the offensive spirit which cannot fail to affect the spirits of their comrades in front who are being forced back, and will also have a corresponding influence upon the resolution of the enemy's threatened advance.

It is this moral as well as physical support which will stay the retreat of our men and even carry them forward again, and will instil hesitation and fear into the enemy's mind and cause him certainly to retreat in his turn or at least to stay his further advance.

9. The first and clearest duty of all those in command of troops in support and reserve is to push on within supporting distance of the troops in front and, on the slightest sign of wavering or retreat in the leading waves, to at once, deploy and advance all or part of their force.

10. The above points must be made clear to all; and their duty to their comrades, to the uniform they have the honour to wear, and to their great and beloved Country, must be impressed upon all our young Officers and N.C.Os. by lectures, and on all possible occasions.

The great moral superiority of the British over the Bosch must never be forgotten. No Bosch will come on if our troops show a firm front and make energetic use of their rifles, and the Bosch cannot stop the British soldier if the latter means to advance.

11. In all training schemes the men must be habitually exercised in meeting a sudden counter-attack by steady fire. Two men advancing with flags will be sufficient to represent the counter-attack.

In Company, Battalion or Brigade attacks, the supports and reserve must also be frequently practised in meeting counter-attacks by deploying and advancing through the waves in front of them.

12.   Officers in charge of these exercises will occasionally test the training of support and reserve troops by suddenly ordering the leading waves of the attack to halt and commence falling back. The supporting troops on seeing the check in front will at once deploy and advance with a cheer, carrying with them the retiring men who will turn and commence to advance again when these supporting troops reach them.

    Whenever this is done those troops which are ordered to fall back must understand that they do so only in order that the supports and reserves may receive proper training. They must on no account be allowed to think that their retirement is justifiable.

13.   I direct that a copy of this paper be given to every Commanding Officer, and that every Brigadier will first read it to his Commanding Officers and impress upon them most carefully the points referred to.

    These will afterwards assemble their Officers and read the paper to them, and impress upon them the far-reaching consequences of these matters to the whole Army.

H.P. Gough.

General,
Commanding Fifth Army.

WAR DIARY OF GENERAL STAFF 38TH (WELSH) DIVISION

INTELLIGENCE SUMMARY. VOLUME XXIII.

Army Form C. 2118.

(Erase heading not required.)

Place	Date	Hour	Summary of Events and Information	Remarks and references to Appendices
CROIX DU BACQ	OCTOBER. 1917.			
	1st.		Our artillery was fairly active and fired in punishment for hostile artillery and trench mortar fire. Hostile artillery showed normal activity. One of our patrols occupied posts in NEEDLE TRENCH in N.10.d., without opposition during the night and withdrew before daylight; no enemy were seen. Hostile aircraft less active; bombs were dropped in the vicinity of SAILLY during the evening.	
	2nd.		Our artillery was fairly active. Hostile artillery very quiet, except in the ARMENTIERES SECTION when it was normal. Hostile aircraft activity was below normal. Our patrols were very active during the night, 10 were out during the night. No enemy patrols were seen.	
	3rd.		Hostile artillery was quiet in the Right and Centre Sections, but normal in the left Section. Our artillery fired in registration and retaliation and also on enemy movement and works. Our snipers obtained a certain hit on a German at N.8.b.65.15. Our patrols were as usual very active. No hostile patrols were seen. Hostile aircraft activity was below normal.	
	4th.		Hostile artillery was quiet except in the Left Section where it was normal. Hostile T.M. and M.G. activity was normal. As usual we had many patrols out during the night. No hostile patrols were seen. Hostile aerial activity was below normal.	
	5th.		Hostile artillery was normal in the Left Section and quiet in the other Sections. A heavy hostile T.M. barrage was put down behind our lines in C.17.a. and c. at 4.30.a.m. No infantry section followed. 2 British fighters had to land behind our lines during the day. One landed at 12.50.p.m. at H.12.d. and the other at 4.p.m. at H.18.c. Both machines were practically undamaged. One of our patrols entered NOVEL TRENCH at 2.30.p.m. and penetrated as far as N.14.b.9978. finding the trenches derelict and unoccupied.	
	6th.		Hostile artillery was normal except for some shelling of ARMENTIERES with 100 rounds of 21.c.m. How. and of battery position in H.23.a. and b. with 200 rounds 15.c.m. T.M. and M.G. activity was normal on both sides. One of our patrols encountered an enemy patrol 30 to 40 strong and dispersed it with rifle fire.	
	7th.		Hostile artillery was quiet in the Right and Centre Sections but was normal in the Left Section. Our artillery was engaged in wire cutting in front of INCLEMENT TRENCH and carried out a destructive shoot on enemy trenches in C.29.a. and c. in which T.M's co-operated. M.G. activity was normal on both sides. One hostile aeroplane was driven down out of control behind the enemy lines in the FLEURBAIX SECTION. 3 bombs were dropped by hostile planes on BAC ST MAUR at 9.15.a.m. causing 17 casualties. Our patrols were as usual very active,	

WAR DIARY or INTELLIGENCE SUMMARY.

Army Form C. 2118.

Page 2.

Place	Date	Hour	Summary of Events and Information	Remarks and references to Appendices
CROIX DU BAC.	OCTOBER 1917.			
	7th.		NECKLACE TRENCH, NEEDLE TRENCH, NEEDLE AVENUE and INCOME TRENCHES were entered. One patrol penetrated as far as MOUQUET FARM. Our snipers obtained a certain hit at I.11.a.66.75. on a German who was observing with field glasses.	
	8th.		G.S.O.2. went on leave. Under cover of heavy T.M. and artillery barrage enemy raiding party of about 60 strong raided our lines in N.6.a. between TIN BARN AVENUE and ABBOTS LANE. They crossed our line but were engaged with Lewis Gun and rifle fire by one of our posts and were forced to retire in disorder leaving one dead German, of 78th Landwehr Sturmtrupp, in our wire. Hostile artillery and T.M's were active during the day. Our patrols entered NECKLACE and NEPHEW TRENCHES and found them unoccupied. Our snipers obtained 2 certain hits.	
	9th.		Hostile artillery were practically inactive. Our artillery carried out wire-cutting and destructive shoots. Our patrols entered INCOME and INCARNATE TRENCHES but were prevented from penetrating further by strong wire. Our machine guns brought down a hostile plane in I.11.c.	
	10th.		Hostile artillery was inactive in the Right and Centre Sections but normal in the Left Section. Hostile aircraft showed considerable activity in the afternoon. One of our patrols penetrated the enemy lines as far as ORCHARD BARN. Our snipers obtained 4 certain hits on Germans.	
	11th.		Operation Order 141 issued re attachment of Battalion of C.E.P. Hostile artillery was more active. FLEURBAIX was shelled also a battery position in H.16.a. The front in the Left Section also received a good deal of attention. Hostile aircraft were active over the Left Section. One of our patrols entered NECKLACE TRENCH and penetrated as far as N.15.b.60.80.	
	12th.		Hostile artillery activity was below normal except in the Left Section. Our artillery carried out wire cutting and destructive shoots with good effect. Our patrols were very active as usual.	
	13th.		Hostile artillery was very active in the Left Section. Our artillery and T.M's carried out wire cutting and destructive shoots. Our snipers obtained a certain hit on a German. One of our patrols entered NEPHEW TRENCH and penetrated as far as N.15.b.65.64.	
	14th.		GENERAL RUAL and his A.D.C. and COLONEL MERRILL U.S.A. ARMY arrived for instruction.	
	15th.		Our artillery and T.M's active wire cutting and destructive shoots. LIEUT-COLONEL MUNBY D.S.O., reported as G.S.O.1. vice LIEUT-COLONEL H.E. ap.RHYS PRYCE, C.M.G., D.S.O., promoted Brigadier-General to command 113th Infantry Brigade vice BRIGADIER-GENERAL PRICE-DAVIES., V.C., D.S.O. Hostile artillery more active. Our Stokes Mortars carried out a shoot on INCLEMENT TRENCH	

Army Form C. 2118.

WAR DIARY
or
INTELLIGENCE SUMMARY.
(Erase heading not required.)

Page 3.

Place	Date	Hour	Summary of Events and Information	Remarks and references to Appendices
CROIX DU BAC.	OCTOBER 1917.			
	15th.		One of our patrols entered CENTAUR TRENCH and meeting a number of the enemy put them to flight killing or wounding several, and securing a prisoner, who escaped upon the escort being wounded. Another patrol entered NECK TRENCH but found no signs of the enemy.	
	16th.		BRIGADIER GENERAL PRICE-DAVIES, V.C., C.B., D.S.O., left for England. Enemy artillery and M.G. activity normal, but T.M's and Aircraft less active. One of our patrols engaged hostile post without result. Enemy patrol scattered by one of our patrols. Our artillery and T.M's mainly active with wire cutting.	
	17th.		LIEUT-COLONEL H.E.ap.RHYS PRYCE, V.M.G., D.S.O., left Divisional Headquarters to assume command of 113th Infantry Brigade. BAC ST MAUR shelled during the morning and early afternoon, and some of our battery positions were heavily shelled during the day. One of our patrols dispersed a hostile working party. E.A. rather more active.	
	18th.		O.O.142 issued regarding attachment of Battalion C.E.P. Out artillery carried out a shoot in retaliation for shelling of BAC ST MAUR yesterday. Normal T.M., M.G. and Aircraft activity on both sides. O.O.143 issued re attachment of Battalion C.E.P.	App 2
	19th.		Hostile activity of all sorts less active than usual to-day. A German patrol was rounded up outside our wire in I.16.b. 2 prisoners of 6th Coy. 2nd Battn. 77th R.I.R. 2nd Guard Reserve Division being captured. (1 an 'offizier Stellvertreter'). Our artillery carried out wire cutting and destructive shoots in the ARMENTIERES and BOIS GRENIER SECTIONS.	App 3
	20th.		Hostile artillery less active but T.M. active in the FLEURBAIX front. M.G. and aircraft normal on both sides. Our patrols active. Our artillery mainly active with wire cutting.	
	21st.		Enemy artillery M.G's and T.M's and Aircraft quiet. Enemy T.M's active in the BOUTILLERIE SECTOR. Our artillery and T.M's active with wire cutting. Our artillery patrols were active.	
	22nd.		G.O.C. leaves for England for one months leave. Brigadier-General ALEXANDER assumes temporary command of the Division. Normal activity of all sorts on both sides. Our artillery and T.M's mainly engaged in wire cutting. Our patrols were active.	
	23rd.		O.O.144 issued regarding second period of attachment of 4th and 17th Battalions 5th Bde.C.E.P. Hostile artillery, trench mortars, machine guns and aircraft activity a little below normal. ARMENTIERES slightly shelled. Our artillery and trench mortars continued wire cutting and destructive shooting.	App 4
	24th.		Enemy attempted a raid on one of our posts in H.9.d. After a brief encounter the enemy party was driven off leaving one dead man in our trenches. None of our men were missing and only	

WAR DIARY or INTELLIGENCE SUMMARY.

Army Form C. 2118.
Page 4.

Place	Date	Hour	Summary of Events and Information	Remarks and references to Appendices
CROIX DU BAC.	OCTOBER 1917. 24th.		only 4. were wounded. Identification - 6th Company 2nd Battn, 299 R.I.R. 50th Reserve Divn. Hostile artillery was more active especially in the ARMENTIERES SECTION. Our artillery was again active with wire cutting and destructive shoots. All other activity normal on both sides. An enemy patrol was dispersed in O.29.a.	App 5
	25th.		G.S.O.2. Returned from leave. Hostile artillery below normal. Enemy trench mortars only active in retaliation for T.M's. Enemy machine guns more active in BOIS GRENIER SECTION. Enemy aircraft and patrols inactive. Our artillery and trench mortars busy with wire-cutting. All other activity normal.	
	26th.		O.O.145 issued regarding attachment of 4th and 17th Bn. 5th Bde. C.E.P. Hostile artillery, trench mortars and aircraft inactive, but machine guns active during the night in the FLEURBAIX SECTION. Our artillery busy with wire cutting and Trench Mortars and machine guns busy in preparation for our raid. One of our patrols found the enemy post at the head of NEGATIVE DRIVE unoccupied. We attempted a raid on the enemy line in N.6.b. but was only partially successful. No identifications and our casualties 1 officer and 6 O.R. wounded.	App 6
	27th.		G.S.8064 issued regarding attachment of 5th Trench Mortar Battery C.E.P. Enemy artillery showed increased activity in the BOIS GRENIER SECTION and ARMENTIERES SECTION. Hostile trench mortars inactive. Hostile aircraft more active. Our artillery and trench mortars engaged in destructive shoots. Our machine guns aircraft and patrols active. An enemy patrol enhaged one of ours resulting in 2 casualties to our party. O.O.146 issued regarding gas operation by 1st Special Company R.E.	App 63
	28th.		G.S.8068 issued regarding withdrawal of 10th Bn. C.E.P. on completion of period of training. Enemy activity in general quiet. Our artillery busy with wire cutting. At 9.30.p.m. we carried out a successful gas bombardment on areas I.27.b.,C.23.,and C.29. Hostile trench mortars retaliated rather heavily in the BOIS GRENIER SECTION, but only slightly in the ARMENTIERES SECTION.	App 1
	29th.		G.S.8102 issued regarding handing over of Sub-section to 10th Battn C.E.P. for period of 6 days. 2 wounded prisoners of 5th Coy.,2nd Battn., 77 R.I.R. 2nd Guard Reserve Division were taken early in the morning in our trenches I.16.b. in an attempted enemy patrol enterprise. We suffered only 1 O.R. wounded.	
	30th.		G.S.O.1. left for 8.84 14 days leave to England. Conference of Brigadiers at Divisional Headquarters.	

Army Form C. 2118.

WAR DIARY
or
INTELLIGENCE SUMMARY.
(Erase heading not required)

Page 5.

Instructions regarding War Diaries and Intelligence Summaries are contained in F. S. Regs., Part II. and the Staff Manual respectively. Title pages will be prepared in manuscript.

Place	Date	Hour	Summary of Events and Information	Remarks and references to Appendices
CROIX DU BAC	OCTOBER 1917.			
	30th.		Hostile artillery active in the ARMENTIERES SECTION but hostile trench mortars generally inactive. Enemy machine guns active in the BOIS GRENIER SECTION and ARMENTIERES SECTION. Our artillery and trench mortars active with wire cutting. One of our patrols dispersed an enemy patrol at N.9.c.55.50. killing one from whom an identification was obtained - 2nd Coy. 1st Bn. 229 R.I.R. 50th Reserve Division.	
	31st.		Enemy guns were busy with counter-battery work in the ARMENTIERES SECTION during the morning. Our artillery continued wire cutting operations in the BOIS GRENIER and ARMENTIERES SECTIONS during the morning. Our artillery continued wire cutting operations in the BOIS GRENIER SECTION and ARMENTIERES SECTION. Our trench mortars co-operated in wire cutting. Machine guns, aircraft and patrolling normal on both sides. G.S.8145 issued regarding attachment of 5th Light Trench Mortar Battery C.E.P. to 113th Infantry Brigade.	

1/11/17.

T.Harington Captain.
Lieut,
General Staff 38th (Welsh) Division.

Vol 24.

General Staff,
38th Division.
November 1917.

SECRET

FILE No. G.12.

Sub-Nos. 185

SUBJECT. ~~Minor Operations~~

Sub-head. ~~Proposed Raid by 11 N. Lanc R.,~~
~~120th Bde., 40th Div.~~

~~II Corps~~

Referred to	Date.	Referred to	Date.

ORIGINAL

Army Form C. 2118.

WAR DIARY
or
INTELLIGENCE SUMMARY.
(Erase heading not required.)

GENERAL STAFF
38th (Welsh) Division.
VOLUME XXIV.

Instructions regarding War Diaries and Intelligence Summaries are contained in F.S. Regs., Part II. and the Staff Manual respectively. Title pages will be prepared in manuscript.

Place	Date	Hour	Summary of Events and Information	Remarks and references to Appendices
CROIX DU BAC.	NOVEMBER 1917.			
	1st.		Some counter battery work was done by the enemy against our guns in the ARMENTIERES SECTION. Trench mortars, machine guns and aircraft normally active on both sides. 11 patrols went out from our lines. 2 enemy patrols were encountered and dispersed. Hostile artillery quiet. No aircraft activity on either side. Enemy patrolling greater than usual. O.O. 147 issued re arrival of 59th F.A. Brigade from 11th Division.	App 1
	2nd.		Enemy artillery and trench mortars were quiet except for some retaliation for our wire cutting. An enemy patrol dispersed leaving one wounded prisoner of 78th Landwehr Regt, 38th Landwehr Division in our hands.	App 2
	3rd.		O.O. 148 issued regarding Raid by 115th Infantry Brigade on German Front and Support Lines. Our artillery and trench mortars continued wire cutting in the BOIS GRENIER Section, and ARMENTIERES Section. Enemy artillery quiet during the day. No enemy patrols encountered. The body of a dead German of the 77th R.I.R. 2nd Guards Reserve Division was found by a patrol at I.11.c.50.55. last night. Our artillery continued wire cutting on wire in front of INCANDESCENT and INCH TRENCHES and CENSORS NOSE. 2 German patrols were heard moving near their wire in the Right Section. No encounters took place.	App 3
	4th.			
	5th.			
	6th.		Our artillery and trench mortars continued wire cutting on INCANDESCENT and INCH TRENCHES and CENSORS NOSE. Hostile artillery quiet, though there was one heavy counter battery shoot in the ARMENTIERES SECTION. Our patrols went out along the whole front reconnoitring enemy wire. Enemy showed no activity and there were no patrol encounters.	
	7th.		We carried out a successful raid with a strong force against INCANDESCENT R TRENCH and SUPPORT in I.11.a. early this morning. 12 prisoners were captured, heavy casualties inflicted, and great havoc wrought in the enemy trenches. In the Centre Sector a small raiding party entered INCLEMENT TRENCH at I.23.a.2.5. but found that the enemy had evacuated his trench at this point. Bangalore Torpedoes were successfully exploded in enemy wire in front of INCH and INCIDENT TRENCHES covering our operations in other sections. In the raid in the ARMENTIERES SECTION we obtained identifications of the 15th R.I.R. 2nd Guards Reserve Division. Units normal.	
	8th.		A patrol in C.23.c. found a dead German of the 91st R.I.R. 2nd Guard Reserve Division. Artillery Trench Mortars and Machine Guns co-operated in forming a box barrage in conjunction with the raid on INCANDESCENT TRENCH. Hostile retaliation (T.M.) for special operation was very light. O.O. 149 issued re withdrawal of 59th F.A. Brigade. Enemy artillery unusually active against battery areas in the ARMENTIERES SECTION. /over	

Army Form C. 2118.

WAR DIARY
or
INTELLIGENCE SUMMARY.

Page 2.

(Erase heading not required.)

Place	Date	Hour	Summary of Events and Information	Remarks and references to Appendices
CROIX DU BAC.	NOVEMBER 1917.			
	8th.(continued).		Over 100 rounds 15.c.m. and 10.5.c.m. being fired. (T.M's) Intermittent fire in short bursts by ourselves and the enemy. Our patrols active; enemy showed no initiative. Enemy aircraft active over front line and back areas during the morning. Bombs were dropped on BAC ST MAUR, on ROUGE DE BOUT- SAILLY ROAD, and on our support line (CORDONNERIE SECTION). Raid 7/8th October. According to further reports received an explosion in an ammunition dump at 1.11.b.05.78. was caused by our bombardment. Prisoner states there was a small dump of T.M. shells near this point. O.O.150 issued re discharge of gas on enemy.	app 4 app 5
	9th.	4.p.m.	GOC 58th Division held a conference with G.O.C' Brigades. G.S.8302 issued regarding second attachment of 4th and 17th Battalions C.E.P. holding a subsection with responsibility for defence. Hostile artillery active in RUE MARLE and CHAPELLE D'ARMENTIERES areas searching for battery positions. Over 600 gas bombs were discharged on enemy trenches in I.21. Enemy T.M's more active than usual along whole front especially in retaliation for gas bombardment during the night. Bombs dropped in the morning near BAC ST MAUR north of the River LYS. Patrols out along the whole Divisional front. Enemy patrol was seen in C.29.a. and dispersed by L.G. fire.	app 6
	10th.		O.O.151 issued regarding discharge of gas shells on enemy front and support lines in I.21.c. Our front line in Right Section N.8.c. lightly shelled in the afternoon. Enemy T.M. displayed sudden activity against our trenches in I.14.b. and I.10.c. at 4.45.p.m. A strong enemy patrol was seen in I.26.b. but lost sight of in the darkness.	app 7
	11th.		G.S. 10/4 issued regarding date of arrival of 17th Battalion C.E.P. in British Area. Our artillery carried out destructive shoots on INCANDESCENT and INCREASE SUPPORT TRENCHES. Retaliated for hostile T.M. fire and registered on special targets. Hostile artillery active throughout the day against battery areas in the ARMENTIERES SECTION over 1000 rounds 10.5.c.m. and 15.c.m. being fired. Our Heavy T.M's carried out destructive shoots on a T.M. emplacement in I.26.b. and against trenches and wire in I.22.a. and I.11.d. Enemy aircraft showed considerable activity during morning, bombs were dropped on Support Line I.15.b. and near LE LE SEQUEMAU A.30.c. Patrols were out along the whole front. Enemy heard wiring in I.5.c. and a covering patrol was seen. Rapid fire was opened by our patrol and the enemy retired. In response to an S.O.S. call our artillery fired on barrage lines in the Left Section from 8.10.a.m. to 8.50.a.m. yesterday morning. Enemy Field Artillery put down a heavy barrage on our front and support lines in C.28. at 8.a.m. lasting 30 minutes. Enemy Heavy Artillery /active	
	12th.			

Army Form C. 2118.

WAR DIARY
or
INTELLIGENCE SUMMARY.

(Erase heading not required.)

Page 3.

Place	Date	Hour	Summary of Events and Information	Remarks and references to Appendices
CROIX DU BAC.	NOVEMBER 1917.			
	12th.		against Battery areas in the FLEURBAIX and ARMENTIERES SECTIONS. Enemy gas shells were fired on CHAPELLE D'ARMENTIERES and DESOLANQUE FARM. Our heavy and light T.M's carried out destructive shoots o in ARMENTIERES SECTION. Enemy machine guns co-operated with their artillery at 8.a.m. by sweeping front and support lines in I.28. Enemy aircraft active. One plane flew over our lines in left section. S.O.S. call at 8.a.m. was sent out by an unknown power buzzer probably an enemy instrument. No infantry action followed. G.S.O.1. returned from leave in England.	
	13th.		Marked decrease in enemy artillery activity. 10.30.p.m. and 11.p.m. enemy artillery and trench mortars carried out shoots with intensive bombardments with H.E. and gas on our trenches in RUE DU BOIS area and at 3.30.a.m. on our trenches in the Left Sector. At the same time gas shells were fired on various targets along whole Divisional front. Our artillery replied vigorously in kind. After 2.30.a.m. Situation quiet. Hostile machine guns unusually active on areas subjected to gas bombardment during the night. Enemy patrols moving near their own wire heard in the Right and Left Sections. No encounters took place.	
	14th.		Enemy artillery fired some gas shells on our support and subsidiary lines but was only fairly active with trench mortars and machine guns. Our snipers obtained 14 victims and one of our patrols encountered a hostile party. No identification obtained however. During the night 5 of our patrols occupied the enemy's abandoned front line in N.10. and remained until 4.a.m.	
	15th.		G.S.S.10/7 issued regarding 5th Light Trench Mortar Battery C.T.P. returning to PORTUGUESE AREA.	app 8
	16th.		Enemy Artillery rather more active but all other activity normal. Enemy Trench Mortars carried out an organised shoot in the Left Section. Our guns active generally along the whole front and our T.M's carried out successful shoots in the Left and Centre Sections.	
	17th.		G.S.S.10/13 issued regarding XI Corps H.Q. and Corps Troops will be relieved by XV Corps H.Q. and Corps Troops.	app 9
	18th.		Our artillery, Trench Mortars and Machine Guns and patrols were normally active. Enemy artillery active on ARMENTIERES with 10.5.c.m. How. and gas shells, but was otherwise quiet.BRIGADIER-GENERAL ALEXANDER returns to Corps and BRIGADIER-GENERAL THOMPSON assumes command of the Division. Our artillery and trench mortars were active in retaliation for enemy activity and on special targets.	

Army Form C. 2118.

WAR DIARY
or
INTELLIGENCE SUMMARY.

Page 4.

(Erase heading not required.)

Instructions regarding War Diaries and Intelligence Summaries are contained in F.S. Regs., Part II and the Staff Manual respectively. Title pages will be prepared in manuscript.

Place	Date	Hour	Summary of Events and Information	Remarks and references to Appendices
CROIX DU BAC.	NOVEMBER 1917.			
	18th. (contd).		Our patrols were also active and a 'land mine' was laid on an enemy track. Enemy artillery showed an increase in the Left Section but only scattered fire reported in the Right and Centre Sections. Enemy T.M's showed marked activity in the BOIS GRENIER SECTION and M.G's were more than usually active during the night.	
	19th.		The 77th R.I.R. 2nd Guard Reserve Division identified by the capture of 4 wounded other ranks. They formed part of a patrol which had lost its way. We were active generally with artillery, trench mortars, machine guns, sniping and patrolling work. Hostile artillery showed normal activity in the ARMENTIERES SECTION, some gas shells being used, but not unusually active in the other sections. Enemy aircraft impeded our retaliation shoots.	
	20th.		Enemy artillery and trench mortars active in the ARMENTIERES SECTION. Enemy machine guns more active than usual.	
	21st.		Enemy artillery and trench mortars were rather more active in the ARMENTIERES SECTION but only moderately in the other sections.	
	22nd.		G.O.C. returned from leave. The Division comes under the command of the XV Corps from 4.p.m. Our artillery and trench mortars active with retaliatory work. The body of a German Officer (1st Coy, 1st Battn, 77 R.I.R., 2nd Guard Res. Division) brought in by one of our patrols. Enemy guns active in the ARMENTIERES SECTION some gas being used. Quiet in other sections. An enemy patrol was dispersed and the above identification secured.	
	23rd.		Our artillery responded to an S.O.S. call sent up by Division on our right. Body of a machine gunner of 1st Battalion 77 R.I.R. found in I.16.b. Hostile artillery and trench mortars again very active in the ARMENTIERES SECTION but inactive in the other sections, except for a T.M. bombardment in the FLEURBAIX SECTION.	
	24th.		Our artillery, trench mortars and machine guns and patrols active generally. Enemy party about 30 strong attempted a raid on our post at I.5.a.50.65. about 5.30.a.m. but was dispersed by our L.G. fire.	
	25th.		Our artillery and trench mortars were active in retaliation for hostile shelling. An enemy patrol dispersed by fire from one of our patrols.	
	26th.		Hostile artillery mainly active in the ARMENTIERES SECTION and trench mortars mainly active in the FLEURBAIX SECTION and BOIS GRENIER SECTION. Enemy machine guns unusually active in the ARMENTIERES SECTION during the night. No hostile patrols encountered.	
			/27th.	

Army Form C. 2118.

WAR DIARY
or
INTELLIGENCE SUMMARY.

(*Erase heading not required.*)

Page 5.

Place	Date	Hour	Summary of Events and Information	Remarks and references to Appendices
CROIX DU BAC.	NOVEMBER 1917.			
	27th.		Our artillery was again busy with a destructive shoot Trench Mortars assisting. G.S.O.3. starts for leave. G.O.C. 2nd Portuguese Division visits Divisional Commander.	
	28th.		Our artillery and trench mortars continued destructive shoots. Other activity normal. Chief of Portuguese Staff visits Divisional Headquarters. G.O.C., R.A. Corps visits Divl. Commander. G.S.S. 10/4 issued regarding 17th Battalion C.E.P. returning to the Portuguese area on 1st December.	App 10.
	29th.		Our artillery was active with destructive and counter battery shoots and our T.M's were active generally. Numerous patrols were out on the Divisional front. Our machine guns brought down an enemy plane. Enemy attempted to enter our lines under cover of a T.M. bombardment but was immediately repulsed by our Lewis Guns and rifle fire. No casualties to us and no identifications. Corps Commander visits G.O.C. and goes round line with G.S.O.2.	App 11.
	30th.		G.S.S. 10/4 issued regarding 17th Battalion C.E.P. remaining in ERQUINGHEM. Our artillery and trench mortars active generally. 10 patrols were out on the Divisional front. Hostile artillery was again somewhat active in the ARMENTIERES SECTION and on a battery position.	

21/12/17.

[signature]
Lieut,
for General Staff 38th (Welsh) Division.

War Diary

SECRET

38th Division No.S.S.111/5.

Subject :- Report on Raid carried out on the night 7th/8th November by the 10th (S) Battalion South Wales Borderers.

XI Corps

1. The raid was carried out by about 270 men of the above Battalion supported by 8 Batteries of 18-prs., 2 Batteries of 5.9", 1 Light T.M. Battery and 1½ Batteries of Medium Mortars.

2. The wire was well cut by the Field and Heavy Artillery and Trench Mortars. The portion in front of the enemy's support line was cut by 6" Howitzers. Wire had also been cut on other portions of the front.

3. Gas bombardments took place simultaneously on 3 portions of the front, and a small raid was also carried out by the 113th Infantry Brigade and 6 Bangalore torpedoes were successfully let off in the enemy's wire to draw his attention off the raid.

4. The Raiding Party obtained all its objectives except on the extreme left of the enemy's Support Line where they were unable to get through the wire.

5. 50 of the enemy were killed and 12 prisoners brought back.

3 concrete dug-outs were blown up by the R.E. One of these dug-outs had a machine gun in it and some of the enemy who would not come out.

In addition to the known casualties inflicted on the enemy there must have been others as some were fired at running away and they had to get through our barrage.

6. Prisoners stated that they had relieved the Company occupying the trenches raided 3 days earlier than normal owing to the heavy casualties caused by our Artillery fire.

/7.

(2)

7. The barrage and counter-battery work was good and there was little retaliation until the party began to withdraw.

Hostile fire died down very soon after our Artillery ceased firing.

8. No. 1 Special Company R.E. carried out their Gas bombardment skilfully.

9. Great credit is due to Lieut. Colonel HARVEY, Commanding the 10th (S) Battalion South Wales Borderers, who trained the Raiding Party, and to Captain COBB, 10th (S) Battalion South Wales Borderers who commanded it.

All ranks, and the R.E. who accompanied the party, did their work with great determination. They were out to win and did so.

10. Our casualties were :-

	Killed.	Wounded.	Died of Wounds.	Missing.
Officers.	-	3	-	-
Other ranks.	7	42	1	-

12th November 1917.

Brigadier General,
Commanding 38th (Welsh) Division.

NARRATIVE OF THE ATTACK OF THE PILCKEM
RIDGE BY THE 38TH (WELSH) DIVISION.

The Division was holding the British Line from the YPRES - PILCKEM ROAD to BOESINGHE inclusive, when towards the end of May it was informed that a big attack would be delivered by the British on the YPRES front and that advantage should be taken of the coming attack of the Second Army on the MESSINES - WYTSCHAETE RIDGE to dig such assembly trenches as would be necessary. These trenches were dug towards the end of May and the beginning of June and our line advanced all along this front to within 200 yards of the enemy front line, from in some places, a distance of 300 yards further off.

The enemy's attention was drawn to these trenches but he did comparatively little firing upon them, and it was thought that he must have considered them as a ruse to try and draw attention from the attack upon the MESSINES - WYTSCHAETE RIDGE.

In June the Division was informed of the definite role that it would have to play in the coming Battle.

It then left the VIII Corps and joined the XIV Corps and in course of time handed over the BOESINGHE Sector to the Guards Division, who were to fight on their left.
Towards the end of June the Division left the Line and proceeded to the ST.HILAIRE area to train for the coming Battle.

A replica of the trenches and strong points to be attacked was laid out on the ground between ENQUIN and DELETTE and the Brigades were practiced over the same in their respective roles. Opportunity was also taken to practice the machine gun barrage and this was found extremely useful, as none of the machine gunners had hitherto done any firing for long periods at a time. On the 19th and 20th July the Division returned to its Sector in the line, taking over from the 29th Division, to whom its thanks are due for carrying on such work as was necessary in preparation for the attack.

From the period the Division was in the Line until the day of the actual attack on the 31st July a considerable number of

/losses

losses occurred from shell fire and gas shells. The Germans had introduced new gas of the Mustard type which proved much more serious than at first sight it appeared to be. Matters however, proceeded well and all arrangements were completed some days before the attack actually took place.

On the morning of the 27th July Aeroplane reports indicated that the Germans had evacuated their trenches and consequently it was arranged that this Division and the Guards should send forward patrols at 5.30. in the afternoon to test the accuracy of the above report.

The 15th Welsh Regt and the 15th Royal Welsh Fusiliers were detailed to each find 2 platoons for this work.

At the appointed hour they moved forward and found no Germans in the front line but after proceeding beyond this discovered that the support and reserve lines and also the German Second Line system were strongly held. The Platoons however, pushed on untill they fully developed the enemy's strength, which on the western slope of the PILCKEM RIDGE was found to be 2 Battalions.

In the front of the Guards owing to the severity of the shelling the enemy had withdrawn from his front system and consequently it was decided that the ground gained by the Patrols should be held and arrangements were consequently made by which the left of the Division was linked up with the right of what the Guards had gained east of the YSER CANAL, so as to facilitate their further attack.

On the night 30/31st July the troops were brought into their assembly positions and were concentrated without a hitch by 2.54.a.m. on the 31st July.

/The

The general dispositions of the Division were as under :-

114th Brigade on the right and the

113th Brigade on the left with the

115th Brigade in reserve.

Tasks allotted to the first two Brigades were to attack the BLUE LINE, the BLACK LINE and the GREEN LINE.

In the second objective was included the village of PILCKEM and the third brought them half way between the STEENBEEK and PILCKEM VILLAGE. On this line being attained the 115th Infantry Brigade were to push forward two battalions and capture the STEENBEEK and its crossings.

The troops suffered but little loss before the attack commenced and this is attributed to the plentiful bombardment by gas shell of enemy batteries.

Zero was at 3.50.a.m. and at that hour the 10th Welsh Regt on the right, and the 13th Welsh Regt on the right centre, the 13th Royal Welsh Fusiliers on the left centre and the 16th Royal Welsh Fusiliers on the left moved forward to the attack.

The BLUE LINE was captured with but little opposition, most of the enemy encountered being found in dugouts in CAESAR'S SUPPORT. These were taken prisoners with the exception of those who showed fight.

The advance to the BLACK LINE was carried out by the 15th Welsh Regt on the right and the 14th Welsh Regt on the right centre.

In the 113th Brigade who had not so many trenches to encounter this attack was carried out by the remaining two Companies in both the 13th Royal Welsh Fusiliers and 16th Royal Welsh Fusiliers. The opposition met in this advance was severer than that met in the advance on the BLUE LINE. The centres of resistance were MARSOUIN FARM and STRAY FARM on the right and the village of PILCKEM on the left. In all these places there were several

/concrete

concrete machine gun emplacements but the men working very well outflanked them and compelled the garrisons to surrender.

The BLACK LINE was captured up to time and was immediately consolidated.

The advance to the GREEN LINE was carried out by half Battalions of the 15th and 14th Welsh Regt. on the right and by the 15th Royal Welsh Fusiliers on the left.

Considerable trouble was met from the direction of RUDOLPHE BARM which was in the area allotted to the 51st Divn. That Division was either not up or a gap existed and consequently a Platoon of the 15th Welsh Regt. was detailed to attack the FARM. This was successfully accomplished. The enemy, with the exception of some 15 men who surrendered, either ran away or were shot.

The neighbourhood of IRON CROSS was strongly held and the 14th Welsh Regt suffered somewhat heavily in rushing it. They had however, the satisfaction of killing with the bayonet some 20 of the enemy and taking 40 prisoners and 3 machine guns in this neighbourhood. This done the 14th Welsh Regt pushed on to U.28.c.10.35. where an enemy Dressing Station and 16 men wounded and 22 unwounded were captured.

The 15th Royal Welsh Fusiliers commenced their advance from the BLACK LINE at the correct time but on nearing BATTERY COPSE were met with such heavy fire that in a short time only a few Officers were left and our barrage began to run away from the men. The men, however, struggled forward and established themselves on the IRON CROSS RIDGE.

During the period that the 114th and 113th Brigades were attacking up to the IRON CROSS RIDGE the 11th South Wales Borderers and the 17th Royal Welsh Fusiliers, both of the 115th Infantry Brigade were gradually working their way forward until they were close up to the IRON CROSS RIDGE from which they launched their attack, on the STEENBEEK.

/This

This attack was successfully carried out in the face of considerable opposition from concrete shelters inside the houses, most of which were made by machine guns. All were however, outflanked by the infantry and the garrisons compelled to surrender and the STEENBEEK was reached and parties pushed out to cover and hold its crossings.

The losses amongst our men were however severe and consequently the General Officer Commanding the 115th Infantry Brigade ordered one Company of the 16th Welsh Regt to reinforce the 17th Royal Welsh Fusiliers and one company of the 10th South Wales Borderers to reinforce the 11th South Wales Borderers. From 2.p.m. onwards, the Germans were seen to be massing for Counter attack and this attack developed at 3.10.p.m. and one Company of the 11th South Wales Borderers which had occupied AU BON GITE were forced to retire to the western side of the STEENBEEK. The remainder of the line repelled the attack, the Artillery and Machine Gun barrage helping largely. Rifle fire was successfully employed in wiping out some 100 Germans who had got through our barrage.

During the course of the afternoon the weather which had been dull and cloudy changed for the worst and rain began to fall steadily and continued more or less for the next 3 days, rendering operations extremely difficult owing to the slippery and muddy state of the ground, which clogged the movement of the Infantry.

The morning of the 31st July was quiet so far as hostilities were concerned but in the course of the afternoon the enemy again attempted a counter attack, but this was broken up by Artillery and Machine Gun fire before it had time to mature.

The heavy shelling and the state of the weather and the many casualties experienced by the 115th Brigade necessitated

/us

us being relieved.

On the night of the 1st/2nd August the 113th Brigade took over the front line. From this date to the 6th August there is but little to record whatever, theweather during this period being so bad that operations became impossible. On the 6th the Division was relieved in the line by the 20th Division and withdrew to PROVEN where it rested and commenced to train.

The Division remained at PROVEN until the 19th and 20th August, when it relieved the 20th Division, who in the meanwhile had taken LANGEMARCK.

The line taken over ran through WHITE TRENCH and BEAR TRENCH, EAGLE TRENCH being in the hands of the Germans.

In conjunction with larger attacks on the right an attack was made at 1.55.p.m. on the 27th August by the 16th Welsh Regt. on EAGLE TRENCH.

The weather/had been moderately fine in the morning became so bad during the course of the day that when the time came to advance, the men who had been lying in shell-holes which were gradually filling with water found great difficulty in getting out and advancing and keeping up with the barrage. The barrage got away from them and they came under the fire of Machine Guns from the direction of PHEASANT FARM and were unable to reach their objective.

No further operations were conducted on the front of the Division and the remaining period in the line passed without event except for the usual daily shelling.

The Division was relieved on the 11th September by the 20th Division and moved to PROVEN and left PROVEN on the 13th September for CROIX DU BAC.

The success in taking PILCKEM RIDGE may be attributed to the excellent work done by the Artillery in breaking down the wire and smashing up trenches and emplacements and also to the way in which the men rapidly outflanked numerous concrete dugouts

/met

Page 7.

met in the captured area. The first enumeration showed that there were 280 of these concrete structures.

Opposed to the Division on the morning of the 31st July was the German 3rd Guards Division, just arrived in the line the day before in place of the 23rd Reserve Division worn out by our preparatory activity.

Of the 3rd Guards Division, the Guards Fusilier Regiment (the notorious 'Cockchafers' so popular in Berlin) which was holding PILCKEM itself received particularly rough treatment at the hands of the Division. All three Battalions were met and broken in turn and of this Regiment alone 400 prisoners were taken as well as many killed.

Of the other Regiments of the 3rd Guards Division the Lehr Regiment was surprised while still relieving the 392nd I.R., 23rd Reserve Division, and prisoners of both Regiments were taken, while a few prisoners were taken of the 9th Grenadiers who were in reserve and who suffered heavy losses in counter attacking the STEENBEEK. In addition a number of prisoners were taken of the 73rd Fusiliers (Hanoverians), 111th Division, who just over-lapped our left front, making a total of close on 700 prisoners. The 3rd Guards Division had to be withdrawn immediately after the Battle.

In the course of the subsequent operations between the 20th August and the 11th September prisoners were taken from the 119th Grenadier and 125th Infantry Regiments of the 26th (Wurtemberg) Division and from the 185th Infantry Regiment of the 208th Division which relieved the 26th Division, withdrawn exhausted, from the effects of our shell fire.

Fifth Army G.A. 790/4
XIV Corps No.G.44/3.
38th Division No.G.S. 6858.

XIV Corps.

      The following letter of congratulation has been received by the Army Commander, and is communicated for information of all ranks :-

                                G.H.Q. British Armies in France,
                                         1st August 1917.

General Sir H. Gough.

      My warmest congratulations to yourself and to the Comdrs. Staffs and troops under your command on the great success gained yesterday.   The severity of the fighting and the very heavy losses suffered by the enemy will force him to expend his remaining reserves rapidly in the effort to stay our advance and this is even more important than the gain of ground, great as that was -

      You and all ranks under your command may well be proud of and fully satisfied with such a splendid day.

                                             (Signed) D. HAIG.
                                                      Field Marshal.

                                     (Signed) M WETHERLY, Major
                                        for Major-General, G.S.

                (2).

113th Bde	19th Welsh Regt.	A.P.M.	38th Div "Q".
114th Bde	A.D.M.S.	D.A.D.O.S.	
115th Bde	Signals.	D.M.G.O.	
38th Div Arty.	Div Train.	Sniping Coy.	
C. R. E.	176th M.G. Coy.	S.S.O.	

      For information.

                                       (Signed) F.J. HARINGTON,
                                               Captain,
                                    for Lieut-Colonel,
                     General Staff 38th (Welsh) Division.

H.Q., XIV Corps.
August 4th 1917.

My Dear Blackader,

I must put in writing, for what it is worth, my intense appreciation of the noble fight put up by the 38th Division on 31st July.

From the moment I saw the wonderful change that your Division had wrought in the defences of the Northern half of the "YPRES SALIENT", I was certain that they were to be trusted to do more important work.

They have wiped that Salient off the Map.

I cannot thank you and your Staff enough for your admirable work, and I shall make a point of personally thanking each of your Brigadiers and C.O's as soon as I can.

Believe me,
Yours most gratefully,
(Sd) CAVAN.

(2).   38th Division No.G.S. 6867.

113th Bde	A.D.M.S.
114th Bde	38th Div "Q".
115th Bde	38th Div Train.
G.O.C., R.A.	19th Welsh Regt.
C. R. E.	Signals.

I forward herewith a copy of a private letter from the Corps Commander, the contents of which I should like made known to the Units under your command.

I need scarcely say what a pleasure it is to me to know that the good work of all in the Division has been so highly appreciated by higher authority.

As this is a private letter, I naturally must ask you to take steps to see that no further use is made of it than communicating its contents as above.

(Signed) C.G. BLACKADER,
Major-General,
Commanding 38th (Welsh) Division.

5/8/17.

Fifth Army G.A. 657/275.
2nd August 1917.
XIV Corps G. 44/3.

XIV Corps.
----

1.   The Army Commander wishes to offer his heartiest congratulations to the troops under his command on the success gained by them on July 31st.

2.   For the fortnight prior to the attack the enemy has maintained a heavy and continuous Arty. fire, including an unprecedented use of H.V. guns against back areas, and a new form of gas shell, all of which caused severe casualties.   Despite this fact that the forward area was dominated by the enemy at all points, the necessary preparations for the battle were completed and the difficult forward march and assembly of nine Divs. successfully carried out and the assault launched.   Thid alone constitutes a performance of which the Army may well be proud.

3.   As a result of the battle and the enemy has once again been driven by the 1st French Army and ourselves from the whole of his front system on a front of about 8 miles, and we are now firmly established in or beyond his second line on a front of 7 miles.

4.   We have already captured 5448 prisoners, including 125 officers.   Up to date the capture of 8 guns, 10 T.M's and 36 machine guns have been reported.

5.   In addition we have inflicted extremely heavy casualties on the enemy.   Owing to losses during our preliminary bombardment he was forced to bring up 6 fresh Divisions.   Since then 3 more Divisions have been withdrawn shattered.

   Thus, in a fortnight, we have disposed of 7 or 8 Divisions, and severely handled 10 more, several of which must be shortly withdrawn.

6.   The Second Army on our right and the 1st French Army on our left have been as successful as ourselves.   The French captures to date number 157 prisoners, and 3 guns.   The Second

Army have also taken 390 prisoners and several machine guns.

Despite the weather onnthe day of the battle we shot down 5 enemy machines and 1 balloon, losing only 1 machine ourselves.

(Signed) R. T. COLLINS, Lt.Col.
for Major-General, G. S.

Copies to :-

Infantry Brigades.
38th Div Artillery.
C. R. E. 38th Div.

SECRET.

38th Division No. G.S. 7197.
XIVth Corps No. G.55/2.
115th Bde., B.M.

38th Division.

1. Herewith 18 copies of Fifth Army letter S.G.671/26 for distribution down to Battalion Commanders.

2. This stirring paper can be summed up in the two following simple principles -

    (a) If leading troops are seen to be retiring, it is the duty of the nearest Battalion in support to go forward at once without waiting for orders from the Brigade.

    (b) On reaching objective, every man not detailed for consolidation will shoot at every German he sees.

3. Training on these lines will be initiated at once.

                                (sd.) E. SEYMOUR, Captain for
                                          Brigadier General,
3rd September, 1917.   General Staff, XIV Corps.

(2).

115th Brigade.

In forwarding these points made by the Army Commander the Major General directs that all training must be devoted to instilling an Offensive Spirit in Officers, N.C.O's. and men.

They must be taught how to meet an enemy counter attack by advancing with the bayonet and when the enemy turn and run our troops must at once lie down and open rapid fire.

Special attention is directed to paragraph 13 of the Army Commander's letter.

                                  (Sd.) R.S. Follett, Major,
                                       for Lieut. Colonel,
4th September, 1917.   General Staff, 38th (Welsh) Division.

38th Division No. G.S.6864.

113th Brigade	Div. Train
114th Brigade	A.P.M.
115th Brigade	D.A.D.O.S.
38th Div. Arty.	D.M.G.O.
C.R.E.	Sniping Coy.
19th Welsh Regt.	176th M.G.Coy.
A.D.M.S.	38th Div. "Q".
Signals	

The following letter and telegrams of congratulations have been received by the G.O.C. and are communicated for information of all ranks :-

"The Corps Commander thanks every Officer and man in the XIV Corps for their splendid efforts today. R.E., the Field and Heavy Artillery and Infantry share the chief honours of an advance of 2½ miles.

Labour Companies and all sorts of transport drivers deserve the fullest recognition also, for the way they have stuck to their job under harassing fire.

(Sd) F.GATHORNE HARDY,
Brigadier-General,
General Staff, XIV Corps."

31st July 1917.

"Please convey to all ranks my congratulations on great success of WELSH DIVISION today.

EDWARD P. H.Q., XIV Corps."

31st July 1917.

"Many congratulations on your successful day from General PLUMER and Staff Second Army.

31st July 1917."

H.E. Pryce
Lieut. Colonel,
General Staff, 38th (Welsh) Division.

4/8/1917.

XI Corps No. A.128/466

The G.O.C. 38th Division

    Since the Division under your Command was for over six months in the XI Corps, I hope you will permit me to congratulate you and all ranks in your Division on your splendid achievments in the recent Battle of YPRES.

    I hear that the Division advanced over two miles, held all the ground they had gained, and beat off two hostile counter-attacks. It must have been a great satisfaction to you all to have been engaged against, and to have smashed up the celebrated German Cockchafers.

    I wish you the best of good fortune and continued victory.

9th August 1917.
                          (sd) R.HAKING, Lieut. Gen.
                              Commanding XI Corps.

(2)

Lieut. Gen. Sir R.C.B.HAKING, K.C.B.
    Commanding XI Corps

    On behalf of all ranks of the 38th (Welsh) Division I beg to thank you for your very kind congratulations on the part they played in the recent operations.

    Anticipating your permission I have communicated the contents of your letter to them, and I am quite sure they appreciate very highly the good wishes, as well as the praise that their late Corps Commander bestows on them.

                            (sd) C.G.BLACKADER,
                                Major General,
12/8/1917.
                      Commanding 38th (Welsh) Divn.

Sent to all Units

CONFIDENTIAL.

Fifth Army No. G.A. 837/1
G.H.Q. No. O.A. 70.
XIV Corps No. G.154/4
38th Division No. G.S.7049

Fifth Army

Captured documents detailing the results of the investigation of British prisoners disclose the fact that in many cases individuals have been given information prior to operations which it is unnecessary and very dangerous for them to know.

Although it is essential for everyone taking part in an attack to know everything necessary to enable him to carry out his task, and to co-operate with the action of his neighbours, it is equally essential to ensure that no one knows more of the general plan and objectives of the operation than is absolutely necessary.

It is impossible to lay down definite rules as to the amount of information which should be imparted to the various individuals, units, and formations, in an Army, but the Field-Marshall Commanding-in-Chief looks to Army Commanders to impress on the Commanders and Staffs of all formations the necessity, whenever an order or instruction in connection with forthcoming operations is written or circulated, to limit the information concerning the plan to what is absolutely necessary for the recipient to know for the efficient execution of his duties.

Subordinates should only be made acquainted with such necessary information at the latest possible moment with due regard to the efficient performance of their duties, thus avoiding the dangers inherent to the premature knowledge of secret information.

Adv. G.H.Q.
20th August 1917.

(sd) L.E.KIGGELL, Lieut.-Genl.
C.G.S.

(2)

113th Brigade   19th Welsh Regt.
114th Brigade   C.R.E.
115th Brigade   176th M.G.Coy.

Forwarded for your information.

In this connection please see the attached copy of G.H.Q. letter No. O.B./2015 of 5th April 1917.

The attention of all ranks should be drawn to "Extracts from General Routine Orders" page 70, para. 11. Arrangements must be made for its communication to all reinforcements on arrival

This paragraph should be read to the men periodically.

Sufficient copies are enclosed for issue down to Coys.

Lieut. Colonel,
General Staff, 38th (Welsh) Division.

24/8/1917.

SECRET

Copy No. 11

38TH (WELSH) DIVISION ORDER NO. 109.

1. Gas will be discharged from Gas Projectors on the Divisional Front on the first favourable night on or after the night 20th/21st July.
   All preparations for the discharge will be completed by dawn on 20th July.

2. A simultaneous discharge on all fronts will be attempted, but the discharge of gas on targets for which the wind is favourable will not be stopped because of unfavourable wind conditions on other targets.

3. Captain H.MAY (No. 2 Special Company R.E.) is detailed to control operations on the Corps front.
   O.C. Special Companies R.E. and Captain MAY are authorised to frank messages "Operations, Priority" during these operations.

4. About 3.p.m., formations and units concerned will be warned, whether a discharge is likely to take place or not that night. The message "NIGHTJARS will probably operate" = "Gas will probably be discharged to-night". This will be confirmed or modified after 7.p.m.

5. The time of discharge will be 2.a.m.
   Should a sudden change in the wind make the conditions unfavourable at this hour, the discharge will be cancelled for the night, and should the wind be favourable, it will take place at the same hour on the following night.

6. The decision as to whether conditions are favourable for discharge at the appointed time on any part of the front rests finally with the Company or Section Commander of the Special Company R.E. at the emplacements, who will be kept informed of the weather conditions on neighbouring fronts.

7. The distribution of projectors and targets on the Division front will be as follows :-

	Installed at	Target.
350 projectors	C.7.c.70.05.	Telegraph House, CANCER TRENCH, PILCKEM MILL.
320 projectors	C.13.b.0.0.	House 19 and CACTUS RESERVE from C.7.b.5.4. to C.8.a.3.2.

8. "WIND DANGEROUS" will be ordered for all troops East of the YPRES - BOESINGHE Railway from midnight 19th/20th July and will be maintained until the conclusion of the discharge which will be notified to all concerned.

   ACKNOWLEDGE.

   Lieut. Colonel,
   General Staff, 38th (Welsh) Division.

   Issued to Signals at :- 6.30 p.m.

   Copies to :- (See overleaf)

D.O. 109.   (2)

Copies to :-

       G.O.C.   XIV Corps "G"
       G.S.O.1.   XIV Corps "Q"
       G.S.   Guards Divn.
       "Q"   20th Divn.
       Signals   29th Divn.
       38th Div: Arty.   51st Divn.
       38th Heavy Bombt.Group.   "Q" Special Coy. R.E.
       C.R.E.   *Captain MAY.*
       113th Brigade   *(No 2 Special Coy)*
       114th Brigade
       115th Brigade   *173rd Tunnelling Coy R.E.*
       19th Welsh Regt.
       176th M.G.Coy.
       A.D.M.S.
       D.M.G.O.
       A.P.M.
       Div:Gas Officer.

Vol. 25

General Staff.
38th Division.
December 1917.

Army Form W.3091.

Cover for Documents.

Nature of Enclosures.

113th, 114th, 115th Infantry Bdes

~~Orders~~

Notes, or Letters written.

Army Form C. 2118.

WAR DIARY

INTELLIGENCE SUMMARY

GENERAL STAFF
38TH (WELSH) DIVISION.
VOLUME XXIV.

Instructions regarding War Diaries and Intelligence Summaries are contained in F.S. Regs., Part II and the Staff Manual respectively. Title pages will be prepared in manuscript.

ORIGINAL

Place	Date	Hour	Summary of Events and Information	Remarks and references to Appendices
CROIX DU BAC.	DECEMBER 1917.			
	1st.		Silent raid attempted on our post at N.10.b.05.20. but was instantly driven off by the garrison of the post. 3 prisoners of 1st Battn. 79 Reserve 85th Landwehr I.R. 38th Landwehr Division left with us. Our casualties nil.	
	2nd.		A patrol encounter at 9.45.p.m. resulted in our capturing 1 unwounded and 1 fatally wounded prisoner. Both belonged to 78th Landwehr I.R. Conference at Corps H.Q.	
	3rd.		Our artillery active on destructive shoots and T.M's on wire cutting. One of our patrols entered enemy trench about I.11.a.60.55. and found it to be unoccupied.	
	4th.		E.A. dropped 8 bombs on I.20.c. at 3.p.m. MAJOR FOLLET G.S.O.2. left Division to take up an appointment as G.S.O.2. X Corps. O.O. 152 issued regarding relief of 114th Infantry Brigade.	
	5th.		Hostile artillery activity above normal. FLEURBAIX shelled during the day and subjected to a heavy Gas shell bombardment from 6.50.p.m. to 8.10.p.m. A number of parachute balloons were liberated from enemy lines which dropped propaganda newspapers.	
	6th.		A patrol encounter resulted in our capturing 1 wounded and 1 unwounded prisoner of the 10th Coy. 3rd Battalion 14th I.R. 4th Division thus establishing the relief of the 2nd Guard Reserve Divn. Conference of Brigadiers at Divisional H.Q.	
	7th.		1st Battery 5th Group Portuguese Artillery arrived in Divisional area.	
	8th.		CAPTAIN TOWER, M.C., joins the Division as G.S.O.2. vice MAJOR FOLLETT D.S.O.	
	9th.		Enemy patrol encountered in NO MANS LAND and dispersed by rifle fire.	
	10th.		Under cover of a T.M. Bombardment enemy entered our line at I.26.a.95.52 between 2 posts. No encounter occured and the only identification we obtained was some grenades. Our casualties were one slightly wounded.	
	11th.		FLEURBAIX SECTION handed over to the 2nd Portuguese Division ay 6.a.m. G.O.C. 2nd Australian Division visits Divisional Commander.	
	12th.		An enemy patrol of 1 N.C.O. and 2 O.R. endeavoured to enter our lines but was driven off leaving the N.C.O. (unwounded) in our hands. Identification - 8th Coy.2nd Bn 49.I.R. 4th Divn.	
	13th.		Bad visibility resulted in little artillery activity.	
	14th.		Bad visibility resulted in little artillery activity. One unwounded prisoner belonging to 8th Coy 2nd Bn 14 I.R. 4th Divn. was captured in an attempted raid. This raid was carried out at 5.30.a.m. by a party consisting of 1 officer and 20 O.R. and They attempted a silent raid on our lines in the ARMENTIERES SECTION but were driven off by Artillery, rifle and M.G.fire. We suffered no casualties.	
	15th.		1 enemy aeroplane brought down by us. Enemy attempted raid on post held by Portuguese and British troops but was repulsed. 2 Press representatives join the Division to obtain information as	

Army Form C. 2118.

WAR DIARY
or
INTELLIGENCE SUMMARY.
(Erase heading not required.)

Page 2.

Place	Date	Hour	Summary of Events and Information	Remarks and references to Appendices
CROIX DU BAC.	Dec.1917. 15th (contd). 16th.		to History of the Welsh Troops. One of our gun positions heavily shelled. Our gun busy with a destructive shoot in conjunction with the Heavies. Conference at Corps H.Q., G.O.C. and G.S.O.1. attending.	
	17th.		Enemy plane brought down by one of our planes. G.O.C. 1st Anzac Corps visits Divisional H.Q. and Divisional Commander. Warning Order GSS.10/25 issued re 114th Infantry Brigade to Relieve Left Brigade 2nd Portuguese Division. O.O.153 issued. 114th Infantry Brigade will relieve Left Brigade 2nd Portuguese Division.	app 2 app 3
	18th.		One of our battery positions heavily shelled. O.O.154 issued re 9th Aust.Inf.Brigade will relieve 115th Infantry Brigade.	app 4
	19th. 20th.		ARMENTIERES shelled with 300 rounds. Owing to the fog a party of 5 Australians wandered into NO MANS LAND and only one returned having encountered a strong hostile patrol. We sent out a search party and again an enemy patrol was encountered and dispersed. As a result of this encounter we secured one wounded prisoner and one dead German both of the 1st Battalion 14thIR. In addition to the 2 missing men one Australian Officer was killed in the trenches. Portuguese in the FLEURBAIX SECTIOn relieved by 114th Infantry Brigade. Command of SECTION passing to G.O.C., 114th Inf.Bde. at 6.a.m. 115th Infantry Brigade in the ARMENTIERES SECTION relieved by the 9th Australian Infantry Brigade.	app 5
	21st.		BRIGADIER-GENERAL H.E. ap RHYS PRYCE, C.M.G., D.S.O., proceeds on leave to ENGLAND on one months leave. LIEUT-COLONEL COCKBURN 17th R. W. F., assuming command of the Brigade during his absence. O.O.155 issued regarding relief of the Divisional Artillery by 3rd Australian Divisional Artillery in the ARMENTIERES SECTION.	
	22nd.		Hostile artillery more active. 2 enemy planes forced to descend by our planes. One seen to crash at I.31.d.98.10.	
	23rd.		BRIGADIER-GENERAL HARMAN 114th Infantry Brigade returns from leave. G.S.O.1. 12th Division visits Divisional headquarters. 4 Junior U.S. Officers attached to Division for 3 days.	
	24th.		Our artillery in co-operation with the Heavies fired bursts at 5.p.m. and 9.p.m. on enemy blockhouses. 3 of the enemy seen near our wire and found German rifle but no sign of any Germans. Patrol promptly went out and found German rifle but no sign of any Germans. Relief of Divisional Artillery complete in the ARMENTIERES SECTION.	
	25th.		Our artillery in co-operation with the Heavies fired on enemy blockhouses in N.16.a. and c. A very quiet day.	
	26th.		Presents from G.O.C. to children of CROIX DU BAC. MAJOR GENERAL ALKEN, U.S.A. with chief /of Staff	

Army Form C. 2118.

WAR DIARY
or
INTELLIGENCE SUMMARY.

Page 3.

(Erase heading not required.)

Place	Date	Hour	Summary of Events and Information	Remarks and references to Appendices
CROIX DU BAC.	DEC.1917.			
	26th. (contd.)		and A.D.C. attached to Divisional Headquarters for 12 days.	
	27th.		2 explosions caused by our artillery in CHATEAU RICHE (N.11.d.) Enemy artillery very quiet.	
	28th.		During the morning our artillery carried out successful shoot with aeroplane observation on N.24.b. and N.14.b. Hostile aircraft active, on one occasion fired machine gun on road near GRIS POT. CAPTAIN HARINGTON, D.S.O., G.S.O.3., returned from leave.	
	29th.		Low visibility prevented observation beyond the enemy front line. Our artillery active with destructive shoots and harassing fire at night.	
	30th.		Our artillery carried out a destructive shoot on INCOMPLETE SUPPORT, DRIVE and INDEX TRENCH. A burst of 7 rounds gun fire from Group guns and Hows. was made on OIL TRENCH and dugouts at midnight.	

January 1918.

[signature]

Captain,
General Staff 38th (Welsh) Division.

Vol. 26.

General Staff.
38th Division.

January 1918

Army Form W.3091.

Cover for Documents.

Nature of Enclosures.

~~38th Div. Orders,~~

~~Instructions etc~~

Notes, or Letters written.

ORIGINAL.

Army Form C. 2118.

WAR DIARY of GENERAL STAFF
38TH (WELSH) DIVISION.

INTELLIGENCE SUMMARY.

VOLUME XXV.

Instructions regarding War Diaries and Intelligence Summaries are contained in F. S. Regs., Part II and the Staff Manual respectively. Title pages will be prepared in manuscript.

Place	Date	Hour	Summary of Events and Information	Remarks and references to Appendices
CROIX DU BAC.	JANUARY.1918.			
	1st.		Our artillery was active in shoots on LA MARLAQUE FARM (N.17.b.) NATTY TRENCH (N.15.) NEGRO TRENCH (N.23.b.) OIL TRENCH (O.2.c.) INDEX SUPPORT (O.1.a.) GRAND MAISNIL FARM (I.33.d.) and LA VALLEE I.34.d. Our 6" trench mortars carried out a successful shoot on the wire and parapet of INDEX TRENCH (O.1.a. and I.31.c.) Hostile 77.m.m. guns were more active and fired on our lines in N.10.c., N.5., I.31.b., H.36. and I.25.c. and d. Hostile aircraft were fairly active during the morning.	App.1.
	2nd.		O.O.156 issued – 115th Infantry Brigade will vacate the ESTAIRES AREA on Jany 6th. CAPTAIN CHARLES assumed temporary duties of Brigade Major 114th Infantry Brigade vice CAPTAIN BUCKNALL to ENGLAND on Staff Course. Our artillery active with harassing fire, and enemy artillery activity mainly confined to retaliation.	App.2.
	3rd.		With the exception of one heavy shoot on LA CROMBALOT enemy guns were fairly quiet. Our artillery mainly active on hostile M.G's and T.M's. Corps Commander visits G.O.C.	
	4th.		Conference at Corps Headquarters, G.O.C. G.S.O.1. and C.R.E. attending. Hostile guns very quiet and our guns active on hostile T.M's movement and dugouts. One of our patrols entered enemy lines at N.10.c. but found same unoccupied.	
	5th.		Hostile artillery almost completely silent; our guns and T.M's active in retaliation for hostile T.M. shelling. At 7.45.p.m. we assisted the Division on our right in replying to a heavy enemy bombardment on their left Battalion front. One hostile patrol encountered and dispersed by rifle fire from our patrol.	
	6th.		Artillery and Trench Mortars on both sides quiet. Our patrols active otherwise no Infantry activity on either side. ~~American General and Staff leave~~ General ALLAN G.S.O. *Aust. A.S. Army*	
	7th.		Hostile artillery and trench mortars again quiet. Our guns engaged enemy Trench Mortars and gave covering fire for a wire cutting shoot by T.M's. Enemy patrols heard, but none encountered.	
	8th.		Enemy artillery again quiet and T.M's only normally active. Our guns active in retaliation for enemy T.M's, and our T.M's continued wire cutting. An enemy patrol approached one of our posts but quickly withdrew on being fired upon.	
	9th.		O.O.157 issued – Relief of Division by 12th Division.	

Army Form C. 2118.

WAR DIARY
INTELLIGENCE SUMMARY.

Page 2.

Place	Date	Hour	Summary of Events and Information	Remarks and references to Appendices
CROIX DUBAC.	JANUARY 1918.			
	9th.		Little artillery activity on either side. Our T.M's engaged in wire cutting; hostile T.M's quiet. Our patrols active but no enemy Infantry activity reported.	
	10th.		Hostile artillery rather more active; our guns active on special targets and in response to S.O.S. call. At 3.30.a.m. under cover of a T.M. and artillery bombardment, a party of about 30 Germans approached our line, and 20 succeeded in entering the trench at I.31.b.6.2., but were quickly ejected by the garrison. We suffered no casualties; no identifications obtained.	
	11th.		Our artillery engaged hostile T.M's and our T.M's were active with retaliatory fire. Hostile artillery quiet but trench mortars fairly active. No hostile infantry activity reported. Enemy attempted to raid PAUL POST I.31.b.6.2., but was driven off by M.G. and rifle fire.	App 3
	12th.		Our artillery carried out several aeroplane shoots and engaged enemy working parties.	App 4
	13th.		Hostile artillery generally quiet. O.O.158 issued - Move of 114th Infantry Brigade to MERVILLE AREA, for Training. O.O.159 issued - Move of 2 Batteries 38th Div.Artillery to Field Firing Area at WESTREHEM. 114th and 115th Infantry Brigades move to ESTAIRES NORTH and ESTAIRES SOUTH AREA respectively. 114th Infantry Brigade relieved in the line by 36th Infantry Brigade 12th Division. 113th Infantry relieved by 37th Infantry Brigade. 113th Brigade become Divisional Reserve.	
	14th.		Hostile artillery generally quiet. Divisional Headquarters close at CROIX DU BAC and open at MERVILLE, being relieved by 12th Division. 38th Div.Artillery come under orders of 12th Division.	
MERVILLE.	15th.		113th Infantry Brigade move to MERVILLE NORTH AREA.	
	16th.		G.S.O.1. and G.S.O.2. visit Brigades at Training. Ground very wet, only allowing Musketry in billets.	
	17th.		All Brigades training and building ranges, etc. Divisional Artillery out of the line. Brigades training, - Musketry and Platoon Drill.	
	18th.		Corps Commander visits Divisional Commander. 114th Infantry Brigade move to GUARBECQUE. 113th and 115th Infantry Brigades are Training and working on ranges and bayonet courses.	
	19th.			
	20th.		Corps Commander inspected 114th Infantry Brigade on the march, to ST HILAIRE AREA. 113th and 115th Infantry Brigades training.	
	21st.		G.S.O.1. visited 113th Infantry Brigade at training. G.S.O.2. visited went to ENGUINEGATTE to see 114th and 115th Machine Gun Companies. G.S.O.3. visited Sniping Coy.	

Army Form C. 2118.

WAR DIARY
INTELLIGENCE SUMMARY.
(Erase heading not required)

Page 3.

Instructions regarding War Diaries and Intelligence Summaries are contained in F. S. Regs., Part II. and the Staff Manual respectively. Title pages will be prepared in manuscript.

Place	Date	Hour	Summary of Events and Information	Remarks and references to Appendices
MERVILLE.	JANUARY. 1918.			
	22nd.		G.S.O.1. went round the Battalions in the ST HILAIRE AREA with GENERAL HARMAN.	
	23rd.		Conference of Brigadiers at Divisional Headquarters at 5.p.m. All Brigades at Training; Musketry drill and Physical Training in the mornings and recreational training during the afternoons.	
	24th.		Major General Commanding returns from leave. G.S.O.1. goes on a fortnights leave. All Brigades training.	
	25th.		Corps Commander inspects 114th Infantry Brigade at training. Brigades Training. Hostile aeroplanes active by day and night in Reserve Area.	
	26th.		O.O.160 issued – 113th Brigade will relieve 114th Infantry Brigade in ST HILAIRE AREA. 113th and 176th Machine Gun Companies will relieve 114th and 115th Machine Gun Companies at ENGUINEGATTE.	App 5.
	27th.		Conference at Corps Headquarters attended by G.O.C., G.S.O.2, C.R.A. and C.R.E. Brigades training. GSS.10/83 issued – Move of Divisional Sniping Company to ST HILAIRE AREA, on 29th and 30th insts.	App 6.
	28th.		B.G,G.S., XV Corps visited the Major General. O.O#161 issued – Move of one Battalion 114th Infantry Brigade from ST HILAIRE AREA to 57th Division area, on 29th Jan; to move on LYS Line	App 7.
	29th.		G.O.C. inspects 114th Infantry Brigade at training in ST HILAIRE AREA. Practice Barrage scheme carried out by Divisional Artillery at Artillery range WESTREHEM. GSS.10/53/1 issued – 129th and 131st Field Ambulances will remain at their present sites, and will not move with their respective Brigade Groups. 13th Welsh Regt moved by lorry to 57th Division area (PONT NIEPPE) for work on the LYS LINE. Divisional Sniping Company stage at GUARBECQUE.	App. 8.
	30th.		114th and 115th Machine Gun Companies move to GUARBECQUE. Divisional Sniping Company move to AUCHY AU BOIS. G.O.C. inspects Battalions of 113th Infantry Brigade. G.S.O.3. visited 114th Infantry Brigade.	
	31st.		G.S.O.2. and G.S.O.3. visited 115th Infantry Brigade and 13th Welsh Regt. For orders regarding the reorganisation of Number of Infantry Battalions in Infantry Brigades See Appendix 9.	

January 9th 1918.

M Bring [signature]
Captain,
General Staff 38th (Welsh) Division.

Vol. 27.

General Staff.
38th Division.

February 1918.

Army Form W.3091.

Cover for Documents.

Nature of Enclosures.

~~38 T/M Arty Orders~~

Notes, or Letters written.

WAR DIARY or INTELLIGENCE SUMMARY

GENERAL STAFF 38TH (WELSH) DIVISION. Army Form C. 2118.

VOLUME XXVI

(Erase heading not required)

Place	Date	Hour	Summary of Events and Information	Remarks and references to Appendices
MERVILLE.	FEBRUARY.1918.			
	1st.		113th Brigade move to GUARBECQUE. 114th Brigade move to LES LAURIERS. G.O.C. inspects Brigades on the march. B.G., G.S., XV Corps visited Divisional Headquarters. Orders received for 2 Companies 114th Infantry Brigade to move to PONT DE NIEPPE for work on the LYS LINE.	
	2nd.		115th Infantry Brigade hold a Horse Show. G.S.O.,1., Training, First Army, visited Divisional Headquarters. 113th Infantry Brigade move to ST HILAIRE AREA. Hostile aeroplanes very active after dark.	
	3rd.		2 Companies 14th Welsh Regt go to PONT DE NIEPPE for work under 57th Division. Orders received that 2nd R.W.F. will join Division on the 6th instant. Hostile aeroplanes dropped a bomb close to 14th Welsh Regt H.Q. No damage.	
	4th.		G.O.C. visits 113th Infantry Brigade in the ST HILAIRE AREA.	
	5th.		GSS.12/10. issued regarding moves to take place on 5th and 6th instant. 14th Welsh Regt Divisional Machine Gun Officer returns from CAMIERS with MAJOR LYTTLETON, who is to command the Divisional Machine Gun Battalion. G.S.O.2. 57th Division visits Divisional Headquarters to discuss taking over their line. 2nd R.W.F. arrive in ESTAIRES, and come under orders of the G.O.C. 115th Infantry Brigade.	
	6th.		Divisional Signal Company hold sports. G.S.O.1. returns from leave. G.O.C. 114th Infantry Very wet. Training in billets.	
	7th.		Brigade reconnoitres 57th Division trenches.	
	8th.		G.OLC's 114th and 115th Infantry Brigades visited Divisional Headquarters. O.O.162 issued regarding relief of 57th Division by the 38th Division. MAJOR TALLENTS, D.S.O., Lancashire Fusiliers arrives to take up duty as G.S.O.2. exchanging with CAPTAIN B.C.B.TOWER, M.C., Royal Fusiliers to 34th Division	
	9th.		Brigades at training. Corps Commander inspected 2nd R.W.F. Orders received from Corps that disbanded Battalions will work under Divisions, after taking over the line. Brigades training. GENERAL HARMAN, 114th Infantry Brigade, proceeds to CAMIERS for Machine Gun Course.	
	10th.		G.O.C. attended the march past of the 2nd Battalion Royal Welsh Fusiliers after Church Parade at MERVILLE.	
	11th.		G.S.O.2. visited 57th Division. Staff Exercise at Corps H.Q. in connection with action of Reserve Division in case of hostile attack. CAPTAIN B.C.B.TOWER,M.C.,Royal Fusiliers, left Division to take up duty as G.S.O.2. 34th. Division.	

Army Form C. 2118.

WAR DIARY
or
INTELLIGENCE SUMMARY.

Page 2.

(Erase heading not required.)

Instructions regarding War Diaries and Intelligence Summaries are contained in F. S. Regs., Part II, and the Staff Manual respectively. Title pages will be prepared in manuscript.

Place	Date	Hour	Summary of Events and Information	Remarks and references to Appendices
MERVILLE.	FEBRUARY. 1918.			
	12th.		Conference at Corps Headquarters to discuss scheme of previous day. G.O.C. and G.S.O.1. 57th Division, visited Divisional Headquarters.	
	13th.		Rugby Football match Welsh Division versus New Zealand Division. G.S.O.1. and G.S.O.2. went round the line in the ARMENTIERES SECTOR. 113th Infantry Brigade move from ST HILAIRE AREA to GUARBECQUE. 115th Infantry Brigade move from ESTAIRES to WEZ MACQUART SECTION relieving the 170th Infantry Brigade.	
	14th.		G.S.O.2. and Divisional Machine Gun Officer went round the line in the ARMENTIERES SECTION. G.S.O.3. visited 57th Division to takeover Maps. 114th Infantry Brigade move to HOUPLINES SECTION relieving 171st Infantry Brigade. 113th Infantry Brigade move to ESTAIRES AREA.	
	15th.		G.S.O.1. goes round the line with O.C., Machine Gun Battalion. 113th Infantry Brigade take over the L'EPINETTE SECTION relieving 172nd Infantry Brigade.	
STEENWERCK.	16th.		Divisional Headquarters take over from 57th Division, moving to STEENWERCK. 5 M.P's visit ARMENTIERES.	
	17th.		G.S.O.1. went round Machine Gun positions in HOUPLINES SECTION with O.C., 38th Battalion Machine Gun Corps. CHAPELLE D'ARMENTIERES heavily shelled.	
	18th.		G.S.O.3. went round the SWITCH LINES with Brigade Major 115th Infantry Brigade. Conference of Brigadiers at Divisional Headquarters. HOUPLINES and CHAPELLE D'ARMENTIERES heavily shelled.	
	19th.		G.O.C. went round Battle Zone with O.C., Machine Gun Battalion.	
	20th.		G.S.O.1. and G.S.O.2. and C.R.E. went round the HOUPLINES SECTION.	
	21st.		G.S.O.3. went round the Right Brigade front. Slight Trench Mortar activity in the WEZ MACQUART SECTION, otherwise a very quiet day.	
	22nd.		G.O.C. and G.S.O.1. went up the line. Great aerial activity on both sides: one enemy machine brought down. A few rounds of L.H.V. over ERQUINGHEM.	
	23rd.		Windy with poor visibility and a slight drizzle. A quiet day. G.O.C. and G.S.O.1. attended Corps Conference.	
	24th.		G.S.O.1. and G.S.O.2. went round the Right Section. Hostile artillery put down a barrage on our front and support lines in the WEZ MACQUART SECTION. Enemy put down a heavy barrage at 4.p.m. on I.10. and I.15. Corps Commander visited Divisional Headquarters and HOUPLINES SECTION.	
	25th.	4.am.	Following a heavy Artillery and Trench Mortar Barrage the enemy raided our trenches in I.5.c	

Army Form C. 2118.

WAR DIARY
of
INTELLIGENCE SUMMARY.
(Erase heading not required.)

Page 3.

Instructions regarding War Diaries and Intelligence Summaries are contained in F. S. Regs., Part II. and the Staff Manual respectively. Title pages will be prepared in manuscript.

Place	Date	Hour	Summary of Events and Information	Remarks and references to Appendices
STEENWERCK.	FEBRUARY.1918.			
	25th. (continued).		taking 2 of our men, and leaving 1 dead and 1 wounded prisoner belonging to 1st Battn. 138.I.R. 42 Division in our hands.	
	26th.		Divisional artillery Conference at Divisional Headquarters at 5.p.m. Hostile Artillery fired 150 15.c.m. shells into HOUPLINES.	
	27th.		Wire received from Corps that deserter reports attack by Germans will start before dawn at GHELUVELT on 28th. Hostile Artillery more active on HOUPLINES.	
	28th.		G.S.O.2. and G.S.O.2., Corps went round the Centre and Left Sections. Divisional Cross Country Run Competition (Winners C Battery 122nd Brigade R.F.A.) G.O.C. and G.S.O.1. inspected practice for 17th R. W. F. raid.	

/3/18.

Captain,
General Staff 38th (Welsh) Division.

GLOSSARY.

Abbaye, Abbᵉ	Abbey.
Abreuvoir, Abʳ	Watering-place.
Abri de douaniers	Customs-shelter.
Aciérie	Steel works.
Aiguilles	Points (Ry.)
Allée	Alley, Narrow road.
Ancien -ne, Ancⁿ	Old.
Aqueduc	Aqueduct.
Arbre	Tree.
" éventail	" fan-shaped.
" déchiré	" bare.
" fourchu	" forked.
" isolé	" isolated.
" penché	" leaning.
Arbrisseau	Small tree.
Arc	Arch.
Ardoisière, Ardʳᵉ	Slate quarry.
Arrêt	Halt.
Asile	Asylum.
" des aliénés	Lunatic asylum.
" de charité	
" des pauvres	Asylum.
" de refuge	
Auberge, Aubᵍᵉ	Inn.
Aune	Alder-tree.
Bac	Ferry.
" à traille	
Bains	Baths.
Place aux bains	Bathing place.
Balise	Boom, Beacon.
Banc de sable	Sand-bank.
" vase	Mud-bank.
Baraque	Hut.
Barrage	Dam.
Barrière	Gate, Bill.
(Machine à) Bascule	Weigh-bridge.
Bassin	Dock, Pond.
" d'échouage	Tidal dock.
Bassin de radoub	Dry dock.
Bateau phare	Light-ship.
Blanchisserie	Laundry.
B.M. (borne milliaire)	Mile stone.
Bⁿ (borne kilométrique)	
Boulangerie	
Fabᵗ de boulons	Bolt Factory.
Bouée	Buoy.
Brasserie, Brasᵉ	Brewery.
Briqueterie, Briqʳ	Brickfield.
Brise-lames	Breakwater.
Bureau de poste	Post office.
" de douanes	Custom house.
Butte	Butt, Mound.
Cabane	Hut.
Cabaret, Calᵗ	Inn.
Câble sous-marin	Submarine cable.
Calvaire, Calʳᵉ	Calvary.
Canal de dessèchement	Drainage canal.
Canal d'irrigation	Irrigation canal.
Fabᵗ de caoutchouc	Rubber factory.
Carrière, Carʳᵉ	Quarry.
" de gravier	Gravel-pit.
Caserne	Barracks.
Champ de courses	Race-course.
" manœuvres	Drill-ground.
" tir	Rifle range.
Chantier	Building yard.
Chantier de construction	Ship yard. Dock yard.
Chapelle, Chˡˡᵉ	Slip-way. Chapel.
Charbonnage	Colliery.
Château d'eau	Water tower.
Chaussée	Causeway.
Chemin de fer	Highway. Railway.
Cheminée, Chⁿᵉᵉ	Chimney.
Chêne	Oak tree.
Cimetière, Cimʳᵉ	Cemetery.
Clocher	Belfry.
Clouterie	Nail factory.
Colombier	Dove-cot.

Coron	Workmen's dwellings.
Cour des marchandises	Goods yard.
Couvent	Convent
Crassier	Slag heap.
Croix	Cross.
Darse	Inner dock.
Démoli -e	Destroyed.
Détruit -e, Détʳ	
Déversoir	Weir.
Digue	Dyke, causeway.
Distillerie, Distⁱᵉ	Distillery.
Douane	Custom-house.
Bureau de douane	
Entrepôt de douane	Custom warehouse
Dynamitières, Dynᵐ	Dynamite magazine.
Dynamiterie	Dynamite factory.
Écluse	Sluice, Lock.
Écluselle, Eclˡˡᵉ	Shice.
École	School.
Écurie	Stable.
Église	Church.
Émaillerie	Enamel works.
Embarcadère, Embʳᵉ	Landing-place.
Estaminet, Estamᵗ	Inn.
Étang	Pond.
Fabrique, Fabᵗ	Factory.
Fabᵗ de produits chimiques	Chemical works.
Fabᵗ de faïences	Pottery.
Faïencerie	
Ferme, Fᵉ	Farm.
Filature, Filᵉ	Spinning mill.
Fonderie, Fondⁱᵉ	Foundry.
Fontaine, Fontⁿᵉ	Spring, fountain.
Forêt	Forest
Forme de radoub	Dry dock.
Forge	Smithy.
Fosse	Mine, Pit.
Fossé	Moat, Ditch.
Four	Kiln.
" à chaux	Lime kiln

Four à coke	Coke oven.
Ganterie	Glove Factory.
Gare	Station.
Garenne	Warren.
Garnison	Garrison.
Gazomètre	Gasometer.
Glacerie	
Fabᵗ de glaces	Mirror Factory.
Glacière	Ice factory.
Grue	Crane.
Gué	Ford.
Guérite	Sentry-box, Turret.
" à signaux	Signal-box (Ry.)
Halte	Halt.
Hangar	Shed, Hangar.
Hôpital	Hospital.
Hôtel-de-Ville	Town hall.
Houillère	Colliery.
Huilerie	Oil factory.
Imprimerie, Impʳⁱᵉ	Printing works.
Jetée	Pier.
Laminerie	Rolling mills.
Ligne de haute marée	High water mark.
" de basse marée	Low
Maison Forestière, Mⁿ Fʳᵉ	Forester's house.
Malterie	Malt-house.
Marbrerie	Marble works.
Marais	Marsh.
Marais salant	Saltern. Salt marsh.
Marché	Market.
Mare	Pool.
Meule	Rick.
Minière	Mine.
Monastère	Monastery.
Moulin, Mⁿ	Mill.
" à vapeur	Steam mill.
Mur	Wall.

Nacelle	
Orme	
Orphelinat	
Ouvrière	
Ouvrage	
Ouvrages	
Papeterie	
Parc	
" aéronautique	
" à charbon	
" à pétrole	
Passage à niveau	
Passerelle	
Pépinière	
Peuplier	
Phare	
Pilier, Pilᵉ	
Plaine d'aviation	
Pompe	
Poncea	
Pont	
" levis	
Poste	
Station	
Poteau Pᵘ	
Poterie	
Poudrière, Pʳᵉ	
Magasin à poudre	
Prise d'eau	
Puits	
" artésien	
" d'aérage	
" ventilateur	
" de sondage	
Quai	
" aux bestiaux	
" aux marchandises	
" des voyageurs	
Raccordement	
Raffinerie	

TRENCH MAP.

St. JULIEN.
28 N.W. 2.
EDITION 5. A

Scale 1:10,000

	2		N.E.	4	2		N.E.	4	2		N.E. 4
	1	21	3		1	29	3		1	37	3
	2	N.W.	4	2		N.E.	4	2		N.E.	4
	1	20	3		1	28	3		1	36	3
	2	S.W.	4	2		S.E.	4	2		S.E.	4
	1	19	3		1	27	3		1	35	3

INDEX TO ADJOINING SHEETS. ZONE, CALL, W, X, Y, Z.

- Coke oven
- Glove Factory.
- Station.
- Warren.
- Gasworks.
- Gasometer.
- Mirror Factory.
- Ice factory.
- Oven.
- Fort.
- Sentry-box, Turret.
- Signal-box (Ry.)
- Halt.
- Shed, Hangar.
- Hospital.
- Town hall.
- Colliery.
- Oil factory
- Printing works.
- Pier.
- Rolling mills.
- High water mark.
- Low
- Forester's house.
- Malt-house.
- Marble works.
- Marsh.
- Saltern.
- Salt marsh.
- Market.
- Pool.
- Rick.
- Mine.
- Monastery.
- Mill.
- Steam mill.
- Wall.

- Nacelle — Ferry.
- Orme — Elm.
- Orphelinat — Orphanage.
- Oseraies — Osier-beds.
- Ouvrage — Fort.
- Ouvrages hydrauliques — Water works.
- Papeterie — Paper-mill.
- Parc — Park, yard.
- " aérostatique — Aviation ground.
- " à charbon — Coal yard.
- " à pétrole — Petrol store.
- Passage à niveau P.N. — Level-crossing.
- Passerelle, Pass" — Foot-bridge.
- Pepinière — Nursery-garden.
- Peuplier — Poplar tree.
- Phare — Light-house.
- Pilier, Pil" — Post.
- Plaine d'exercice — Drill ground.
- Pompe — Pump.
- Ponceau — Culvert.
- Pont — Bridge.
- " levis — Drawbridge.
- Poste de garde — Coast-guard station.
- cotier
- Poteau I"" — Post.
- Poterie — Pottery.
- Poudrière, Poud" — Powder magazine.
- Magasin à poudre —
- Prise d'eau — Water supply.
- Puits — Pit-head, Shaft, Well.
- " artésien — Artesian well.
- " d'airage —
- " ventilateur — Ventilating shaft.
- " de sondage — Boring.
- Quai — Quay, Platform.
- " aux bestiaux — Cattle platform.
- " aux marchandises — Goods platform.
- Raccordement — Junction.
- Raffinerie — Refinery.
- " de sucre — Sugar refinery

- Remblai — Embankment.
- Remises (des Machines) — Engine-shed.
- Réservoir, Rés" — Reservoir.
- Route cavalière — Bridle road.
- Rubanerie — Ribbon Factory.
- Ruine
- Ruines
- En ruine — Ruin.
- Ruiné-e
- Sablière — Sand-pit.
- Sablonnière, Sablon"
- Sapin — Fir tree.
- Saule — Willow tree.
- Saunerie — Salt-works.
- Scierie, Sci" — Saw-mill.
- Sondage — Boring.
- Source — Spring.
- Sucrerie, Suc" — Sugar factory
- Tannerie — Tannery.
- Tir à la cible — Rifle range.
- Tissage — Weaving mill.
- Tôlerie — Rolling mill.
- Tombeau — Tomb.
- Tour — Tower.
- Tourbière — Peat-bog, Peat-bed.
- Tourelle — Small tower.
- Tuilerie — Tile works.
- Usine à gaz — Gas works.
- " d'électricité — Electricity works.
- " métallurgique — Metal works.
- " à agglomérés — Briquette factory.
- Verrerie, Verr" — Glass works.
- Viaduc — Viaduct.
- Vivier — Fish Pond.
- Voie de chargement
- " de déchargement
- " d'évitement — Siding.
- " formation
- " manoeuvre

Vol. 28.

General Staff.
38th Division.
March 1918.

Army Form W. 3091.

Cover for Documents.

Natures of Enclosures.

~~C.R.E's Orders etc~~

Notes, or Letters written.

WAR DIARY or INTELLIGENCE SUMMARY.

GENERAL STAFF 38TH (WELSH) DIVISION Army Form C. 2118.

VOLUME XVII.

Place	Date	Hour	Summary of Events and Information	Remarks and references to Appendices
STEENWERCK.	MARCH.1918.			
	1st		Commander in Chief visited Divisional Headquarters. Hostile artillery less active, probably owing to bad visibility.	
	2nd		115th Infantry Brigade raided enemy's trenches in I.16.d. killing 5 and bringing in 1 wounded prisoner of 131 I.R. The raid was not so successful as it should have been owing to zero being put on 10 minutes and this information did not reach all the batteries in time, with the result that there were two barrages. All our raiding party returned, but two men were seriously wounded and 10 men slightly wounded.	
	/3rd		Corps Commander visited Divisional Headquarters. G.O.C. and G.S.O.2. inspected 114th Infantry Brigade raiding party practising over replica trenches. 5 M.P's visited ARMENTIERES SECTION.	
	4th		G.O.C. went round the Battle Zone. G.S.O.3. visited the front line posts in the WEZ MACQUART SECTION. B.G.,G.S. visited Divisional Headquarters. Officer of 113th Infantry Brigade attached to Divisional Headquarters for a fortnight to practise decoding Playfair. Machine Gun Battalion H.Q. open at ARMENTIERES.	
	5th		G.O.C. and C.R.E. went up the line. G.S.O.1. visited 114th Infantry Brigade to discuss scheme of proposed raid.	
	6th		Corps Commander visited Divisional Headquarters. G.O.C. visited Sniping Coy. O.C. "N" Special Coy R.E. visited Divisional H.Q. and 113th Infantry Brigade with a view to letting off gas prior to the 113th Infantry Brigade raid. Hostile artillery active in the HOUPLINES SECTION.	
	7th		Hostile artillery showed a considerable increase in activity during the afternoon and evening. Our artillery was chiefly engaged in retaliation both day and night. During the night hostile F.A. fired short concentrations of gas and H.E. on the area of HOUPLINES. Hostile aircraft was very active over our own and enemy lines. Visibility was bad owing to haze.	
	8th		Hostile F.A. again showed abnormal activity especially in the HOUPLINES SECTION, the areas C.16.d., C.17.c. and C.21. being heavily shelled during the morning. CHAPELLE D'ARMENTIERES and trenches in WEZ MACQUART SECTION received much attention also. Our artillery was engaged in retaliation and in co-operation with the Trench Mortars carried out a successful shoot on the enemy's wire in front of INCANDESCENT TRENCH. Hostile aircraft was active behind the enemy's lines but only 4 crossed our lines.	
	9th		The G.O.C. took up temporary command at Corps H.Q. and GENERAL THOMPSON took over duties as Divisional Commander. Hostile F.A. continued abnormally active against our forward areas especially the HOUPLINES SECTION where our trenches were systematically shelled at a rapid /rate	

WAR DIARY or INTELLIGENCE SUMMARY.

Army Form C. 2118.

Page 2.

Place	Date	Hour	Summary of Events and Information	Remarks and references to Appendices
STEENWERCK.	MARCH 1918.			
	9th. (continued.)		Shelling of the forward area in the WEZ MACQUART SECTION was also above normal. This artillery activity was maintained during the night. Under cover of a very heavy T.M. and artillery bombardment the enemy penetrated our line in the EPINETTE SALIENT and raided 3 of our posts. A few of our men were reported missing. The enemy put up a harassing fire on all the roads in our back areas. Some gas was also expended. Our artillery carried out 6 concentrated group shoots in retaliation and replied vigorously at 4.30.a.m. to their bombardment. Hostile aircraft were active but mostly flying high behind the enemy's lines.	
	10th.		Under cover of a very heavy bombardment the enemy's infantry attempted to raid our line in the WEZ MACQUART and HOUPLINES SECTIONS at about 5.a.m. In the former they were driven off but in the latter a hostile party estimated at 150 succeeded in penetrating our line and attacked two of our posts. The enemy were speedily ejected. Hostile F.A. was less active; mostly harassing fire. RUE ALLEE (I.7.b.) was shelled with about 200 rounds H.E. and gas shells and ARMENTIERES in vicinity of NOTRE DAME CHURCH was shelled for 2½ hours with 10.5.c.m. Hows air bursts.	
	11th.		At 9.30.p.m. we carried out a minor operation against CENTAUR TRENCH. During the day our artillery fired 4 concentrated group shoots in retaliation for hostile shelling. Hostile artillery activity generally showed a marked decrease. F.A. continued scattered harassing fire on our forward system in all 3 sections. Hostile aircraft continued active.	
	12th.		We successfully repulsed an enemy raid on our line in WEZ MACQUART SECTION and captured one unwounded prisoner (I Pioneer Bn. No.26, 41 Division) at 5.15.a.m. During the day our F.A. carried out 5 concentrated group shoots in retaliation. We also carried out wire cutting in co-operation with Trench Mortars. Hostile aircraft were active. CAPTAIN C.G.CONSTABLE arrived and attached to 'G' temporarily.	
	13th.		G.O.C. returned from Corps to the Division. Hostile artillery much less active. Our artillery carried out 3 concentrated group shoots and in co-operation with trench mortars carried out effective wire cutting in front of INCANDESCENT TRENCH and SUPPORT.	
	14th.		Hostile F.A. was again very active during the day, though the number of batteries taking part appeared to be small. HOUPLINES was shelled all day. Our artillery carried out 4 concentrated group shoots in retaliation and in co-operation with Trench Mortars, and carried out wire cutting in I.11.a. and C.29. During the night we carried out harassing fire and counter preparation. Hostile Artillery was quiet during the night. Hostile aircraft were inactive. Visibility low.	
	/15th.			

Army Form C. 2118.

WAR DIARY
or
INTELLIGENCE SUMMARY.
(Erase heading not required)

Page 3.

Place	Date	Hour	Summary of Events and Information	Remarks and references to Appendices
STEENWERCK.	MARCH 1918.			
	15th.		Corps Commander, B.G.G.S. and 12th Divisional Commander visited G.O.C. at 11.a.m. G.S.O.2. left for Machine Gun Course CAMIERS. At 10.7.p.m. under cover of an artillery Trench Mortar and Machine Gun barrage a party, 2 companies strong, raided INCANDESCENT TRENCH and SUPPORT (I.11.a.) with complete success. At least 30 of the enemy are reported to have been killed in the trenches and dugouts. 15 prisoners and 2 machine guns were brought in, and 2 concrete dugouts were blown up. Our casualties were not heavy. At the same time a successful feint raid with dummy figures was carried out on CENTRAL and INANE TRENCHES.	
	16th.		Corps Commander visited G.O.C. at 4.p.m. Officers from G.H.Q. (O) visited G.O.C. at 1.p.m. G.O.C. and G.S.O.1. went back to area in WEZ MACQUART SECTION. Hostile artillery activity was normal and consisted chiefly of harassing fire by 77.m.m. guns on our forward area. During the morning 40 rounds of gas shells were fire d on HOUPLINES and the CEMETERY in C.28.a. During the night a H.V. gun was active from 7.p.m. to 11 p.m. on the ERQUINGHEM - ARMENTIERES ROAD. Our artillery fired on hostile movement, dispersed a working party in C.23.b. and successfully registered the dumps in I.30.b. with aeroplane observation. At 5.10.p.m. a hostile gun opened fire at a rapid rate on C.28.a. The gun was observed firing from a dip in the ground or dug in pit at about C.30.c.7.1. with thick wire and camouflage in front of the position. The heads of 3 men could be seen. No flash could be detected, but the gun made a loud report and a large volume of smoke. On our shelling the men ran - they wore a light blue uniform and German steel helmets. It is thought to have been a Trench gun of 5.3. or 5.7.c.m. Calibre.	
	17th.		G.O.C. went on leave to ENGLAND and BRIGADIER-GENERAL H.E.ap Rhys PRYCE C.M.G.,D.S.O. took over command of the Division. Enemy F.A. carried out their usual harassing fire on the forward system, their activity being a little above normal on the Right Section. 70 rounds 77.m.m. gas shells were fired on I.2.b.60.40.(ARMENTIERES). Aircraft generally was more active. Visibility was good throughout the day.	
	18th.		Very warm and bright. Hostile F.A. was again fairly active. A battery of ours in I.2.8. was shelled with 200 rounds of 10.5.c.m. How. and another position at I.8.a. was shelled with 100 rounds 77.m.m. gun. About 600 rounds were fired on CHAPELLE D'ARMENTIERES. At 1.55.pm 100 rounds of gas shell were fired into HOUPLINES. Our artillery retaliated actively.	
	19th.		Raining hard all day. Visibility very bad. Hostile artillery showed a marked decrease in activity except in the WEZ MACQUART SECTION where about 300 rounds of 77.m.m. gun and Hows were fired on front trenches. From 8.26.p.m.to 9.pm. a 15.c.m.H.V.gun fired 15 rounds on the	

Army Form C. 2118.

WAR DIARY
or
INTELLIGENCE SUMMARY.

(Erase heading not required.)

Page 4.

Place	Date	Hour	Summary of Events and Information	Remarks and references to Appendices
STEENWERCK.	MARCH 1918.			
	19th.		on the vicinity of STEENWERCK. About 10.p.m. 430 4" gas bombs were fired onto I.5.b. and at 11.p.m. gas projectors fired onto RUELLE de LA NOIX (I.17.b.)	
	20th.		BRIGADIER-GENERAL W.A.M. THOMPSON C.B.,C.M.G.,left for ENGLAND for 6 months tour of duty, and his duties will be carried out by LIEUT.-COLONEL W.C.B.RUDKIN C.M.G.,D.S.O., Hostile artillery very quiet on forward trenches. Field Artillery was more active in the afternoons. A 15.c.m. gun shelled STEENWERCK with about 12rounds of shrapnel.	App I
	21st.		At 5.a.m. a general gas bombardment was opened along the whole front. With the exception of slight shelling of C.22. the forward areas were not affected, practically all the shelling being on the Field battery area, where all the batteries were affected except one in I.7.d. Shelling died down by 7.30.a.m. and no gas shells after 9.a.m. Germans commenced their offensive. An enemy party was dispersed and left one prisoner in our hands.	App 2
	22nd.		Corps Commander inspected 16th R.W.F. and complimented them on their raid.	
	23rd.		A patrol of the Sniping Company dispersed a hostile patrol capturing one wounded prisoner of 102 I.R. 32 Division, in C.17.c. 2 attempts were made to raid our posts in I.10.b. and d. at 1.40.a.m. and 4.45.a.m. One of these was driven off and the other succeeded in capturing 3 of our men. An exceptionally quiet day. G.S.O.2. returned from CAMIERS.	App 3
	24th.		O.O.163 issued regarding withdrawal of 147th (Army) Brigade R.F.A. Corps Commander visited Divisional Headquarters. B.G. G.S. called on Divisional Commander. Orders received for 147th (Army) Brigade R.F.A. to leave Division the same evening. A very quiet day.	
	25th.		O.O.164. issued regarding changes in dispositions. B.G. G.S. visited Divisional H.Q. and held a Conference, arranging for the re-adjustment of the Divisional front into 2 Brigade fronts. G.S.O.1. and C.R.A. delivered lectures on Divisional Area. A quiet day.	
	26th.		GSS.5/58 issued regarding relief of 14th (SWANSEA) Battn Welsh Regt in the line on the night 27/28th March 1918. Adjustment of line into 2 Brigade front complete. Hostile Artillery very quiet.	
	27th.		Corps Commander went round the WEZ MACQUART SECTION. Hostile artillery again inactive.	
	28th.		10th S.W.B. carried out a successful raid in C.21.c.capturing 6 prisoners belonging to 369 I.R. 10th ERSATZ Division. Our casualties 6 slightly wounded. About 6.a.m. enemy put down	

Army Form C. 2118.

WAR DIARY
or
INTELLIGENCE SUMMARY.

Page 5.

(Erase heading not required.)

Instructions regarding War Diaries and Intelligence Summaries are contained in F. S. Regs., Part II. and the Staff Manual respectively. Title pages will be prepared in manuscript.

Place	Date	Hour	Summary of Events and Information	Remarks and references to Appendices
STEENWERCK.	1918.			
	28th.		down a heavy barrage on the FLEURBAIX - ARMENTIERES LINE. Warning order for move of the Division on night 29/30th. sent out. O.O. 165 issued. G.O.C. returns from leave.	Ouif X
	29th.		Two minor enterprises were attempted, but both were unsuccessful in obtaining an identification. 113th Infantry Brigade were relieved in Reserve, and move to DOULIEU AREA. O.O. 166 issued cancelling O.O. 165. - Division to leave XV Corps area by rail, entraining on the night March 31st/1st April 1918.	
	30th.		115th Infantry Brigade relieved by 170th Infantry Brigade 57th Division, at 2.a.m., and move to NOUVEAU MONDE. 115th Infantry Brigade move by bus at 2.p.m. to HAVERSKERQUE AREA. 113th Infantry Brigade move by bus at 3.p.m. to STEENBECQUE AREA. 30/31st March 1918 - 114th Infantry Brigade move from the front line to MERVILLE AREA to entrain.) Divisional Headquarters move to MERVILLE. G.O.C. 34th Division takes over command of the Left Sector XV Corps at 10.a.m.	
MERVILLE.	31st.		31st March / 1st April - Division leaves XV Corps area and entrains for V Corps Area.	

Harington

Captain,
General Staff 38th (Welsh) Division.

GENERAL STAFF

38th (Welch) DIVISION

APRIL 1918

Report on Operations 19th to 25th April 1918.
Operation Orders.

WAR DIARY
INTELLIGENCE SUMMARY

GENERAL STAFF 38TH (WELSH) DIVISION.
VOLUME XXVIII.

Army Form C. 2118.

Instructions regarding War Diaries and Intelligence Summaries are contained in F.S. Regs., Part II. and the Staff Manual respectively. Title pages will be prepared in manuscript.

(Erase heading not required.)

Place	Date	Hour	Summary of Events and Information	Remarks and references to Appendices
MERVILLE. TOUTENCOURT.	APRIL 1918. 1st.		Divisional Headquarters close at MERVILLE 3.p.m. and open at TOUTENCOURT same hour. D.O.187 issued - The Division belongs to V Corps and will relieve the 47th and 2nd Divisions.	app 1
	2nd.		113th Infantry Brigade move to FORCEVILLE: 114th Infantry Brigade move to TALMAS: 115th Infantry Brigade move to HEDAUVILLE. Orders received from V Corps that the Division will be in 3rd Army Reserve. Divisional Sniping Company reformed.	
	3rd.		D.O.168 issued cancelling D.O.187:- Moves to take place on 3rd April,1918. 113th Infantry Brigade move to TOUTENCOURT. G.O.C., 115th Infantry Brigade evacuated to C.C.S. COLONEL COCKBURN assumes command of the Brigade. G.O.C. visits 114th Infantry Brigade. Corps Commander visits Divisional Headquarters. One company 38th Battalion,M.G.C. ordered to go into the line.	app 2
	4th.		19th Welsh Regt (GLAMORGAN PIONEERS) and one Field Coy R.E. ordered to move to WARLOY. Orders received at midnight for the Division to be prepared to move at an hours notice.	
	5th.	12.20.a.m.	G.49 issued - From 5.a.m. the Division will be prepared to move at an hours notice. Orders issued for 114th Infantry Brigade to take up position of readiness in HERISSART, and 113th Infantry Brigade between CONTAY and WARLOY. 113th and 114th Sections of Divisional Sniping Coy join their Brigades. One company of the Div.M.G.Battn, joins 113th Infantry Brigade and one company 114th Infantry Brigade. (See G.55.) 2nd Australian Division and 12th Division attacked N.W. of ALBERT. 113th Infantry Brigade moves back to MIRVAUX, and 114th Infantry Brigade to TALMAS. 47th Division and 63rd Division engaged in AVELUY WOOD.	app 3
	6th.		115th Infantry Brigade moves back from HERISSART to HEDAUVILLE to TOUTENCOURT - HERISSART area. 'A' Company 38th Bn.M.G.C. move to their H.Q. at PUCHVILLERS - MILLENCOURT LINE. 115th Infantry Brigade find working parties for the ENGLEBELMER - MILLENCOURT LINE.	
	7th.		G.A.7. issued - Move of 115th Infantry Brigade. Working party (strength 600) found by 115th Infantry Brigade for work on ENGLEBELMER - MILLENCOURT LINE. 113th and 114th Infantry Brigades at training. M.G.Battn, move from PUCHEVILLERS to RUBEMPRE (less 'C' Coy in the line.)	app 4
	8th.		Corps Commander visits Divisional Headquarters.	
	9th.		G.109 issued 113th Infantry Brigade to move to HARPONVILLE on 10th instant, and for 1 Battalion of 115th Infantry Brigade to move to WARLOY on 10th, and 1 company M.G.Battn to VADENCOURT. 331st Coy.A.S.C. and 333rd Coy.A.S.C. move to SEPTONVILLE. Division to relieve 12th Division in the line, night 11/12th.	app 5

WAR DIARY

INTELLIGENCE SUMMARY.

(Erase heading not required.)

Page 2.

Army Form C. 2118

Place	Date	Hour	Summary of Events and Information	Remarks and references to Appendices
TOUTENCOURT.	April 1918. 10th.		115th Infantry Brigade move to HARPONVILLE; 114th Infantry Brigade move to HENENCOURT with one Battalion at WARLOY to relieve 35th Brigade in 12th Division Reserve. D.O.169 issued - The Division (less Artillery) will relieve the 12th Division in the line from E.2.central to W.15.a.3.7.	app 6.
	11th.		The Division proceeds to move into the line, 113th Infantry Brigade in the left Section with 2 front battalions in the line and 1 in reserve. 114th Infantry Brigade on the right with 2 front battalions in the front line and 1 in reserve. 115th Infantry Brigade move to Divisional Reserve in HENENCOURT. Normal activity in front line.	
CONTAY.	12th.		G.152. issued - Command will pass to G.O.C., 38th (Welsh) Division at 8.a.m. 12th instant. Divisional H.Q. moves to CONTAY, G.O.C. taking over command of the line at 8.a.m. Visibility good. We carried out vigorous harassing fire on approaches. B.G.,G.S. Harassing fire on MILLENCOURT, HENENCOURT, BOUZINCOURT and SENLIS MILL. B.G.,G.S. visited Divisional Headquarters.	app 7
	13th.		Visibility very low. Our artillery inactive during the day, but vigorous harassing fire by night: 300 rounds per battery 18-pdr and 200 per battery 4.5" Hows. Hostile artillery exceptionally quiet all day. 3 E.A. over our lines. From Patrol Reports and Airphotos, the enemy line west of the ANCRE appears to consist of a series of isolated posts disposed in depth; some of these posts are organized shell holes.	
	14th.		Enemy harassing fire on BOUZINCOURT, SENLIS, HENENCOURT. Retaliation for our vigorous night, fire was practically nil. No counter battery work by the enemy.	
	15th.		Hostile artillery below normal. HENENCOURT lightly shelled. 'CRASH' on BOUZINCOURT for 10 minutes. Army Commander visits Divisional H.Q.; also Corps Commander.	
	16th.		Conference at Divisional H.Q. attended by G.O.C. 35th Division, G.S.O.1. 35th Division, B.G., G.S. V Corps. Virgin on ALBERT CATHEDRAL fell at 3.45.p.m. G.S.O.3. reconnoitred Left Brigade front. Our night firing was continued, with some gas shelling. No enemy gun above 10.5.c.m. firing.	
	17th.		G.O.C. 113th Infantry Brigade with G.O.C. at Conference. 3 low flying enemy aircraft reported. G.S.O.1. and G.S.O.2. make a special reconnaissance. Enemy artillery activity quiet, but showed slight increase on previous days.	
	18th.		G.S.O.1. went to Corps Conference. Our usual harassing fire carried out. 115th Infantry Brigade relieved 113th Infantry Brigade in the Left Section of the Line. - D.O.170.	app 8
	19th.		Enemy employed usual harassing fire on roads and valleys and was slightly more active than usual, especially on Left Brigade front. One E.A. low over SENLIS.NORD CHIMNEY in ALBERT so destroyed.	

Army Form C. 2118.

WAR DIARY
or
INTELLIGENCE SUMMARY.
(Erase heading not required.)

Page 3.

Instructions regarding War Diaries and Intelligence Summaries are contained in F. S. Regs., Part II. and the Staff Manual respectively. Title pages will be prepared in manuscript.

Place	Date	Hour	Summary of Events and Information	Remarks and references to Appendices
CONTAY.	April 1918.			
	20th.		113th Infantry Brigade practice their scheme; G.O.C. and G.O.C., 35th Division present. Hostile artillery slightly more active. 14 enemy aircraft over our lines during the day. Our aircraft very active. Enemy 10.5. How. registering our trenches on right Brigade front. Corps Commander visited Divisional Commander. O.O.171 issued - On the evening of the 22nd April the 38th and 35th Divisions will capture and consolidate the line W.21.b.central - 16.a.0.0. - 10.c.0.7. - 4.c.8.0. - 4.b.1.3.	Opp 9.
	21st.		Hostile artillery in the SENLIS, WARLOY VALLEY during the night and early morning. 113th Infantry Brigade takes up its position in the line as Left Brigade.	
	22nd.		Hostile artillery not particularly active during the day. 113th Infantry Brigade carried out successful minor operation at 7.30.p.m. in conjunction with 35th Division. 2 officers 83 other ranks prisoners and 2 machine guns. We advanced 250 yards on a front of 1000 yards south of AVELUY WOOD.	Opp 10.
	23rd.		4.40.a.m. enemy made a local attack on the salient we made by our new line. Attack broken up and 4 prisoners taken. Enemy artillery active. 500 4.2's on MILLENCOURT. Heavy barrage on Left Brigade front. D.O.172 issued - Reliefs and moves to take place.	
	24th.		Divisional Order 172 postponed 24 hours except Serial Nos.1, 2 and 3. Hostile artillery below normal throughout the day. Desultory shelling of BOUZINCOURT, also CHLORINE gas shells on BOUZINCOURT. Left Battalion shelled at night. Enemy reported digging in opposite 113th Infantry Brigade front.	
	25th.		Corps Commander visited Divisional Commander. G.O.C. visited 115th Infantry Brigade. 115th Infantry Brigade relieve 113th Infantry Brigade in the Left Section. Slight hostile activity in the SENLIS - WARLOY VALLEY. 113th Infantry Brigade become Divisional Reserve. D.O.173 issued cancelling D.O.172. 19th Welsh Regt (GLAMORGAN PIONEERS) will move to their original bivouacs in V.3.central.	Opp 11.
	26th.		114th Infantry Brigade relieved in the Right Section by a Brigade of the 2nd Australian Division. 114th Infantry Brigade move to WARLOY & CONTAY. Our front line registered by artillery and trench mortar salvoes on HERENCOURT WOOD.	Opp 12.
	27th.		113th Infantry Brigade move to HERISSART and MIRVAUX Area. 114th Infantry Brigade move to TOUTENCOURT. BOUZINCOURT CHURCH TOWER destroyed by hostile artillery. Mustard gas on SENLIS VILLAGE from 10.p.m. to midnight.	
	28th.		GSS.10/63/1. issued - Warning Order for relief of 55th Division.	Opp 13

Army Form C. 2118.

WAR DIARY
INTELLIGENCE SUMMARY.
(Erase heading not required.)

Page 4.

Place	Date	Hour	Summary of Events and Information	Remarks and references to Appendices
CONTAY.	APRIL 1918.			
	28th.		Corps Commander (LIEUT-GENERAL SHUTE) visits Divisional Commander. Hostile artillery showed slightly increased activity.	
	29th.		Conference of Brigadiers at Divisional Headquarters. At 8.25.a.m. abnormal movement was seen on the ALBERT - LA BOISSELLE ROAD, which was engaged by aeroplanes and artillery. D.O.175 issued - relief of 35th Division by 38th Division. The command of part of the line taken over by 115th Infantry Brigade will pass to G.O.C.,38th Division on night 1/2nd May. Command of the remainder of 35th Division front will pass to G.O.C., 38th Division on completion of the relief on night 2/3rd May 1918.	app 14.
	30th.		Corps Commander's Conference at TOUTENCOURT attended by G.O.C., G.S.O.1., A.A.&.Q.M.G. and Brigadiers Generals Commanding 113th and 114th Infantry Brigades. Hostile artillery otherwise quiet. BOUZINCOURT and the vicinity of SENLIS MILL shelled. Panorama given to G.O.C. 38th(Welsh)Division showing Overview Contour.	app 15

April 1918.

F.J. Harington
Captain,
General Staff 38th (Welsh) Division.

Appendix 1 — *War Diary*

SECRET
COPY NO. 47

38TH (WELSH) DIVISION ORDER NO. 168

Reference Sheet 57 D. S.E.
and 1/100,000 Map LENS Sheet

2nd April 1918

1. 38th Division Order No. 167 is cancelled.

2. The following moves will take place to-morrow, 3rd instant.

   (a) 113th Brigade Group will return to the TOUTENCOURT - HERISSART AREA to the same billets as before, marching by ACHEUX and LEALVILLERS at any time desired; time to be notified to this office.

   (b) 114th Brigade Group will remain in present billets.

   (c) 115th Brigade and 151st Field Coy. R.E. and 'C' Coy. 38th Bn. M.G.Corps will remain in present area, and come under orders of Brigadier General Commanding 115th Brigade.
   38th Bn. M.G.Corps, less 'C' Coy, will move to an area to be notified later.
   'A' Coy. 38th Bn. M.G.Corps will rejoin Headquarters 38th Bn. M.G.Corps by any route and at any time desired.

   (d) 333rd Coy. 38th Div. Train will move to TOUTENCOURT and join 331st Coy.

3. Regulation intervals to be maintained on the march.

   ACKNOWLEDGE

   J. E. Munby
   Lieut-Colonel,
   General Staff, 38th (Welsh) Divn.

Issued to Signals 8.45 p.m.
Copies to :-

G.O.C.
G.S. (3)
"Q" (3)
12th Div. Arty.
36th (Army) Bde. R.F.A.
48th (Army) Bde. R.F.A.
C.R.E.
38th Signals
113th Brigade (2)
114th Brigade (2)
115th Brigade (2)
38th Bn. M.G.Corps
19th Welsh Regt.)
(GLAMORGAN Pnrs.)
38th Div. Train
S.S.O.
A.D.M.S.
D.A.D.V.S.

D.A.D.O.S.
A.P.M.
38th Sniping Coy.
38th Gas Officer
Camp Comdt.
235th Employment Coy.
French Mission
V Corps (2)
V Corps R.A. (2)
D.A.D.P.S. V Corps
2nd Division
17th Division
47th Division
63rd Division
1st N.Z. Division
12th Division
No. 3 Sec: 38th D.A.C.

War Diary

MESSAGES AND SIGNALS.

PRIORITY
and
S.D.R.

Appendix 2

```
113th Brigade                A.D.M.S.
114th Brigade                D.A.D.V.S.
115th Brigade                A.P.M.
C.R.E.                       D.A.D.O.S.
38th Bn., M.G.C.             38th Div: Sniping Coy.
19th Welsh Rgt.              38th Gas Officer.
38th Signals.                Camp Comdt.
38th Div: "Q"                235th Employment Coy.
38th Div: Train              French Mission.
S.S.O.                       No. 3 Sec: 38th D.A.C.
```

G. 49.   5th.

From Five.a.m. today Fifth April, 38th Divn. will be prepared to move at one hours notice AAA Acknowledge by return.

38th Division.
12-20.a.m.

T.W. Owens, Lt.
Lieut. Colonel,
General Staff, 38th (Welsh) Divn.

Appendix 3   War Diary

MESSAGES AND SIGNALS.

PRIORITY.

Lt.Col.
G.S.

113th Brigade   C. R. E., 38th Divn.
114th Brigade
115th Brigade   38th Div: "Q"
38th Bn. M.G.C.
19th Welsh Regt.   (Copy to G.O.C.)

G. 55.   5th.

Hostile attack threatened from direction of ALBERT and MAROEUIL AAA.
113th Brigade will move to position of readiness between WARLOY and VARDINCOURT at once and on arrival there will reconnoitre country and defences between BAISIEUX and HENENCOURT AAA.
114th Brigade will move at once to position of readiness near HERISSART. AAA.
38th Bn.M.G.C. will send one company to join each of these Brigades at above places and to come under orders of Brigadier. AAA.
Brigades will report time first troops move and time when concentrated. AAA. After concentration they will be at half hours notice AAA.
115th Brigade and remainder Divisional Troops stand fast. AAA.

Addrd. 3 Bdes, M.G.Bn., Pnrs, C.R.E., "Q". Rep'd remainder *of recipients of G. 49 of today*

ACKNOWLEDGE by return.

38th Divn.

10-50.a.m.

J.E. Munby
Lieut. Colonel,
General Staff, 38th (Welsh) Divn.

Appendix 4

MESSAGES AND SIGNALS.

Prefix ____ Code ____ Words ____
Office of origin. ____ Sent at ____
To ____
By ____

113th Bde.	A.D.M.S.
114th Bde.	D.A.D.V.S.
115th Bde.	A.P.M.
C.R.E.	D.A.D.O.S.
38th Bn. M.G.C.	38th Div: Sniping Coy.
19th Welsh Regt.	38th Div: Gas Offr.
38th Div: Signals	Camp Comdt.
38th Div: "Q"	235th Employt. Coy.
38th Div: Train	French Mission
S.S.O.	No. 3 Sec:, 38th D.A.C.
333rd Coy. A.S.C.	35th Divn.
105th Inf. Bde.	38th M.T. Coy.

G.A.7.   7th.   AAA

115 Bde less working parties will march at six p.m. today by WARLOY to billets in TOUTENCOURT and HERISSART   AAA   Baggage wagons and cookers may march at any time and by any route desired   AAA   Working parties will march by WARLOY on completion of work to rejoin Brigade   AAA
105 Brigade is marching from TOUTENCOURT at six p.m. by VARENNES to HEDAUVILLE   AAA   On arrival of 115 Bde at TOUTENCOURT and HERISSART 333rd Coy. A.S.C. now at TOUTENCOURT will become part of 115th Bde. Group   AAA   Addressed All units 38th Divn repeated 35th Divn and 105th Brigade for information.

38th Div.

1 p.m.

J.E. Munby
Lieut-Colonel,
General Staff, 38th (Welsh) Division.

appendix 5

War Diary

MESSAGES AND SIGNALS

Prefix _____ Code _____ Words _____
Office of origin. _____ Sent at _____
To _____
By _____

113th Bde.	A.P.M.
114th Bde.	D.A.D.O.S.
115th Bde.	38th Sniping Coy.
C.R.E.	38th Gas Officer
38th Bn. M.G.C.	Camp Comdt.
19th Welsh Regt.	235th Employment Coy.
38th Div. Signals	French Mission
38th Div. "Q"	No. 3 Sec: 38th D.A.C.
38th Div. Train	
S.S.C.	
A.D.M.S.	
D.A.D.V.S.	

G.109   9th,   AAA

113th Inf. Bde. will move to-morrow at any time and by any route desired to HARPONVILLE AAA Tents for two Battalions will be delivered at HARPONVILLE to-morrow under divisional arrangements AAA 331 Coy. A.S.C. to TOUTENCOURT Area AAA 131 Fd. Ambce now at CLAIRFAYE remains there and becomes part of 113th Bde. Group instead of 129 Fd. Ambce AAA Brigade will commence work on eleventh inst. on the BAIZIEUX - FORCEVILLE Line and BAIZIEUX SWITCH under instructions from C.R.E. AAA Added 113th Bde. Reptd all Units 38th Div.

38th Div.

7.50 p.m.

J.E. Munby
Lieut-Colonel,
General Staff, 38th (Welsh) Division

War Diary *appendix 6*

SECRET
COPY NO. 50

38TH (WELSH) DIVISION ORDER NO. 169

Ref: Maps Sheet 11, 1/100,000 62.D.1/40,000   10th April 1918.
Sheet 57 D. 1/40,000

1. The Division (less Artillery) will relieve the 12th Division (less Artillery) in the line from E.2.central to W.15.a.3.7. in accordance with the attached table.

2. The 12th Division Defence Scheme will be taken over and acted upon until further orders, with the exception that from the 12th instant inclusive onwards the action of the reserve brigade will be as follows :-

    One Battalion will occupy the Corps Line in each Brigade Section, and will be prepared to move forward to the old French Line running through D.6.b., V.30.b. and d., V.24.b. and d., and W.13. should the reserve battalions of the Brigades in line move forward.

    The Battalion at WARLOY will be moved to a position of assembly near MILLENCOURT.

    115th Inf. Brigade will reconnoitre the Corps Line, and adjacent country to-morrow.

3. Details of relief will be arranged between Brigades direct.

4. Command of the line will pass to G.O.C. 38th Division at 10 a.m. 12th instant, at which time 38th Divisional H.Q. will open at CONTAY.

5. Command of Machine Gun Companies will be exercised in the same manner as when the Division was last in the line except that the Company stationed at HENENCOURT will be under the orders of the Brigadier General Commanding the Reserve Brigade.

6. ACKNOWLEDGE

J.E. Munby
Lieut-Colonel,
General Staff, 38th (Welsh) Divn.

Issued to Signals at 6.16 p.m.

Copies to :- All Units, 38th Division.   Area Comdts :-
    V Corps   TOUTENCOURT
    V Corps R.A.   HERISSART
    V Corps H.A.   RUBEMPRE
    D.A.D.P.S., V Corps   PIERREGOT
    12th Division   CONTAY
    17th Division   VADENCOURT
    35th Division   WARLOY
    47th Division   HARPONVILLE
    63rd Division   HEDAUVILLE
    2nd Aust. Div.   SENLIS
    R.T.O., BELLE EGLISE.   HENENCOURT

TABLE OF RELIEFS AND MOVES TO ACCOMPANY 38TH DIV. ORDER NO 169.

Serial No.	Date (April)	Unit.	To	In relief of	Remarks.
1.	10th.	114th Brigade H.Q. Sniping Sec. T.M.Bty. 2 Battns. 1 Battalion	HENENCOURT. WARLOY	35th Brigade.	Will be in 12th Div: Reserve.
2.	11th.	115th Brigade.	HENENCOURT & WARLOY	114th Brigade	
3.	11th.	D Coy. 38th Bn.MGC.	HENENCOURT.	One Coy. 12th Bn.MGC.	Will be in 12th Div: Reserve.
4.	11th.	A Coy. - do -	WARLOY.		Will be under orders of Res.Bde.
5.	11th.	19th Welsh Rgt.	SENLIS	5th Northants Regt.	
6.	11th.	123rd Fd.Coy.RE.	SENLIS		To work under orders of 113th Bde.
7.	11th.	151st - do -	SENLIS		To work under orders of 114th Brigade. Orders as to taking over details of work in hand are being issued by C.R.E. Transport will not move.
8.	11th.	129th Fd. Ambce.	WARLOY.	Fd.Ambce., 12th Div.	
9.	11/12th.	114th Brigade.	Line RIGHT.	36th Brigade.	
10.	11/12th.	115th Brigade.	Line LEFT.	37th Brigade.	
11.	12th.	38th Div: Train.	HARPONVILLE.	12th Div: Train.	
12.	12th.	No.3 Sec.38th DAC.	CONTAY.		
13.	12th.	130th Fd. Ambce.	RUBEMPRE.		
14.	12th.	A Coy. 38th Bn.MGC.	Corps Line.		
15.	12th.	B Coy. - do -	HENENCOURT.	One Coy. 12th Bn.MGC.	
16.	12/13th.	D Coy. - do -	Line RIGHT.	D Coy. 38th Bn.MGC.	
17.	12/13th.	C Coy. - do -	Line LEFT.	One Coy. 12th Bn.MGC.	Will be under orders of Res. Bde.
18.	12/13th.	124th Fd.Coy.RE.	Will remain at LA VICOGNE for the present.		- do -
19.		131st Fd.Ambce.	Will remain at CLAIRFAYE.		

10th April 1918.

J.F.Plunkett
Lieut. Colonel,
General Staff, 38th (Welsh) Division.

"War Diary appendix 7

MESSAGES AND SIGNALS

Prefix   Code   Words
Office of Origin.   Sent at
                           To
                           By

113th Bde.   12th Div. Arty.
114th Bde.   V Corps
115th Bde.   V Corps R.A.
38th Bn. M.G.C.   V Corps H.A.
38th Signals
C. R. E.
19th Welsh Regt.
A. D. M. S.
38th Div. "Q"
12th Div.
17th Div.
35th Div.
47th Div.
63rd Div.
2nd Aust. Div.

G.132   11th   AAA

Amendment to 38th Div. Order 169 AAA Para. 4 AAA Command will pass to G.O.C. 38th Div. at 8 a.m.

38th Div.

9.50 p.m.

E.T. Allen Major
Lieut-Colonel,
General Staff, 38th (Welsh) Divn.

Appendix 8   *War Diary*

SECRET
COPY NO. 40

38TH (WELSH) DIVISION ORDER NO. 170

Ref: Map Sheet 57 D. 1/40,000   18th April 1918

1. 115th Brigade will relieve 113th Brigade in the line to-day and to-night.
   All details to be arranged between Brigades direct.
   All ammunition and trench stores will be handed over and receipt obtained, and forwarded to this office by 113th Brigade.
   Trench maps and air photos will not be handed over.
   The two Companies 10th Battalion South Wales Borderers now attached to 113th Brigade will cease to be so attached from the completion of the relief.

2. After relief 113th Brigade will withdraw to the positions occupied by 115th Brigade, except that the two Companies now in WARLOY may remain there if desired until further orders.

3. After being relieved in the line 113th Brigade will become Divisional reserve and will take over the duties laid down in 38th Division Instructions for Defence No. 1.

4. The Company 38th Battalion Machine Gun Corps, now attached to 115th Brigade, will remain in its present position and will come under the orders of 113th Brigade after the completion of the above relief.

5. ACKNOWLEDGE.

J. E. Munby
Lieut-Colonel,
General Staff, 38th (Welsh) Division.

Issued to Signals at 6 a.m.

Copies to all Units 38th Division
              V Corps
              V Corps R.A.
              V Corps H.A.
              12th Division
              17th Division
              35th Division
              63rd Division
              12th Div. Arty.
              Area Comdt. WARLOY.

Appendix 9

SECRET

38th Division No. S.S.125/2.

AMENDMENT NO. 1 to 38TH DIVISION ORDER NO. 171.

Amendment to "TABLE of MACHINE GUN ACTION" issued with 38th Division Order No. 171 dated 20-4-1918 :-

First two pairs of guns - Target after final objective is taken, <u>for</u> "Road at W.22.<u>b</u>.3.2" <u>read</u> "Road at W.22.<u>a</u>.3.2."

F.J. Harington Captain
for Lieut. Colonel,
20th April, 1918.   General Staff, 38th (Welsh) Division.

Copies to all recipients of D.O. 171.
To list of addressees add :- A.D.M.S., 38th Div.
                35th Bn.M.G.C.
                "B" Coy.12th Bn.M.G.C.

SECRET
COPY NO.

38TH (WELSH) DIVISION ORDER NO. 171

Ref: Map, Sheet 57 D, S.E., 1/20,000   20th April 1918

1. On the evening of the 22nd instant the 38th and 35th Divisions will capture and consolidate the line W.21.b.central - 16.a.0.0. - 10.c.0.7 - 4.c.8.0. - 4.b.1.3.
   The dividing line between the Divisions is a line drawn East and West through W.10.c.0.7.

2. The attack on that part of the objective allotted to 38th Division will be carried out by Brigadier General Commanding 113th Brigade who will have under his command for this task -

          113th Brigade
          One Battalion of 115th Bde. (from completion of relief
                                                 mentioned in para. 8 (a)
                                                 till further orders).
          19th Welsh Regt. (GLAMORGAN Pioneers).

3. The 19th D.L.I. (of 35th Division) have been ordered to capture and consolidate the line W.10.c.0.7 - W.9.b.9.3, and will come under the orders of the Brigadier General Commanding 113th Bde. from Zero until this line is captured.

4. Orders for artillery action will be issued by the C.R.A. 12th Divisional Artillery.

5. Machine gun action will be as given in attached table.
   'A' Coy. 38th Bn. M.G.Corps will move into position as shown in the table on the night 21st/22nd, and will remain in these positions till 4 a.m. 23rd April.

6. Collecting Station for walking wounded will be established at Cross Roads V.16.a.8.8., and an additional R.A.P. will probably be established at W.19.c.1.8.

7. The 38th Divisional Signal Coy. will maintain communication with 113th Brigade Command Post at V.23.a.9.8 by wire, wireless and visual (visual through T.S. at SENLIS MILL).

8. For the purpose of the above operations the following reliefs will take place on the night 21st/22nd instant.

   (a) 113th Brigade will relieve 115th Brigade (less one Battalion) and will relieve troops of the 35th Division in the front and support trenches as far North as W.9.c.4.7. All details of relief to be arranged between Brigades concerned. After relief 115th Brigade (less one Battalion) will withdraw to Divisional Reserve, and will maintain one battalion at V.28.b. and one at V.16.d.

/ 8. (b)

Page 2

8. (b) The half of 'B' Coy. 12th Bn. M.G.Corps now at WARLOY will relieve 'A' Coy. 38th Bn. M.G.Corps, and will come under the orders of Brigadier General Commanding 115th Brigade until 8 a.m. 23rd instant by which time it will be relieved by 'A' Coy. 38th Bn. M.G.Corps, and will withdraw to WARLOY. Details of relief to be arranged by O.C. 38th Bn. M.G.Corps.

9. ACKNOWLEDGE

E. Wallen Maj.
for Lieut-Colonel,
General Staff, 38th (Welsh) Divn

Issued to Signals at **8** p.m.

Copies to :-

G.O.C.
113th Brigade
114th Brigade
115th Brigade
12th Div. Arty.
38th Bn. M.G.Corps
C. R. E.
38th Div. Signals
19th Welsh Regt.)
(GLAMORGAN Pnrs.)
38th Sniping Coy.
38th Div. 'A' & 'Q'
A.D.M.S.

V Corps
V Corps R.A.
V Corps H.A.
35th Division (2)
2nd Aust. Div.
12th Division.

35 Bn. M.G.C.
'B' Coy. 12 Bn. M.G.C.

TABLE OF MACHINE GUN ACTION. (38th Divn. Order. No. 171.)

GUNS.	In action at.	TARGETS AT ZERO.	TARGET after final objective is taken.
38th Bn.MGC.(A Co.)			
2 guns.	W.19.d.4.6.	Hostile Communication trench W.15.d.6.2. - 8.5.	Road at W.22.b.3.2.
2 "	"	Gulleys W.9.d.1.2. to 6.5. and W.9.d.3.0. to 6.5.	"
8 "	W.20.a.1.9.	Road W.15.d.9.0. - Cross Roads W.15.b.9.2.	Bank W.16.c.9.2. - a.9.2. (10 guns)
4 "	W.13.d.7.8.		Road W.16.a.9.2. (2 guns)
35th Bn.MGC.			
2 guns.		W.16.b.1.7. - W.16.a.8.9.	Remain on same target.
2 "		W.16.b.2.8. - W.10.c.9.1.	Remain on same target.
4 "	W.3.d.7.7.	Along road W.15.b.9.2. - W.9.d.9.0.	
2 "	W.2.d.	Along road W.22.a.1.8. - W.15.d.7.5.	

All guns will lift off their Zero target at the same time that the Heavy Artillery barrage lifts off that target.

Rate of fire (of 38th Bn.MGC guns) on targets after the final objective is taken will be 100 to 50 rounds per gun per minute for same duration as the Artillery protective barrage; guns of 38th Bn. MGC. will open at a rapid rate on their "final objective" targets in response to S.O.S. signal during the night.

S.M. Allen
for Lieut. Colonel,
General Staff, 38th (Welsh) Division.

20th April 1918.

SECRET.   38th Division.No.S.S.125/4.

Amendment No.2 to Divisional Order No.171.

Para 6.   for W.19.c.1.8. road W.13.c.3.6. (usual H.Q. of the
          Reserve Battalion, Left Brigade).

Para 7.   Add "Runners (found by 115th Brigade under instructions
          already issued) will work from the Brigade command
          post to a D.R. post at V.16.a.central".

Table of Machine Gun Action.
          Delete first sentence of footnote and substitute
          "Guns will lift off their zero targets at the following
          times :-
          C.T.W.15.d.6.2 at zero + 10
          Gulleys   "   " + 5
          Road W.15.d.9.0 - b.9.2. at zero + 15.
                W.15.b.9.2.- W.9.d.9.0. at zero + 15.) 35 Bn.
                W.22.a.1.8 - W.15.d.7.5 "   " + 8.)

          In second para of footnote for "for same duration
          as the Artillery protective barrage" substitute
          "until zero + 75".

ACKNOWLEDGE.

21/4/1918.
                                              Lieut.Colonel.
                                General Staff.38th (Welsh) Division.

Copies to all recipients of Divisional Order No.171.

Appendix 10

MESSAGES AND SIGNALS.

PRIORITY. to 113)
              114) Bdes
              115)

E.S.Allent Maji L'Col of 38 Bn MGC.

Prefix _____   Code ____ Words ____
Office of Origin. ____   Sent at ____
                          To ____
                          By ____

"Q"	19th Welsh Regt.	Gas Officer.	V Corps.
63rd Div Arty	Div Train.	Camp Commdt.	V Corps R.A.
C.R.E.	S.S.O.	236th Employment.	V Corps H.A.
Signals.	A.D.M.S.	French Mission.	D.A.D.P.S., V Corps
113th Brigade	D.A.D.V.S.	3 Secn 38th D.A.C.	12th Division.
114th Brigade	D.A.D.O.S.	63rd Division.	17th Division.
115th Brigade	A.P.M.	2nd Aus.Divn.	35th Division.
38th Bn.M.G.C.	Sniping Coy.	R.T.O. RAINCHEVAL SIDING.	
Area Comdt. TOUTENCOURT.		Area Comdt. RUBEMPRE.	
Area Comdt. HERISSART.		Area Comdt. CONTAY.	
		Area Comdt. WARLOY.	

G.318.   24th.   AAA

38th Divisional Order 172 postponed 24 hours except Serial Nos. 1, 2 and 3.

38th Div.

5.p.m.

E.S.Allen Maj.
Lieut-Colonel.
General Staff 38th (Welsh) Division.

GENERAL STAFF,
V CORPS.
No. GA 635
Date 23-4-18

SECRET
COPY NO. 32

38TH (WELSH) DIVISION ORDER NO. 172

Ref: Maps Sheet 57 D., 1/40,000
     Sheet 62 D., 1/40,000

23rd April 1918

1. Reliefs and moves will take place as laid down in attached table.

2. Command of the line from right boundary to W.15.d.5.0. will pass to 2nd Australian Division at 6 a.m. 25th instant.
Remainder of present Division front will remain under command of General Officer Commanding 38th Division.

3. The normal composition of Brigade Groups will be changed. Brigade Groups will be as under after arrival in billets and camps :-

   113th Bde. Group :- 113th Bde. and 130th Fd. Ambce.

   114th Bde. Group :- 114th Bde. and 129th Fd. Ambce.

4. Regulation intervals will be maintained on the march.

5. Divisional Headquarters will remain at CONTAY.

6. ACKNOWLEDGE

J.S. Munby
Lieut-Colonel,
General Staff, 38th (Welsh) Divn.

Issued to Signals at 6.10 p.m.

Copies to :- All Units 38th Division
            V Corps
            V Corps R.A.
            V Corps H.A.
            D.A.D.P.S., V Corps
            12th Division
            17th Division
            35th Division
            63rd Division
            2nd Aust. Div.
            63rd Div. Arty.
            R.T.O. RAINCHEVAL SIDING.

Area Comdts :-
            TOUTENCOURT
            HERISSART
            RUBEMPRE
            CONTAY
            VARLOY

BILLET TABLE ISSUED WITH 38TH DIVISION ORDER NO. 142.

Serial No.	Unit	Date (April)	From	To	R.O.R.O.	Billeted by.	Instructions.
1.	R.E. (See 13+14(RE)	24th.	Line	TOUTENCOURT Camp U.1.c.	Any	R.E. 2nd Aust. Div.	Additional tentage will be provided.
2.	19th Welsh Rgt. 24th. (Pioneers)		(H.Q.,V.3.cent)Camp HERISSART	Via WARLOY.-CONTAY			No roller. In tents.
3.	H.Q. & H.Q. Secn. 24th. Sniping Coy.		WARLOY.	TOUTENCOURT.ViaVADENCOURT.		5th Aust.I.Bde.	Billet from Town Major. Other Secns.remain with their Brigades. Comes under orders of 115th Brigade.
4.	2nd R.W.F.	Night 24/25.	Line.	—	Any.	6th Aust.I.Bde.as far N.as W.26.d.0.6. Remainder (incldg. Res:Bn:) by 5/Aust. Inf. Brigade.	
5.	114th Bde.	Night 24/25.	Right Front Line (H.Q.— V.20.d.6.4.)	Bivouacs of Res:Bde.	—	5/Aust:I.Brigade.	
6.	113th Brigade as far N. as W.15.d.5.0.	Night 24/25	Line.	TOUTENCOURT Via PUCHEVILLERS	—		Camp, U.1.c.
7.	114th Brigade	25th.	WARLOY.	TOUTENCOURT Via CONTAY.			
8.	38th Div:Train (less 353 Coy.)	25th.	TOUTENCOURT	M.36.d.			
9.	38th Bn.MGC. Guns covering the front taken over by 2/A.Div.	Night 25/26.	Line.	WARLOY.	Any.	2nd Aust:Div:.	
10.	Remainder 113th Brigade.	Night 24/25.	Line.	WARLOY.	Any.	115th Brigade.	
11.	Serial No.9. less 1 Coy. detailed for defence of HENENCOURT RIDGE.	26th.	WARLOY.	TOUTENCOURT Via VADENCOURT			Billets from Town Major.
12.	113th Brigade	26th.	WARLOY	HERISSART & MIRVAUX.	Any.		2 Bns.billets HERISSART. 1 Bn. & T.M.B.billets MIRVAUX. H.Q. at MIRVAUX or HERISSART as desired.
13.	129th Fd.Ambce.	26th.	WARLOY.	TOUTENCOURT. CONTAY.		2nd Aust:Div:.	Div:H.Q., Mob:Vet:Secn., No.3 Sec:, 38th D.A.C. 130th and 131st Fd.Ambces and 333 Coy. A.S.C. Billets.

The following Units remain in present position :—

J. F. Mundy
Lieut.Colonel,
General Staff, 38th (Welsh) Division.

23rd April, 1918.

GENERAL STAFF.
V CORPS.
No. GA 635
Date 23/4/18

SECRET
COPY NO. 31

38TH (WELSH) DIVISION ORDER NO. 172

Ref: Maps Sheet 57 D., 1/40,000
     Sheet 62 D., 1/40,000

23rd April 1918

1. Reliefs and moves will take place as laid down in attached table.

2. Command of the line from right boundary to W.15.d.5.0. will pass to 2nd Australian Division at 6 a.m. 25th instant.
   Remainder of present Division front will remain under command of General Officer Commanding 38th Division.

3. The normal composition of Brigade Groups will be changed. Brigade Groups will be as under after arrival in billets and camps :-

   113th Bde. Group :- 113th Bde. and 130th Fd. Ambce.

   114th Bde. Group :- 114th Bde. and 129th Fd. Ambce.

4. Regulation intervals will be maintained on the march.

5. Divisional Headquarters will remain at CONTAY.

6. ACKNOWLEDGE

Noted.

J.S. Munby
Lieut-Colonel,
General Staff, 38th (Welsh) Divn.

Issued to Signals at 6.10 p.m.

Copies to :- All Units 38th Division   Area Comdts :-
             V Corps   TOUTENCOURT
             V Corps R.A.   HERISSART
             V Corps H.A.   RUBEMPRE
             D.A.D.P.S., V Corps   CONTAY
             12th Division   HARLOY
             17th Division
             35th Division
             63rd Division
             2nd Aust. Div.
             63rd Div. Arty.
             R.T.O. RAINCHEVAL SIDING.

Copy sent to R.
23/4/18.

RELIEF TABLE ISSUED WITH 38TH DIVISION ORDER NO. 172

Serial No.	Unit	Date (April)	From	To	Route	Relieved by	Instructions
1.	R.E. (Coy 124 Fd.Coy R.E.)	24th.	Line	TOUTENCOURT Camp U.l.c.	Any	R.E. 2nd Aust. Div.	Additional tentage will be provided.
2.	19th Welsh Rgt. (Pioneers)	24th.	(H.Q.,V.3.contl) Camp HERISSART	Via WARLOY.—CONTAY — HERISSART	No roller.	In tents.
3.	H.Q. & H.Q. Secn. Sniping Coy.	24th.	WARLOY.	TOUTENCOURT. Via VADENCOURT.	—	—	Billet from Town Major. Other Secns. remain with their Brigades. Comes under orders of 115th Brigade.
4.	2nd R.W.F.	Night 24/25.	Line.	—	—	5th Aust. I. Bdo.	
5.	114th Bdo.	Night 24/25.	Right Front Line (H.Q.— V.20.d.6.4.)	Bivouacs of Res:Bde.	Any.	6th Aust. I. Bdo. as far N. as W.26.d.0.6. Remainder (incldg. Res:Bn:) by 5/Aust. Inf. Brigade. 5/Aust:I.Brigade.	
6.	113th Brigade as far N. as W.15.d.5.0.	Night 24/25.	Line.	—	—	—	Camp, U.l.c.
7.	114th Brigade	25th.	WARLOY.	TOUTENCOURT Via CONTAY.	—	—	
8.	58th Div: Train (less 353 Coy.)	25th.	TOUTENCOURT	M.36.d.	PUCHEVILLERS	—	
9.	38th Bn. M.G.C. Guns covering the front taken over by 2/A.Div.	Night 25/26.	Line.	WARLOY.	Any.	2nd Aust: Div:.	
10.	Remainder 113th Brigade.	Night 24/25.	Line.	WARLOY.	Any.	115th Brigade.	
11.	Serial No.9. less 1 Coy. detailed for Defence of HENENCOURT RIDGE.	26th.	WARLOY.	TOUTENCOURT	Via VADENCOURT	—	Billets from Town Major.
12.	113th Brigade	26th.	WARLOY.	HERISSART & MIRVAUX.	Any.	—	2 Bns.billets HERISSART. 1 Bn. & T.M.B billets MIRVAUX. H.Q. to MIRVAUX or HERISSART as desired.
13.	129th Fd.Ambce.	26th.	WARLOY.	TOUTENCOURT.	CONTAY.	2nd Aust:Div:.	Billets.

Div:H.Q., Mob:Vet:Secn., No.3 Secn:, 38th D.A.C. 130th and 131st Fd.Ambces and 333 Coy. A.S.C.

The following Units remain in present position :-

J.E. Munby
Lieut.Colonel,
General Staff, 38th (Welsh) Division.

23rd April, 1918.

"C" FORM.
MESSAGES AND SIGNALS.

Army Form C. 2123.
(In books of 100.)

Prefix ..... Code ..... Words 33
Charges to Collect
Service Instructions

Received. From JCH By Sigs

Sent, or sent out At ..... m. To ..... By .....

Office Stamp.

Handed in at JCH Office 5.20 p.m. Received 5.13 p.m.

TO **5 Corps.** GA 635

Sender's Number.	Day of Month.	In reply to Number.	AAA
G 218	24th		

38th Divisional order 172 postponed 24 hours except serial nos 1 2 and 3

FROM 38th Div
PLACE & TIME 5 pm

5.45pm

"C" FORM.
MESSAGES AND SIGNALS.
Army Form C. 2123.

Prefix	Code	Words	Received From	Sent, or sent out At	Office Stamp
Charges to Collect			By	To	26.V.18
Service Instructions				By	

Handed in at......... Office.........m. Received.........m.

TO 5th Corps

Sender's Number	Day of Month	In reply to Number	AAA
541	26th		

Reference Para 3a of
order 179 aaa Relief
Complete

Qa 635/1

FROM 38 Div
PLACE & TIME 2.40a

SECRET

38th Division No. GSS. 2/5

REPORT ON OPERATIONS, 38TH (WELSH) DIVISION
PERIOD 19th APRIL – 28th APRIL (Both inclusive).

19th Aprl.)
20th Aprl.)   Harassing fire employed by artillery of both sides.

21st Aprl.   115th Brigade relieved 113th Brigade in the Left Section and relieved the right of the 35th Division as far as W.9.c.5.8. for the purpose of operations due to take place the following day.
For the same purpose the 113th Brigade was reinforced by one Battalion (2nd Battn. R.W.F.) of the 115th Brigade and took up "battle frontages" as follows :-
   Holding the line from W.21.c.8.0. – W.21.central
      2 Companies 2nd Battn. R.W.F.

   On front of attack :-
      Right   13th Battn. R.W.F.
      Centre   16th Battn. R.W.F. supported by
                  2 Cos. 14th Battn. R.W.F.
      Left   2 Cos. 14th Battn. R.W.F.
      Reserve 2 Cos. 2nd Battn. R.W.F. in W.20.a.
                  and W.13.d.

22nd Aprl.   The following operations was carried out under the orders of V Corps and in conjunction with an attack made by 35th Division on our left.
   Objective W.21.b.central – W.16.a.0.0. – W.10.c.0.8.
   Zero   7-30.p.m.
   Narrative Two companies of the right Battalion of the 35th Division (19th D.L.I.) came under the orders of 38th Division from Zero till 8.a.m. and were put under the orders of the 115th Brigade.
Remainder of the Right Brigade (104) of 35th Division were put under the orders of 38th Division for the same period.
   There was no preliminary bombardment.
   Attacking troops advanced under cover of a barrage formed as follows :-
   By Corps Heavy Artillery
   By Field Artillery from right to left :- 63rd Bde., 82nd Bde., 34th Bde., 48th Bde., and one Bde., 35th Div: Arty.
   By 38th Battn. M.G.C. (16 guns)
   By 35th Battn. M.G.C. (10 guns)
   Immediately on leaving our front trenches our Infantry came under very heavy M.G. fire from hostile positions in shell-holes along the high ground in W.15. and from W.10. and suffered some 700 casualties.
      They, however, reached and consolidated the following line:-
         W.21.b.central – W.15.central – Cross Roads W.15.a.4.8. – W.9.central.
      Captures :- 3 Officers, 83 Other Ranks and 6 machine guns.
   As a result of this operation the high ground in W.15. was practically denied to the enemy for observation purposes and a point at W.21.bcentral was reached and held from where good observation can be obtained by us into the ANCRE Valley.

23rd Aprl.   At 7-30.p.m. the enemy put down a heavy barrage behind our front trenches in W.21. and launched a counter-attack against our new position in W.21.b.; this was driven off by our Artillery, M.G. and rifle fire.

24th Aprl.   Early this morning the attempt of the previous evening was repeated by the enemy with the same result, and the capture of 4 prisoners by us.
25th Aprl.   115th Brigade relieved the 113th Brigade this night.

                         (sd) C.G.BLACKADER,   Major General,
26th April 1918.   Commanding 38th (Welsh) Division.

Copies to 114th Brigade
         115th Brigade

Appendix 11

SECRET

Copy No. 49

38TH (WELSH) DIVISION ORDER NO. 173.

Ref: Maps, 1/10,000, Sheets 57D. & 62D.   25th April, 1918.

1. 38th Division Order No. 172 is cancelled.

2. The 19th Welsh Regt. (GLAMORGAN PIONEERS) will move today to their original bivouacs in V.3. etc.
   Orders for the return move of 123rd and 151st Field Ccs. R.E. will be issued by the C.R.E.

3. (a) 115th Brigade will, tonight, relieve 113th Brigade in the line from V.21.c.5.0. to the Left Divisional Boundary.

   (b) Details of relief will be arranged between Brigades direct.

   (c) All trench maps, photos, trench stores and ammunition will be handed over and copies of receipts forwarded to this office.

   (d) The battalion and one company of 115th Brigade at present under orders of 113th Brigade will revert to the command of 115th Brigade from completion of relief.

4. After relief 113th Brigade will be in Divisional Reserve and will occupy bivouacs in V.16, V.21, and V.28 and will be prepared to act in accordance with 38th Division Instructions for Defence No. 1. para. 1.

5. 38th Division letter No. GSS. 10/62 of yesterday is cancelled.

All units 38th Division to <u>acknowledge.</u>

J. E. Munby
Lieut. Colonel,
General Staff, 38th (Welsh) Division.

Issued to Signals at 12-15.p.m.

Copies to :- All Units 38th Division.
All other recipients of D.O. 172.

Appendix 12. War Diary

SECRET

Copy No. 52

38TH (WELSH) DIVISION ORDER NO. 174.

26th April 1918.

Ref: Maps, 1/40,000,
Sheets 57.D. & 62.D.

1. The Division (less Artillery) will be relieved by troops of the 2nd Australian Division from the present right boundary to the grid line running East and West through W.15.c.5.0.

2. Command of the above part of the line will pass to G.O.C., 2nd Australian Division at 6.a.m. 27th instant. The remainder of the present Division front will remain under the command of the G.O.C., 38th Division.

3. Reliefs and moves will take place in accordance with the attached table.
Details of reliefs will be arranged between Brigades direct.
All trench maps, photos, trench stores and ammunition will be handed over and receipts forwarded to this office.

4. Regulation intervals will be maintained on the march.
The normal composition of Brigade Groups will be changed. After arrival in billets and camps Brigade Groups will be as under :-

  113th Brigade Group - 113th Brigade and
              130th Field Ambulance.

  114th Brigade Group - 114th Brigade and
              129th Field Ambulance.

5. Divisional Headquarters will not move.

6. ACKNOWLEDGE.

E. Allen, Major, for
Lieut-Colonel,
General Staff 38th (Welsh) Division.

Issued to Signals at 1.30 a.m.

Copies to :- All Units 38th Division.
      All other recipients of D.O.173.
      Rear Infantry Brigade Headquarters.

RELIEF TABLE ISSUED WITH 38TH DIVISION ORDER NO 174.

Serial No.	UNIT	Date (April)	From	To	Relieved by	Instructions.
1.	R.E. (less 124th Fd.Coy.RE.)	27th.	Line.	TOUTENCOURT Camp U.l.o.	R.E., 2nd Aust:Div:.	Additional tentage will be provided.
2.	19th Welsh Regt. (Pioneers)	27th.	(H.Q.,V.3.central)	Camp HERISSART.	No relief.	In tents.
3.	114th Brigade.	Night 26/27.	Right Front Line (H.Q.,V.20.d.6.4)	T.M.B. & 2 Bns. 6/Aust.I.Bde.as far N. WARLOY; 1 Battn.as W.26.d.0.6. Remainder (incldg.Res.BN.) by 5th Aust.Inf.Brigade. CONTAY.		
4.	115th Brigade. as far N. as W.15.d.5.0.	Night 26/27.	Line.	Bivouacs in V.21. until those in V.16.are vacated by 113th Brigade.	5/Aust.I.Bde.	
5.	114th Brigade.	27th.	WARLOY & CONTAY	TOUTENCOURT	-	Camp U.l.o.
6.	38th Div:Train (less 333 Coy.)	27th.	TOUTENCOURT.	M.36.d.	-	
7.	38th Bn.MGC. Guns covering the front taken over by 2nd. Aust. Division.	Night 27/28.	Line.	WARLOY.	2nd Aust: Divn.	-
8.	Serial No. 7.loss 1 Coy. detailed for Lof ence of HENENCOURT RIDGE.	28th.	WARLOY.	TOUTENCOURT.	-	Billets from Town Major.
9.	113th Brigade.	27th.	Reserve.	HERISSART and MIRVAUX.	-	2 Bns.billets HERISSART. 1 Bn.&T.M.B.billets MIRVAUX. H.Q. to MIRVAUX or HERISSART as desired.
10.	129th Fd.Ambce.	28th.	WARLOY.	TOUTENCOURT.	2nd Aust. Divn.	Billets.

The following Units remain in present position :- Div:H.Q.,Mob:Vet:Secn; No.3.Secn.D.A.C. 130th and 131st Fd.Ambces. and 333rd Coy. A.S.C.

Appendix 13.

SECRET

38th Division No. GSS. 10/63/1.

113th Brigade	38th Bn. M.G.C.
114th Brigade	38th Div: "Q"
115th Brigade	35th Division (For information)
C. R. E.	

WARNING ORDER FOR RELIEF OF 35TH DIVISION.

1. **FRONTAGES.**
   The Division will be on a three Brigade front as under :-
   115th Brigade from present Right to W.9.c.central.
   113th Brigade from W.9.c.central to grid line between W.3. and W.9.
   114th Brigade from Grid line between W.3. & W.9. to grid line between Q.33. & W.3.

2. **RESPONSIBILITY AND WORK.**
   Each Brigade will be responsible for the defence of its own area as far back as the MILLENCOURT - ENGLEBELMER Line inclusive; for work they will be responsible as far back as the line W.14.c.0.0. - W.8.c.0.0. - Q.32.d.5.0. Each Brigade will have half a Field Coy. R.E. under command of the Brigadier for work in front of this line and will place half a Battalion at the disposal of the C.R.E. for work in rear of this line.

3. **DISPOSITIONS.**
   Each Brigade will maintain one Battalion in reserve in bivouacs approximately as under :-
   V.16.d., V.5.a., P.35.a.
   Those Battalions will not be employed either tactically or for work in front of the MILLENCOURT - ENGLEBELMER Line without permission of the General Officer Commanding the Division.
   Three Machine Gun Companies will occupy positions as far back as the MILLENCOURT - ENGLEBELMER Line inclusive; the fourth Company will be in reserve but will have positions allotted to it in that line.

4. **RELIEF.**
   Night 1st/2nd. 115th Bde. will extend to the left.
   113th Bde. will relieve Left Battn. of Right Bde., 35th Divn. and Right Bn. of Left Bde., 35th Division.
   38th Bn.MGC. will relieve half the guns of the 35th Division.
   Night 2nd/3rd. 114th Bde. will relieve the two left Battns. of the 35th Division.
   38th Bn.MGC. will relieve the remaining guns of 35th Division.

5. **HEADQUARTERS.**
   It is desirable that Brigade H.Q. should be located as under :-
   Right as at present, Centre V.12.c. or V.17.a., Left V.6.d.

6. **CONFERENCE.**
   The above orders are provisional only until ratified at a conference which will be held at Div: H.Q. at 4-30.p.m tomorrow (29th) which Brigadiers and C.R.E. will attend.

7. **MAPS.**
   Maps showing the trenches of the new area and also showing the present dispositions and Defensive arrangements of 35th Division are enclosed herewith.
   ACKNOWLEDGE.

J.E. Munby

28th April 1918.
Lieut. Colonel,
General Staff, 38th (Welsh) Division.
Copy to 38th Div: Signals.

Appendix 14.

SECRET
─*─*─*─*─
38th Division No. GSS. 10/63.

AMENDMENT NO. 1 to 38TH (WELSH) DIVISION ORDER NO. 175.

1. Add to para. 2.
   104th I.Bde., less 1 Battn., will be under the orders of G.O.C.38th Divn. from completion of relief until 10.a.m. 3rd May.

2. Add to para. 4.
   There is no restriction as to route.

3. Table.
   In column 3 of Serial Nos. 1 and 5, add "less 1 Battalion".
   Add Serial numbers as follows :-

1.	2.	3.	4.	6.
14.	2nd May.	1 Battn. 113th Bde.	Bivouac near HEDAUVILLE.	To arrive by 2.p.m.
15.	3rd May.	1 Battn. 114th Bde.	Bivouac near HEDAUVILLE.	To arrive by 10.a.m.

4. 113th and 114th Brigades to acknowledge.

F. J. Harington Captain
for Lieut. Colonel,
29th April 1918.   General Staff, 38th (Welsh) Division.

Copies to all recipients of D.O. 175.

SECRET
COPY NO. 48

38TH (WELSH) DIVISION ORDER NO. 175

Ref: Map, 1/40,000, Sheet 57D.   29th April 1918.

1. The Division (less Artillery) will relieve the 35th Division (less Artillery) in the line from W.15.a.5.6 to P.34.d.4.0; reliefs and moves will take place as laid down in attached table.

2. The command of that part of the line taken over by 115th Infantry Brigade will pass to G.O.C. 38th Division on completion of that relief on night 1st/2nd May.
   The command of the remainder of 35th Division present front will pass to G.O.C. 38th Division on completion of relief on night 2nd/3rd May.

3. After relief the boundaries between Brigades will be :-

   Between 115th Bde. and 2nd Aust Div. - Grid line between W.15 & 21.

   Between 115th Bde. and 113th Brigade - E. & W. line drawn through W.9.c.central.

   Between 113th Bde. and 114th Brigade - The road at W.3.d.6.1 - W.3.central - W.2.b.central - thence along the BOUZINCOURT - MARTINSART road to the grid line between W.1. and W.7, thence due West.

   Between 114th Brigade and 17th Div. - The grid line between Squares Q and W.

4. Regulation intervals will be maintained on the march.

5. All details of relief will be arranged between Brigades direct.

6. All trench maps, air photos, trench stores and ammunition will be taken over and lists forwarded to this office.

7. Divisional Headquarters will remain at CONTAY.

8. ACKNOWLEDGE

                                    Lieut-Colonel,
                        General Staff, 38th (Welsh) Divn.

Issued to Signals at 8.45 p.m.

Copies to :- All Units 38th Division   47th Division
             V Corps   63rd Division
             V Corps R.A.   2nd Aust. Div.
             V Corps H.A.   R.T.O. RAINCHEVAL SIDING.
             D.A.D.P.S. V Corps   Area Comdts :- TOUTENCOURT
             12th Division   HERISSART
             17th Division   HEDAUVILLE.
             35th Division (2)

RELIEF TABLE TO ACCOMPANY 38TH DIVISION ORDER NO. 175.

1. Serial No.	2. Date. (MAY)	3. UNIT.	4. TO	5. In relief of	6. Remarks.
1.	1st.	113th Brigade (less 1 Bn.)	Bivouac near HEDAUVILLE less 1 Bn. to V.17.b.	106 I.Bde.	To arrive by 2.p.m. Transport to HARPONVILLE.
2.	1st/2nd.	One Coy.38th Bn.MGC.	Line, Left.	Right Bn.105th I.Bde.	Remains under command of 115th Brigade.
3.	1st/2nd.	One Bn. 115th Brigade	Line.		Transport no change.
4.	1st/2nd.	113th Brigade.	Line.	Left Bn.105th I.Bde. Right Bn. 104th I.Bde.	To arrive by 2.p.m. (*)
5.	2nd.	114th Brigade.(less 1 Bn)	Bivouac near HEDAUVILLE	105th I.Bde.	
6.	2nd/3rd.	114th Brigade	Line.	104 I.Bde., less 1 Bn.	
7.	2nd/3rd.	One Coy.38th Bn. MGC.	Line, Centre.		
8.	2nd/3rd.	One Coy.38th Bn. MGC.	Reserve and ENGLEBELMER Line.		
9.	1st.	19th Welsh Regt. (Pioneers)	Original bivouacs in V.3. etc.		Transport to HARPONVILLE.
10.	1st.	123rd & 151st Field Coy. R.E.	Bivouacs in V.8.	R.E., 35th Division.	Transport to HARPONVILLE.
11.	1st.	Div:Sniping Coy.H.Q. and H.Q. Section.	V.4.b.8.1.	35th Div:Observation Group.	
12.	2nd.	331st and 332nd Coys. A.S.C.	U.2.c.		
13.	—	H.Q. 38th Bn.M.G.C. No.3 Sec.38th D.A.C. Field Ambulances. 124th Fd.Coy. R.E.	NO CHANGE.		

NOTE - (*) = Transport to U.11.c. (Serial No. 5)

29th April 1918.

Army Form A. 2607.

CENTRAL REGISTRY.

Central Registry No. and Date. Attached Files.

Moves **38 DIV²**

SUBJECT, AND OFFICE OF ORIGIN.

SECRET

Referred to	Date.	Referred to	Date.	Referred to	Date.
				P. A.	Date.

Schedule of Correspondence.

Inter-Office Minutes.

NOTE.—Inside sheets to be attached to this page.

NOT TO BE WRITTEN ON.

"C" Form.
MESSAGES AND SIGNALS.
Army Form C. 2123.
(In books of 100.)
No. of Message ....

| Prefix | Code | Words 104 | Received From EaR By aB | Sent, or sent out At .... m. To .... By | Office Stamp |

Charges to collect

Service Instructions. Priority

Handed in at EaR .... Office 6.50 p.m. Received 7.37 p.m.

TO 4 Corps

Sender's Number | Day of Month | In reply to Number | AAA

Refce GB210 not sent to LUGGER and MANDRAKE aaa MANDRAKE less EAGLE but with HQ and three Sections MT Co will be transferred from ONYX to PEARL aaa MT Co by Road by ARBROATH and WEMBLEY remainder by rail aaa Entraining commences midnight 31/1st April aaa Detrain WEMBLEY and GATESHEAD aaa To be accommodated in LUGGER area E of ELTHAM-WEMBLEY Road to be allotted FLAGSHIP by LUGGER aaa MANDRAKE will be in PEARL reserve administered by FLAGSHIP aaa addd 10 and 5 Corps Reptd 1st Army 17th Div and 4 Corps and 38 Div

FROM
PLACE & TIME Third Army 6.5 p.m.

"C" Form
MESSAGES AND SIGNALS.
Army Form C. 2123.

Prefix	Code	Words 70	Received From CAR	Sent, or sent out At	
Charges to collect			By	To	
Service Instructions	Rly			By	
Handed in at			Office 5/10	Received	

TO: 4 Corps

*Sender's Number	Day of Month	In reply to Number	AAA
9B360	2		

Reference PEARL wire 9B299 dated 31st aaa MANDRAKE will not be released from PEARL Reserve and will not be used in front line but may be used to relieve reserve troops aaa LUGGER will report when GANNET of DAFFODIL now in line will be ready to move to ARBROATH area aaa ACKNOWLEDGED aaa Added 5 Corps Reptd 4 and 10 Corps

FROM PLACE & TIME: Third Army 5 pm

4th Corps.

GB 268   30.

Rpt GB 270 not sent to 5th. Corps + 38th. Divn.
38th Divn (less Arty) lent with HQ and 3 Sections
M.T. Co. will be transferred from First Army
to 3rd Army. M.T. Co. by road by FREVENT
and DOULLENS remainder by rail. Entraining
commences midnight 31/1st. April. Detrain
DOULLENS & MONDICOURT. To be accomodated in
5th Corps area E. of AMIENS - DOULLENS road
to be allotted by X Corps by 5th. Corps. 38th Divn
will be in 3rd Army Reserve administered by X
Corps. Addsd X & 5th Corps repto 1st Army 17th. C.
and 4th Corps & 38 Divn

Third Army   ✓
            6.5 pm

X Not rcd. gaws

(6339) Wt. W160/M3016 1,500,000 10/17 McA & W Ltd (E 1898) Forms W3091.   Army Form W.3091.

Cover for Documents.

Nature of Enclosures.

~~113 Inf. Bde Orders~~

Notes, or Letters written.

Vol. 30.

General Staff.
38th Division.
May 1918.

ORIGINAL

WAR DIARY of GENERAL STAFF 38th (Welsh) Division

INTELLIGENCE SUMMARY

VOLUME XXIX.

(Erase heading not required.)

Army Form C. 2118

Instructions regarding War Diaries and Intelligence Summaries are contained in F.S. Regs., Part II. and the Staff Manual respectively. Title Pages will be prepared in manuscript.

Vol 30

Place	Date	Hour	Summary of Events and Information	Remarks and references to Appendices
CONTAY.	MAY. 1918 1st.	1.30.a.m.	At 1.30.a.m. 17th Royal Welsh Fusiliers advanced their line under cover of a T.M. barrage & W.15.a.80.30. to C.80.80. 113th Brigade (less 1 Battalion) move to line Centre Section. G.S.O.2. and D.A.Q.M.G. inspect draft at Reinforcement Camp.	
	2nd.		One Battalion 113th Infantry Brigade move from MIRVAUX to Brigade Reserve. 114th Infantry Brigade (less 1 Battalion) move to Line Left Section. Hostile artillery engaged BOUZINCOURT and V.12. Divisional Sniping Coy obtained 3 hits during day.	
	3rd.		15th Welsh Regt move up into Reserve to 114th Infantry Brigade. Battery position in V.16.c. heavily engaged. 115th Infantry Brigade H.Q. lightly shelled by salvoes. Great aerial activity. G.S.O.1. went round the line Right Section.	
	4th.		Enemy shelling intermittent on SENLIS MILL, MARTINSART and BOUZINCOURT, and on battery areas along HEDAUVILLE ROAD. Enemy machine guns active by night in AVELUY WOOD. 6 E.A. over our lines in the evening.	
	5th.		G.O.C. visits Brigades.	
	6th.		BOUZINCOURT fairly heavily shelled by 10.5.c.m. and 15.c.m. Intermittent shelling on our battery areas. 10 E.A. over our lines. Our patrols found the enemy very alert. MARTINSART and HEDAUVILLE heavily shelled. Front line 113th Infantry Brigade heavily shelled in the afternoon. E.A. active.	
TOUTENCOURT.	7th.		Divisional Headquarters moves from CONTAY to TOUTENCOURT.	
	8th.		A few crashes on BOUZINCOURT. 12 E.A. over Centre Brigade during the evening. Patrols found enemy posts very alert. S.0176. Operation in Aveluy wood. Opp I Hostile artillery very active. Crashes on BOUZINCOURT and HEDAUVILLE. 300 rounds and some gas on battery areas. Heavy barrage at midnight on Centre and Right Brigade fronts.	
	9th.	4.a.m.	Under heavy barrage enemy attacked Right Battalion Right Brigade (also Right Flank Battalion). Enemy repulsed by our Lewis guns, though he penetrated on Right Flank Battalion front, from which he was later ejected. Hostile artillery active. Barrage on Right and Centre Bdes.	
	10th.		Patrols found enemy quiet. Our snipers obtained 25 certain hits 114th Brigade operation in AVELUY WOOD unsuccessful. No shelling of battery areas in reply to our barrage. G.O.C., 114th during the operation. Infantry Brigade visited all the companies in the line who had taken part in the attack. All Company Commanders were of opinion that the failure was due to our protective barrage coming down on top of the attackers.	
	11th.		Many crashes by the enemy artillery on front and support lines. Our snipers obtained 9	

Army Form C. 2118.

WAR DIARY
or
INTELLIGENCE SUMMARY

(Erase heading not required.)

Page 2.

Place	Date	Hour	Summary of Events and Information	Remarks and references to Appendices
TOUTENCOURT.	MAY 1918.			
	11th continued.		certain hits. G.O.C. visits G.O.C. 114th Infantry Brigade with a view to investigating the failure of the attack on AVELUY WOOD.	
	12th.		G.O.C. visited all Brigades. G.S.O.1 went round AVELUY WOOD. G.S.O.1. visited 47th Division. G.O.C., 63rd Division visited Divisional Commander. Warning Order received regarding relief of 38th Division by 35th Division. Usual enemy artillery crashes. An hours bombardment on front and support lines of the Centre and Right Brigades.	app I.
	13th.		G.S.O.2. visits Divisional Wing. "N" Special Company, R.E. attached to 113th Infantry Bde. 400 rounds on SENLIS area. Observers report unusual movement on Divisional front. GSS.10/66 issued regarding moves to be completed by noon 15th instant. GSS.10/66/1 issued regarding/relief of 38th Division by 35th Division.	app II. app III. app IV.
	14th.		Our snipers obtained 12 certain hits. Embankments behind MARTINSART heavily shelled. 150 rounds into SENLIS by day. Villages in forward area shelled by night. Our aircraft very active.	
	15th.		Usual enemy fire on forward villages. 12 E.A. over our lines. D.O. 177 issued regarding relief of Division by 35th Division.	app V.
	16th.		Enemy shelling confined to occasional crashes. 50 rounds Yellow Cross gas on MARTINSART WOOD. Our aircraft very active.	
	17th.		G.S.S. 2/33. Report on Operations for week ending 16/5/18.	
	18th.		O.C., 14th Royal Welsh Fusiliers viewed ground from Front line AVELUY CENTRE with a view to proposed raid. Our artillery carried out usual night programme.	
	19th.		G.O.C., visits 113th Infantry Brigade. 14th Royal Welsh Fusiliers and 16th Royal Welsh Fusiliers under cover of an artillery barrage carry out successful raid. 1 prisoner, 1 machine gun captured. Considerable retaliation to our raid bombardment. 100 rounds of all calibres on MARTINSART WOOD. SENLIS and HEDAUVILLE frequently shelled during the night.	
		G.O.C. and G.S.O.1. extended exercise for Brigadiers and Commanding Officers for carrying out counter-attack. Commanding Officers work out same scheme with Company Officers in the afternoon. 113th Infantry Brigade relieved in the line. Enemy put down heavy Artillery and Trench Mortar barrage about 9.40.p.m., but no Infantry attack followed. 114th and 115th Infantry Brigades relieved in the line. Hostile artillery more active at night. Some gas shelling of T.13. Divisional Headquarters close at TOUTENCOURT and open at	
HERISSART.	20th.	4.15.p.m.	Following received from Corps reference Divl. order 477. Command will Pass	app VI.

Army Form C. 2118.

WAR DIARY
or
INTELLIGENCE SUMMARY

(Erase heading not required.)

Page 3.

Place	Date	Hour	Summary of Events and Information	Remarks and references to Appendices
HERISSART.	MAY 1918. 21st.		and Divisional Headquarters close at TOUTENCOURT and open at HERISSART, on completion of relief. 114th Infantry Brigade move into TOUTENCOURT (less 1 Battalion) employed on work under C.R.E., V Corps. 115th Infantry Brigade move to HERISSART.	
	22nd.		All Brigades training. A second Battalion of 114th Infantry Brigade move up into forward area for work on burying cable. 2 machine gun companies report to 63rd Division for special operation.	
	23rd.		114th Infantry Brigade practises taking up Reserve Positions. MAJOR-GEN.L R.A. T.A. CUBITT, C.M.G., D.S.O., R.A., assumes command of the Division (from commanding 57th Infantry Brigade. Lecture by Corps Chemical Adviser.	
	24th.		G.O.C. inspected Brigades at training. Corps Commander met G.O.C. and inspected the men at Musketry.	
	25th.		115th Infantry Brigade and 2 R.E. companies have a rehearsal Ceremonial Parade. G.O.C. and G.S.O.1. visit 115th Infantry Brigade at training.	
	26th.		G.O.C. visited Divisional Artillery and (with G.S.O.2.) Divisional Reinforcement Camp. 14th Welsh Regt relieved 13th Welsh Regt, working in forward area.	
	27th.		Conference of Brigadiers at 9.15.a.m. to discuss details of tactical scheme with "Tanks" taking place to-morrow. Army Commander inspects 115th Infantry Brigade at 2.0.p.m. Corps Commander inspects 115th Infantry Brigade at 3.p.m. Conference held in connection with Musketry Competitions. 38th Divisional Artillery hold gymkhana at GEZAINCOURT.	
	28th.		115th Infantry Brigade (morning) and 115th Infantry Brigade (afternoon) take part in tactical exercise with tanks. G.O.C. attends both demonstrations. BRIGADIER-GENERAL HARMAN, D.S.O., acts as Chief Umpire. Corps Commander attends afternoon scheme. This proved a very valuable exercise to all.	
	29th.		Corps Commander inspects 38th Battalion Machine Gun Corps during the morning. G.S.O.2. holds Rifle Competition Conference at 6.p.m. Corps Commander inspected 114th Infantry Brigade, G.O.C. in attendance. G.O.C. also visited 2nd Royal Welsh Fusiliers, 17th Royal Welsh Fusiliers and 10th South Wales Borderers.	
	30th.		G.S.O.2. 63rd Division visits Divisional Headquarters. G.S.O.2. and G.S.O.3. reconnoitre ranges for rifle Competition. G.S.42 issued regarding attachment of personnel; abolishment of Divisional Sniping Company; and establishment of a Divisional Reception Camp.	

Army Form C. 2118.

WAR DIARY
or
INTELLIGENCE SUMMARY

Page 4.

(Erase heading not required.)

Instructions regarding War Diaries and Intelligence Summaries are contained in F. S. Regs., Part II. and the Staff Manual respectively. Title Pages will be prepared in manuscript.

Place	Date	Hour	Summary of Events and Information	Remarks and references to Appendices
	MAY 1918.			App IX
HERISSART.	31st.		O.O.178 issued - 58th Division will relieve 63rd Division in the MESNIL SECTOR. 115th Infantry Brigade carry out Tactical Schemes. 113th Infantry Brigade inspected by Corps Commander. 4 Vickers guns moved up to 35th Division area to assist in operation.	

[signature]
Captain,
Act/General Staff 38th (Welsh) Division.

COPY.   10/5/18.

Statement by Liaison Officer,
       157 Bde. R.F.A.

   Ruring reconnaissance of the front line on 10/5/18 between 12-30 and 12-40 p.m. I heard six heavy shells (about 6" and H.E.) far behind our line about W.4.a.40.40.
   During a further reconnaissance of the assembly positions at about 7.30.p.m. conclusive evidence was found of 18-pdr shells having fallen on the assembly line.
   Taking these facts into consideration and in view of the short time available for re-organization and registration it would seem absolutely impossible to have repeated the attack before dark.

                                   (sd) G.PHILLIPS.,
                                            Capt., R.F.A.
                          Arty Liaison Officer to 114th Inf.Bde.

Records of No.131 Field Ambulance show :-

           158 shell wounds.
            27 bullet.
            31 unclassified.

Of these last, 15 were multiple wounds and probably due to shells. The remaining 16 might be either.

Allowing them to be bullet, it would give

            Shell   173
            Bullet   43

                    216
                    ======

                                   (sd) A.G.THOMPSON, Colonel,

                          A.D.M.S., 38th (Welsh) Division.

C O P Y.   SECRET.

38th Div.G.   A.H.21.

REPORT ON OPERATION BY 114TH INFANTRY BRIGADE 10th May 1918.

The operation carried out this morning on the S.W. portion of AVELUY WOOD by this Brigade, was I regret to say a complete failure.

The moral of both Officers and men both before and after the attack was excellent and very good.

As soon as the Artillery had died away I sent my Brigade Major CAPTAIN BUCKNELL also the Artillery Liaison Officer CAPTAIN PHILLIPS up to the front to go round our new line and bring me back as soon as possible a full report both on the action and the present situation.

The report they brought me back was most disquieting, so in company with the Division Liaison Officer, CAPTAIN HARRINGTON, I went first to LIEUT-COLONEL PARKINSON's Headquarters, this officer being in command of the operations.

He was out, having gone up the line some two hours previous to this to reconnoitre the new line.

I decided to go on to the wood to meet him there, taking with me as guide LIEUT.THOMAS, 15th Welsh Regt., the Battalion Liaison Officer.

On my way up I met LIEUT-COLONEL PARKINSON returning, having issued his orders regarding re-organising and preparing to repeat the attack at an early hour (7.p.m.)

He told me what orders he had given which were briefly that companies were to reform on their original line as quickly as possible and to report as soon as this was done.

I approved of this.

I asked what he attributed the failure to, and he replied to one cause only, with that handing me one of our 18-pdr fuzes; I told him I had heard a remark to this effect but was going up myself to verify the statement as far as possible.

Having issued him with some further instructions as to the forming up for the fresh attack and the probable Zero hour, I went on to the WOOD.

I did not have far to go before I found evidence of some large and new craters in the vicinity of W.4.c. and R.34.c., they were not in my opinion the crater of the 106 fuze.

On going a little further I got to the assembly position where I found several 18-pdr cases and again near the forming up positions.

I then saw all the officers who were left, asking them for an account of the fight and their reasons for the failure.

According as to which part of the line they were in I was told-
That the left flank protective barrage was short, actually falling on their line of advance.
That the barrage seemed to come down on them in rear of the "creeping barrage", the third wave following the second being caught in it. That heavy shell, probably 6" or 4.5" fell actually on their assembly position.
That heavy shell fell on, and shrapnel burst over RUNNERS RIDE.
That smoke shell fell in the wood from Zero plus 10 seconds onwards throughout the operation in W.4.c.
The last statement the R.A. Liaison Officer and myself can both confirm

(2)

I further questioned very many of the N.C.O's and men, who all told me that the only thing that stopped them was artillery fire.

I then questioned all the stretcher bearers I could find as to whether the wounds were caused by rifle and machine gun fire or artillery, they said they were hardly any rifle bullet wounds.

The Medical Officer also said this.

Whether the shell fire was enemy fire or not, must be proved by the experts.

I attach a brief report by the R.A. Liaison Officer, CAPTAIN PHILLIPS.

There was also an R.A. Officer on the Staff of 63rd Division (?) who confirms the smoke shell and short shooting. I do not know his name.

I left the WOOD at about 4.p.m. and from what I had seen & realised the companies and platoons would not be re-organized before 5.p.m., the actual hour being 5.40.p.m. I also estimated 1½ hours would be required for forming up, which meant Zero could not be before 8.p.m.

On return to my advanced Headquarters I reported verbally also in writing to the Division and sent the Division Liaison Officer straight back so that he could give first hand information.

Shortly after this I got the order not to carry out any further attack so issued disposition orders and again went forward to satisfy myself that all was well, when I came away I left my Brigade Major in the wood to see that all was completed according to my orders.

The re-distribution was completed by 1.a.m. on 11th May 1918.

Apart from the question of the shell fire, I cannot help feeling that some of the failure may be due to lack of leadership on the part of junior N.C.O's.

The attack was carried out by section at 30 yards interval which meant that everything depended on the section leadership, the Officers could do no more than lead the section they were actually with, those on their flanks being almost out of sight and certainly out of hearing due to artillery and machine gun fire.

The Captain of the left flank company is missing and I have every confidence in saying that had it been possible for that company to go forward CAPTAIN STRANGE would have done it.

The estimated casualties are :-

	Officers.			Other ranks.	
	K.	W.	M.	K.	W. and M.
14th Welsh Regt.	-	1	1		47
15th Welsh Regt.	1	6	2		112
19th Welsh Regt.	-	2	-		50

No report has been received from Lt.Col.T.W.PARKINSON as yet.

(sd) A.HARMAN, Brig-Genl.,
Commdg. 114th Inf.Bde.

10-5-18.

Appendix V

SECRET

38th Division No. GSS. 2/33

V Corps

REPORT ON OPERATIONS FOR WEEK ENDING 16/5/1918

1. Our Artillery has continued to carry out harassing fire and 'Crashes' by night. Enemy working parties and movement on roads have been engaged.

2. Patrols have been out each night. We raided an enemy post at W.15.a. on the night 8th/9th May killing two of the occupants, but at 12.30 a.m. on 9th May, under cover of a heavy M.G. and T.M. barrage, the enemy succeeded in again driving us out.

Our snipers have obtained 64 hits during the past week.

At 8 p.m. on 15th May an enemy patrol approached our lines, but was driven off leaving one dead man belonging to the 1st Marine Regiment, 3rd Naval Division.

3. 10th instant

We attacked in AVELUY WOOD with the object of establishing a line running roughly along the ride W.4.c.8.1 to W.4.b.2.4. Zero hour was 9 a.m. Force employed, one and a half Battalions.

The position of assembly was along a ride running from W.4.a.6.9 to W.4.b.3.7, and the attack was made in a Southerly direction. There was no preliminary bombardment.

The troops advanced under a Creeping Barrage formed from the flank by 17th Divisional Artillery, and one Company 38th Bn. M.G.Corps. The Protective Barrage was formed by the 35th Divisional Artillery and V Corps Artillery, while destructive bombardments on known hostile positions in and near the wood were carried out also by 35th Divisional Artillery and V Corps Artillery. Harassing and sniping fire was maintained by one Company 35th Bn. M.G.Corps, and all known hostile positions on the remainder of the Divisional Front were kept under fire by 3" Stokes Mortars of the remaining two Infantry Brigades, and by the Artillery of the Division on our right.

The attack gained the first objective and advanced as far as W.4.a.3.0 - W.4.a.8.2 having met with a certain amount of opposition. But considerable casualties appear to have been caused hitherto by our own barrage which was falling short. Our shells continued to fall on, and in rear of our troops, and caused them to withdraw to our original line.

It was found that the disorganisation caused by casualties, and the density of the wood, were so great that it was decided to abandon the attack.

16th May 1918.

Major-General,
Commanding 38th (Welsh) Division.

Army Form W.3091.

Cover for Documents.

Nature of Enclosures.

~~Inf Bde Orders~~

Notes, or Letters written.

Vol. 31.

General Staff,
38th Division.

June 1918.

ORIGINAL.

Vol 31

Instructions regarding War Diaries and Intelligence Summaries are contained in F.S. Regs., Part II. and the Staff Manual respectively. Title pages will be prepared in manuscript.

WAR DIARY
OF
GENERAL STAFF 38TH (WELSH) DIVISION
INTELLIGENCE SUMMARY
VOL. XXX.

Army Form C. 2118.

Place	Date	Hour	Summary of Events and Information	Remarks and references to Appendices
HERISSART.	JUNE, 1918.			
	1st.		Brigades continued training as under :- 113th Infantry Brigade and 115th Infantry Brigade, Musketry and eliminating rounds of the A.R.A. Competitions. 114th Infantry Brigade Musketry and Company schemes.	
	2nd. 3rd.		G.O.C. inspected transport of the 38th Bn.M.G.Corps. Church parades. Divisional Rifle Meeting was held. Result of competitions see Appendix Reconnaissance of the line (MESNIL SECTOR) carried out by General Staff. 2nd Battalion 115th Infantry Brigade moved from HERISSART AREA to ACHEUX WOOD. Pioneer Battalion moved from HERISSART to VARENNES.	APP.
	4th.		Training was continued by 114th Infantry Brigade and by one Battalion 115th Infantry Brigade. 1 Battalion of 115th Infantry Brigade moved from HERISSART to Reserve Area Centre Brigade MESNIL SECTOR. 2 Battalions 115th Infantry Brigade moved from ACHEUX WOOD into the line in relief of 189th Infantry Brigade 63rd Division. Relief complete at 7.0.p.m.night 4/5th. 2 Battalions 113th Infantry Brigade moved from RUBEMPRE to ACHEUX WOOD. 2 Companies 38th Bn.M.G.C. moved from TOUTENCOURT to line in relief of Right and Left Coys. 63rd Battn. M.G.C.	
	5th.		Relief of 63rd Division in the MESNIL SECTOR was completed and G.O.C. 38th Division took command of the line. Divisional Headquarters closed at HERISSART at 7.p.m. and re-opened at LEALVILLERS at same hour. 38th Division Order 179 issued to Signals at 8.30.p.m.	APP. 2
LEALVILLERS.	6th.		The night was quiet, but there were small bursts of hostile shell fire occasionally. The dawn patrol R.A.F. reported the Divisional front quiet. The Divisional front was organized into a two Brigade front, with one Brigade in Reserve. This was completed by 4.55.a.m. 7th.	
	7th.		G.O.C. accompanied by G.S.O.1. reconnoitred the front of the Right Brigade. During the night there was some hostile artillery fire, but otherwise it was quiet. G.O.C. accompanied by G.S.O.2. reconnoitred the front of the Left Brigade and saw all Brigadiers. *Activity during the day was confined to slight and intermittent artillery fire by both sides. During the night there was nothing to report except intermittent shelling by both sides.	
	8th.		G.O.C. visited all Brigade Headquarters. At 10.15.a.m. the Division on our Right carried out a raid on the enemy's positions and we co-operated with artillery and Machine Gun fire. /9th.	

Army Form C. 2118.

WAR DIARY
or
INTELLIGENCE SUMMARY.
(Erase heading not required.)

Page 2.

Instructions regarding War Diaries and Intelligence Summaries are contained in F.S. Regs. Part II. and the Staff Manual respectively. Title pages will be prepared in manuscript.

Place	Date	Hour	Summary of Events and Information	Remarks and references to Appendices
LEALVILLERS.	JUNE, 1918.			
	9th.		There was some retaliatory fire on our front during the night, probably on account of our activity during the raid. The day was fairly quiet apart from some shelling of ENGLEBELMER. G.O.C. visited the trenches of the Right Brigade. At 5.p.m. 6 of the enemy attempted to rush one of our sentry posts in AVELUY WOOD, but were driven off by rifle fire. A reconnaissance of this area was immediately made and a cap and revolver marked 139 R. 10.C. were found. The identification was normal.	
	10th.		Apart from usual harassing fire by both sides the night was quiet. During the day hostile artillery was active, shelling our battery positions. Our Artillery shelled the enemy's back area. G.O.C. held a Conference of Brigade Commanders at H.Q. 115th Infantry Brigade.	
	11th.		There was slight gas shelling of one of our battery positions near ENGLEBELMER. One man is missing from our post. Under cover of a barrage the enemy raided the trenches of the Right Brigade.	
			Apart from slight shelling, nothing of importance occurred during the day, till 4.p.m. when a party of the enemy under cover of artillery fire tried to raid one of our Posts in AVELUY. The enemy was driven off leaving one * dead man in front of the post. His body was recovered. Identification - 139 I.R. 24 Saxon Division. 38th Division Order 180 issued to signals at 6.a.m.	APP. 3.
	12th.		The night was quiet. During the day usual artillery activity of a harassing nature took place. There was slight gas shelling of the Right Brigade Sector in AVELUY WOOD. (BLUE X).	
	13th.		There was some gas shelling of our trenches and the vicinity of Right and Left Brigade H.Q. both BLUE and YELLOW CROSS gas being used. Otherwise the night was quiet. The 114th Infantry Brigade relieved the 115th Infantry Brigade in the Right Brigade Sector. Replica marked out for special operation.	
	14th.		The night passed quietly. During the day there was slight shelling of our forward trenches. Otherwise it was quiet. The Evening Patrol Aeroplane reported considerable movement of M.T. behind the enemy's lines in the neighbourhood of POZIERES, FRICOURT, BECORDEL. At about 6.25.p.m. a small hostile biplane dropped 4 bombs on the support trenches of the Left Brigade.	
	15th.		The night was quiet, on the Divisional front, but an S.O.S. signal to the south was observed at 2.a.m.. It did not extend. The day passed quietly. Owing to low clouds andconsiderable wind aerial observation was difficult.	

/16th.

WAR DIARY or INTELLIGENCE SUMMARY.

Army Form C. 2118.

Page 3.

Place	Date	Hour	Summary of Events and Information	Remarks and references to Appendices
LEALVILLERS.	JUNE 1918.			
	16th.		The night was quiet. The G.O.C. visited the line of the Left Brigade and Headquarters 113th, 114th and 115th Infantry Brigades, and H.Q., 13th Welsh Regt. At 6.a.m. a hostile plane dropped 3 small bombs on MESNIL. There was considerable aerial activity between 6.a.m. and 10.a.m. 2nd and 14th Battalions Royal Welsh Fusiliers practised at night on the replica for the special operation.	
	17th.		The night was quiet apart from some slight shelling of one of our battery positions in ENGLESART VALLEY. During the day the usual harassing fire of tracks and valleys took place. There was more H.V. gun activity than usual.	
	18th.		The night was quiet. At 9.15.a.m. one of our planes was brought down by hostile A.A. fire and crashed behind the German trenches. 2nd and 14th Royal Welsh Fusiliers practised over replica. G.O.C. was present. At 3.p.m. The Corps Commander (LIEUTENANT-GENERAL SHUTE) inspected the troops practising over the replica. The day was quiet and nothing more than the usual activity was reported.	App 5
	19th.		The night was quiet and there was nothing to report. G.O.C. reconnoitred front line of the INTERMEDIATE SYSTEM and the PURPLE SYSTEM north of the ENGLEBELMER - MARTINSART ROAD and visited 113th and 114th Infantry Brigade H.Q. In the afternoon G.O.C. went to the Divisional Reception Camp at VALHEUREUX accompanied by G.O.C., 115th Infantry Brigade and G.S.O.2. The activity during the day was normal. During the evening hostile H.V. guns were active on back areas, from 7.30.p.m. A Chinese attack was carried out in AVELUY WOOD from 12.midnight till 2.50.a.m. The enemy's retaliation to our fire was not heavy, on the Divisional front.	App 4
	20th.		After the Chinese attack the shelling was intermittent during the remainder of the night. G.O.C. visited all Brigade H.Qrs. The weather was variable during the day, but during the fine intervals both sides carried out harassing fire. At 10.p.m. ☆ the 2nd and 14th Battalions Royal Welsh Fusiliers moved from the bivouacs in the vicinity of FORCEVILLE and marched to the assembly positions for a raid on the enemy's positions along the railway line running N. from AUTHVILLE to HAMEL. At 2.5.a.m. under cover of artillery, T.M. and M.G. Barrages the troops advanced to their objectives, only to find them to be unoccupied. One machine gun was captured and several dugouts bombed or blown up. Identification NIL. Our casualties were slight. At 9.45.p.m. a hostile patrol lay in wait for our visiting /patrol	

WAR DIARY
INTELLIGENCE SUMMARY

Army Form C. 2118.

Page 4.

Place	Date	Hour	Summary of Events and Information	Remarks and references to Appendices
LEALVILLERS.	JUNE, 1918.			
	20th. (continued.)		patrol 2 N.C.O's and 1.O.R. near a post in AVELUY WOOD, and on their approach opened fire wounding all three: the other rank is missing. Afterwards there was only slight retaliation for raid and this ceased at about 2.40.a.m. The night was quiet. G.S.O.3. returned from leave and G.S.O.2. proceeded on leave. G.O.C. visited 2nd and 14th Royal Welsh Fusiliers and interviewed several of the officers and men who partook in the raid. During the day there was practically no shelling of the forward positions but HEDAUVILLE, FORCEVILLE and ENGLEBELMER received some attention. The night passed quietly.	app 6
	21st.			
	22nd.		Apart from some slight hostile T.M. activity on the Right Brigade front there was only the usual harassing fire during the day. The weather was bad and there was no aerial activity. The 115th Infantry Brigade relieved the 113th Infantry Brigade in the MESNIL Left Sector. On relief the 113th Infantry Brigade came into Divisional Reserve.	
	23rd.		Apart from some artillery activity in the neighbourhood of HILL 142 during the morning, the day was quiet. H.V. guns were active on FORCEVILLE during the early part of the night. G.O.C. visited the trenches of both front line Brigades in the morning.	
	24th.		The night passed quietly. A patrol of the 2nd Royal Welsh Fusiliers endeavoured to locate and cut out a hostile post. They got into the enemy's trenches and on their way found an abandoned post containing rifle, bayonet and cap. These were brought in. Although the patrol remained in the enemy's lines 45 minutes no other trace of the enemy was seen. There was a slight increase in hostile aircraft activity, probably due to improvement in the weather. During the day the artillery of both sides carried out usual harassing programmes.	
	25th.		During the day there was a slight increase in hostile artillery activity, as compared with that of previous few days. This activity continued till about 9.30.p.m. when it gradually died down. A small raiding party (2 platoons) of 2nd Royal Welsh Fusiliers endeavoured to cut out a hostile post N. of HAMEL, but were held up by wire during which time the enemy got away. As they ran they were fired upon and it is believed that 3 of them were hit. The raiders remained in the enemy trench for 55 minutes, but nothing further was seen of the enemy. One rifle was found and brought back. We had no casualties.	
	26th.		There was rather more hostile artillery activity than usual during the night. /The 2nd	

WAR DIARY
INTELLIGENCE SUMMARY.

Army Form C. 2118.
Page 5.

Place	Date	Hour	Summary of Events and Information	Remarks and references to Appendices
LEALVILLERS.	JUNE, 1918.			
	26th.		(continued). The 2nd Royal Welsh Fusiliers with one company attempted to cut out a suspected hostile post near HAMEL. They entered the enemy's trenches and remained there for over an hour but found no trace of the enemy. A small party of the enemy approached one of our posts in AVELUY WOOD but were engaged by rifle fire and driven off. At about 4.30.a.m. 27th one of the enemy was seen in our lines and was shot; his body was secured. (Identification 3rd Battn. 1st MARINE INFANTRY REGT.) This confirms the rumour that the 24th Saxon Division has been relieved.	
	27th.		The night was quiet. There was a slight decrease in the activity of hostile artillery during the day. Hostile planes were active during the morning and evening. A fighting patrol of 2nd Royal Welsh Fusiliers endeavoured to raid the enemy's trenches in the vicinity of HAMEL, but encountered strong resistance from rifles and bombs. They returned to our lines and re-organised and attempted the raid with the same result. The party returned to our lines at 2.30.a.m. after being out 4½ hours. The remainder of the Divisional front was covered by reconnoitring patrols which did not encounter the enemy.	app. 7
	28th.		Quiet night. The Divisional front was organised into a one Brigadefront, and after midnight 27/28th the dispositions were as follows:- Line Brigade - 125th Infantry Brigade, Support - 114th Infantry Brigade, Reserve Brigade - 113th Infantry Brigade. During the early morning E.A. were active over our lines and some long distance reconnaissance planes passed high over the Divisional area going west. Hostile artillery activity was normal.	
	29th.		The night was quiet. During the day the activity of both sides was normal. H.O.C. reconnoitred the BROWN LINE from FORCEVILLE to BEAUSART. Corps Commander visited G.O.C. at 1.p.m.	
	30th.		There was considerable gas shelling during the night, ENGLEBELMER in particular receiving attention. The gas was chiefly BLUE CROSS followed by YELLOW CROSS. G.O.C. held a Conference of G.O's.C. Brigades, and Battalion Commanders at Support Brigade H.Q. During the night the 12th Division on our Right carried out a minor operation with success. Our artillery and M.G's co-operated. Hostile retaliation was not heavy.	app. 8

June 1918.

Abernay Jones. Captain,
General Staff 38th (Welsh) Division.

War Diary

38th Division No. GSS. 2/33

V Corps

REPORT ON OPERATIONS FOR WEEK ENDING 13/6/1918

1. Our Artillery has continued to carry out 'crashes' and harassing fire by night.
Movement behind the enemy's line has also been successfully engaged.

2. Hostile Artillery during the period under review has confined its activity to slight and intermittent harassing fire by day and night. On two occasions only has gas shelling been reported, when both BLUE and YELLOW CROSS gas was used. Some 'crashes' have been fired; all in the vicinity of ENGLEBELMER.
On the night of the 8th instant there was some retaliatory fire on our front system, probably the result of our co-operation with the Division on our left in their enterprise on that night.

3. The Divisional front has been patrolled nightly, but the enemy was not encountered.
At about five p.m. on the evening of the 9th inst. 6 of the enemy attempted to rush one of our posts in AVELUY WOOD. They were engaged by rifle fire and driven off. A reconnaissance of the ground later produced a cap and a revolver marked 139 I.R. 10th C. (Identification normal).
At about 9 p.m. on 11th instant, a party of the enemy, under cover of artillery fire, raided one of our posts in AVELUY WOOD (Q.34.d.9.6). One of our men is missing.
At 3.35 p.m. on the 11th instant, after heavy artillery fire, the enemy attempted to raid our post at Q.34.d.45.60. The leader was killed, and his body recovered. He belonged to 139 I.R. (Identification normal).

13/6/1918.

Major-General,
Commanding 38th (Welsh) Division.

38th Division No.GSS.2/33.

V Corps.

REPORT ON OPERATIONS FOR WEEK ENDING 20/6/18.

1. Our Artillery has, during the period under review, carried out the usual harassing fire and "crashes" by day and by night.

On night of 19/20th June our artillery co-operated in the "Chinese attack" on the enemy positions east of AVELUY WOOD, and No.2.Special Company R.E., fired 296 4" Stokes gas shells on the line of the railway in Q.29.b. in conjunction with the above.

2. Hostile artillery activity has not shown any material increase during the past week but there has been slightly more shelling of our forward trenches.

Gas shelling was reported four times and both BLUE and YELLOW Cross were used. Gas shelling was confined to valleys, and ENGLEBELMER VILLAGE.

Retaliation for our shelling during the "Chinese Attack" was slight and consisted of 4.2's, Light and Heavy T.M's.on the front line and forward communication trenches, and 77.m.m. on the support lines.

3. The Divisional front was patrolled nightly.

The enemy was encountered twice and shots were exchanged. We did not suffer casualties on either occasion.

20/6/18.
Major-General,
Commanding 38th (Welsh) Division.

38th Division No.GSS.2/33

V Corps.

REPORT ON OPERATIONS FOR WEEK ENDING 26/6/18.

1.   Our Artillery fire during the past week has been normal and has consisted chiefly of harassing fire by day and night.
        Working parties have been engaged and dispersed and individual movement and transport has also been fired upon with success.
        On the night 20/21st inst. our artillery co-operated in a raid on the enemy's trenches and put down a barrage in support of the Infantry. At 3-30 a.m. on the same night they fired on "S.O.S." lines in accordance with the Raid Scheme.

2.   Hostile Artillery has shown increased activity on only two occasions during the period under review - on June 24th and between 6 a.m. 25th and 6 a.m. 26th.
        Except once when CHARLES AVENUE was heavily shelled, hostile artillery has shown a tendency to shoot more on back areas than during the two previous weeks.
        Gas shelling has been reported on four occasions; Yellow, Blue, and Green Cross shells have been used. The concentrations were, however, only slight.
        Retaliation for our operation on 20/21 June was only slight.

3.   Patrols have been active on the Divisional Front each night.
        Four small expeditions into the enemy's trenches have been attempted, but though on each occasion our party entered their trenches the enemy was only encountered once. On two occasions articles of equipment and rifles were brought back to our trenches, but no identification was secured.
        On the night 20/21st June, three companies of 2nd R.W.F. (115th Brigade) and the whole of the 14th R.W.F. (113th Brigade) carried out a combined raid on the enemy's posts and dugouts on the line Q.35.B.5.5. to Q.23.d.5.0. The raid was supported by the following troops from other Divisions:-
                Corps Heavy Artillery.
                Artillery of Flank Divisions.
                35th Bn.M.G.Corps.
                One Section No.3 Special Coy R.E.
                No. 12 Squadron M.G.Corps.
        Zero was at 2-5 a.m.
        The objective was reached along the whole line except on the extreme right where the raiders were held up by a hostile T.M.Barrage. On the approach of our raiders small parties of the enemy were seen retiring and were fired upon; they left one machine gun in our hands. One hostile post heavily wired held out and as the wire was too thick to cut in the time available, the garrison was engaged with rifle grenades, rifle fire and bombs, and descended into a dugout after losing at least two men hit.
        Eight dugouts were demolished by parties of R.E. who accompanied the raiders carrying mobile charges.
        The raid withdrew as arranged at 2-35 a.m.
        Casualties 47, all caused by hostile artillery fire which he opened on the objective.

4.   On night 20/21st a small enemy party lay in wait on the parapet of a Communication Trench leading to one of our posts in AVELUY WOOD (Q.35.A.20.00.) and fired upon a visiting patrol of 2 N.C.Os and 1 O.R. Both N.C.Os. were wounded, and the O.R. was also seen to fall. The O.R. is missing.

27/6/18.   Major-General,
                        Commanding 38th (Welsh) Division.

Vol. 32.

General Staff,
38th Division.

July 1918.

(6339) Wt. W160/M3016 1,500,000 10/17 McA & W Ltd (E1898) Forms W3091.   Army Form W.3091.

Cover for Documents.

Nature of Enclosures.

~~45 Inf Bde Orders~~

Notes, or Letters written.

ORIGINAL Vol XXXI App I

WAR DIARY OF GENERAL STAFF 38th (Welsh) Division
INTELLIGENCE SUMMARY.

Army Form C. 2118.
VOLUME XXXI

(Erase heading not required.)

Instructions regarding War Diaries and Intelligence Summaries are contained in F.S. Regs... Part II. and the Staff Manual respectively. Title pages will be prepared in manuscript.

Place	Date	Hour	Summary of Events and Information	Remarks and references to Appendices
LEALVILLERS.	JULY 1918. 1st		The night was quiet on our front, but there was considerable artillery activity on the Right Division front in connection with their operation. Our artillery co-operated. The day was exceedingly quiet, practically no activity being reported.	
	2nd.		During the night the enemy counter-attacked the Division on our Right and forced them to yield some of the ground taken the previous night. 113th Infantry Brigade relieved 115th Infantry Brigade in the Line. At about 10.p.m. the enemy attempted to raid two of our posts in AVELUY WOOD. They were engaged with rifle fire and driven off. It is believed that casualties were inflicted on them. LEALVILLERS was heavily shelled by H.V. gun. Some casualties were suffered. The day was very quiet.	
	3rd.		The night was quiet on our front, but the enemy further counter-attacked the Division on our Right and forced them to retire to their original position. The day was particularly quiet. The G.O.C. visited front line of the whole Divisional sector and also all Brigade H.Q.	
	4th.		The night was quiet. During the early morning considerable movement was seen behind the enemy's lines. This was probably due to the relief of the 3rd Naval Division. This movement was engaged by Artillery. The day was quiet, but there was considerable aerial activity during the evening.	
	5th.		The night was quiet apart from some artillery activity at 12.30.a.m. in support of a raid by the Division on our Left, in which our artillery co-operated. There was only slight activity by day; this included shelling of MESNIL.	
	6th.		The night passed quietly. During the day activity of both sides was normal. Enemy shelled area just North of MESNIL with 5.9 Hows. Division on our right reported a new gas shell - gas said to smell like "mint".	
	7th.		The night was quiet. During the day hostile artillery activity was only slight apart from two heavy "crashes" on ENGLEBELMER. Our artillery was active throughout the day. Visibility was poor. At 11.10.p.m. the Right Supporting Division had a practice "Stand-to". This was cancelled at 6.a.m. G.O.C. held a Conference at Divisional H.Q. following were present. G.O.C., G.S.O.1., G.O's.C. 113th 115th Bdes., A.A.&.Q.M.G., C.R.A., C.R.E., A.D.M.S.	AQ/88
	8th.		The night passed quietly. At 4.15.a.m. the enemy shelled our positions in the vicinity of AVELUY WOOD and MESNIL with T.M's, 4.2" and 77.m.m. This bombardment lasted till 5.30.p.m. The remainder of the day was very quiet. There was some aerial activity in the early morning. During the afternoon one of our patrols endeavoured to rush a hostile post N. of AVELUY WOOD but were prevented by wire. The two sentries were however shot. /9th.	

Army Form C. 2118.

WAR DIARY
or
INTELLIGENCE SUMMARY.

(Erase heading not required.)

Page 2.

Instructions regarding War Diaries and Intelligence Summaries are contained in F.S. Regs., Part II. and the Staff Manual respectively. Title pages will be prepared in manuscript.

Place	Date	Hour	Summary of Events and Information	Remarks and references to Appendices
LEALVILLERS.	JULY 1918.			
	9th.		The night was quiet. During the day hostile artillery was inactive. Visibility was good in the morning but became bad from noon onwards. 2nd Royal Welsh Fusiliers carried out a rehearsal for minor operation, on replica near FORCEVILLE: G.S.O.2. present. During the night the enemy fired some gas shells on FORCEVILLE - HEDAUVILLE Road otherwise the night was quiet. 115th Infantry Brigade (less 2nd Royal Welsh Fusiliers) relieved	
	10th.		113th Infantry Brigade (less 13th Royal Welsh Fusiliers) in the front line night 9/10th July. Apart from a few H.V. shells on VARENNES during the afternoon hostile artillery was inactive. At 12.45.p.m. E.A. brought down the VARENNES balloon in flames. 2nd Royal Welsh Fusiliers carried out final practice for minor operation. Corps Commander, G.O.C., and G.S.O.1. present. Afterwards 2nd Royal Welsh Fusiliers proceeded to their assembly positions in the INTERMEDIATE SYSTEM. 00 189. 00 190	Aff II III
	11th.		The night was quiet. During the day hostile artillery activity showed a slight decrease. 2nd Royal Welsh Fusiliers spent the day in their assembly positions preparatory to moving up for the raid on hostile positions around HAMEL. At 11.p.m. under cover of artillery and machine gun barrages 2nd Royal Welsh Fusiliers raided the enemy's trenches and reached their objectives without much opposition. 1 wounded and 18 unwounded prisoners and 1 machine gun were captured. Our casualties were slight. After raid 2nd Royal Welsh Fusiliers returned to billets near FORCEVILLE. 00 191	Aff IV
	12th.		After the barrage for the raid died down the night was quiet. Hostile reply to our barrage was weak and consisted of T.M's and M.G's chiefly. G.O.C. visited 2nd Royal Welsh Fusiliers and 114th Infantry Brigade. Corps Commander visited G.O.C. at Divisional Headquarters. Army Commander. (GENERAL BYNG) issued his congratulations for successful raid. Hostile artillery showed slight increase in activity. 00 192 Warning order that 21st Division would relieve 38th Division received.	Aff V
	13th.		During the night N Special Coy.R.E. discharged 600 gas projectors on HAMEL and trenches in vicinity. 63rd Division on our left carried out successful raid on which our artillery and machine guns co-operated. G.O.C. visited 113th Infantry Brigade and 2nd Royal Welsh Fusiliers and afterwards inspected the wagon lines of 121st Brigade R.F.A. /Hostile	

Army Form C. 2118

WAR DIARY
or
INTELLIGENCE SUMMARY

(Erase heading not required.)

Page 3.

Place	Date	Hour	Summary of Events and Information	Remarks and references to Appendices
LEALVILLERS.	JULY 1918.			
	13th. (contd).		Hostile artillery was quiet during the morning, but showed a slight increase in activity during the afternoon. 38th Div.Operation Order No.193 issued.	
	14th.		2nd Royal Welsh Fusiliers relieved 13th Royal Welsh Fusiliers as support Battalion of Brigade in Line. Enemy Artillery very quiet. G.O.C. visited all Brigades. Quiet day and night. O.O.193	Off VI
	15th.		G.O.C. with A/G.S.O.2. visits PURPLE LINE and INTERMEDIATE SYSTEM. CAPTAIN KING, M.C., Brigade Major 115th Infantry Brigade joins Division with view to acting G.S.O.2.	
	16th.		Orders received cancelling relief arrangements and substituting fresh ones to the effect that Division would be relieved by 17th and 63rd Divisions. No abnormal hostile activity. Divisional Order No.194 issued. G.O.C. visits S. part of Corps Defences.	Ord. Off.
	17th.		Quiet day. G.O.C. inspects part of BROWN LINE to be occupied by 113th Infantry Brigade. A/G.S.O.1. visits 115th Infantry Brigade. O.O.195 issued. Enemy artillery active during the night. O.O.195	App VII
	18th.		G.O.C. visits all Brigades, and inspects some refilling points and wagon lines. Situation quiet generally. Relief of Division by 17th and 63rd Divisions commences. One of our Sniping Posts rushed by hostile patrol and one sniper captured.	
	19th.		Divisional relief completed. Command of Div.Artillery passes to flank Divisions. M.G.Battalion relieved. Defence Scheme as Right Supporting Division issued.	
	20th.		Corps Commander and B.G., G.S., visit G.O.C. G.S.O.1. returns from leave in ENGLAND. Training commences. E.A. dropped a bomb on U.I.e.. No casualties.	OO.196. App.14
	21st. 22nd.		Two Brigades training, and one on work BROWN LINE. (HEDAUVILLE). G.O.C. visits 115th Infantry Brigade at training. G.S.O.1. and G.S.O.2. visited HERISSART AREA with a view to placing all Trench Mortar Batteries under D.T.M.O. for training purposes. MAJOR G.E.TALLENTS, D.S.O. assumed duty as G.S.O.2.Training at G.H.Q. MAJOR M.KING, M.C., assumes duty as officiating G.S.O.2. 38th Division.	
	23rd.		Very little training possible owing to wet weather. G.S.O.1. visited all Brigades. Meeting at Divisional Headquarters of Sports Committee.	
	24th.		G.O.C. attended Semi-final of Divisional Boxing Competition. Brigades training.	
	25th.		G.O.C., G.S.O.1. and C.R.A. attend Corps Conference at VAL VION CHATEAU. 114th and 115th Infantry Brigades carry out tracer bullet demonstration.	

Army Form C. 2118.

WAR DIARY
or
INTELLIGENCE SUMMARY.

Page 4.

(Erase heading not required.)

Place	Date	Hour	Summary of Events and Information	Remarks and references to Appendices
LEALVILLERS.	JULY 1918.			OP/ x
	26th.		G.O.C. visited 17th Division in connection with proposed raid on whole of Corps front. Lectures alone possible possible owing to wet weather. R.E. sports. Final of Divisional Boxing Competition at TOUTENCOURT.	
	27th.		Two Brigades training, one Brigade on work near HEDAUVILLE. Corps Commander visited G.O.C.	
	28th.		Conference at Divisional Headquarters attended by Brigadiers and O.C., M.G.Battalion to discuss attack scheme on Corps front. LIEUT.FERRIS, R.M.A., reported for duty as Divisional Educational Officer.	
	29th.		Corps Commander and G.O.C. inspected 14th Welsh Regt in Battalion attack scheme. 63rd Division leave Corps and 38th Division become Right and Left Supporting Division. 00109 Divisional Order No. 197 issued regarding moves of 113th and 115th Infantry Brigades.(29th) 115th Infantry Brigade move to ACHEUX. 113th Infantry Brigade move to RAINCHEVAL and ARQUEVES. G.O.C. inspects 114th Infantry Brigade in Battalion Tactical Exercise.	
	30th.		114th Infantry Brigade holiday and Sports Meeting (to celebrate the capture of PILCKEM July 1917.)	
	31st.		G.S.O.2. arranges ground for replica in connection with proposed scheme by 114th Infantry Brigade for capturing high ground N.W. of ALBERT.	

July 1918.

T. J. Hering
Captain,
General Staff 38th (Welsh) Division.

War Diary

SECRET

38th Division No. GSS. 2/33

V Corps

WEEKLY REPORT ON OPERATIONS

Week ending 10th July 1918

1. Our Artillery fire has been normal during the past week. The usual harassing fire has been carried out, and some 'crashes' have been fired on SUNKEN ROAD Q.36.d.4.9 and Q.36.c.0.2.
   Movement has been engaged with success on four occasions.
   Destructive shoots have also been carried out on enemy's works and defences.

2. Hostile Artillery activity has shown a slight decrease by day, but an increase has been noticed during the night.
   Activity by day has been confined chiefly to scattered harassing fire on the forward trenches and tracks.
   By night harassing fire has been fairly heavy, and, in addition, some crashes have also been fired on Valleys, and the Railway running N. from MESNIL.
   Between 4.45 and 5.30 a.m. on 8th July, there was a heavy concentrated bombardment of Q.28.c., Q.34.a. and CUTHBERT AVENUE, consisting of 77 mm, 10.5 cm. and M.T.M's; about 300 rounds were fired. This shoot was observed by E.A.
   Gas has been reported on two occasions; YELLOW and BLUE CROSS and PHOSGENE being used.
   The PURPLE System in Q.25. and Q.31 has also received some attention, chiefly during the night.

3. Our patrols have been active nightly along the whole Divisional Front.
   On night of 6th/7th July one of our patrols rushed an enemy post at Q.29.d.50.30. The two occupants ran away, and no identifications were secured, though the enemy were fired on.
   On night of 7th/8th July one of our reconnoitring patrols encountered a party of the enemy estimated at 40 moving towards our lines. Posts were warned and fire opened upon them. A reconnaissance of the ground afterwards did not produce an identification.
   A daylight patrol on afternoon of 8th July shot two sentries in the trench leading to our lines from Q.35.b.55.60.

4. On night of 8th/9th July at 1.45 a.m. a party of about 12 of the enemy attempted to raid our Post at Q.35.a.70.35. Fire was opened and the enemy dispersed.
   Otherwise, hostile Infantry was inactive. They were, however, alert in their Posts when they were approached by our patrols.

11th July 1918.

Major-General,
Commanding 38th (Welsh) Divn.

Copies to :- 17th Division
             63rd Division

SECRET.

COPY NO. 6

OPERATION ORDER No. 171

2nd BATTALION ROYAL WELSH FUSILIERS.

115TH INFANTRY BRIGADE
10th JUL 1918
No. BM 9117

Ref. Map 57D.S.E. 1/20,000.

1. **Objective and General plan.**
    On the night 11/12th July 1918, (Zero will be notified later)
    (a) The 2nd Batt. R.W.F. will carry out a raid on HAMEL, with a view to killing Germans, obtaining identifications, capturing enemy material, and inflicting damage to dugouts and works.

    (b) <u>Area</u>. Right Boundary:- The Railway.
        Left Boundary:- Q.23.c.10.60. to Q.23.a.90.80.

    (c) <u>Objective</u>. A line from Q.24.a.0.2. to Q.23.a.9.8.

    (d) <u>Direction of attack</u>. N.E.

    (e) <u>Strength</u>. One Battalion - 3 Companies assaulting.
                      1. Coy. forming defensive Right flank.

    (f) <u>Formation</u>.
        The 3 assaulting Companies will assault in three lines, the first line will consist of, 2 platoons per Company, and will go straight to the objective.
        The Second and Third lines will each consist of, one platoon per Company, and will go straight to their respective areas, for mopping up.
        The Right Flank Company, will be formed up in column of Platoons, each platoon at Zero, going straight to its objective.

2. (a) <u>Troops to be used</u>.
       Infantry. 1. Battalion.
       R.E. with 10 mobile charges.
       Covered by:-
           R.F.A. & R.G.A. as per programme.
           M.Gs, 12 Batteries of 8 guns each.
           L.T.M.B., 8 guns.

   (b) <u>Preparation of exit from our trenches</u>.
       There will be prepared on the night before the raid takes place, section boards and tapes, the latter giving direction, from Front line trench, through forming up area, and a suitable number of yards (10/15 yards) beyond. These tapes will be run out either by section Commanders, or their second-in-command of leading line at Zero minus 60. Covering parties, will occupy the whole Front line trench, at the same time.

   (c) <u>Forming up</u>. At Zero minus 15, all troops will be formed up in front of HAMEL OUTPOSTS, ready to advance at Zero.

   (d) <u>Direction</u>. Every Officer must check the direction of advance by Compass at the forming up position. The compass should be used as far as possible both in the advance and withdrawal.

   (e) <u>Task</u>. The first line will assault and seize the objective, pushing out strong covering parties in front, and up enemy C.Ts., where there are several M.G. positions, and is responsible for cleaning up the objective.
       The second and third lines clean up their respective areas in rear, to which each Platoon is detailed.
       Frontage of each of the three assaulting Companies, 175 yards.

   (f) The first line will attack in small columns.
       The 2nd and 3rd lines will advance in small columns.
       Distance between 1st and 2nd line, will be 20 yards.
       Distance between 2nd and 3rd line will be 30 yards.

(g)/.

page (2)

(g) **Mopping up.**

Owing to the enemy holding the village, by a system of mobile outposts, the two rear platoons of each Company are detailed to mop up their respective areas. There are no trench lines to enable definite names to mop up definite trenches. Each mopping up section, should carry two sandbags to collect identities, and booty.

(h) Lewis Guns will be used to defend the Right flank, and will fire on the Bridges and any active enemy MG's in MILL ROAD. Eight Lewis Guns will be pushed out in front of the objective, alternate guns firing North and N.E. respectively.

(i) No posts or Strong points will be constructed.

(j) Four L.T.M.Bs will fire into the reverse slope of the Bank in Q.29.b.
   Zero to Zero plus 5 - 10 rounds per gun per minute.
   Zero plus 5 to Zero plus 60 - 2 rounds per gun per minute.
   4 L.T.M.Bs on wire in Q.25.a. Hurricane fire Zero to Zero plus 2.

(k) Distribution of strength and duties of various parties.

(i) **Assaulting Coys.**   Right Front Coy.   4 Officers 115 O.R.

LEFT PLATOON			RIGHT PLATOON		
1 Officer & runner.			One Officer & runner.		
Bombers & R.G.	Bombers L.G.	etc.	Bombers etc.	L.G.	Bombers & R.G.
1.N.C.O. & 8 men.	1.N.C.O. & 7 men.	1.N.C.O. & 8 men.	1.N.C.O. & 8 men.	1.N.C.O. & 6 men.	1.N.C.O. & 9 men.

1st MOPPING UP WAVE.

Coy. H.Q.   1 Officer, 1.C.S.M. and 2 runners.

Left Section.	Centre Section.	Right Section.
1.N.C.O. & 5 men. 2 Stretcher Brs.	1.N.C.O. & 7 men.	1.N.C.O. & 5 men. 2. R.E's.

2nd MOPPING UP WAVE.

1. Officer, 1 N.C.O. and 1 runner.

Left Section.	Centre Section.	Right Section.
1.N.C.O. & 8 men.	1.N.C.O. & 7 Men. 2. R.E's. 2.S.B's.	1.N.C.O. & 6 men. 2. R.E's.

Two Checkers in.

(k) **LEFT FRONT COMPANY.**   4 Officers 112 O.R.

LEFT PLATOON			RIGHT PLATOON		
1 Officer & runner.			1 Officer & runner.		
L.G.	Bombers.	R.G.	R.G.	Bombers.	L.G.
1.N.C.O. & 10 men.	1.N.C.O. & 6 men.	1.N.C.O. & 8 men.	1.N.C.O. & 6 men.	1.N.C.O. & 6 men.	1.N.C.O. & 10 men.

FIRST MOPPING UP WAVE.   1 Officer and runner.

LEFT SECTION.	CENTRE SECTION.	RIGHT SECTION.
1.N.C.O. & 9 men. 2. R.E's.	1.N.C.O. & 6 men. 2. S.B's.	1.N.C.O. & 6 men.

2nd Mopping/.

Page (3)

LEFT FRONT COY (cont'd)

SECOND MOPPING UP WAVE. 1. Officer & 2 runners.

LEFT SECTION.	CENTRE SECTION.	RIGHT SECTION.
2.N.C.Os & 6 men.	1.N.C.O. & 6 men.	1.N.C.O. & 6 men.

Coy. H.Q. C.S.M. 2 S.B's. 2 Checkers in.

CENTRE COMPANY. 4 Officers 114 Other ranks.

LEFT PLATOON.			RIGHT PLATOON.		
1 Officer and runner.			1 Officer and runner.		
Bombers etc.	L.G.	Bombers etc.	Bombers etc.	L.G.	Bombers etc.
1.N.C.O. & 6 men.	1.N.C.O. & 9 men.	2.N.C.O. & 6 men.	1.N.C.O. & 6 men.	1.N.C.O. & 9 men.	1.N.C.O. & 6 men.

FIRST MOPPING UP WAVE.

LEFT SECTION.	CENTRE SECTION.	RIGHT SECTION.
1.N.C.O. & 9 men. 2. R.E's.	1.N.C.O. and 8 men. O.C. COY., 2 runners and C.S.M.	1.N.C.O. & 6 men. 2. R.E's.

SECOND MOPPING UP WAVE. 1 Officer 1 runner.

LEFT SECTION.	CENTRE SECTION.	RIGHT SECTION.
1.N.C.O. & 6 men.	1.N.C.O. & 9 men. 2. R.E's.	1.N.C.O. & 6 men.

4 Stretcher Bearers. 2 Checkers in. 2 Signallers.

RIGHT FLANK COMPANY. 4 Officers 108 other Ranks.

LEFT FLANK PLATOON. 1. Officer 1 Runner.

L.G.	Riflemen.	R.G..
1.N.C.O. & 9 men.	1.N.C.O. & 5 men.	1.N.C.O. & 6 men.

LEFT CENTRE PLATOON. 1 Officer and one runner.

L.G.	Riflemen.	R.G.	Coy. H.Q.. 1. Officer
1.N.C.O. & 7 men.	1.N.C.O. & 6 men. 2.R.E's.	1.N.C.O. & 7 men.	2 Runners. C.S.M. 4. S.B's.

RIGHT CENTRE PLATOON. 1 Officer and 1 Runner.

L.G.	Riflemen.	(R.G.
1.N.C.O. & 7 men.	1.N.C.O. & 6 men. 2 R.E's.	1.N.C.O. & 7 men.

RIGHT FLANK PLATOON. 1.N.C.O. and 1 runner.

L.G.	Riflemen.	R.G.
1.N.C.O. & 6 men.	1.N.C.O. & 6 men.	1.N.C.O. & 7 men.

---

(1) Carrying parties. - Nil.

(3) (a) Raid Headquarters. (advanced) - Q.25.c.80.00.
Raid Headquarters (Rear) - Q.22.d.40.00.
Brigade Headquarters. P.24.d.30.40.
(b) Forward Dumps. 700 rounds, Stokes.

(4) <u>ARTILLERY</u>. Machine Guns and Trench Mortars as explained.

(5) (a) Location on <u>11/7/18</u>. Troops will move up to and be accommodated in the forward system before daylight on the 11th inst.

"A" & "C"/.

"A" and "C" Companies in QUAKER ALLEY, the former leading.
"D" and "B" Companies in front line of INTERMEDIARY SYSTEM, former on the Left.

(b) Communications.
(i) From HAMEL to Advanced Raid H.Q. - by runner, and to INTERMEDIARY Station at Q.22.d.90.90. - By lamp.
(ii) From Advanced Raid H.Q. to Rear Raid H.Q. and to INTERMEDIARY Station, by wire and runner.
(iii) From INTERMEDIARY STATION to Rear Raid H.Q. by wire. To Brigade H.Q. - By lamp.
(iv) From Rear Raid H.Q. to Brigade H.Q. by lamp and buried cable.
(v) From Battalion H.Q. Q.22.c.90.10., by Power Buzzer.

Personnel.

	Advd. Raid H.Q.	INTERMED-IARY STN.	Rear Raid H.Q.	HAMEL.
Signallers.	3.O.R.	3.O.R.	4.O.R.	2.O.R.
Runners.	3.O.R.	1.O.R.	3.O.R.	Coy. Runners.

(c) Medical. R.A.P. is at Q.28.c.60.20. Evacuations from R.A.P. under arrangements made by A.DM.S. via CUTHBERT AVENUE and ENGLEBELMER.
The reserve bearers, 8 in number, and the stretcher bearers Corpl, will be stationed along HAMEL OUTPOSTS, and proper points as regards the raid.
Walking wounded will be looked after by these bearers in HAMEL OUTPOST and will evacuate via CRAB TRENCH and CHARLES AVENUE, to Road at Q.21.c.50.30. where there will be R.A.M.C. men stationed to direct them to A.D.S. at ENGLEBELMER.

(d) Prisoners. Any prisoners captured will be sent back at once by the quickest route to Rear Raid H.Q; from where, their identity will be wired to Brigade H.Q.
They will be made use of to carry M.Gs captured or wounded cases to that point. From Rear Raid H.Q., they will be marched to Brigade H.Q. where the A.P.M. will take them over.

(e) Equipment and dress.
Rifle and Bayonet, Bandoliers, Box Respirators in the 'Alert' position, Steel helmets.
Each Platoon of the first line will have a Rifle Grenade Section and Rifle Grenades will be distributed as required with sections. All rifles will be loaded, one round in chamber, 9 in magazine.
Bombs. First, second, and third waves will carry bombs on the scale of 2 per man.
Wirecutters. Every other man in the first wave will carry wirecutters. 2 per section will be carried by Moppers up.
All identities and papers will be removed, except that all ranks will wear two special raid discs, for facilitating checking in.
All ranks will also wear a strip of white tape fastened across the sling of their Box Respirators on the back, as a means of recognition.

(6) Watches, will be synchronized at Brigade H.Q. on Zero day at 10a.m. and 5.p.m., and within the Battalion at 12.Noon and 7.p.m.

(7) Exploding of Mobile charges.
These will be laid directly objectives are occupied and exploded by the R.E. responsible after the wave has passed, or time given for all to get clear. Three short sharp blasts on a whistle will indicate that the fuze has been lit.

(8) Signal for withdrawal. Watches must be considered the principle factor in this respect, but a Thermite Bomb will also be fired from CRAB TRENCH over the line of final objectives at Zero plus 60.

(9) Checking in. Will be conducted at the MESNIL-AUCHONVILLERS Rlys at (a) Junction of CHARLES AVENUE.
(b) Junction of GRASS AVENUE.
The R.S.M. will supervise this duty, which will be performed by the two men detailed by Companies for the work.

page (5)

(10) Password.   " REGGIE "

   A signal cord will be issued later.

(11. Acknowledge.

J. B. Cockburn
                     Lieut. Colonel.
               Commanding 2nd. Batt. R.W.Fusiliers.

Issued at 4 0pm.
by D.R.L.S and Runner. 10/7/18.

Copy No. 1. C.O.
"   "   2. "A" Company.
"   "   3. "B" Company.
"   "   4. "C" Company.
"   "   5. "D" Company.
"   "   6. 115th Inf. Bde.
"   "   7. Q.M. & T.Officer.
"   "   8. 2nd in Command.
"   "   9. Left Battalion.
"   "   10. Right Battalion.
"   "   11. 17th Bn. R.W.F.
"   "   12.
"   "   13. File.
"   "   14. War Diary.

Report on Raid carried out by
9th R.W.F.
on Night of 11-12 July 1915

I. General Preparations for Raid as detailed in various Brigade & Batt'n instructions.

II. Plan — Drawn up & forwarded under Brigade instructions including action of Artillery M.Gs & T.M.s

III. <u>Execution</u>

In putting the Plan so carefully drawn up into execution very few difficulties presented themselves.

There was certainly a very bad storm towards evening which made the trenches very slippery and the going more difficult than it otherwise would have been, but on the whole the night was propitious and the hour of ZERO just enabled the forming up to be completed after sufficient darkness had set in.

The forming up positions were firstly covered by parties sent from each Coy & immediately after Tape men appointed to lay the tapes for each section to form up on carried out their duties

with the result that when the Companies arrived at their areas no confusion whatever occurred and the forming up was completed in absolute silence throughout. At ZERO hour the Artillery opened and the Battalion at once moved forward in the order laid down –
Tape Men were allotted to each Coy & these men followed the rear mopping up party laying out the tapes for the return journey from HAMEL.
At ZERO + 4 the M.G. Barrage commenced and continued till ZERO + 70
Our L.T.M. also carried out their allotted task at the appointed time.
The covering fire of the Artillery M.Gs & T.Ms left nothing to be desired while the Counter Battery work proved too good for the enemy whose only retaliation consisted of a few light field guns and T.Ms which appeared to fire without any definite object and generally the enemy seemed unable to grasp the situation

regretted that a certain number of men were missing but there is little doubt that most if not all of these were killed at the or about the same time as Lieut Sloyd also when a L G team with their gun were almost all destroyed by a T.M. Bomb the gun ~~under~~ Since the covering parties and all who were in the Rear during the withdrawal seemed Confident that there ~~was~~ were no wounded left behind I did not send out the Patrols I commenced to form in case there were & men Reported missing.

The Red light sent out with 'A Coy' for the purpose of giving direction on flank of withdrawal does not appear to have been Seen -

The O/c Coy being wounded it probably was not put up as he intended adjusting it himself in a Suitable place.

JBC

Every Company attained their objective and overcame argued all all obstacles and the considerable resistance offered by the enemy. It is difficult to estimate the enemy's actual losses in killed but there is little doubt fully 50 were either bayoneted or destroyed by Bombs & Mobile Charges thrown into the Cellars.

At Z+60 the Artillery Barrage stopped and the withdrawal took commenced covered by sections told off for the purpose, the withdrawal was most brilliantly executed & reflects the greatest credit on Company Platoon & Section leaders.

There was no noise or confusion of any kind nor did the British enemy obtain any clue as to what was occurring or he would undoubtedly have opened from his positions North of HAMEL

At Z+70 the M.G. Barrage ceased and the withdrawal shortly after the covering parties entered our trenches — It is

Adjt. Dosa.

Report on Raid "B" Co.

The forming was very good and was completed by 10·45 p.m.

At 11 p.m. the barrage opened & the sections went forward at a very steady pace keeping touch the whole way until opposition was met with.

The whole Co attacked very well & with great confidence going straight through to final objective after mopping up the posts. The first line mopped up their own posts with the assistance of 1st line mopping up party.

The Objective was reached about 11-30 p.m.

The withdraw was given to time and carried out in an organised manner no rush at all.

All other information was given in answer to the list of questions which was sent round yesterday.

7-80 A.M.

13/1/18.

J. Montgomerie Lt.
"B" Co

Májt.
Dora

Report on Raid 11/12 July from C Company
Right Assaulting Company

The Company formed up on direction tapes and was in position at 2-16.

On barrage opening all parties moved off together and touch was kept for the first 200x. ~~At this point~~

On crossing the German line running West to East Q23d1.3 - 25.30 the two right sections pressed forward and crossed German second line trench at Q23d4.7 and moved up road to cross roads Q23d4.9. The road running north east was used as a right guide and Germans were encountered in trenches at Q23b5.3. These ran down into a dug out which was promptly bombed and while a search round was being made enemy Trench Mortars knocked out the greater portion of one section and the Lewis Gun.

2/Lt Lloyd was hit at this stage and L/Cpl Metcalfe and one or two other men then encountered three Germans who were taken prisoner. The mopping up party attached had not kept up and L/Cpl Metcalfe brought two of the prisoners back — The mopping up party had been broken up and casualties suffered by one of the R.E.'s throwing down his Mobile Charge into a dug-out in which three Germans were hiding.

The centre of the Company was held up for a short time by encountering a German post at Q23d 05.40. This was dealt with but the party was held up by two belts of wire between this trench and the plantation Q23d 4.6

The trench running behind the hedge N to S & W to E immediately before reaching Cross roads was searched and five prisoners taken. The house and cellar on east of road was searched but the entrance was blown in and the cellar could not be demolished. The orchard behind this trench was carefully gone through and the cellar on corner was bombed. No R.E.'s were available for demolishing with this latter party of moppers up

The left sections of the Company crossed the German line at Q23d 05.70 and moved up into the village between hedges being the boundaries of gardens. They crossed the road at Q23d 25.95 and bombs were thrown into a dug out apparently disused across the road in the trench. The sections moved on and crossed second road and moved on to objective. The moppers up who had followed closely behind searched ground north of second road and between roads capturing one prisoner and leaving one other German with his leg off.

The various sections withdrew at Zero + 60 from their various positions in an orderly manner and arrived back in our trenches at Z + 75.

Prisoners taken 9

MW Radford
Capt
OC C Coy

To Adj. D Coy

Report on Raid:

The assembling of the company in the front line trench & the forming up outside in front was performed with practically no confusion or noise.

The advance to the first road was very steady. It was very difficult to maintain touch owing to the darkness. M.G. fire was met with before the 1st road was reached, from the right flank, but no casualties were caused. Prisoners were taken between the 1st & 2nd roads, numbering in all 8 Boches. 3 Cellars were blown up, also a ruined house. There were a large number of dugouts already blown in. As the 2nd road was approached, Boches were seen to be running away behind our barrage. The enemy T.Ms at this moment opened on their front line running W & E of the village & for about a quarter of an hour the fire was heavy. The withdrawal was well carried out.

D Coy casualties. Total 1 killed 4 wounded

12/7/18   S.W. Charlton Capt. Comd D Coy

Adjt. Dosa

Report on Raid "A" Coy.

The forming up was completed successfully by 10.45 p.m. At 11 p.m. when the barrage opened the coy. moved forward but were held up a little by the rough country. Very little wire was encountered. Each platoon reached its objective each having encounter with enemy on the way. Germans were killed and 6 prisoners taken. Final objective was reached at 11.30 p.m.

The ~~order~~ to withdraw was given at 12 midnight and was carried out in good order.

The red lamp was not visible on the withdrawal but the sections found their way.

All other information, also recommendations, have been given in answer to list of questions sent round 12/7/18

13/7/18

Jas Knowland
2nd Lt
for O.C. "A" Coy.

REPORT ON RAID OF HAMEL VILLAGE BY 2ND. BN. ROYAL WELSH FUSILIERS ON NIGHT 11TH/12TH JULY.

SECTION I.   **GENERAL PREPARATIONS**

1. A replica of the area was laid out with tapes by 6th July at P.33.a. & d.
   On this replica all known Machine Guns, Trench Mortars, Dugouts and prominent landmarks were shown by boards and partial excavations.

2. The troops practised on the replica by day & by night.
   Enemy were represented by men firing blank S.A.A.
   Our barrage was represented by men waving flags, who conformed to the lifts of the barrage.

3. On the five nights previous to the raid, selected Officers and N.C.O's patrolled the enemy's line on the frontage of attack.
   The position to be raided was further reconnoitred by day from our lines by every Officer and a large percentage of N.C.O's.

4. Every man was provided with a large scale map, on which was clearly shown his objective and distance in yards he had to go.

5. Artillery preparations were according to plan.

SECTION II.   **PLAN.**

1. From patrol reports it had been ascertained that the enemy altered his dispositions nightly. The plan of attack was, therefore, based on the supposition that the enemy held all posts in which he had been located from time to time, which necessitated an attack of 1 Battalion in depth.

2. (a) Patrols had previously established the fact that the enemy did not hold the Railway on the Western edge of the marsh in strength, thus facilitating an attack on an East & West line.
   (b) The enemy's wire faced roughly North & South and his previous barrage lines had been noted as being on our trenches, running roughly North & South.
   (c) Two main roads in the Village run East to West but the line of the hedges run North & South.
   (d) Provided one could ensure the safety of the Right Flank near the Railway, for the purpose of forming up, it was decided to attack from an East & West line in a Northerly direction, securing the following advantages -

    (i) Utilizing the hedges for direction.
    (ii) Utilizing the roads as stage in reaching the objective.
    (iii) Getting inside his main wire facing West.
    (iv) Getting to a flank of his main barrage line on our trenches running North & South.
    (v) Attacking the steep bank frontally & thus ensuring touch within the Battalion.

   (e) The plan based on para. '(d)' was for the leading waves to go straight to their objective & succeeding waves to "mop up" areas in rear.

Page 2.

(f) Preliminary action of the Artillery over a period of six days was to make all positions and posts for the enemy on the Railway (Right Flank) untenable and to drill him to be accustomed to bursts of fire on HAMEL.

This action was justified by the results. The enemy was not alarmed by our bombardment and no enemy posts or patrols on the Right Flank interfered with our forming up.

SECTION III.   EXECUTION.

1. (a) The execution was carried out in every way according to rehearsal and orders, and was brilliantly carried out.

(b) The forming up positions were covered by parties from each Company.

(c) The troops moved to the Outpost Line, and thence straight to their forming up positions. Guides & Notice Boards being placed in the Outpost Line to mark the flanks of each Company.

(d) The forming up was completed in absolute silence by Zero minus 15.

(e) On the Battalion moving forward at Zero, "tape men" ran out tapes from the Outpost Line on each Company flank to act as a guide for direction on the return to our trenches.

(f) Every Company reached its objective overcoming considerable resistance by the enemy posts in the Forward System — further to the rear the enemy was completely surprised and either came out of his dugouts and surrendered or was bombed in his dugouts and the entrances blown in by the charges carried by parties of R.E., attached to "mopping up" parties.

In particular, the Company Headquarters at Q.23.b.4.2. (on the occupants refusing to come out) were destroyed and the exits effectually blocked.

In all, 18 dugouts were destroyed.

(g) On the final objective little resistance was met with, the enemy was seen running to his rear into our Artillery and Machine Gun barrage.

(h) The actual number of enemy killed exceeded 50 and the total prisoners that reached our lines was 19.

(j) The withdrawal was commenced at Zero plus 60 minutes, at which time, the Artillery barrage ceased. The withdrawal was covered by sections detailed for the purpose. There was no noise or confusion of any sort and the enemy obtained no clue as to what was happening.

(k) Our casualties occurred from bombs from the sentry groups in the Outpost Line, and primarily from T.M. fire on the centre of HAMEL fired from a direction North East of HAMEL. This T.M. fire opened at Zero plus 30 minutes when he had evidently ascertained we were in HAMEL but ceased at about Zero plus 45 minutes.

Some casualties were also caused by M.G. fire from the slope on the Eastern side of the ANCRE, and from a M.G. at Q.23.a.7.3., which was rushed and captured, the team were all killed.

TOTAL CASUALTIES

	Killed	Wounded
Officers	1	3
O.R's.	12	44

2. Appendix "B" deals with salient points of the co-operation of other Arms & action of enemy.

/Section IV.

SECTION IV. NOTES & LESSONS.

1. The Section in file is the best way of attacking a Village by night. Section leaders were able to control their men. Lateral connecting files are necessary.

2. An occasional "Very" Light fired by the assaulting troops would have been of assistance in picking up general position.

3. Accurate "Checking in" immediately after raiders have returned is difficult, wounded men go by the shortest route, "Checking in" stations should be well to the rear.

4. There was a tendency for "moppers up" detailed for a further objective to delay and capture prisoners on their way - this brings the attack to a leap frog attack which is slower and more difficult.

5. Forward Collecting Station for prisoners must be marked on replica and all ranks know its position.

6. Replica should, if possible, embody the features of the area to be attacked as to banks, hedges, etc., rather than comprising the area as a whole.

++++++++++++++++++

14.7.1918.   Brigadier-General,
                   Commanding, 115th Infantry Brigade.

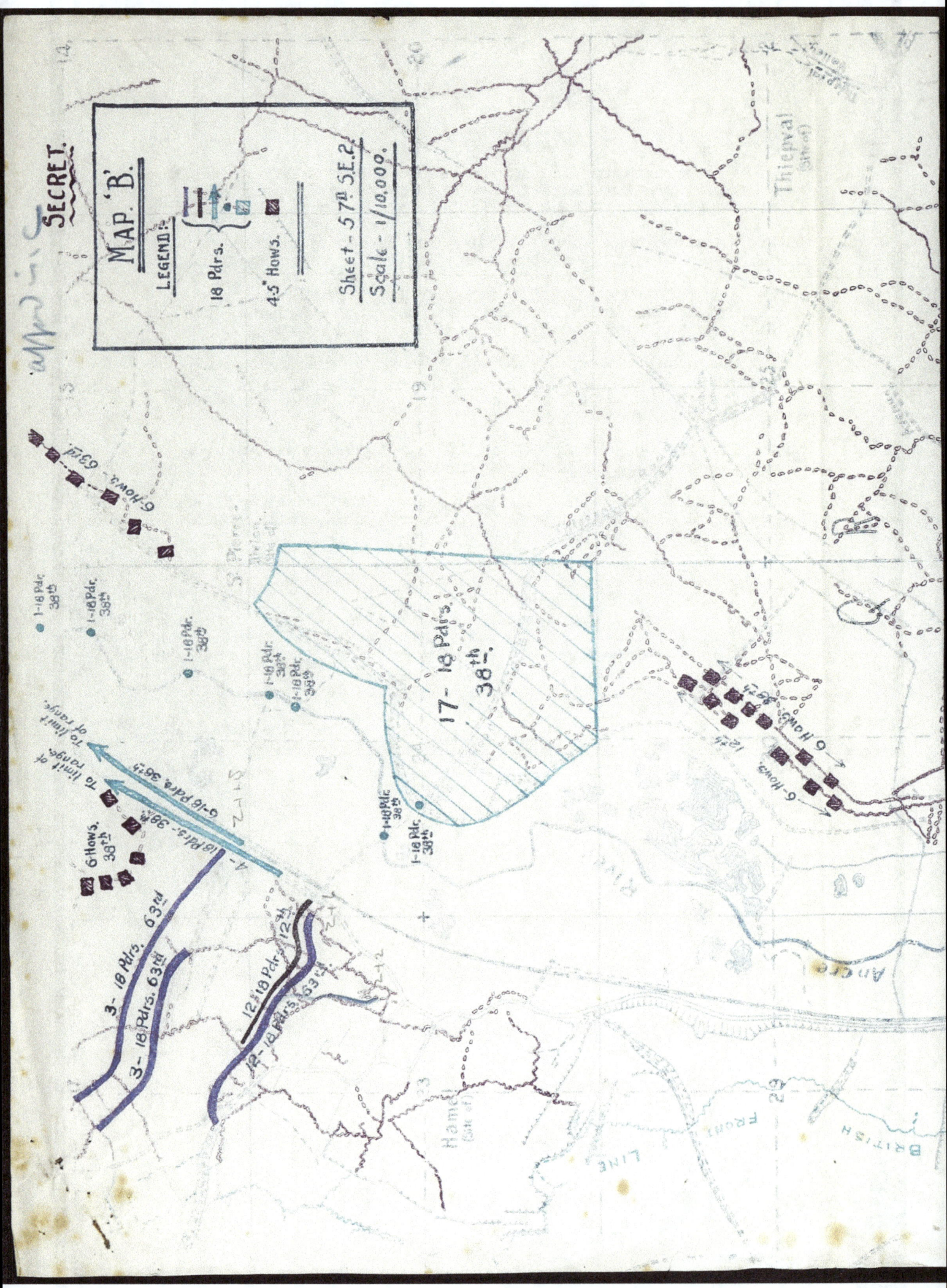

SECRET

RAID BY 2ND. R.W.F.

1. The 2nd. R.W.F., will, at a date and hour to be notified later, carry out a raid on HAMEL.

2. AREA & OBJECTIVE

   Right Boundary. The Railway.
   Left Boundary.   Q.23.c.10.60. to Q.23.a.9.8.
   Objective.   A line from Q.24.a.0.2. to Q.23.a.9.8.

3. The direction of attack will be North East.

4. STRENGTH.

   1 Battalion, i.e., 3 Coys. assaulting and 1 Coy. forming a defensive flank.

5. FORMATION.

   The 3 assaulting companies will assault in three lines.
   The First Line will consist of 2 platoons per Company.
   The Second & Third Lines will each consist of 1 Platoon per Company (See Map)
   Right Flank Coy. will be formed up in column of Platoons, each Platoon moving at ZERO to its position on Railway (See Sketch).

6. DUTIES OF EACH LINE

   The First Line will assault and seize the objective pushing out strong covering parties in front & is responsible for "cleaning up" anything found on the objective.
   The Second & Third Lines will follow at 20 yards distance and will "clean up" the areas for which each party is detailed.

7. FORMING UP.

   At Z minus 15, all troops will be formed up in front of HAMEL OUTPOSTS, ready to advance at ZERO. The O.C., 2nd. R.W.F., will provide his own covering parties

8. ARTILLERY.

9. M.G's.

10. MEDICAL.

11. SIGNALS.

12. L.T.M's.

(2)

13. <u>WITHDRAWAL</u>.

At Z plus 60 troops will commence to withdraw, during which period, the covering parties on the North & East will be responsible for the safety of the remainder.

14.

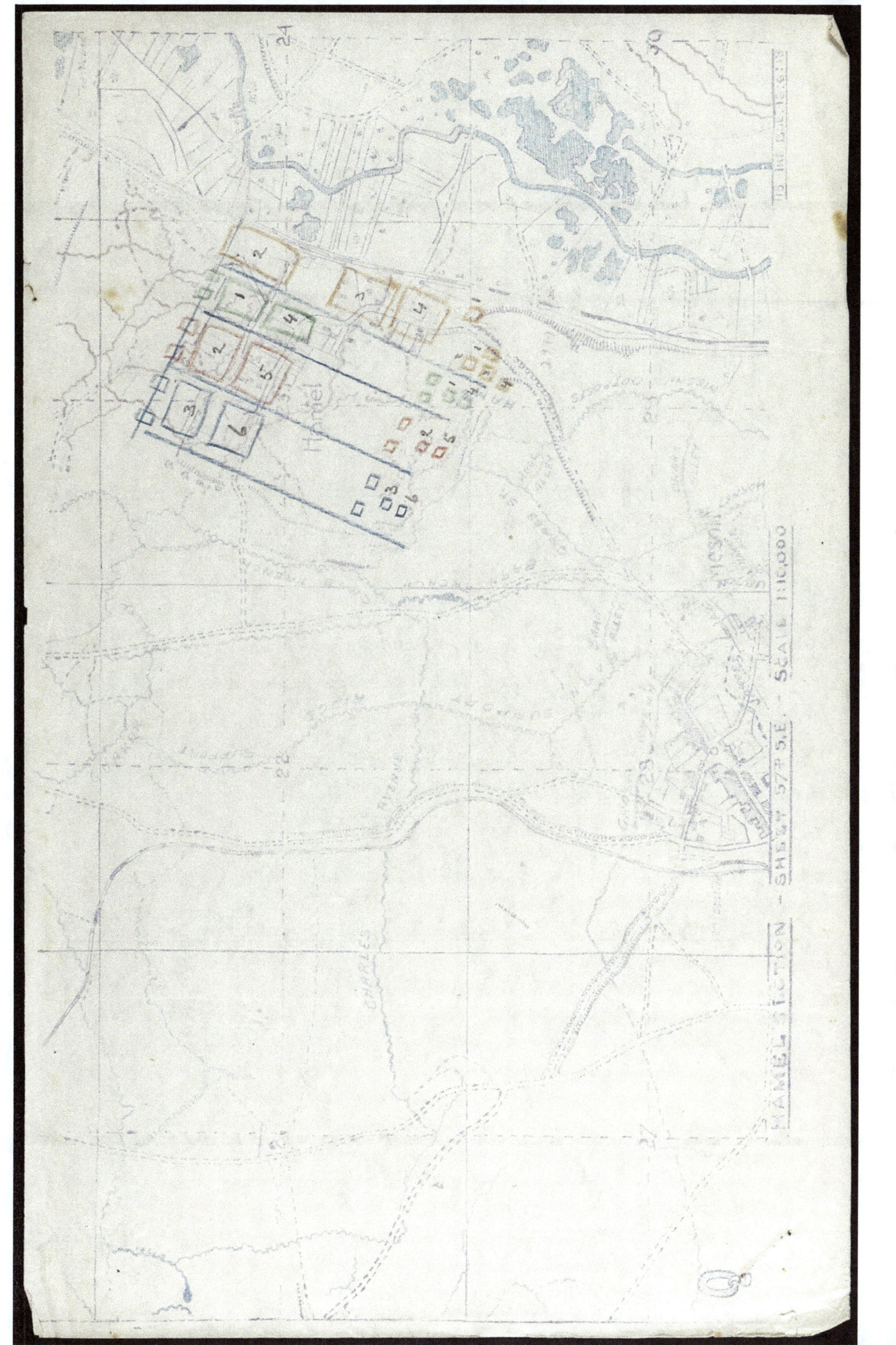

115th Infty. Bde. B.M. 9206.

38th Division.

Herewith report on Raid by 2nd. Bn. Royal Welsh Fusiliers on HAMEL, night 11th/12th July, together with the following Appendices:-

Appendix	"A".	Salient Points.
"	"B".	Brigade Orders.
"	"C".	Artillery Barrage Maps.
"	"D"	Machine Gun Barrage.
"	"E"	Straight Line diagram of Communications.
	F	General map of operation

(Signed W B Woulfe)

14th July, 1918.

Brigadier-General,
Commanding, 115th Infantry Brigade.

REPORT ON RAID OF HAMEL VILLAGE BY 2ND. BN. ROYAL WELSH FUSILIERS ON NIGHT 11TH/12TH JULY.

SECTION I.   GENERAL PREPARATIONS

1. A replica of the area was laid out with tapes by 6th July at P.33.a. & d.
    On this replica all known Machine Guns, Trench Mortars, Dugouts and prominent landmarks were shewn by boards and partial excavations.

2. The troops practised on the replica by day & by night.
    Enemy were represented by men firing blank S.A.A.
    Our barrage was represented by men waving flags, who conformed to the lifts of the barrage.

3. On the five nights previous to the raid, selected Officers and N.C.O's patrolled the enemy's line on the frontage of attack.
    The position to be raided was further reconnoitred by day from our lines by every Officer and a large percentage of N.C.O's.

4. Every man was provided with a large scale map, on which was clearly shewn his objective and distance in yards he had to go.

5. Artillery preparations were according to plan.

SECTION II.   PLAN.

1. From patrol reports it had been ascertained that the enemy altered his dispositions nightly. The plan of attack was, therefore, based on the supposition that the enemy held all posts in which he had been located from time to time, which necessitated an attack of 1 Battalion in depth.

2. (a) Patrols had previously established the fact that the enemy did not hold the Railway on the Western edge of the marsh in strength, thus facilitating an attack on an East & West line.
    (b) The enemy's wire faced roughly North & South and his previous barrage lines had been noted as being on our trenches, running roughly North & South.
    (c) Two main roads in the Village run East to West but the line of the hedges run North & South.
    (d) Provided one could ensure the safety of the Right Flank near the Railway, for the purpose of forming up, it was decided to attack from an East & West line in a Northerly direction, securing the following advantages -

        (i) Utilizing the hedges for direction.
       (ii) Utilizing the roads as stage in reaching the objective.
      (iii) Getting inside his main wire facing West.
      (iv) Getting to a flank of his main barrage line on our trenches running North & South.
       (v) Attacking the steep bank frontally & thus ensuring touch within the Battalion.

    (e) The plan based on para. '(d)' was for the leading waves to go straight to their objective & succeeding waves to "mop up" areas in rear.

(f) Preliminary action of the Artillery over a period of six days was to make all positions and posts for the enemy on the Railway (Right Flank) untenable and to drill him to be accustomed to bursts of fire on HAMEL.

This action was justified by the results. The enemy was not alarmed by our bombardment and no enemy posts or patrols on the Right Flank interfered with our forming up.

SECTION III. EXECUTION.

1. (a) The execution was carried out in every way according to rehearsal and orders, and was brilliantly carried out.

(b) The forming up positions were covered by parties from each Company.

(c) The troops moved to the Outpost Line, and thence straight to their forming up positions. Guides & Notice Boards being placed in the Outpost Line to mark the flanks of each Company.

(d) The forming up was completed in absolute silence by Zero minus 15.

(e) On the Battalion moving forward at Zero, "tape men" ran out tapes from the Outpost Line on each Company flank to act as a guide for direction on the return to our trenches.

(f) Every Company reached its objective overcoming considerable resistance by the enemy posts in the Forward System – further to the rear the enemy was completely surprised and either came out of his dugouts and surrendered or was bombed in his dugouts and the entrances blown in by the charges carried by parties of R.E., attached to "mopping up" parties.

In particular, the Company Headquarters at Q.23.b.4.2. (on the occupants refusing to come out) were destroyed and the exits effectually blocked.

In all, 18 dugouts were destroyed.

(g) On the final objective little resistance was met with, the enemy was seen running to his rear into our Artillery and Machine Gun barrgae.

(h) The actual number of enemy killed exceeded 50 and the total prisoners that reached our lines was 19.

(j) The withdrawal was commenced at Zero plus 60 minutes, at which time, the Artillery barrage ceased. The withdrawal was covered by sections detailed for the purpose. There was no noise or confusion of any sort and the enemy obtained no clue as to what was happening.

(k) Our casualties occurred from bombs from the sentry groups in the Outpost Line, and primarily from T.M. fire on the centre of HAMEL fired from a direction North East of HAMEL. This T.M. fire opened at Zero plus 30 minutes when he had evidently ascertained we were in HAMEL but ceased at about Zero plus 45 minutes.

Some casualties were also caused by M.G. fire from the slope on the Eastern side of the ANCRE, and from a M.G. at Q.23.a.7.3., which was rushed and captured, the team were all killed.

TOTAL CASUALTIES

	Killed	Wounded
Officers	1	3
O.R's.	12	44

2. Appendix "B" deals with salient points of the co-operation of other Arms & action of enemy.

/Section IV.

SECTION IV.   NOTES & LESSONS.

1.   The Section in file is the best way of attacking a Village by night. Section leaders were able to control their men. Lateral connecting files are necessary.

2.   An occasional "Very" Light fired by the assaulting troops would have been of assistance in picking up general position.

3.   Accurate "Checking in" immediately after raiders have returned is difficult, wounded men go by the shortest route, "Checking in" stations should be well to the rear.

4.   There was a tendency for "moppers up" detailed for a further objective to delay and capture prisoners on their way - this brings the attack to a leap frog attack which is slower and more difficult.

5.   Forward Collecting Station for prisoners must be marked on replica and all ranks know its position.

6.   Replica should, if possible, embody the features of the area to be attacked as to banks, hedges, etc., rather than comprising the area as a whole.

++++++++++++++++++

14.7.1918.   Commanding, 115th Infantry Brigade.
                                        Brigadier-General,

APPENDIX A

OUR ARTILLERY.

Did it start to time ?	Yes.
Did it cease at Zero plus 60 ?	Yes.
Was it of use as a recall Signal ?	Yes.
Any short shooting ?	No.
Were the men up to the barrage ?	Yes.
Any Remarks ?	H.E. better as a line than Shrapnel.

OUR MACHINE GUNS.

Any short shooting ?	No.
Any Remarks ?	Gave great confidence to the men.

OUR L.T.M's on Q.23.a.

Did they start to time ?	Yes.
Did they cease fire before troops reached them ?	Yes.

OUR HEAVY T.M's. 9.4".

Did any Heavy T.M. bombs fall in HAMEL between Zero and Zero plus 60 ?	No.

ENEMY ARTILLERY FIRE.

Time of opening fire ?	Zero plus 3.
Fire opened on ?	Outpost line of CRAB TRENCH.
General barrage Line ?	Principally on RIDGE & RIDGE SUPPORT TRENCHES.
Nature of Fire ?	4.2 and shrapnel; slow rate of fire; not more than 4 rds per min. per gun.
Any Remarks.?	Retaliation very weak.

ENEMY M.G's.

Time of opening fire ?	Zero plus 4.
Approx. No. of Guns ?	8.
Guns fired from ?	(1) Q.23.a.7.4. and (2) Q.23.d.5.9. (3) Q.30.b.

(1)

1 = 1 gun
2 = 3 guns
3 = 4 guns
Total 8 guns.

ENEMY M.G's. (contd.)

Guns ceased fire at Zero plus ?   Zero plus 10.

ENEMY T.M's.

Time of opening fire ?   Zero plus 30.

Fire opened on ?   Q.23.b.3.0. & area 100 yds E & W and in front of BEAUMONT AND CRAB TRENCH.

Enemy fired from ?

Fire ceased ?   Zero plus 45.

How was direction kept ?	Compass & line of hedges very useful.
What was the 'Going' like in No Man's land ?	Surface good and only natural obstacles met with.
Was the pace too quick or too slow ?	Right pace
Were landmarks as laid down in replica of use ?	Yes.
Did all Companies reach their objective ?	Yes.
Where did casualties chiefly occur ?	HAMEL VILLAGE. N.E. Corner.
What were most casualties caused by ?	T.M's.

No. of enemy killed ?	54, excluding those blown up in dugouts.
Where were the greatest number of enemy encountered ?	Eastern edge of HAMEL.
Were they in dugouts or in the open ?	
Did the enemy try to retire or run away ?	Yes.
Was enemy wire an obstacle ?	Practically Nil.
What other unexpected obstacles were met with ?	Steep bank - & thick hedge
Were the direction tapes of use ?	Yes.
Action of R.E's ?	20 dugouts or shelters were blown up.

SECRET.

38th Division. No. GSS. 2/33.

V Corps.

WEEKLY REPORT ON OPERATIONS
Week ending 17th July 1918.

1.   At 11.p.m. 11th July 2nd Battalion Royal Welsh Fusiliers raided the village of HAMEL and trenches around it.
The troops were formed up in front of HAMEL OUTPOSTS by 10.45.p.m. and advanced at 11.p.m. under cover of an accurate artillery and M.G. barrage.   The objective which was a line drawn from Q.24.a.0.2. to Q.23.a.9.8. and was reached at all points; several dugouts were bombed and blown up.   One wounded and 18 unwounded prisoners were captured all belonging to the 29th R.I.R., of the 16th Reserve Division.   In addition a large number of the enemy were killed and one Machine gun brought back.
Our patrols have been active nightly along the whole Divisional front.   13/14th - 4 enemy sentries were shot and on night 14/15th an enemy patrol was dispersed and the leader shot.

2.   Our artillery fire has been normal.   All guns co-operated in the raid on HAMEL on the night of the 11/12th.   The ANCRE crossings have been successfully engaged on several occasions with good results, particularly the new bridges in W.5.b.   All guns fired concentrations on road Q.18.c. where enemy cookers were reported to stop.   Enemy T.M's in HAMEL and Railway Q.35.b. have been silenced.

3.   Hostile artillery has been generally quiet.   Light harassing fire on forward areas predominating.
Reply to our raid on HAMEL was weak.   During the night 12/13th a concentration of 400 rounds Green Cross and H.E. was fired on a battery position in Q.31.b. with 10.5., and night 14/15th 1500 rounds of Yellow, Blue and Green Cross was fired on ENGLEBELMER Q.21. and 22.   The PURPLE SYSTEM in Q.25. and 31. has received a certain amount of attention.   Night 16/17th there was a heavy shoot with 15.c.m. on area Q.28.a. and c.
   Hostile machine guns and trench mortars have been normal.

4.   Only 2 enemy patrols have been encountered.   Both were dispersed; these were on the night 10/11th and evening of the 14th respectively.

5.   Hostile activity in the air has increased somewhat. Low flying planes have been active over forward system and 4 of our balloons have been brought down.

6.   The enemy's attitude remains purely defensive and no work of importance has been observed.

19/7/18.
Major-General,
Commanding 38th (Welsh) Division.

S E C R E T.   115th Brigade No. BM/B/399.

                                        115TH INFANTRY BDE
                                        25 JUN 1918
                                        No. BM 1795

Headquarters,
    38th.(Welsh) Division.

         Herewith report on Raid carried out by 14th Battalion
Royal Welsh Fusiliers, on the 20th/21st June, 1918, in conjunction
with the 2nd Battalion, Royal Welsh Fusiliers.

I.   GENERAL PREPARATIONS FOR RAID.

         The 14th Battn. R.W.F. were withdrawn from the line to
Reserve Area about FORCEVILLE, on the 12th/13th June.
         A replica was laid out in Q.27, on which the Battalion
carried out practices by night and day until the 19th instant.

II.   PLAN.

         The objective of the Raid was the Railway running from
Q.29.d.,40.45. to Q.25.b.,67.00, and the Road between
Q.29.b.,90.70. and Q.29.b.,80.80., with a view to killing or
capturing Germans, blowing up dugouts, capturing Machine Guns,
and obtaining identifications.
         The 115th Infantry Brigade were to raid in conjunction
on our Right.
         The general plan was for the Infantry to rush the
position from MESNIL and HAMEL OUTPOSTS under cover of a Smoke
Barrage from 4" Stokes Mortars, and a discharge of Rifle Grenades
from our Front Line, combined with an Artillery, Machine Gun and
Trench Mortar Barrage on all positions from which the enemy might
interfere with the Raid by fire or counter-attack.
         On the previous night at 3.a.m., 4" Stokes Mortars
discharged Gas mixed with Smoke on the objective and neighbouring
points, so as to make the enemy think on the night of the Raid,
when they saw the Smoke, that Gas was being discharged, and put
on their Respirators.

III.   EXECUTION.

         Under unfavourable weather conditions caused by a constant
drizzle which set in at 10.50.p.m and continued until 3.50.a.m.,
three Companies 14th Battn. R.W.F. (Left, Centre and Right) at
2.5.a.m. 21st June 1918, raided the enemy's advanced posts, Machine
Gun positions, dugouts, and the Railway between Q.29.d.,45.50. and
Q.25.d.,55.00.
         Right Company had three objectives :-
(a)   Dugout in Embankment Q.29.d.,35.60.
        Dugout in Railway Embankment Q.29.d.,42.62.
(b)   Machine Gun at Q.29.d.,35.75., dugouts Q.29.d.,40.90., and
        40.98., and dugout in Railway Q.29.d.,45.80.
(c)   Machine Gun at Q.29.b.,32.25., dugouts Q.29.b.,40.10. and
        Railway.

        Report.

         No enemy were seen or encountered, and no Rifle or Machine
Gun fire met with. The suspected dugouts in the embankment were
merely shelters and 'cubby' holes. Two small dugouts were found
on the road at Q.29.d.,40.68. and two at Q.29.d.,40.90. These were
demolished by the R.E. Section.

                                        / A wire
                                        P.T.O.

Page 2.

A wire barricade was found across the road at Q.29.d.,40.55., and several sections of old trenches in embankment between the road and the railway. Concertina wire, running Northwards, was encountered on bank Q.29.b.,30.20., it was much trampled down and formed no obstacle. The bank was about 30 feet deep and steps were found near this point.

The retirement was carried out without any difficulty.

Centre Company had two objectives :-

(a) Machine Gun at Q.29.b.,34.45., dugout Q.29.b.,40.45., and dugout on Railway Q.29.b.,55.30.
(b) Machine Gun in shell hole Q.29.b.,45.58., dugout Q.29.b.,45.60. and dugout, railway Q.29.b.,57.45.

Report.

No enemy were seen or encountered.

A little loose wire found at Q.29.b.,30.45. formed no obstacle. Machine Gun Post at Q.29.b.,34.45. was found to be disused and partly covered with grass. The bank here is steep with a drop of about 30 feet. The Railway Embankment at Q.29.b.,52.45. is 8 to 10 feet. The suspected dugout at Q.29.b.,45.50. was found to be a small cave with three entrances, unoccupied, and containing no identifications. It was demolished by the R.E. Section.

The enemy put down a 77.mm. barrage on embankment running North and South at Q.29.b.,05.45.

Left Company had three objectives :-

(a) Shell hole position Q.29.b.,45.68. and 4 dugouts running East on Road Q.29.b.,60.60. to 75.60.
(b) Machine Gun at Q.29.b.,50.80., dugout Q.29.b.,55.80., and Machine Gun on Railway Q.29.b.,60.80.
(c) Machine Gun at forked roads Q.23.d.,47.00., and then to Railway Q.29.b.,65.95.

Report.

(a) On reaching the embankment a Machine Gun and Team were located at Q.29.b.,60.65. The team, on being shot at, ran away, leaving their Gun behind, and escaped owing to the Raiders encountering loose wire which impeded their progress. Rifle fire was continued on them as they ran away, but without visible results. The Gun was captured. A detour was made for the dugouts on the road at Q.29.b.,65.60., which were found unoccupied and containing no identifications.

(b) On reaching first objective, a weak spot was found in enemy wire. Some enemy were seen retreating to a Post near the Railway. They were followed and shot at, whereon they withdrew still further. Progress here came to a standstill as the enemy put down a 7.7 barrage on his advanced posts and the Railway.
It is estimated that the enemy here lost 4 killed or wounded.

(c) When 30 yards from the forked roads a very thick belt of wire consisting of concertinas, gooseberries, and loose wire was encountered in a borrow pit or depression. An attempt was made to cut through, but the wire was too thick and loose. The enemy were seen in the Post and were immediately bombed.

/ One of them

(c) continued.

One of them was shot with a rifle when firing a "Very" Light and was seen to fall. Part of the Raiders worked round towards the rear of the post, but failed to find an opening in the wire. The enemy ran to a dugout in an embankment within the wire, and one other man was seen to fall, apparently dead. No entrance through the wire being found, the dugout was engaged with smoke bombs and grenades, and it is hoped that the whole eight were killed or wounded.

Our Artillery and Machine Guns fired mainly on the flanks of the attack, and were successful in keeping down all flanking fire so much so that none of our casualties were due to Machine Gun or Rifle fire.

IV.   NOTES AND LESSONS.

1.   The enemy retaliated chiefly on the embankment of the objective, Support Lines Q.29.a., and Q.28.b. with 10.5.cm.Hows: and with Trench Mortars on Front and Support Lines Q.23.a. and Q.22.b.

2.   The usual pyrotechnic display started at 2.6.a.m., on the Right and Left flanks Golden Rain, innumerable Green and Reds bursting into two were used, one Red bursting into four Reds.
   It was not until 2.15.a.m. that any Lights were sent up on the front being raided, and then only one Red Light and a "Very" Light were seen.

3.   It would appear that the enemy do not hold the embankment and the Railway between their trenches near AVELUY WOOD and about Q.29.b.,80.65.

4.   On a misty night the Thermite Bomb does not show up sufficiently well to be used as a signal for retirement.
   Retirement was made by the Watch and the cessation of the barrage.

5.   Further training is required for Section Commanders so that they will take charge of their Sections. In the heat of a fight there is a tendency to individual effort which, if restrained or guided as necessary by Section Commanders, would ensure more complete results by the combined action of the whole section.

6.   The value of careful training and rehearsals were once more emphasised.

7.   The operation was carried out in accordance with programme, and all arrangements worked well, and reflected great credit on the Officers, N.C.Os. and men concerned.

V.   Copy of Brigade Order with Map showing forming up positions and objectives, is attached. *(not attached)*

VI.   CASUALTIES.

Our casualties were :- Wounded - 2 Officers and 18 O.R.
Missing :- 3 Other Ranks (believed killed).

H E Pryce
Brigadier General,
Commanding 115th Infantry Brigade.

22nd June 1918.

Copies to :-

115th Inf. Bde.
War Diary.

HQ GS38D
Dupl
Aug' 18

On His Majesty's Service.

D.A.G.
B 3rd Echelon

No. 122

ORIGINAL

WAR DIARY of GENERAL STAFF 38th (Welsh) Division

Army Form C. 2118.

INTELLIGENCE SUMMARY.

VOLUME. XXXII

(Erase heading not required.)

Instructions regarding War Diaries and Intelligence Summaries are contained in F.S. Regs., Part II. and the Staff Manual respectively. Title pages will be prepared in manuscript.

Place	Date	Hour	Summary of Events and Information	Remarks and references to Appendices
LEALVILLERS.	AUGUST 1918.			
	1st.		Army Commander, Corps Commander and Divisional Commander inspected 113th Brigade at training.	
	2nd.		G.O.C. attended Corps Conference at 17th Division H.Q. TOUTENCOURT to discuss the necessary action owing to the enemy's retirement to the RIVER ANCRE.	
	3rd.		Divisional Recreational Sports; championship won by R.A.M.C. D.O.198 issued.	APP. 1
	4th.		Medal presentation by G.O.C. to 114th Infantry Brigade. Divisional Horse Show and Race Meeting.	
	5th.		115th Brigade go into AVELUY Right Brigade Section. 113th and 114th Brigades carry out Training Programme and Tracer Bullet Demonstration.	
	6th.		113th and 114th Brigades and 38th Div.Artillery go into the line. 113th Brigade AVELUY LEFT: 114th Brigade AVELUY CENTRE: Command passed from G.O.C. 17th Division to G.O.C. 38th Division at 4.15.p.m.	
	7th.		G.O.C. accompanied by G.S.O.2. went round PURPLE LINE during the morning. G.S.O.1. inspected M.G. Emplacements in the afternoon. G.S.O.3. went round Divisional O.P's during the morning.	
	8th.		G.O.C. went round the line and visited Brigades. BRIG-GENERAL HARMAN, C.M.G., D.S.O., G.O.C. 114th Infantry Brigade left for ENGLAND for 6 months exchange: BRIG-GENERAL T.ROSE PRICE from G.S.O.1. 55th Division assumed command of 114th Infantry Brigade. G.S.S.2/33 issued "Report on Operations.	APP. 2
	9th.		G.O.C. held a Conference of Brigadiers at 114th Brigade H.Q. for the purpose of thinning out line. Hostile artillery very quiet. G.O.C. and G.S.O.2. visited the Divisional Reception Camp in the afternoon. Fires and many explosions in ALBERT. D.O.200 issued.	APP. 3
	10th.		Patrols successfully reconnoitred the crossings of the RIVER ANCRE. Several explosions from delay fuzes in AVELUY and in the direction of AUTHUILLE. Line thinned out: one Battalion of each Brigade in front system, with one Battalion in Support and one in Reserve.	
	11th.		Hostile artillery harassed BOUZINCOURT and HEDAUVILLE.	
	12th.		A very quiet day. G.O.C. visited Corps School. 38th M.T.Company held sports at BERNEUIL. G.O.C. attended.	
	13th.		G.O.C. proceeded on leave and BRIG-GENERAL H.E. ap RHYS PRYCE, C.M.G., D.S.O., assumed command of the Division during his absence. The day was quiet. G.O.C. visited all Brigades.	
	/14th.			

Army Form C. 2118.

WAR DIARY
or
INTELLIGENCE SUMMARY.

Page 2.

(Erase heading not required.)

Place	Date	Hour	Summary of Events and Information	Remarks and references to Appendices
LEALVILLERS.	AUGUST 1918.			
	14th.		Quiet night. Message received to the effect that enemy was withdrawing on the front of the Centre Division of the Corps on our Left, in the SERRE-PUISIEUX AU MONT Sector. Patrols were endeavouring to keep touch. In the afternoon a message was received saying that enemy was withdrawing on the front of the Division on our left. Patrols had pushed forward. Many low reconnaissances carried out by R.A.F; few enemy seen and several explosions not caused by artillery were observed in the neighbourhood of OVILLERS-LA BOISSELLE. Division on our Right reported at 8.30.p.m. that enemy were still in ALBERT and fired upon our patrols. G.O.C. visited all Brigades. Corps Commander visited G.O.C. at 4.30.p.m.	APP. 4. APP. 5.
	15th.		The day was quiet, apart from some slight harassing fire on BOUZINCOURT and on the HEDAUVILLE ROAD. During the night our patrols crossed the ANCRE and found touch with the enemy. Between 10.p.m. and midnight there was some artillery activity on the Outpost line. Aerial activity during the day was above normal. D.O.201 issued. D.O.202 issued.	
	16th.		Division was disposed on a one Brigade front as follows :- Front Line. 115th Infantry Brigade. BROWN LINE. 114th Infantry Brigade. TOUTENCOURT. 113th Infantry Brigade. (in Div.Reserve). During the day artillery activity of both sides was normal. Our heavies bombarded certain selected targets. Our patrols endeavoured to find touch with the enemy on the east bank of the ANCRE. One patrol succeeded in crossing the river but was fired upon by a hostile post.	
	17th.		The night was fairly quiet only light harassing fire being reported. Our patrols were active. Corps Commander visited G.O.C. at 11.15.a.m. G.O.C. carried out a Staff Exercise with 114th Brigade on the BROWN LINE. Divisional Artillery carried out experimental co-operation with a Kite Balloon with view to ascertaining if it is possible to start a barrage by Signal from a Balloon.	
	18th.		Quiet night. Our patrols active along the Divisional Front. Orders issued for the departure of the 318 American Regiment on 19th August.	
	19th.		G.S.O.2. attended Conference at 18th Divisional H.Q. G.O.C. and G.S.O.2. attended Corps Commanders Conference at VAL VION (BEAUQUESNE). G.O.C. held a conference at Divisional H.Q. at 6.p.m. The following were present :- G.O's.C. 113th 114th 115th Brigades; C.R.A.; C.R.E.; G.S.O.1., G.S.O.2., A.A.& Q.M.G., O.C. Signals. D.O.203 issued. D.O.204 issued.	APP. 6. APP. 7.

/20th.

WAR DIARY or INTELLIGENCE SUMMARY.

Army Form C. 2118. Page 3.

(Erase heading not required.)

Place	Date	Hour	Summary of Events and Information	Remarks and references to Appendices
LEALVILLERS.	AUGUST 1918.			
	20th.		Quiet night. 114th Brigade relieved the Left Brigade 115th Brigade and the Right Brigade 110th Brigade (21st Division). Divisional Order 205 issued. (Action of Division in event of enemy withdrawing on our front). Order 207 issued to effect that patrolling must be vigorously carried out in order to ascertain any change in enemy's dispositions or intentions. D.O.206 issued regarding local attacks by 18th and 21st Division.	APP. 8 APP. 9 APP. 10
	21st.		D.O.208 issued. Our patrols were active on the whole Divisional front and kept touch with the enemy. Order 208 issued, re crossing the ANCRE. Brigades to be prepared to force crossings over the RIVER ANCRE and seize high ground on East bank of the river. Our artillery was active. Hostile artillery made only a feeble reply to our fire. O.O.209 issued.	APP. 11
	22nd.		O.O.210. issued. Some of our patrols effected crossings over the RIVER ANCRE with great difficulty. These patrols were reinforced with about 4 sections of riflemen, who maintained these positions against hostile counter-attack. Order 211 issued. 113th Infantry Brigade to attack in conjunction with 18th Division on right, and capture the line of RUBBER LANE and hostile post at CRUCIFIX CORNER. D.O.212 issued.	APP. 12 APP. 13 APP. 14
	23rd.		At 4.45.a.m. 113th Brigade attacked in conjunction with 18th Division. Assembly carried out without incident. At 9.45.a.m. all objectives were taken, and strong patrols pushed out towards OVILLERS. 115th Brigade took overline over RUBBER LANE from CRUCIFIX CORNER to OLD CHALK PIT just east of AVELUY VILLAGE. 7 machine guns were captured by 113th Brigade also 2 77.m.m. guns, and 194 prisoners. 114th Brigade on left had heavy fighting throughout the day on east bank of the RIVER ANCRE between our outposts and parties of enemy in considerable strength. Order 213 issued for attack by 113 114 and 115th Brigades in conjunction with attacks by Divisions on flanks on 24th August. Objectives :- 113th Brigade. LA BOISSELLE.) Right attack. 115th Brigade. OVILLERS.) 114th Brigade. High ground S.E. THIEPVAL.) Left attack.	APP. 15
	24th.		The ground in the vicinity of AUTHUILLE and AUTHUILLE WOOD(forming a pocket between two converging attacks)to be mopped up by 115th Brigade. Attack started at 1.a.m. Two Brigades R.F.A. 62nd Division under orders of 38th Division. Attack started successfully and all Brigades were on objectives by 4.p.m. The enemy strongly resisted attack at OVILLERS and THIEPVAL but was overcome after heavy fighting. Patrols were pushed out towards CONTALMAISON, POZIERES, TULLOCH CORNER and MOUQUET FARM. Corps Cyclists came into action under orders of 115th Infantry Brigade. /Divisional	APP. 16

Army Form C. 2118.

WAR DIARY
or
INTELLIGENCE SUMMARY.

(Erase heading not required.)

Page 4.

Place	Date	Hour	Summary of Events and Information	Remarks and references to Appendices
	AUGUST 1916.			
HEDAUVILLE.	24th (continued).		Divisional Headquarters moved from LEALVILLERS to HEDAUVILLE opening there at 10.30.am. Divisional Order 214 issued. Orders for further attack to general line. - CONTALMAISON - BRAZENTIN LE PETIT - HIGH WOOD in conjunction with 17th Division on Left and 18th Division on Right.	APP. 17 APP. 18
	25th.		During the morning the Right Brigade advanced their line and captured CONTALMAISON at about 5.am. Centre and Left Brigades held up by Machine Gun fire from HIGH WOOD.	
USNA REDOUBT.			Divisional H.Q. closed at HEDAUVILLE and opened at USNA REDOUBT at 3.30.p.m. At 10.55.p.m. line held by Division ran as follows :- Eastern edge of MAMETZ WOOD, BRAZENTIN LE PETIT and BRAZENTIN LE PETIT WOOD. 114th Brigade held line 1000 yards west of HIGH WOOD. Enemy held BRAZENTIN LE GRAND and WOOD and HIGH WOOD. Further advance ordered at 4.a.m. on 26th. 113th Brigade directed on LONGUEVAL, with view to forcing enemy holding HIGH WOOD to withdraw. Ammunition was dropped by R.A.F. for use of Machine guns, to-day, which proved to be very useful.	
	26th.		At 10.45.a.m. HIGH WOOD was reported clear of the enemy, having been captured by 10th Battalion Royal Welsh Fusiliers. At 9.40.a.m. 113th Brigade reported they had captured BRAZENTIN LE GRAND and were advancing on LONGUEVAL. This information was confirmed by Adj. 10th South Wales Borderers who came to Divisional Headquarters to report the situation. At 12.50.p.m. 114th Brigade were reported to be moving on MORVAL; this was not confirmed. At 2.p.m. Right Brigade reported further advance held up by machine gun fire from DELVILLE WOOD.	APP. 19
CONTALMAISON.			Divisional Headquarters moved from USNA REDOUBT to CONTALMAISON, opening there at 4.p.m. 6th Dragoon Guards attached to Division were ordered to attack on foot. At about 6.30.p.m. the enemy heavily counter-attacked our troops from the direction of TRONES WOOD and DELVILLE WOOD. Counter attack was unsuccessful and we took some prisoners of 87th Division. Order 216 issued. Advance to continue as under :- 113th Brigade directed on GINCHY, to attack at 4.a.m. 114th Brigade on MORVAL. 115th Brigade to be in Divisional Reserve and move in close support of 114th Brigade.	
	27th.		Our line at 11.35.p.m. ran from N. edge of BERNAFAY WOOD - northwards through point 1000 yds West of LONGUEVAL to point 1000 yards east of HIGH WOOD. LONGUEVAL was reached but further advance LIEUT-COLONEL,J.B.COCKBURN COMMANDING 2nd Royal Welsh Fusiliers wounded near HIGH WOOD. Attack started at 4.a.m. under Artillery barrage. Left Brigade reached line of LONGUEVAL - FLERS ROAD. held up by M.G. fire from DELVILLE. /This line	

Army Form C. 2118.

WAR DIARY
or
INTELLIGENCE SUMMARY.

(Erase heading not required.)

Instructions regarding War Diaries and Intelligence Summaries are contained in F. S. Regs., Part II. and the Staff Manual respectively. Title pages will be prepared in manuscript.

Page 5.

Place	Date	Hour	Summary of Events and Information	Remarks and references to Appendices
CONTALMAISON.	AUGUST 1918.			
	27th.	(continued).	This line remained unchanged throughout the day. Order 217 issued. Proposing new dispositions as follows :- 113th Brigade - Right Front. 114th Brigade - Left Front. 115th Brigade and 19th Welsh Regt (Glamorgan Pioneers) in Reserve and to be prepared to relieve 113th and 114th Brigades in line on August 28th. Total prisoners captured since August 23rd 20 Officers 1262 other ranks.	APP. 20
	28th.		The night was fairly quiet. Our line remained unchanged during the morning. In the afternoon artillery fired a concentrated bombardment on LONGUEVAL after which our troops entered the village and found it unoccupied. Patrols were then pushed forward about 500 yards. Apart from this operation there was no change in our line. Enemy was reported to be preparing a line of resistance running from ARROW HEAD COPSE - East of GUILLEMONT along line of GUILLEMONT - GINCHY ROAD to a point about 1000 yards N. of GINCHY. Artillery and machine guns harassed this line during the night.	App 21
	29th.		Order 218 issued - ordering continuation of attack at 5.15.a.m. 115th Brigade to advance and occupy GINCHY moving S. of DELVILLE WOOD. 115th Brigade to advance on left of 113th Brigade N. of DELVILLE WOOD and occupy trench system N. of GINCHY. 114th Brigade to mop up DELVILLE WOOD. Advance to be carried out under barrage fire of R.F.A. and machine guns. Practically	
		9.a.m.	Both leading Brigades reported all going well, hostile retaliation/Nil.	
		8.a.m.	Objectives taken and patrols pushed forward, to general line, BOULEAUX WOOD - MORVAL.- 114th Brigade ordered to stand fast. 113th Brigade directed on MORVAL and 115th Brigade on LES BOEUFS. In the evening our line ran round West of MORVAL, East of LES BOEUFS. Divisional order 219 issued. Division to continue advance as under :- 114th Brigade. Advance Guard. 115th Brigade. In Support. 113th Brigade. In Divisional Reserve.	APP. 22
	30th.		Advance to continue at 5.30.a.m. Advance Guard was held up by heavy Machine Gun fire from Spur east of MORVAL. G.O.C. did not intend to press advance under ###### circumstances. BRIG-GENERAL W.B.HULKE, D.S.O., Commdg. 115th Infantry Brigade wounded near LES BOEUFS. LIEUT-COLONEL NORMAN D.S.O. assumed command of 115th Infantry Brigade. There was continuous and heavy shell and machine gun fire on /our positions	

WAR DIARY
or
INTELLIGENCE SUMMARY.

Army Form C. 2118.

Page 6.

(Erase heading not required.)

Instructions regarding War Diaries and Intelligence Summaries are contained in F. S. Regs., Part II. and the Staff Manual respectively. Title pages will be prepared in manuscript.

Place	Date	Hour	Summary of Events and Information	Remarks and references to Appendices
CONTALMAISON.	AUGUST 1918.			
	30th (contd).		our positions all day and our line remained unchanged. Divisional Order 220 issued. 114th Brigade to relieve troops of 113th Brigade in line on night 30th/31st.	APP. 23
	31st.		Patrols of 114th Brigade attempted to enter MORVAL in early morning but were held up by heavy Machine Gun Fire. LIEUT-COLONEL PARKINSON, Commanding 15th Welsh Regt wounded. During the afternoon hostile machine gun fire continued but was not so marked; from MORVAL Enemy appeared to have reinforced the garrison of MORVAL. Situation remained unchanged for the rest of the day. Attack to be resumed at 4.45.a.m. 1st September under Barrage of R.F.A. and machine guns, as under :- 114th Brigade Objective MORVAL and trenches E thereof. 115th Brigade Objective ROAD east of MORVAL to LE TRANSLOY. Final objective Southern edge SAILLY SAILLISEL VILLAGE. 113th Brigade to relieve 114th Brigade East of MORVAL by 6.a.m. and 114th Brigade will withdraw West of MORVAL. Order No.221 issued.	Opp 74
West of HIGH WOOD.			Divisional Headquarters moved to from CONTALMAISON to just West of HIGH WOOD, opening there at 11.a.m.	
	August 1918.			

General Staff 38th (Welsh) Division.

Captain, A. C. G.

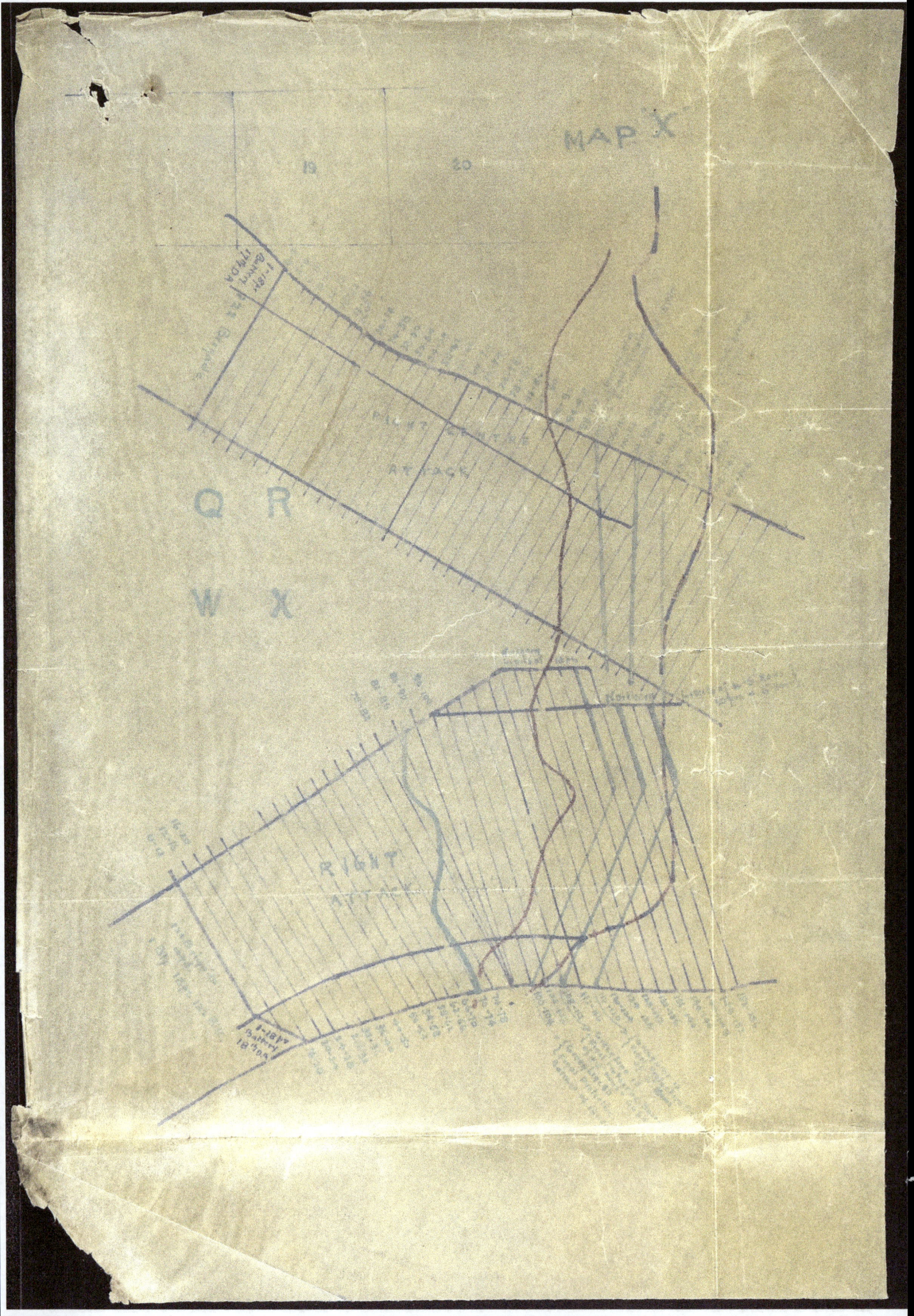

withdrawal

SECRET.

38th Divisional Artillery O.O. No.72.

Copy No. 22

Reference 57D S.E. 1/20,000   14th August 1918.

1. (a) The enemy has withdrawn opposite the Left Divisional front. Troops of 21st Division are now in Q.6 and Q.12. No signs of withdrawal have been observed on front of 38th Division or on that of 18th Division (on our Right). The enemy was reported to be still in ALBERT at 3 p.m.

2. (a) Troops of 21st Division (on our Left) are to push forward to-night to the line THIEPVAL – R.7.c. and if unoccupied to the line R.26.central – R.20.central – R.7.c.

   (b) 18th Division is pushing out patrols to-night.

3. (a) To-night, 14th/15th August 115th Infantry Brigade is to send out strong patrols to occupy the high ground about X.13.a & c.: 113th Infantry Brigade is to send out similar patrols to occupy the high ground about R.31.central.

   (b) If these places are secured, the enemy will probably have retired from the Ridge and at a time to be subsequently fixed 114th Infantry Brigade is to cross the River ANCRE and occupy the high ground on the line THIEPVAL – OVILLERS-LA-BOISSELLE – LA BOISSELLE (all inclusive)

   (c) In the event of the patrols not securing the above objective, the Infantry of 38th Division is to be disposed on 15th inst. as follows:-
   115th Infantry Brigade in GREEN SYSTEM on a 3 battalion front, each battalion with two Companies forward and two in the PURPLE SYSTEM.
   114th Infantry Brigade in BROWN SYSTEM.
   113th Infantry Brigade in TOUTENCOURT.

4. (a) 1. In the event of the action detailed in para 3 (b) being put into effect Rear two Sections of each Battery of 121st Brigade will advance to positions between AVELUY WOOD and MARTINSART: those of 122nd Brigade to the area W. and S.W. of MESNIL.

   2. Forward Sections of all Batteries will remain in their present positions until 114th Infantry Brigade has gained its objective. They will then move forward to join their Batteries under orders to be issued by Brigade Commanders.

   3. O.C. 121st Brigade will establish his H.Q. with G.O.C. 114th Infantry Brigade during the operation.

   4. Advanced H.Q's for both Brigades should be established in close proximity to new Battery positions, present Brigade H.Q's retained as Rear H.Q's and communication established through that channel.

   5. O.C. 122nd Brigade will maintain liaison with the Infantry Brigade detailed to support 114th Infantry Bde An officer not below the rank of Captain will be detailed for this purpose.

SECRET

Copy No. 17

38TH (WELSH) DIVISION ORDER NO. 201.

Ref: Map Sheet 57.D. 1/40,000.   15th August 1918.

1. The enemy are reported to have withdrawn to the general line BUCQUOY - PUISIEUX - R.2.
   It is possible that the enemy may withdraw Eastwards from South of the R.ANCRE also.
   The Division on our left have reached the line - Q.6.central - Q.12.central, and are pushing forward patrols tonight to the spur in R.2. and towards the general line BATTERY VALLEY - THIEPVAL. A patrol of that Division crossed the R.ANCRE at Q.24.a.7.3. unopposed and is being followed by a Battalion whose objective is R.26.central.
   The enemy still hold a position round ALBERT Cathedral; the Division on our right is operating against them from the South and have pushed patrols into W.24.

2. With a view to testing whether the enemy has withdrawn, 113th Infantry Brigade will send a Company via AUTHUILLE towards R.31.central and 115th Infantry Brigade a Company via AVELUY towards Cross Roads X.13.a.05.30.

3. If these companies meet no opposition -

    (a) The 114th Infantry Brigade will then advance via AUTHUILLE and AVELUY towards the general line LA-BOISSELLE - OVILLERS-LA-BOISSELLE - THIEPVAL, and will make good the same. Bde.H.Q. will be at the Old Battn.H.Q. Q.28.a.9.5. Q.32.d.2.0.

    (b) The 115th Infantry Brigade will take over the whole present Divisional front and will have the 2nd Battn./ /318 American Infantry Regt. attached to it in accordance with Warning Order (GSS.5/109/A.).

    (c) The 113th Infantry Brigade will concentrate in the BROWN LINE ready to leapfrog through 114th Infantry Brigade to a general line - the cutting in X.17.a. - Windmill, POZIERES and ridge in R.28.West of COURCELETTE.

    A tracing over the 1/20,000 map is attached (Not to Admn.Units) showing in RED the tactical points which must be occupied by the 114th Infantry Brigade and in BLUE the points to be occupied by 113th Infantry Brigade.

    (d) The Divisional Artillery (less the present advanced sections) will move into position in the PIONEER ROAD - MARTINSART - MESNIL VALLEY, 121st Bde.R.F.A. South of MARTINSART, 122nd Bde. R.F.A. North of MARTINSART; D.A.C. to HARPONVILLE.
    4 Sections 60-pdrs. and 4 Sections 6" Hows. will also move into position in the MARTINSART - MESNIL VALLEY.

4. The following troops will be under the orders of 114th Infantry Brigade :-
    "D" Coy. 38th Battn. M.G.C. (Major ADAMSON).
    3 Sections 178th Tunnelling Coy.R.E. (To search for mines etc.)
    "E" Sqdn. 5th Cyclist Regt. (Major FINLAY).
    One Field Coy. R.E.
    The 114th Brigade will NOT wait for these troops to report before moving. These troops will come under the orders of 113th Brigade when that Brigade passes through 114th Bde.

/5.

2.

5. [handwritten: The C.R.E. is commencing the repair of the following crossings Bapts a/6/16th W11 d 36 - a 36 c 17 - a 29 d 82]

5. The C.R.E., on it being ascertained that the 114th Infantry Brigade has crossed the R.ANCRE, will immediately repair the crossings of the R.ANCRE at AVELUY and AUTHUILLE by two Coys. R.E. and the 19th Welsh Regt. (Glamorgan Pnrs.).

6. Dumps of ammunition, supplies and water will be formed in the MARTINSART VALLEY W.3. W.9.

7. Divisional Headquarters will not move. [handwritten: until 113 Bde passes through 114 Bde when they will move to V4 Central]

ACKNOWLEDGE.

J.E. Munby
Lieut. Colonel,
General Staff, 38th (Welsh) Division.

Issued thro' Signals at 1-30.am.

Copies to :- All Units, 38th Division.
    V Corps.
    V Corps R.A.
    V Corps H.A.
    18th Division.
    21st Division.
    15th Sqdn. R.A.F.
    2nd Bn./318th American Inf.Regt.
    318th American Inf.Regt.

    178th Tunnelling Coy.R.E.
    "E" Sqdn. 5th Cyclist Regt. (Major FINLAY).

S E C R E T.   GSS. 1/18/1.
    Amendment No. 1 to D.O. 201.

1. Para. 3. (a).   last line for

                    "Q.28.a.9.5." road "Q.32.d.2.0."

2. Para. 3. (c).   line 1 for

                    "Brown Line" read "TOUTENCOURT".

3. Para. 4.   for ""D" Coy. 38th Bn. M.G.C. (Major ADAMSON)"

                    read "The BROWN Line M.G. Company".

4. Para. 7.   add "until 113 Brigade pass through 114 Brigade
                    when they will move to V.4.central".

5. Para. 5.   Cancel and substitute "The C.R.E. is commencing
                    the repair of the following crossings   night
                    15th/16th - W.11.d.3.6., Q.36.c.1.7.,
                    Q.29.d.8.2."

                                    J.E. Munby
15/8/1918.   Lieut. Colonel,
                            General Staff, 38th (Welsh) Division.

Copies to - all recipients of 38th Div. Order No. 201.

SECRET

38th Division No. GSS. 1/18/2.

113th Brigade.	38th Div: Signals.
114th Brigade.	19th Welsh Regt. (Glamorgan Pnrs.)
115th Brigade.	38th Div: Train.
38th Bn.M.G.C.	38th Div: "A & Q".
38th Div:Arty.	V Corps (For information)
C. R. E.	A.D.M.S.

Reference 38th Division Order No. 201.

1. If 113th Infantry Brigade moves through 114th Infantry Brigade, 113th Brigade will establish Headquarters about R.32.d.

2. The following are suggested as suitable localities for Battalion H.Q. -

	114th Brigade	Right	X.13.a.1.0.
		Centre	X.7.central.
		Left	R.31.central.
	113th Brigade	Right	X.9.d.3.7.
		Centre	TULLOCH CORNER (R.33.d)
		Left	MOUQUET FARM (R.33.b.4.8.)

3. Signalling arrangements will probably be

   <u>WIRE.</u>   Through PIONEER ROAD, AVELUY, NAB VALLEY.

   <u>VISUAL.</u> W.15. to R.32.d.

4. The General Officer Commanding directs that the advance as ordered in Division Order No. 201 to localities as described above be thoroughly practised by 113th and 114th Infantry Brigades, and that formations and all details be worked out and practised now.

15th August 1918.

Lieut. Colonel,
General Staff, 38th (Welsh) Division.

Withdrawal

SECRET   Copy No. 9

38th Division Royal Engineers

OPERATION ORDER NO 66.

Ref. Map :-
Sheet 57.d. 1/40,000   15th August 1918.

In conjunction with 38th Division Order No. 201.

INFORMATION.

1. The enemy are reported to have withdrawn to the general line BUCQUOY - PUISIEUX - R.2.
   It is possible that the enemy may withdraw Eastwards from South of the River ANCRE also.
   The Division on our left have reached the line - Q.6.central. Q.12.a.central, and are pushing forward patrols tonight to the spur in R.2.and towards the general line BATTERY VALLEY - THIEPVAL. A patrol of that Division crossed the R.ANCRE at Q.24.a.7.3. unopposed and is being followed by a Battalion whose objective is R.26.central.
   The enemy still hold a position round ALBERT Cathedral; the Division on our right is operating against them from the South and have pushed patrols into W.24.

2. With a view to testing whether the enemy has withdrawn, 113th Infantry Brigade will send a Company via AUTHUILLE towards R.31. central and 115th Infantry Brigade a Company via AVELUY towards Cross Roads X.13.a.05.30.

3. If these Companies meet no opposition -

   (a) The 114th Infantry Brigade will then advance via AUTUILLE and AVELUY towards the general line LA - BOISSELLE - OVILLERS - LA - BOISSELLE - THIEPVAL, and will make good the same. Bde. H.Q. will be at the old Battalion Headquarters Q.28.a.9.5.

   (b) The 115th Infantry Brigade will take over the whole present Divisional front and will have the 2nd Battalion 318 American Infantry Regiment attached to it in accordance with Warning Order GSS 5/109/A.

   (c) The 113th Infantry Brigade will concentrate in the BROWN LINE ready to leap-frog through 114th Brigade to a general line - The cutting in X.17.a. - WINDMILL POZIERES and Ridge in R.28. West of COURCELETTE.

   A tracing over the 1/20,000 map is attached (Not to Administrative Units) shewing in red the tactical points which must be occupied by the 114th Infantry Brigade and in blue the points to be occupied by 113th Infantry Brigade.

   (d) The Divisional Artillery (less the present advanced sections) will move into position in the PIONEER ROAD - MARTINSART - MESNIL VALLEY, 121st Brigade R.F.A. South of MARTINSART 122nd Brigade R.F.A. North of MARTINSART; D.A.C. to HARPONVILLE. 4 Sections 60 - Pdrs. and 4 Sections 6" Hows. will also move into position in the MARTINSART - MESNIL VALLEY.

4. The following troops will be under the orders of 114th Infantry Brigade :-
   "D" Coy. 38th Battalion M.G.C. (Major Adamson)

3 Sections 178th Tunnelling Coy. R.E. (to search for mines etc.)
E. Squadron 5th Cyclist Regt. (Major Finlay)
One Field Coy. R.E.

The 114th Brigade will NOT wait for those troops to report before moving. These troops will come under the orders of 113th Brigade when that Brigade passes through 114th Brigade.

5. The C.R.E., on it being ascertained that 114th Infantry Brigade has crossed the R.ANCRE, will immediately repair the crossings of the R.ANCRE at AVELUY and AUTHUILLE by 2 Coys. R.E. and the 19th Welsh Regt. (Glamorgan Pioneers).

6. Dumps of ammunition supplies and water will be formed in the MARTINSART VALLEY W.3. W.9.

7. FIELD COMPANY R.E. INSTRUCTIONS. in the event of para.3. sub. para (a) coming into operation :-

123rd Field Coy. R.E. will repair Bridge and Approach at AUTHUILLE Q.35.d.99.70.
O.C. 123rd Field Coy. R.E. will get into touch with O.C. 151st Field Coy. R.E. who has had charge of reconnaissance of ANCRE BRIDGES, and will be able to supply information.

151st Field Coy. R.E. will repair Bridge and Approach at AVELUY W.17.b.20.85

19th Welsh Regt. (Pioneers) will repair :-

(i) Main BOUZINCOURT - AVELUY Road as far as HAMEL - AVELUY Road. Road to be prepared for rough traffic only in the first instance and then improved afterwards.

(ii) MARTINSART - PIONEER Road as far as HAMEL - AVELUY Road

(iii) MESNIL - AUTHUILLE Road as far as HAMEL - AVELUY Road.

(iv) 19th Welsh Welsh Pioneers will assist Field Coys. in making good approaches to bridges if required by R.E. Officers on site.

124th Field Coy. R.E. will get into touch with G.O.C. 114th Infantry Brigade and come under his orders in the event of para.3 sub para. (a) coming into operation, afterwards coming under the orders of G.O.C. 113th Infantry Brigade as in para.4.

All pontoon equipment and teams to be placed at the disposal of O.C. 151st Field Coy. R.E. for bridging at AVELUY CAUSEWAY.

O.C. 151st Field Coy. R.E. will arrange time and rendezvous for Pontoon wagons direct with the other Field Coy. Commanders

8. These orders will be acted upon on the code word "AUCTION" being received from this office.

9. Divisional Headquarters will not move.

Field Coys. R.E. and Pioneers to acknowledge.

```
Copy No.  1.  O.C. 123rd Field Coy. R.E.
 "    "   2.  O.C. 124th Field Coy. R.E.
 "    "   3.  O.C. 124th Field Coy. R.E.
 "    "   4.  O.C. 19th Welsh Regt. (Pioneers)

          For information :-

 "    "   5.  38th Division "G"
 "    "   6.  38th Division "Q"
 "    "   7.  113th Infantry Brigade.
 "    "   8.  114th Infantry Brigade.
 "    "   9.  115th Infantry Brigade.
 "    "  10.  38th Division R.A.
 "    "  11.  C.E. Vth Corps.
```

J Wood

Major R.E.
A/C.R.E., 38th Division.

Time of issue 5 a.m.

SECRET

Copy No. 13.

38TH (WELSH) DIVISION ORDER NO. 205.

Ref: Maps, Sheet 57.D. 1/40,000.
Sheet 57.D. SE. 1/20,000.

20th August 1918.

INFORMATION & INTENTION.
1. It is possible that the enemy may retire suddenly on the Divisional front. Should this happen the Divn. will follow up the enemy. The 21st Division will be on our left and the 18th Division on our right.

PATROLS.
2. The front Brigades will send out patrols daily and nightly to test for the enemy's withdrawal. Special importance is attached to the dawn patrols as it is shortly after dawn that the enemy's rear guards may be expected to retire.

OBJECTIVES DURING ADVANCE.
3. In the event of the enemy withdrawing the first advance of the Division will be conducted in two bounds :-
 (i) To Objective, the line - LA BOISSELLE - OVILLERS-LA-BOISSELLE - THIEPVAL - STUMP RD. where it will link up with 21st Divn. line through SUNKEN RD. to R.9.central.
 (ii) To Objective, the line - THE CUTTING in X.7.a. - POZIERES WINDMILL - Ridge in R.28. West of COURCELETTE.
Objectives of bounds will be consolidated before further exploitation by patrols is made. First Objective will be maintained as a line of resistance until 2nd objective is consolidated.

METHOD OF ADVANCE.
4. The broad outlines of the advance are as follows :-
FIRST BOUND.
Brigades in the line will advance to first objective.
Reserve Brigade will be in position of readiness in V.8. and V.14.
The Divisional Artillery will support the advance from the ridge in W.4 and W.10 and neighbourhood.
SECOND BOUND.
Reserve Brigade will advance to Second Objective passing through the other two Brigades.
Portion of the Divisional Artillery will move to ridge W.12 and W.18, X.7 and X.13.

5. A tracing over the 1/20,000 map has been issued with D.O.201, showing in RED the tactical points which must be occupied by the leading Brigades and in BLUE the points to be occupied by the Brigade in Divisional Reserve when the advance takes place.
Brigades will detail now the Units for garrisoning these tactical points and the numbers required from the R.E. Coy. attached to them to assist the Infty. in making the more important points.

6. The following troops will be attached to each of the leading Bdes.:-
One M.G. Company.
½ "E" Sqdn. 5th Cyclist Rgt. (Major FINLAY)
½ a Fd.Coy. R.E.
The last two will be attached to the Reserve Bde. as it goes through the leading Brigades.

/7.

2.

7. The Divisional Artillery together with four sections 60-pdrs. and four sections 6" Hows., apart from other Corps Artillery that may be available, will support the advance as under -
First Bound from the line - MESNIL - MARTINSART VALLEY.
During the advance on the second objective part of the Divisional Artillery will move via AVELUY to the USNA HILL Ridge.
When in position the remainder of the Divisional Artillery will move via AVELUY to the ridge East of AUTHUILLE.

8. 38th Battn. M.G.C. will support the advance as under :-
FIRST BOUND.
The two Companies in the BROWN Line will move forward, one with each of the leading Brigades and will eventually be disposed by Sections on the R.31 and X.7. ridges whence they can best support the tactical points to be occupied by the Leading Bdes.
The two Companies in the line will advance to prepared positions in Q.35., W.5., and W.10. and W.16. whence they will support the advance of the Leading Brigades as far as the line USNA HILL - Western end of THIEPVAL.
SECOND BOUND.
The Company with the Reserve Brigade will move to X.9. and R.33. where it will support the Brigade on the 2nd Objective.
the general On 2nd Objective being reached the two Coys. that were in the line will move to line X.15. - R.27.
The Coys. supporting the troops in the first objective will remain where they are.
See Appendix 1.

9. The 124th Fd.Coy.R.E. will be attached to the leading Bdes. and will assist in making the main tactical points. On completion of these it will similarly work with the Reserve Bde. on the 2nd Objective.
C.R.E., from maps and aeroplane photos., will now draw out designs for these and the points made by Infantry alone, and make out estimates of material required for the same.
This material will be now stored in the MARTINSART VALLEY.
The 151st Fd.Coy.R.E. will be employed on making fit for wheeled traffic the bridge in AVELUY called CHATEAU BRIDGE and the 123rd Fd.Coy.R.E. will make fit for Infantry in fours the bridge on the road between MESNIL and AUTHUILLE.
The 19th Battn. Welsh Rgt. (Glamorgan Pioneers) will be employed in making -
    (i) The AVELUY - OVILLERS - X.3. - POZIERES Route and
    (ii) The AUTHUILLE - THIEPVAL - MOUQUET FARM Route and
    (iii) ENGLEBELMER - MESNIL MILL Road.
fit for wheeled traffic by temporary expedients.
A detachment of Pioneers will also be detailed to open up water supplies by the villages in the area of advance.

10. Division Signalling arrangements. (See Appendix 2.)
The general outline is -
    (a) Cable through PIONEER RD. AVELUY, NAB VALLEY to R.32.d.
    (b)   - and through MESNIL to AUTHUILLE.
With laterals) (i) from AUTHUILLE WOOD to Bn. Hd.Qrs.First Objective and from
) (ii) R.32.d. to Bn.Hd.Qrs. on 2nd Objective
    (c) Visual stations at Q.25 and Q.28., W.15, R.32.d. with which units may link up.
    (d) Divisional dropping station - O.22.c.8.5 and V.4.c.8.6.

/11.

3.

11. Contact aeroplanes will fly at Zero plus 1, 3, 5 & 7 hours and will call for flares:
   Flares will only be lit by foremost parties East of the ANCRE not West of the ANCRE.
   Aeroplanes will note the point of assembly of enemy preparing to counter-attack by dropping a RED SMOKE Bomb thereon.

12. 178th Tunnelling Coy.R.E. will proceed with the Loading Bdes. and will search for mines, booby traps, etc. in -
   (a) The tactical points to be occupied by the Bdes. crossing the river vide para. 5 and
   (b) On the roads mentioned in para. 9.

13. Prisoners of war and captured documents will be sent to the Cage at HEDAUVILLE. See Appendix 6.

14. Maps to be carried will be the 1/20,000 Sheet 57.D. SE.

15. Brigades will detail, in each Battalion Liaison Platoons whose duty it will be to keep touch with the units on their flanks.

16. Kit will be worn and stored as detailed in S.S. 135 Sectn. XXXI. (See Appendix 3.)

17. Units will move at the strength laid down in Third Army letter No. G.58/111 dated 27-6-18 forwarded under GSS.12/28 d/- 30-6-18. All surplus to the above being sent to VALHEUREUX.

18. Divisional Dumps of Ammunition, stores, rations and water will be formed and maintained in Valley between MESNIL and MARTINSART. (See Appendix 4).

19. Medical arrangements will be as at present. If the 1st Objective is reached dressing stations will be formed at Q.36.c.8.8. and W.11.b.4.2. (See Appendix 5.)

20. Police and traffic control arrangements will be as at present except that on the line USNA HILL - THIEPVAL being reached Divn. will establish control posts at all crossings of the ANCRE. (See Appendix 6.)

21. Units will pay attention to the daily synchronisation of watches as given by signals at 12 noon daily as there will not be time for a regular synchronisation on the day of the advance.

22. All units will be ready to move at two hours notice.

23. Each unit detailed for a tactical point will have with it 12 Rifle Grenade Signals, parachute, three white stars, for signalling its arrival at its point. 6 of these will be fired in the direction of W.15.central near which will be a special O.P. for noticing the advance of units. The remaining 6 are a reserve in case of failures in letting off the others.
   These signals will be let off 200 yds. South of the Strong Points so that their actual position may not be given away to the enemy.
   In addition to these signals units will notify their arrival by message.
   The Special O.P. will inform Brigades concerned and Divisional Headquarters of all arrival signals noted as soon as seen.
   The general position of Infantry Units will also be shown by BLACK and YELLOW flags vide S.S.135 Sec. III, 10 (ii).

/ 24.

4.

24. Wheeled transport will be utilised as much as possible, animals being used as pack animals where this is not feasible. (See Appendix 7.)

25. Headquarters of Division, Brigades and Battalions will be as in Appendix 8 attached.

26. C.R.E. will arrange now for the making of the requisite trench and road signboards. These will be stored with Brigades and placed in position by parties to be detailed in Brigades. Front Brigades will complete now all marking required in the area recently occupied by us West of the ANCRE.

27. Light Trench Mortars will be used to deal with any small rear guard post holding up the advance at any point and subsequently for supporting main tactical points.

28. **SECRECY.** The importance of secrecy is impressed upon all ranks.

29. **ACKNOWLEDGE by wire.**

J. S. Munby
Lieut. Colonel,
General Staff, 38th (Welsh) Division.

Issued thro' Signals at 6.40 pm

Copies to :-

G.O.C.	V Corps.
G.S. (2)	V Corps R.A.
"Q". (2)	V Corps H.A.
38th Div: Arty.	17th Division.
C.R.E.	18th Division.
38th Div: Signals.	21st Division.
113th Brigade (2)	15th Sqdn. R.A.F.
114th Brigade (2)	
115th Brigade (2)	
38th Bn. M.G.C.	
19th Welsh Regt.	
38th Div: Train.	
A.D.M.S.	
A.P.M.	

115TH INFANTRY BRIGADE
20th AUG 1918
No. BM9899

S E C R E T.   Copy No. 13.

38TH (WELSH) DIVISION ORDER No. 206.

Ref. Maps, Sheet 57.D. 1/40,000.
      Sheet 57.D. SE. 1/20,000.   20th August, 1918.

The 18th and 21st Divisions intend to make local attacks to-morrow which may cause the enemy to withdraw from the front of this Division.

The action of the 38th Division Artillery will be as follows to-morrow (reference tracing attached).

5.45 - 8.55 a.m.	Will shoot on blue points. ✓
8.55 - 9.15 a.m. ✓	Smoke shell on brown areas (will not be put down if 21st Division unsuccessful).
9.15 - 9.45 a.m.	Artillery creep forward to Q and R North and South grid line (Blue line).
9.45 - 11.55 a.m. ✓	Artillery will be on targets East of grid line through Q.25.central X.13.central (Red line) mainly in neighbourhood of tactical points to be occupied by us.
11.55 a.m. - 1.55 p.m.	Artillery creep forward to N. and S. grid line between Q.26 and 27 and X.14 & 15 (Green line).
1.55 p.m. onwards. ✓	Artillery will be on main tactical targets East of last line.

ACKNOWLEDGE. Done
                  SG.

J.E. Munby
Lieut. Colonel,
General Staff, 38th (Welsh) Division.

Issued thro' Signals at 8 p.m.

Copies to all recipients of D.O. 205.

Units must know this WSA

To 3 Bns.

For information. Please note that the earliest hour at which the smoke barrage can come down is 8-55 a.m.

ASt.BM

TRACING TO ACCOMPANY
38TH DIV. O. 206

Diet

36   31

R

W   X

6

Sheet 57C SE. Scale 1/20000

Smoke areas .... ⊙

Targets during phase
before patrols advance. ◯

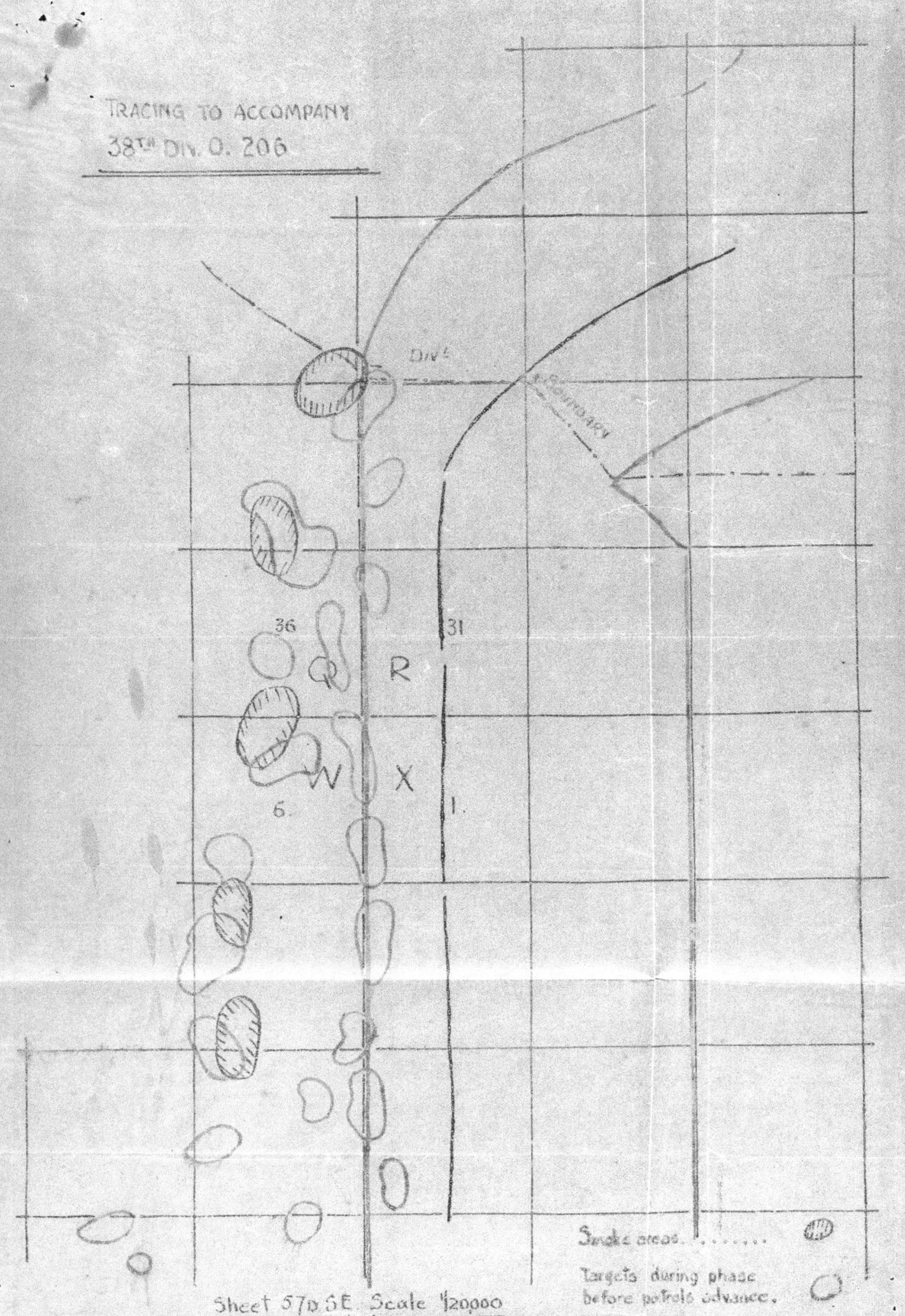

COPY   Spare

SECRET   COPY NO. 13.

38TH (WELSH) DIVISION ORDER NO. 206.

Ref. Maps:- Sheet 57 d, 1/20,000.
Sheet 57 d, S.E. 1/40,000.   20th August, 1918.

The 18th & 21st Divisions intend to make local attacks to-morrow which may cause the enemy to withdraw from the Front of this Division.

The action of the 38th Division Artillery will be as follows tomorrow (Reference tracing attached).

5.45 - 8.55 a.m.	Will shoot on Blue points.
8.55 - 9.15 a.m.	Smoke shell on Brown areas (will not be put down if 21st Division unsuccessful).
9.15 - 9.45 a.m.	Artillery creep forward to Q & N North & South Grid Line (Blue Line).
9.45 - 11.55 a.m.	Artillery will be on targets East of Grid Line through Q.25. Central X.13. Central (Red Line) mainly in neighbourhood of tactical points to be occupied by us.
11.55 a.m.-1.55 p.m.	Artillery creep forward to N & S Grid Line between Q.26 & Q.27 and X.14. & X.15. (Green Line).
1.55 p.m. onwards.	Artillery will be on main tactical targets East of last line.

ACKNOWLEDGE.

Issued thro' Sigs   (Sgd) J.B. Munby, Lt. Col.,
at 8.0 p.m.   General Staff, 38th (Welsh) Division.

(2)

115th Infty. Bde. B.M. 9899.

2nd. R.W.F.
17th R.W.F.
10th S.W.B.

For information. Please note that the earliest time at which the Smoke Barrage can come down is 8.55 a.m.

Captain,
Brigade Major,
115th Infantry Brigade.

20th August, 1918.

115TH INFANTRY BDE
No. 21/AUG1918
No. BM995.

SECRET.
XXXXXXXXXXXXX

21st August 1918.

38th DIVISIONAL ARTILLERY OPERATIONS ORDER No. 77

Reference Sheet 57D 1/40,000
Sheet 57D S.E. 1/20,000

Copy No. **14**

1. (a) 42nd Division Line at 5 p.m. ran L.34.b.9.9. - L.34.central - L.34.c.0.0. (in touch with 21st Division).
    (b) 21st Division has occupied SUNKEN Road in R.**4.a.** and R.3.b. and has 2 Companies in R.3.c. Two Companies have established themselves South of the ANCRE in R.14.a & b.
    (c) 21st Division is to establish and consolidate the general line BAILLESCOURT FME R.3.d. - Railway Crossing over ANCRE R.4.d.4.3. - Sunken Road in R.4.a. Ground gained South of the ANCRE is to be maintained. The Division is to be prepared to advance Southwards on the THIEPVAL RIDGE, should the enemy begin to retire.

2. (a) 115th and 114th Infantry Brigades are to be prepared on receipt of orders from Division to force the crossings over the ANCRE and seize ground on the far side as follows:-
    Force to be employed by each Brigade -
        4 Companies.
        4 L.T.M's
    (b) Patrols (strength one Platoon from each Company) to cross the ANCRE covered by L.T.M. fire where necessary. When these patrols have formed a bridgehead they are to be reinforced by the remainder of their companies.
    (c) Role of these Companies is to seize and hold any ground as far East as the "First Bound" (Vide 38 D.A. O.O. 75).
    (d) If these Companies penetrate sufficiently deeply into the enemy's present position, remainder of their battalions are to follow up without further orders.

3. (a) Arrangements for Artillery Support will be made direct by Group Commanders with Infantry Brigadiers concerned.
    (b) Copies of orders issued by Groups will be forwarded to R.A.H.Q.

4. 121st Brigade will carry out the tasks laid down in 38th D.A. O.O. No.76 para 3. Should 115th Infantry Brigade require support during the time when 121st Bde. is engaged on these tasks, such support will be given by the unemployed two Batteries only.

5. Nothing in this order in any way cancels the proposed action of Infantry Brigades outlined in 38 D.A. O.O. No.75

6. 121st Bde 122nd Bde to ACKNOWLEDGE.

Issued at 11.55 p.m.

J.E. Marston
Major R.A.
Brigade Major, 38th Divisional Artillery.

Copy No. 1 - 5   121 Brigade.   15 114th Infantry Bde.
        6 - 10   122   "   16   V Corps R.A.
        11 S.C.R.A.   17   18th D.A.
        12 R.A. Sigs Officer.   18   21 D.A.
        13   38th Div.   19 & 20 War Diary.
        14   115th Infantry Bde.   21   File.

SECRET.  Copy No. 13

38TH (WELSH) DIVISION ORDER NO. 209.

Ref. Maps, Sheet 57.D. 1/40,000.   21st August, 1918.
Sheet 57.D. S.E. 1/20,000.

1.   As the result of to-day's attack the Third Army has advanced and the line on the IV and VI Corps fronts 5 p.m. was as follows :- 42nd Division L.34.c.0.0. (in touch with 21st Division) - L.34.central - L.34.b.9.9. and then IV Corps line runs due East to the MIRAUMONT - ACHIET LE GRAND Railway and along the West side to East of MOYENNEVILLE joining up with VI Corps at A.27 East of LOGEAST WOOD.

        The 21st Division have occupied the sunken road in R.4.a. and R.3.b. with two Companies and hold the Southern slopes of SERRE - MIRAUMONT Ridge in R.3.c. Two Companies have established themselves to the South of the ANCRE in R.14.a. and b.

2.   The 21st Division will establish and consolidate themselves on the general line BAILLESCOURT FM R.3.d. - Railway crossing over ANCRE R.4.d.4.3. - Sunken Road in R.4.a. and will ensure connection with the Right of the 42nd Division about L.34.c.0.0. The Division will be disposed in depth. The ground gained South of the ANCRE in A.14.a. and b. will be maintained.
        The ground gained during to-day's fighting is to be consolidated in depth.

        The G.O.C. 21st Division will, during the night, establish Bridgeheads South of the ANCRE on the front BEAUCOURT - R.4.d.4.3. - and will construct as many crossings over the river on this front as possible. Touch with the enemy to the South of the railway will be maintained by patrols and the Division will be prepared to advance Southwards on the THIEPVAL Ridge should the enemy commence to retire.

3.   Divisions will ensure that full use is made of all Loop Sets, Amplifiers and Power-buzzers belonging to them and that these are taken well forward.   Full use is to be made of Pigeons.

4.   ACKNOWLEDGE.

                                F.J. Harington Captain
                                       for Lieut. Colonel,
                        General Staff, 38th (Welsh) Division.

Issued thro' Signals 10.20 p.m.

Copies to all Units, 38th Div.
V Corps.
V Corps R.A.
V Corps H.A.
17th Divn.
18th Divn.
21st Divn.

S E C R E T.   Copy No. 14

38TH (WELSH) DIVISION ORDER NO. 208.

Ref. Maps, Sheet 57.D. 1/40,000.   21st August, 1918.
          Sheet 57.D. S.E. 1/20,000.

I.   Brigades will be prepared on receipt of orders from Division Head Quarters to force the crossings over the ANCRE and seize ground on the far side in the following manner.

II. (a).   Force to be employed by each Brigade will be

   4 Stokes Mortars
   4 Companies.

(b).   Battle patrols composed of one platoon from each company will cross the ANCRE covered by fire from the Stokes Mortars where necessary.
   As soon as these patrols have effected a crossing and formed a bridgehead they will be reinforced by the remainder of their companies.

(c).   The role of these companies will be to seize and hold any ground as far as the line laid down for the first bound in D.O. 205.

(d).   The companies to be employed will previously be located in or near our present front line less the battle patrols which should be posted near the AVELUY – HAMEL railway.

(e).   Any arrangements for artillery support will be made direct between Brigadiers and Artillery Brigade Commanders.

(f).   Brigadiers will employ for this operation if desired the M.G. Coy. attached to them under D.O. 205 and these companies will act under their orders. The machine guns mentioned in para. 2 of 38 M.G. Bn. S/851 will move forward to their prepared positions to-morrow before 5 a.m., and will be employed for this operation if desired by Brigadiers who will give the necessary orders through the O's. C. Companies now in the line.

III.   Brigadiers will ensure that where the above companies penetrate sufficiently deeply into the enemy's present position they are followed up by the remainder of the battalions without further orders.

IV.   Nothing in the above order in any way cancels D.O. 207.

V.   ACKNOWLEDGE.

J.E. Munby
Lieut. Colonel,
General Staff, 38th (Welsh) Division.

Issued thro' Signals at 10 20 Pm

Copies to All Units, 38th Division.
V Corps,
V Corps R.A.
V Corps H.A.
17th Divn.
18th Divn.
21st Divn.

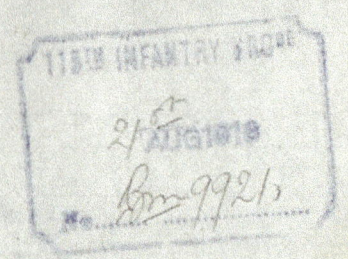

SECRET.

38TH (WELSH) DIVISION ORDER NO.207.

Copy No. 14

Ref. Maps   Sheet 57D 1/40,000
            Sheet 57D S.E. 1/20,000

1.   The remainder of Third Army attacked this morning on a front of about seven miles and drove the enemy back three miles on a front of five miles; at 7-30 this morning our troops were reported on the line COURCELLES - ACHIET-le-PETIT with Cavalry and Tanks in advance.   21st Division took BEAUCOURT and advanced to the line R.2.b., R.3.a., R.3.c., taking prisoner 2 officers and 120 O.R.   The enemy still appears to hold his positions East of the ANCRE, South of MIRAUMONT.

   Our patrols encountered opposition along the whole Division front this morning.

2.   Patrolling will be carried out vigorously by the Brigades in the line to-night and under cover of any mist that there may be to-morrow morning with the object of ascertaining any alteration in the enemy's dispositions.

3.   Harassing fire by Artillery and Machine Guns will be carried out to-night but not against any targets nearer than 1,000 yards East of the Eastern branches of the ANCRE.

4.   If the enemy appears to be withdrawing Brigades in the line will act as ordered in D.O.205.

5.   The gas operations ordered in D.O.204 will not take place till further orders.

6.   ACKNOWLEDGE.   Done

Issued thro' Signals at 1-50 p.m.

                                    J. E. Munby
                                    Lieut-Colonel,
21/8/18   General Staff, 38th (Welsh) Division.

Copies to :- All recipients of Order 205 and
              "N" Special Co. R.E.
              "E" Squadron 5th Corps Cyclists.

APPENDIX 8.

HEADQUARTERS.

Unit.	At present.	For first Bound	For second Bound.
Divl. Hd. Qrs.	O.22.d.central.	V.1.c.2.2.	V.1.c.2.2.
115 Inf. Bde.			
Bde. Hd. Qrs.	V.4.c.4.4.	W.3.d.8.5.	W.3.d.8.5.
Right Battn.	W.13.a.3.6.	X.13.a.1.0.	X.13.a.1.0.
Left Battn.	Q.32.d.2.0.	X.7.central.	X.7.central.
114th Inf. Bde.			
Bde. Hd. Qrs.	P.24.d.3.5.	Q.28.a.9.5.	Q.28.a.9.5.
Right Battn.	Q.32.d.20.00.	R.31.central.	R.31.central.
Left Battn.	Q.28.a.9.3.	R.25.d.5.1.	R.25.d.5.1.
113th Inf. Bde.			
Bde. Hd. Qrs.	V.4.c.8.8.	V.4.c.8.8.	R.32.d.
Right Battn.			X.9.d.3.7.
Centre Battn.			TULLOCK CORNER) R.33.d.)
Left Battn.			MOUQUET FARM R.33.b.4.8.)
38th Bn. M.G.C.	P.27.b.1.2.	Q.28.a.9.5.	R.32.d.

This cancels last sentence of para 5 of B.M. 9883 of 20/8/18.

APPENDIX 7.

1. **TRANSPORT.** - Will be located as follows:-

   Left Brigade.
   ½ Company, 30th Battn. M.G.C.) FORCEVILLE - VARENNES
   ½ "E" Squad. 5th Cyclist Regt.) Valley P.26.27 under
   ½ Field Coy., R.E.) Brigade arrangements.

   Right Brigade.
   ½ Company, 30th M.G.Battn.) N.E. of HEDAUVILLE
   ½ "E" Squad. 5th Cyclist Regt.) P.34.b. under Brigade
   ½ Field Coy., R.E.) arrangements.

   WAGON LINES.
   122nd Brigade, R.F.A. to P.26.a and c. To water at FORCEVILLE.
   121st Brigade, R.F.A. to V.2.d. To water at HEDAUVILLE.
   Nos. 1 and 2 Sections, D.A.C. to V.3.b. To water at HEDAUVILLE.
   No. 3 Section, D.A.C. at P.31.a.4.6.

2. Units will organize pack convoys for carriage of supplies, material, etc. East of the ANCRE in the first instance.

3. Carrying parties will be arranged by Brigades for the final transit of Stores, when animals are unable to be used.

4. On Wagon or Transport Lines changing their locations, Tents and Shelters will be taken.

APPENDIX 6.

PRISONERS OF WAR AND BATTLE STRAGGLER POSTS

1. Battle Straggler Posts, as soon as forward Brigades move, will be established along the line of the ALBERT - MAILLY MAILLET disused Railway and will be located as follows :-

        W.15.b.95.20.
        W.9.d.9.4.
        W.3.d.4.2.
        W.3.b.1.7.
        Q.27.d.7.3.
        Q.26.c.5.9.
        Q.22.c.6.4.
        Q.22.a.6.5.

    Battle Straggler Collecting Station - Q.32.d.2.2.

2. As soon as crossings are effected over the River ANCRE, Brigades in the line will be responsible for detailing a Battle Straggler Post at each crossing. These posts will remain at the Crossings until relieved by A.P.M's Straggler Posts which will move forward from the positions in para.1.

    Prisoners of War will be handed over to Battle Straggler Posts at river crossings and escorts to prisoners will on no account proceed WEST of the River ANCRE.

    Escorts will not exceed the 10% laid down.

    Battle Stragglers will not proceed WEST of the River ANCRE.

    Prisoners of War Cage will be at HEDAUVILLE.

APPENDIX 4

1.   Brigade Dumps will be formed at -

        (a) MESNIL   - Left Brigade.
        (b) HEATHCOTE BANK (W.3.d) - Right Brigade.

2.   A Divisional S.A.A. and Grenade Dump will be formed at Q.33.d.3.1. in which the following will be held and maintained :-

S.A.A.	100,000 rounds.
M.G.,S.A.A.	70,000 rounds.
S.O.S.	100
Flares White.. ...	3,000
Flares Red	2,000
Very Lights... ...	5,000
No.5 Grenades ...	3,000
No.23 Grenades ...	3,000
No.36 Grenades ...	3,000

    The Officer in charge of this Dump will wire his requirements to "Q" Branch, when they will be met.

3.   The two Advanced Brigades will draw the following from the Divisional Bomb Store, HARPONVILLE at once for immediate requirements :-

S.O.S. Rockets. ...	100
No.5 Mills Grenades ...	150 Boxes.

4.   **WATER.**   A Water Dump will be formed at Q.32.d.1.5.

    The importance of returning all empty Petrol Tins to this Dump is emphasised.

5.   The 115th Infantry Brigade will detail 1 Officer, 2 N.C.Os. and 20 other ranks, who will be in charge of both the Ammunition and Water Dumps.

6.   **RATIONS**   Preserved Meat and Biscuit will be delivered at Transport Lines as follows :-

Left Brigade ...	2,000 Rations.
Right Brigade ...	2,000 Rations.
38th Bn. M.G.Corps ...	400 Rations.
124th Field Company R.E.	200 Rations.

    These will form an additional days ration, and will be carried on the man as soon as orders to advance are issued.

    With this exception, the system of supply will be normal.

APPENDIX 3.

The only Stores to be taken will be those laid down in War Establishments and Mobilization Tables.

Packs and Surplus kits will be stored at VARENNES (Cafe de Commerce, Billet D.1 at the Cross Roads).

Accommodation has been sub-divided and allotted to Units.

The O.C., Salvage Company will detail a party to take over Stores at VARENNES.

Baggage Wagons loaded will rejoin their Train Companies.

SECRET
COPY NO. 1

115TH BRIGADE ORDER NO. 258

Ref. Map :- Sheet 57 d, 1/20,000.   22nd August, 1918.

1. Battalions will be prepared, on receipt of Orders from Brigade Headquarters, to force the crossings over the ANCRE and seize the ground on the far side in the manner set down below.   The leading Battalions of the 114th Infantry Brigade, will, under these circumstances, be taking similar action.

2. (a) The force to be employed by each of the leading Battalions will be :-

        2 Stokes Mortars
        2 Companies

(b) At ZERO minus 15 minutes, the leading Battalions will have one platoon opposite each of its two crossings ready to go over at ZERO plus 2 minutes.

(c) The 3 supporting platoons of each of the two Companies detailed by leading Battalions will be in position of readiness for following the leading Platoons when they have crossed and established a Bridgehead.

(d) The role of these Companies will be to seize and hold any ground as far as the line laid down for the First Bound in B.M. 9683 of 20.8.1918.

3. The 2 L.T.M's attached to each Battalion, will, at ZERO, open a hurricane bombardment on the East end of each crossing, lasting for two minutes, after which, the leading Infantry will commence the crossing.

The O.C., L.T.M. detachment, in consultation with O.C., Battalion to whom he is attached, will have his Mortars emplaced in the required positions.

4. The Section M.G., "A" Coy., attached to each Battalion and Reserve Section now in HEATHCOTES BANK will cover the crossings with M.G. Fire, directing their fire especially on enemy trenches in W.6.a. & b., AUTHUILLE WOOD in W.6.d., ROYALTY & RULING trench, from as far West as the guns will allow; junction of ROWLOCK, ROLL, RANCH Trenches at W.12.d.9.2., RAFFLE, ROWLAND & RUB trenches in W.18.b. and trench junctions at W.24.b.3.9.

O.C., Sections attached to Battalions will consult the O.C., Battalions to whom they are attached as to the selection of these targets or any others wished for.

Fire will commence at ZERO and continue until ZERO plus 40 minutes.

Any guns of "B" Coy. M.G.Bn., now in the Line and situated so as to be able to engage these targets, will co-operate.

5. At ZERO all available guns of 121 Bde. R.F.A. will engage trenches and targets on the following lines :-

    (a) Q.36.d.50.43. to W.6.b.25.40.
    (b) W.12.a.00.55. to W.18.b.00.05.
    (c) W.18.d.00.75. to W.28. Central.

Fire will continue until ZERO plus 40 minutes when the barrage will lift to selected targets in rear.

/6.

(2)

6. The 10th S.W.B. will be at ZERO hour be in position as follows,

1 Company	About HEATHCOTES BANK in W.3.b. & d.
1 Company	SAUCHIEHALL Trench & SAUCHIHALL Support in W.9.a
1 Company	SAUCHIHALL Trench & SAUCHIHALL Support Trench from East & West Grid Line through W.8. Central & W.9. Central on the North – and BOUZINCOURT AVELUY Road on the South.
1 Company	Shell Hole & Welsh Trench in W.15.c.

Battalion H.Q., at W.14.b.3.4.
The O.C. 10th S.W.B. will be prepared to move forward to line of Railway in W.11.c., W.17.a. & c., on receipt of Orders from Brigade Headquarters.

The role of the Battalion will probably be :-

(a) To provide Carrying Parties for leading Battalions.
(b) Support either Battalion.
(c) Take over from one or both Battalions on the Objective being reached.

The O.C., 10th S.W.B., will ensure that constant & efficient liaison is kept between himself and forward Battalions and on the flanks at all times, to know the situation.

7. On reaching the Objective (First Bound) leading Battalions will consolidate at once, and dispose their Companies in depth.

8. As soon as Os.C. leading Battalions are satisfied that their 2 Companies have penetrated sufficiently in to the enemy's present position, they will order their remaining 2 Companies to cross and follow without further order from Brigade H.Q.

9. Nothing in this Order in any way cancels Brigade Order No. 257.

10. This Order will only come into Operation on receipt of Code Word "HELL" (followed by ZERO Hour), e.g., "HELL, 11.0 a.m.".

11. ACKNOWLEDGE.

Captain,
Brigade Major,
115th Infantry Brigade.

Issued at 2.15 a.m.
thro' Signals.

DISTRIBUTION

1 Filed.	9 "B" Coy. M.G.Bn.	17 121 Bde. R.F.A.
2 War Diary.	10 55th Brigade.	18 130 Fd. Amb.
3 War Diary.	11 113th Brigade.	19 G.O.C.
4 2nd. R.W.F.	12 38th Division.	20 S.C.
5 17th R.W.F.	13 38th Division.	21 I.O.
6 10th S.W.B.	14 114th Brigade.	22 Bde. Signls.
7 15th L.T.M's.	15 124 Fd. Coy. R.E.	23 C.R.E.
8 "A" Coy. M.G.Bn.	16 151 Fd. Coy. R.E.	24 A.D.M.S.
		25 375th R.F.A

All SOR at 3.45 am
except B Coy MG Bn & 130 FA

[Stamp: 115th INFANTRY BRIGADE, 23rd AUG 1918, No. SM.9953]
115 Inf Bde

SECRET.
~~XXXXXXXXXX~~

Copy No. 15

22nd August 1918.

38th DIVISIONAL ARTILLERY OPERATION ORDER No. 79.

MAP. 57D S.E. 1/20,000.

1. Those portions of 38th.D.A. O.O. No.78 which refer to the attack by 113th.Inf.Bde. and to 38th.D.A. Barrage in support of it are cancelled.

2. (a) Troops of 21st.Division are reported to be in LOGGING SUPPORT (R.13.c. and d.)
   (b) 114th.Inf.Bde. is sending two platoons over MILL CROSSING towards COMMON LANE and to the N. end of THIEPVAL WOOD: also one platoon to CHICKWEED TRENCH. Remainder of battalion is to follow across ANCRE to-night.
   (c) No troops of 115th.Inf.Bde. are yet across the river.
   (d) 18th.Div. line runs W.29.d.9.0. - W.29.d.3.0. - along road to W.29.c.8.9. - thence along Railway to about W.29.a.5.7.
   (e) The enemy is still holding on to a position E.6.b.7.7. - W.24.d.6.5. - thence along RUBBER LANE.

3. On 23rd.August
   (a) 18th.Div. is to attack N.E. with objective TARA HILL.
   (b) 113th.Inf.Bde. is to move up through or N. of ALBERT and attack on left of 18th.Div. with objective RUBBER LANE.
   (c) Boundary between Divisions is the ALBERT - POZIERES Road.

4. Plan of attack of 113th.Inf.Bde. is -
   (a) One Battalion to form up along the Railway Embankment running from W.29.c.7.7. to W.29.a.7.4. between the swamp and the ALBERT - POZIERES Road.
   (b) At Zero + 10 the Infantry, accompanied by tanks, begin to extend Northwards and form up approximately on the N. and S. centre grid line of square W.23.
   (c) On arrival at final objectives patrols are to be pushed out to secure CRUCIFIX CORNER.

5. (a) 38th.D.A. will support the attack of 113th.Inf.Bde.
   (b) Table "A" and Map "A" ~~and table "B"~~ give details of Creeping and Standing barrages ~~respectively.~~
   (c) Vth. Corps H.A. is co-operating.

6. The ALBERT - POZIERES Road will be the boundary between 38th. and 18th.D.A's. 38th.D.A. will not fire S. of this road.

7. (a) On completion of the operation zones will be:-
      121st.Brigade - ALBERT - POZIERES Road to E. and W. grid line dividing squares X.1. and X.7.
      122nd.Brigade - thence to Northern Divisional boundary.
   Vigourous searching Harassing fire will be carried out.
   (b) "S.O.S" lines will be arranged by Group Commanders in consultation with Infantry Brigadiers.
   (c) Both Brigades will be prepared to re-open on the final protective barrage in the event of counter-attack.

8. Paras. 8 and 9 of O.O. 78 still hold good.

9. Zero hour will be 4.45 a.m. 23rd.August. Signal time will be taken.

10. 121 and 122 Brigades to ACKNOWLEDGE.

Issued at 11 p.m.

Brigade Major 38th.Divisional Artillery.

Major R.A.

Copy No.				
1 - 5	121 Bde.	13. 38th.Div.	16	113 Inf.Bde.
6 - 10	122 Bde.	14. 114 Inf.Bde.	17	18th.D.A.
11.	S.C.R.A.	15. 115 Inf.Bde.	18	21st.D.A.
12.	R.A. Signal Officer.		19	V Corps R.A.
			20 - 21	V Corps H.A.

-2-

    (6) In the event of Barrage fire being required Brigade Zones will be in prolongation of the existing zones along the East and West boundaries.

    (7) Reconnaissances of the actual positions to be occupied will be made at dawn. Full advantage should be taken of fire control from O.P's on the high ground East of the River ANCRE.

(b). If 114th Infantry Brigade is not ordered to advance Batteries will remain in their present positions and 121st Brigade will remain in liaison with the 115th Infantry Brigade.

5. (a) Nos. 1 and 2 Sections D.A.C. will move from RAINCHEVAL to lines in U.16.a. Move to be completed by 10 a.m. 15th inst.

    (b) Movements of Battery Wagon Lines, if required, will be made under Brigade arrangements.

6. T.M.B's will await further orders.

7. Present A.R.P. is at U.5.d. A new dump has been established at V.3.d.. The latter will be available in the event of a forward move.

8. Any new locations occupied will be reported at once to R.A.H.Q.

9. R.A.H.Q. will remain in present location.

10. ACKNOWLEDGE.

                                                              Major R.A.

Issued at 11.30 p.m.   Brigade Major, 38th Div: Artillery.

```
Copy No.  1 - 5  -  121st Bde.       38, 39  - War Diary
          6 - 10 -  122nd Bde.       40      - File.
         11 - 15 -  D.A.C.
         16      -  D.T.M.O.
         17      -  S.C.R.A.
         18      -  R.A.Sigs Officer.
         19 - 22 -  38th Div; "G".
         23      -  38th Div; "Q"
         24      -  38th Div; Sigs.
         25      -  S.S.O.
         26      -  330 Coy A.S.C.
         27      -  38th M.T. Coy.
         28      -  Officer I/c 38th Ammn. Sect.
         29      -  D.A.D.V.S. 38th Div;.
         30      -  D.A.D.O.S. 38th Div;
         31      -  A.D.M.S. 38th Div;
         32      -  C.R.E.
         33      -  R.A. V Corps.
         34      -  H.A. V Corps.
         35      -  34th Bde. R.G.A.
         36      -  21st D.A.
         37      -  18th D.A.
```

SECRET

Copy No. 15

38TH (WELSH) DIVISION ORDER No.210.

Ref. Maps. Sheet 57.D. 1/40,000 & 62.D.N.E.
Sheet 57.D. S.E. 1/20,000

22nd August 1918.

1. The III Corps on our right is attacking this morning at 4.45.a.m. with the object of seizing the line F.27.central (2 miles north of BRAY) - ALBERT.
    The 18th Division on our immediate right are to take the line E.6.central - W.29.a.central.
    The Left (55th Brigade) of 18th Division will advance at Zero plus 2 hours. From Zero to Zero plus 2 hours the artillery will bombard the houses about E.2.d.2.8., the HOSPITAL, and the defended locality about W.29.a.7.2.

2. The 113th Infantry Brigade with 124th Field Coy. R.E. less 2 sections and "B" Company 38th Bn.M.G.C. less 2 sections, all under the command of B.G.C., 113th Brigade, will be prepared to move at 7.30.a.m. this morning and to advance through ALBERT and by the river crossings North thereof onto the objective LA BOISSELLE (exclusive) - OVILLERS - X.2.a. and to hold and consolidate this line.

3. 124th Field Coy.R.E. less 2 sections and "B" Company 38th Bn.M.G.C. less 2 sections have been ordered to report at 113th Infantry Brigade H.Q. at 7.a.m. this morning.

4. 113th Brigade will endeavour by means of patrols or posts to obtain touch with any eastward movement of the remainder of our Division and will be ready to assist any such eastward movement.

5. 113th Infantry Brigade H.Q. will be at W.25.b.0.7.

6. The following information has been received as to the crossings north of ALBERT.
    Road bridge over railway W.22.d.7.5. destroyed.
        (Deep cutting here).
    River bridge W.23.c.2.4. gap of 20 feet.
    Footbridge intact at W.23.a.6.9. but difficult of approach from the west owing to floods.
    The officer R.E. making a reconnaissance of these crossings now will report at 113th Brigade H.Q. before 7.a.m. this morning.

7. The advance of 113th Infantry Brigade will be supported by the whole of the 38th Divisional Artillery.
    A barrage programme will be submitted to B.G.C. 113th Infantry Brigade by C.R.A.

8. ACKNOWLEDGE.

J. E. Munby
Lieut-Colonel,
General Staff 38th (Welsh) Division.

22/8/18.

Issued thro' Signals at 2.30.a.m.
Copies to All Units 38th Div.
  V Corps   V Corps H.A.   18th Division.
  V Corps R.A.   17th Division. 21st Division.

SECRET.   Copy No. 14

38th (WELSH) DIVISION ORDER NO. 212.

                                                               22nd August 1918.

Ref.Maps Sheet 57 D 1/40.000.
         Sheet 62 D. NE. 1/20.000.
         Sheet 57 D. SE. 1/20.000.

----

1. A patrol of the 14th Bn Welsh Regt crossed the River ANCRE at Q.29.b.80.10. this afternoon and found CHICKWEED TRENCH and CHICKWEED SUPPORT and CHICKWEED RESERVE unoccupied.

2. Four rifle sections will be sent over to occupy this system and will be followed by a Platoon.

3. The 114th Inf.Brigade will send two Companies up COMMON LANE to-night, starting about 10.30 p.m. to get in touch with the Right Brigade of the Left Division in CANDY AVENUE and will occupy the CHICKWEED System of trenches in Q.30.

4. Bridgeheads will be formed.

5. C.R.E. will arrange to send one Field Coy to bridge the River and improve existing crossings under orders to be issued by G.O.C., 114th Brigade.

6. ACKNOWLEDGE.

                                                 F.J. Harington Captain
                                                 for Lieut.Colonel.
                                                 General Staff, 38th (Welsh) Division.

Issued thro. Signals 9.15 p.m.

Copies to all Units 38th Division.
V Corps.
V Corps R.A.
V Corps H.A.
17th Division.
18th Division.
21st Division.
15th Squadron R.A.F.

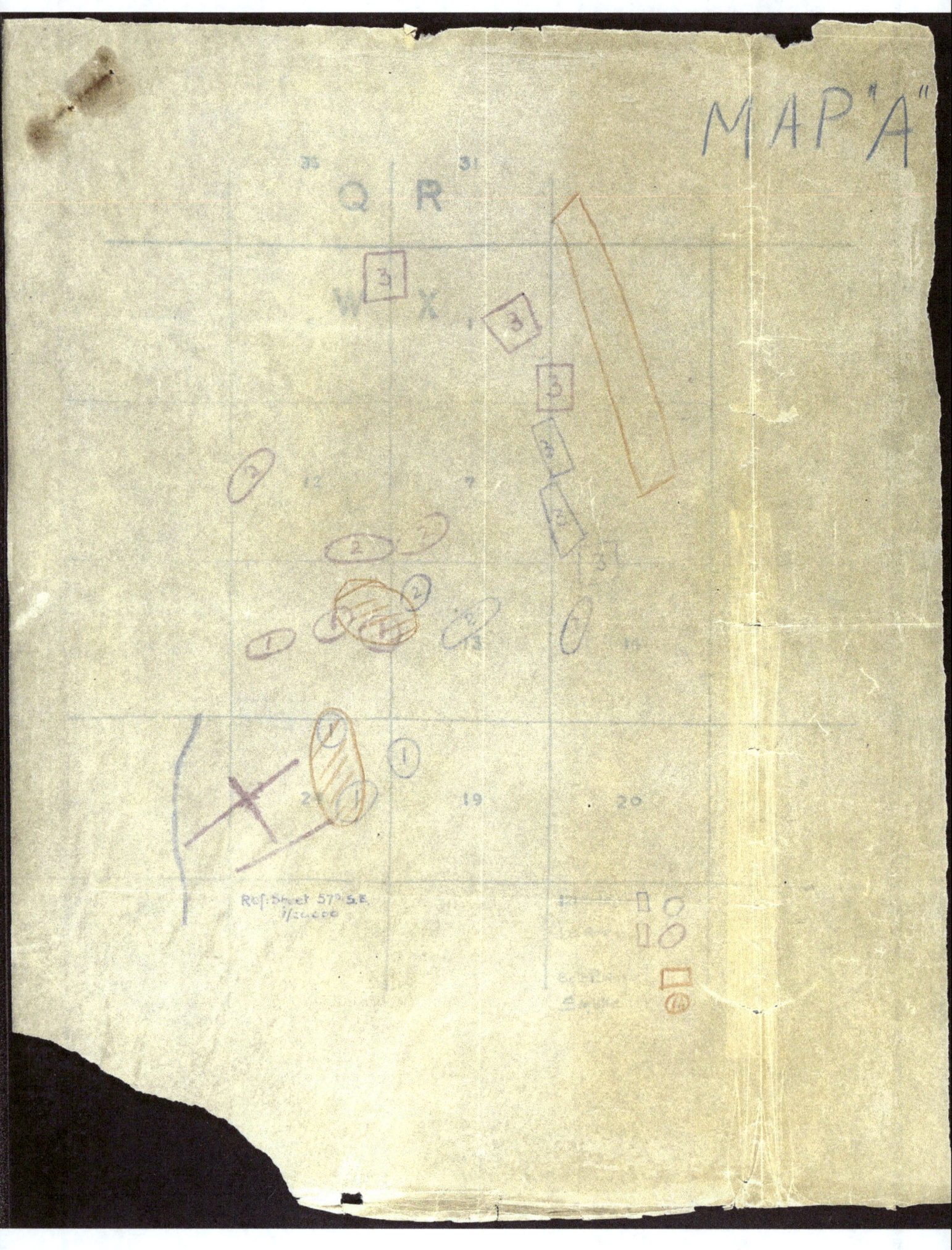

TABLE "A" Cont'd.

Serial No.	Time.	Unit.	Targets.	Rate.	Remarks.
11.	+120 onwards.	"D"/121.) "D"/122.)	On targets East of North and South grid line through R.33.central and X.9.central.	----	
12.	Zero to +30.	248 S.B.	On Trenches on USNA HILL R.24.b.		
13.	+30 to +60.	do	On trenches in R.18.b.		If available.
14.	+60 to +120.		On OVILLERS LA BOISSELLE.		
	+120 onwards.		On objectives E. of N. and S. grid line through R.33.central and X.9.central.		

Serial No.	Time.	Unit.	Targets.	Rate.	Remarks.
				r.p.g.p.m.	
		18-pdr. BATTERIES.			
1.	Zero to + 30.	121st. Brigade. 122nd. Brigade.	On On	1. 1.	
2.	+ 30 to + 60.	121st. Brigade. 122nd. Brigade.	On trenches in areas ditto.	1. 1.	50% "A". 50% "AX".
3.	+ 60 to + 90.	121st. Brigade. 122nd. Brigade.	ditto. ditto.	1. 1.	
4.	+ 90 to + 120.	121st. Brigade. 122nd. Brigade.	ditto. ditto.	1. 1.	
5.	+ 120 to + 140.	121st. Brigade. 122nd. Brigade. }	On	1.	
6.	+ 140 onwards.	121st. Brigade. 122nd. Brigade.	On Targets E. of North and South grid line between squares R.32 and 33 and X.2. and 3.	1.	
		4.5" HOWS.			
7.	Zero to + 30.	"D"/121. "D"/122.	On in R.24.b. On in R.18.b.	Salvo of 3 rds. gun fire then 1 r.p.g.p.m.	Smoke Shell —do—
8.	+ 30 to + 60.	"D"/121. "D"/122.	On On	1. 1.	"BX" "BX"
9.	+ 60 to + 90.	"D"/121. "D"/122.	On On	do do	
10.	+ 90 to + 120.	"D"/121. "D"/122. }	On	do	

SECRET.
XXXXXXXXXX

38th DIVISIONAL ARTILLERY OPERATION ORDER NO. 78

Copy No. 1B

Ref. Sheet 57D S.E.1/20,000   22.8.18.

1. At about 6 a.m. 22nd, 21st Division is to attack THIEPVAL RIDGE from the North under a creeping barrage lasting 2¼ hrs. The final line of the barrage is R.28.b.40.70 - R.21.c.70.15.

2. (a) On 22nd August 18th Division is to attack from South of ALBERT in a N.E. direction.
   (b) Zero hour for this operation is 4.45 a.m.
   (c) 121st Brigade will co-operate with two batteries as already detailed in O.O. No.76.

3. (a) To exploit success gained by 18th Division 113th Infantry Brigade may be ordered to attack the line OVILLERS - LA- BOISSELLE - THIEPVAL.
   (b) In this event the Brigade would cross the railway and River ANCRE between ALBERT and AVELUY and then advance in a N.E. direction.

4. Action of 38th D.A. to support this operation is shown in Table "A" and Map "A" attached.

5. There will be no fire South of the ALBERT - POZIERES - BAPAUME Road.

6. As this area is under complete observation from O.P's Battery Commanders may switch their guns off allotted tasks in order to engage hostile activity.

7. If operation by 113th Infantry Brigade is successful 115th and 114th Infantry Brigades will carry out the "First Bound" as detailed in O.O.75.

8. Brigades will each detail one F.O.O. and party to establish an O.P. on THIEPVAL RIDGE as soon as it is gained.

9. 121st Brigade will be in liaison with 113th Infantry Brigade - H.Q. at W.25.b.0.7.

10. Signal time will be taken.

11. Zero Hour will be notified later. It will probably be after 8 a.m.

12. Brigades to ACKNOWLEDGE.

Issued at 4 a.m.

Brigade Major, 38th Divisional Artillery.
Major R.A.

Copy No.	
1 - 5	121st Bde.
6 - 10	122nd Bde.
11	S.C.R.A.
12	R.A. Sigs Officer.
13 - 15	38th Division.
16	113th Infantry Brigade.
17	18th D.A.
18	21st D.A.
19	V. Corps R.A.
20	V Corps H.A.
21, 22	"A" Bde R.G.A.
23, 24	War Diary.
25	File.

-2-

11. The Code word to put above operation into action will be "FOLLOW". As this Code word may be received at any moment, all Units on receipt of this order will dress and equip so as to be in a state of instant readiness to move.

12. Brigade Headquarters will remain in present position (P.24.d.3.4.) in the first instance; if a move takes place, new location will be Q.28.a.9.3.

13. ACKNOWLEDGE.

Captain
A/Brigade Major,
114th Infantry Brigade.

Issued thro' Signals at 2-30A.M.

DISTRIBUTION

No. 1. 13th Welsh Regiment
 2. 14th   "   "
 3. 15t   "   "
 4. 114th L.T.M.Btty.(At 14th W.R.)
 5. Staff Captain.
 6. B.S.O.
 7. "D" Coy 38th Battn M.G.C.(AT 14th W.R.)
 8. Section 178 Tunnlg Coy (With 14th W.R.)
 9 and 10. 24 Field Coy R.E. (With 13 & 14 W.R.)
 11. 110th Inf Brigade.
 12. 115th Infantry Brigade.
 13. 122nd Bde R.F.A.
 14 and 15 38th Division.
 16 and 17 War Diary.
 18 FILE.

SECRET.

COPY NO. 12

114th INFANTRY BRIGADE ORDER NO.197

Ref Map 57D S.I. 1/20,000   22nd August 1918.

1. 13th and 14th Welsh Regiments with attached troops will be prepared, on receipt of orders from Brigade H.Qrs, to force the crossings of the ANCRE and seize the tactical points mentioned in Order No.196.

2. Battle Patrols of one Platoon from each Reserve Company (4 in all) will cross the ANCRE at, or near the crossings, and with similar objectives to those mentioned in 114th Bde B.M.909. These patrols will if necessary, fight their way up to their objectives. Each patrol will be accompanied by a responsible Officer or N.C.O., and man from each Reserve Company whose duty will be to report to Battalion Headquarters immediately battle patrols have reached their objectives (First Objectives for Nos 2, 3, and 4 Patrols)

3. Battalion Commanders, will without further orders from Brigade Headquarters, will then despatch remainder of Reserve Companies to reinforce Patrols and to occupy the obligatory tactical points. When obligatory tactical points have been occupied, Front line Companies will follow in Support.

4. 1½ Sections "D" Company 38th Battn M.G.Corps; one section 124th Field Company R.E., and ⅔ section 178th Tunnelling Company will accompany Reserve Companies of each Battalion across the ANCRE and will be employed as ordered by Officers Commanding 13th and 14th Welsh Regiments. These Units are now with Battalions.

5. One Section "D" Company 38th Battn M.G.C. will be in Brigade Reserve and will, on receipt of orders, take up a position on Ridge at North end of AVELUY WOOD ready to support advance of battle patrols by direct fire as opportunity offers, by firing on any enemy opposing their advance.
   Such Support will only be given in day-light and if target and patrol are both visible support will be given to all patrols as opportunity offers.

6. 114th L.T.M.Battery (4 Mortars) are being placed in position to-night and from these positions will support advance of battle patrols in same manner as Reserve Machine Gun section (Section 5 above).

7. Separate instructions regarding action of artillery will be issued to Left Group. Artillery fire will be so arranged that it will in no way interfere with advance of battle patrols and Reserve Companies to their objectives.

8. 15th Welsh Regiment (Brigade Reserve Battalion) on receipt of orders from Brigade Headquarters will move to Valley West of MESNIL.

9. On receipt of this order Battalion Commanders will at once order
   (a) Their Battle Patrols to their forward Assembly positions in ANCRE VALLEY as near as possible to crossings.
   (b) Reserve Companies to the general line CASUALTY - BRACKEN - UPTON - BARN TRENCHES, so as to be closer at hand for following up, but not to be visible from enemy side of ANCRE.

10. Orders for action of Reserve Battalion -
    Contact aeroplanes
    Success Signals,
    Maps
    Signal Communications and
    Administrative instructions will be as laid down in
114th Infantry Brigade Order No.196

S.E.C.R.E.T.

38th (Welsh) Division Order. No.211.

22nd August.1918.

I. The attack of the third Corps this morning was successful, their objective was gained and over 1,000 prisoners taken.
The left Brigade of the 18th Division on our immediate right now holds the line of the road from W.29.d.9.0. to W.29.d.3.0. thence along road to road junction W.29.c.8.9. thence along Railway to about W.29.a.8.7.
The enemy is still holding on to a position E.6.b.7.7. W.24.d.6.3. - thence along RUBBER LANE.
The advance of the 113th Brigade ordered in D.O. 210. is postponed until tomorrow and the objectives therein laid down are in abeyance though they may form the objectives for a subsequent operation, for which further orders will be issued

II. The third Corps is renewing the attack at 4.45 a.m. tomorrow
Objectives for 18th Division is the line E.11.d.central - E.6.b.central - W.29.b.8.2.

III The 113th Brigade will attack at the same time as the III Corps and will seize and consolidate RUBBER LANE.
After this objective has been gained 113th Brigade will capture the hostile posts at CRUCIFIX CORNER about W.12.c.0.1. also pushing forward outposts in advance of RUBBER LANE.

IV. 113th Brigade will form up for attack on the line W.29.a. 3.0. - W.29.d.8.7. - passing through or relieving the troops of the 18th Division who now hold that line

V. The Boundary between the III Corps and the 113th Brigade will be the ALBERT- BAPAUME Road (inclusive to III Corps.)

VI. The attack of the 113th Brigade will be supported as follows

(a) The 38th D.A. will bombard the objective at ZERO and will open creeping barrage at ZERO plus 30 with lifts of 100 yards A programme is being prepared by C.R.A.

(b) Two tanks will operate with 113th Brigade under orders given by 18th Division.

(c) In addition to the M.G.Coy. (less 2 sections) acting under the orders of the 113th Brigade the following M.G. action will be arranged under the orders of the O.C., MG Battalion.
8 guns of the Right Machine Gun Company in the line and 8 Guns of the Company attached to 113th Brigade will come into action in squares W.4.,10, and 16 to-night and will open fire at ZERO on such portions of the objectives as are within range. Fire will be direct. This fire will be lifted off the objective when it is seen that our infantry are approaching it. If weather conditions make it impossible to see the objective from the batteries this target will not be engaged at all. After lifting off the objective or if the objective is not engaged this fire will be directed on to the trenches in W.18.b. and maintained on that target till ZERO plus 1½ hours.
Fire will also be directed on to points in AUTHUILLE WOOD from Zero till Zero plus 2½ hours.

SECRET.

38th (Welsh) Division Order. No.211.

22nd August.1918.

I. The attack of the third Corps this morning was successful, their objective was gained and over 1,000 prisoners taken.
    The left Brigade of the 18th Division on our immediate right now holds the line of the road from W.29.d.9.0. to W.9.d.3.0. thence along road to road junction W.29.c.6.9. thence along Railway to about W.29.a.5.7.
    The enemy is still holding on to a position B.6.b.7.7. B.24.d.6.3. - thence along RUBBER LANE.
    The advance of the 113th Brigade ordered in D.O. 210. is postponed until tomorrow and the objectives therein laid down are in abeyance though they may form the objectives for a subsequent operation, for which further orders will be issued

II. The third Corps is renewing the attack at 4.45 a.m. tomorrow
    Objectives for 18th Division is the line N.11.d.central - N.6.b.central - W.6.b.6.5.

III The 113th Brigade will attack at the same time as the III Corps and will seize and consolidate RUBBER LANE.
    After this objective has been gained 113th Brigade will capture the hostile posts at CRUCIFIX CORNER about W.12.c.0.1. also pushing forward outposts in advance of RUBBER LANE.

IV. 113th Brigade will form up for attack on the line W.29.a. 8.0. - W.29.a.5.7. - passing through or relieving the troops of the 18th Division who now hold that line

V. The Boundary between the III Corps and the 113th Brigade will be the ALBERT- BAPAUME Road (inclusive to III Corps.)

VI. The attack of the 113th Brigade will be supported as follows

(a) The 38th D.A. will bombard the objective at ZERO and will open creeping barrage at ZERO plus 50 with lifts of 100 yards A programme is being prepared by C.R.A.

(b) Two tanks will operate with 113th Brigade under orders given by 18th Division.

(c) In addition to the M.G.Coy. (less 2 sections) acting under the orders of the 113th Brigade the following M.G. action will be arranged under the orders of the O.C., MG Battalion.
    8 guns of the Right Machine Gun Company in the line and 8 Guns of the Company attached to 113th Brigade will come into action in squares W.4.,10, and 16 to-night and will open fire at ZERO on such portions of the objectives as are within range. Fire will be direct. This fire will be lifted off the objective when it is seen that our infantry are approaching it. If weather conditions make it impossible to see the objective from the batteries this target will not be engaged at all. After lifting off the objective or if the objective is not engaged this fire will be directed on to the trenches in W.13.b. and maintained on that target till ZERO plus 1½ hours.
    Fire will also be directed on to points in AVELUY WOOD from Zero till Zero plus 1½ hours.

S E C R E T.   Copy No. 13

38th (WELSH) DIVISION ORDER NO. 211.

22nd August, 1918.

I.   The attack of the Third Corps this morning was successful; their objective was gained and over 1000 prisoners taken.
     The left Brigade of the 18th Division on our immediate right now holds the line of the road from W.29.d.9.0. to W.29.d.3.0., thence along road to road junction W.29.c.8.9., thence along railway to about W.29.a.5.7.
     The enemy is still holding on to a position E.6.b.7.7.- W.24.d.8.3.- thence along RUBBER LANE.
     The advance of the 113 Brigade ordered in D.O. 210 is postponed until to-morrow and the objectives therein laid down are in abeyance though they may form the objectives for a subsequent operation for which further orders will be issued.

II. The Third Corps is renewing the attack at 4.45 a.m. to-morrow.
     Objective for 18th Division is the line E.11.d.central - E.6.b.central - W.24.b.8.2.

III. The 113 Brigade will attack at the same time as the Third Corps and will seize and consolidate RUBBER LANE.
     After this objective has been gained 113 Brigade will capture the hostile post at CRUCIFIX CORNER about W.12.c.0.1. also pushing forward outposts in advance of RUBBER LANE.

IV. 113 Brigade will form up for attack on the line W.29.a.9.0. - W.29.a.5.7. passing through or relieving the troops of 18th Division who now hold that line.

V.   The boundary between the Third Corps and the 113 Brigade will be the ALBERT - BAPAUME road (inclusive to Third Corps).

VI. The attack of the 113 Brigade will be supported as follows :-

(a). The 38th D.A. will bombard the objective at Zero and will open a creeping barrage at Zero + 30 with lifts of 100 yards. A programme is being prepared by the C.R.A.

(b). Two Tanks will operate with 113 Brigade under orders given by 18th Division.

(c). In addition to the M.G. Coy. (less 2 Sections) acting under the orders of the 113 Brigade the following machine gun action will be arranged under the orders of the O.C. M.G. Bn.:-
     8 guns of the right M.G. Coy. in the line and 8 guns of the Coy. attached to 115 Brigade will come into action in Squares W.4, 10 and 16 to-night and will open fire at Zero on such portions of the objective as are within range. Fire will be direct. This fire will be lifted off the objective when it is seen that our infantry are approaching it. If weather conditions make it impossible to see the objective from the batteries this target will not be engaged at all. After lifting off the objective or if the objective is not engaged this fire will be directed on to the trenches in W.18.b. and maintained on that target till Zero + 1½ hours.
     Fire will also be directed on to points in AUTHUILLE WOOD from Zero till Zero + 1½ hours.
     O.C. M.G. Coy. will arrange a visual signal station at W.15.b.9.0. which will receive any messages sent by visual by 115 Brigade and communicate them to the batteries; this station can also be reached by wire through 115 Brigade O.P.

VII./

VII. The Headquarters of the 113 Brigade will be at W.25.b.0.7.

VIII. ACKNOWLEDGE.

F. J Harington Captain
for Lieut. Colonel
General Staff, 38th (Welsh) Division.

Issued thro' Signals 8.10 p.m.

Copies to all Units, 38th Division.
V Corps.
V Corps R.A.
V Corps H.A.
17th Division.
18th Division.
21st Division.
15 Squadron R.A.F.

MAP "A"

W | X

Ref Sheet 27a
1/20,000

TABLE "A".

Serial No.	Time.	Unit.	Target.	R to. r.p.g.p.m.	Remarks.
1.	Zero onwards.	All 18-pdr.Btys. 121 and 122 Bdes.	Creeping Barrage - with objectives - lifts and times as shown in Map "A" attached. The Barrage will open on the line A - A.	2.	Shrapnel with long corrector will be fired throughout, except that 1 rd. in 15 will be smoke. H.E. will not be used until after arrival at the final protective barrage. Fire will be maintained on the final protective barrage line for 30 minutes and then gradually die down. Smoke will not be used if the weather is misty.
2.	Zero to +30.	"D"/121.	Area W.24.d.6.9. - W.18.d.3.0.	3 rds gun fire then 1 r.p.g.p.m.	Smoke. If misty "EX".
3.	+30 to +50.	-do-	Dug-outs at W.24.b.7.0. W.24.b.2.9. X.19.d.1.5.	1½.	"EX".
4.	+50 onwards.	-do-	RUMMAGE Trench. RAFFLE Trench.	1½.	"EX".
5.	Zero to +30.	"D"/122.	RAFFLE Trench, ROUTON LANE, RUM Trench.	Salvo, then 3 rds. G.F., then 1 r.p.g.p.m.	Smoke. If misty targets - RIBAID AV. and Trench W.24.c. 7.4. - W.24.a.2.0. "EX".
6.	+30 to +70.	-do-	RIBAID AVENUE.	1.	
7.	+30 to +100.	-do- (2 Hows.)	CRUCIFIX CORNER (W.12.c.).	1.	
8.	+30 to +150.	-do- (2 Hows.)	ROVAJEY Trench (W.12.a.&.c.)	1.	
9.	at +70 to +150	-do- (2 Hows.)	Lift off RIBAID AVENUE on to ROWLOCK Trench.	1.	

TABLE "A" Contd.

Serial No.	Time.	Unit.	Target.	Rate r.p.g.p.m.	Remarks.
10.	At Z 100 to Z 150.	"D"/122. (2 Hows)	Lift off CRUCIFIX CORNER on to ROLL Trench.	1.	
11.	At Z 150.	All fire ceases.			

NOTE:- V Corps H.A. is bombarding CRUCIFIX CORNER, DONNET POST and trenches immediately South lifting off within safety limits in conformity with the F.A. Barrage.

SECRET.   Copy No. 9.

38th Division Royal Engineers

C.R.E's Operation Order No. 67.

23rd August, 1918.

1. The 38th Division together with other troops on both flanks will attack the enemy positions east of the River ANCRE on the night 23/24th August, 1918.
Further particulars and the orders in paras 4 – 10 were communicated verbally to officers Commanding 123 and 151 Field Coys R.E. and O.C. 19th Welsh Regt. (Pioneers) at C.R.E's Conference today.

2. The duties allotted to Field Companies and Pioneers are as under:-

3. 124 Field Coy R.E. has already been detailed as follows :-

    (a) Company, less 2 sections, placed under orders of G.O.C. 113 Infantry Brigade.

    (b) 1 section under orders of G.O.C. 114 Infantry Brigade.

    (c) 1 section under orders of G.O.C. 115 Infantry Brigade.

4. The remaining 2 Field Coys and Divisional Pioneers will work under the orders of the C.R.E. and carry out the following tasks.

5. <u>123 Field Coy R.E.</u> will

    (a) make crossings of the ANCRE fit for Infantry in single file at :
        Q.29.b.8.0.
        Q.24.c.5.0.
It is essential that this work be put in hand immediately it is dark enough and completed as soon as possible.
    (b) Make the road from MESNIL through Q.29.a and b to Q.24.a.1.5, sufficiently good to allow pack animals to reach the MILL road crossing, which starts from that point.
    (c) Make the crossing of the ANCRE good for field artillery at
        Q.36.c.1.3. and Q.36.c.1.7.
    (d) Improve one of the crossings in sub para (a) above, so as to take pack animals.

6. O.C. 19th Welsh Regt. (Pioneers) will place 1 company at disposal of O.C. 123 Field Coy R.E. to assist him in carrying out the work detailed in para 5 (a), (b) and (c). When no longer required by O.C. 123 Field Coy R.E., it will be available for the work detailed in para 8 (a).

7. <u>151 Field Coy R.E.</u> will
    (a) Make the crossing of the ANCRE good for 60 pdrs at W.11.d. 2.6.
    (b) Make the crossing of the ANCRE good for Infantry in single file at W.17.d.1.7.
    (c) Make the crossing of the ANCRE good for Infantry in file and if possible, for Field Artillery at W.28.b.8.5, but work in sub para (a) takes precedence over this.

8. 19th Welsh Regt. will repair the following roads so as to take horse transport, and subsequently, if their condition permits, motor lorries. One company will be employed on each.

    (a) AUTHUILLE - THIEPVAL.
    (b) AVELUY (W.11.d.7.7.) through W.18.a and b - OVILLERS - X.8.b.6.7. - X.9.c.8.9. *also from X.8.6.6.7 & R.33.d.8.3*
    (c) ALBERT - BAPAUME road from X.13.d.0.0. north eastwards.

9. The MILL ROAD crossing of the ANCRE (Q.24.a.4.2.) will be made good for field guns by 17th Division and also the road from there to THIEPVAL.

10. The ANCRE crossings detailed in paras 5 and 7 replace those given in 38th Division Order No. 213 para V11.

Field Coys and Pioneers to acknowledge.

W. Dickinson
Lieut, R.E.
for Lieut. Col. R.E.
C.R.E., 38th (Welsh) Division.

Issued 8.55 p.m.

Copy No. 1. O.C. 123 Field Coy R.E.
" " 2. O.C. 124 Field Coy R.E.
" " 3. O.C. 151 Field Coy R.E.
" " 4. O.C. 19th Welsh Regt.(Pioneers)

For information.

Copy No. 5. 38th Division G.S.
" " 6. 38th Division A. & Q.
" " 7. 113 Infantry Brigade.
" " 8. 114 Infantry Brigade.
" " 9. 115 Infantry Brigade.
" " 10. Chief Engineer, Vth Corps.
" " 11. C.R.E., 17th Division.
" " 12. C.R.E., 18th Division.
" " 13. C.R.A., 38th Division.
" " 14. A.D.M.S., 38th Division.
" " 15. O.C. 38th M.G. Corps.
" " 16. War Diary.
" " 17. File. (C.R.E's copy.)
" " 18. File.
" " 19. File.
" " 20. File.

SECRET.
XXXXXXXXXX

38th DIVISIONAL ARTILLERY OPERATION ORDER NO.81

Copy No...29

23rd August 1918.

1. In the event of success in tonight's operation 38th Division, if not strongly opposed is to advance to the line CONTALMAISON-POZIERES - COURCELETTE.

2. RE-ORGANIZATION OF F.A.
From 12 noon 24th August the Field Artillery covering 38th Division will consist of 4 Brigade Groups, as under :-

121st Brigade	in liaison with	113th Infantry Bde.
122nd Brigade	in liaison with	114th Infantry Bde.
310th Brigade	in liaison with	115th Infantry Bde.
312nd Brigade in action in Divisional Artillery Reserve.		

3. BRIGADE H.Q's.
Artillery Brigade Headquarters, should, whenever possible, be established with Headquarters of affiliated Infantry Brigade. But if all batteries of a Brigade are sited at a considerable distance from Infantry Brigade Headquarters then Artillery Brigade Headquarters will be established close to its batteries. In this event an officer not below the rank of Captain will be detailed as liaison officer with the Infantry Brigade.

4. ADVANCE OF ARTILLERY.

(a) In the event of the attack by 38th Division being successful, the Artillery will begin to move forward across the ANCRE on completion of the barrage.
(b) Brigades will advance by Sections or Batteries, 121st Brigade leading.
(c) 122nd Brigade will move next, but will not start until 121st Brigade is across the river and in action.
(d) Remaining Brigades will move under orders to be issued later.
(e) Areas to be occupied are :-

121st Brigade W.18.
122nd Brigade W.12.

5. BRIDGES.
The route from present positions will be PIONEER Road - AVELUY - Bridge at W.11.d.4.6. This bridge has not yet been constructed but work is in progress. The roads and area East of the Bridge have been very much cut up.
Reconnaissance of the roads to the bridge and routes beyond will begin at Zero hour.

6. More Batteries will not be advanced than can be supplied with ammunition. All arrangements for bringing up ammunition by pack will be made.

7. It should be impressed on all ranks that they should act act with the greatest boldness and that risks which promise good good results should invariably be taken.

/8.

-2-

8. F.O.O's must send reports regularly. Negative reports are as valuable as positive ones.

9. Lewis guns will be taken with every section which moves forward and will be sited for the defence of the position.

10. Ample tools for filling in or bridging trenches will be taken with each section.

11. ACKNOWLEDGE.

J.E. Thurston
Major R.A.
Brigade Major, 38th Divisional Artillery.

Issued at 10 p.m.

Copy No.	1 - 5	121st Brigade.
	6 - 10	122nd Brigade.
	11	38th D.A.C.
	12	S.C.R.A.
	13	R.A. Sigs Officer.
	14 - 18	310th Brigade.
	19 - 23	312th Brigade.
	24	62nd D.A.C.
	25	62nd D.A.
	26	38th Division "G"
	27	113th Infantry Brigade.
	28	114th Infantry Brigade.
	29	115th Infantry Brigade.
	30	V Corps R.A.
	31	V Corps H.A.
	32, 33	War Diary.
	34	File.

SECRET.   Copy No. 13

38TH (WELSH) DIVISION ORDER NO. 213.

                                                       23rd August, 1918.

I.   D.O. 205 is cancelled.

II.   Six Armies (British and French) are attacking to-day between ARRAS and SOISSONS.
      The Corps on our left is attacking IRLES and ACHIET LE GRAND to-day.
      GOMIECOURT has been taken by us to-day.

III. The V Corps will attack to-night 23rd/24th at 1 a.m.
      Objectives and boundaries are shown on the attached map.
      The 18th Division on our right is attacking at the same hour with the object of seizing the line X.25.a. - X.20.a.9.9.

IV.   The Left attack will be carried out by the 21st Division.
      The Centre attack   "   "   "   "   " 17th and 38th Divs.
      The Right   "   "   "   "   "   " 38th Div.

V.   The Right attack will be carried out by the 113 Brigade on the right and the 115 Brigade on the left, the boundary between the two being the road X.13.a.3.6. - OVILLERS (inclusive to 115 Brigade), point X.8.b.9.3. where the track cuts the rod line.
      115 Brigade will attack with one Battalion in front closely supported by another and one in reserve. The support battalion will be employed in forming a left defensive flank and taking and occupying the trench system in the apex of the triangle (made by the boundary lines) in X.2; the reserve battalion will be employed in mopping up the remainder of the country between the left boundary of the right attack and the right boundary of the centre attack paying special attention to any posts which fire on to the crossings of the ANCRE.
      Both Brigades will form up for attack on RUBBER LANE, the dividing line being the sunken road W.18.d.2.7.

VI.   The right half of the centre attack as shown on the attached map will be carried out by 114 Brigade who will form a defensive flank along the right boundary of their attack.

VII. Bridges will be taken in hand by Field Coys. as under :-

By 151 Field Coy.   W.17.c.8.6. footbridge; at once.
   "   "   "   W.11.d.4.6. for all arms   ) immediately that
   " 123   "   W.36.c.1.3 & 1.7. for all arms) these crossings can
   "   "   "   W.29.c.8.3. foot bridge.   ) be approached without
   "   "   "   W.24.c.5.0.   "   ) drawing fire.

      Field Coys. R.E. will send a bridge situation report hourly from receipt of this order 151 Field Coy. to 115 Brigade, 123 Field Coy. to 114 Brigade. C.R.E. will report hourly to Division Head Quarters.

      The bridges made by 151 and 123 Field Coy. R.E. are allotted for use to 115 and 114 Brigades respectively; 113 Brigade will use the crossings in ALBERT.

VIII One section of 124 Field Coy. R.E. is placed under the orders of each of 115 and 114 Brigades forthwith.
      A half section of 178 Tunnelling Coy. is placed under the orders of each of the above Brigades for the purpose of searching for mines etc.
      The Pioneer Battalion will be employed under the C.R.E. on the repair of roads AVELUY - OVILLERS and AUTHUILLE - THIEPVAL - POZIERES.

                                                              IX./

SECRET.

IX.   'E' Squadron V Cyclist Regt. will remain under the orders of 113 Brigade for the present.

X.   M.G. Coys. are placed under the orders of Brigades forthwith.
        Under 113 Brigade. "B" Coy. (remaining two sections to report to the Bde. at once).
           " 114 Brigade. "D" Coy.
           " 115 Brigade. "A" Coy.
        At least half the guns under Brigade orders are to be employed on the final objective of this and any future attacks.
        (For this attack each Brigade will detail one Infantry company as carrying party for its own M.G. Coy.; until bridges are suitable for pack or wheeled transport).
        Guns now in position in the line may be withdrawn from position at once.

XI.   Arrangements for artillery support are being issued by the C.R.A.

XII.   Advanced Headquarters will move as under before Zero.
           114 Brigade to Q.28.a.9.4.
           115 Brigade to W.3.d.8.5.

XIII.   A Staff Officer will visit Brigades, R.A., and M.G. Bn. between 6 p.m. and 7 p.m. to-day for the purpose of synchronising watches.

XIV.   The regimental signallers of the 19th Welsh Regt. (Glamorgan Pioneers) will be attached to the Div. Signal Coy. forthwith.

XV.   Until further orders the aeroplane signal to denote the assembly of hostile troops for counter attack will be a red smoke bomb dropped in the direction of their place of assembly.

                                        J.S. Munby
                                        Lieut. Colonel,
                                        General Staff, 38th (Welsh) Div.

Issued thro' Signals at 2.30 p.m.

Copies to all Units, 38th Division.
V Corps.
V Corps R.A.
V Corps H.A.
17th Division.
18th Division.
21st Division.
'E' Squadron, V Corps Cyclists.
15 Squadron R.A.F.

SECRET. 38th Div. No.GSS.1/18.

38TH (WELSH) DIVISION.

Tactical Instructions in connection with D.O. 213.

1. The final objective is the red line shown on the map issued with D.O. 213.

2. On arrival on the final objective (red line) the boundaries will be as follows :-

   Between the Div. on our right and 38 Div. - The grid line between X.14. and X.20.
   "   "   "   "   "   left "   "   - The grid line between R.27 and R.33.
   (MOUQUET FARM inclusive to 38 Div.)

   Between Brigades, the same boundaries as laid down for the attack extended due East from the point where these boundaries meet the red line.

3. As soon as the protective barrage lifts strong patrols will be pushed forward to the blue and red line and their action must not be limited by this line. On arrival on the final objective the Cyclist Coy. will come under the orders of the Division; they will patrol all roads which are fit for bicycles and will maintain touch with the enemy. They will report information direct to Div. Head Quarters and to the Brigades which are affected by that information.

4. The 21st Division is attacking at 5 a.m. to-morrow with the object of occupying the blue line or a position further East.

5. A sufficient number of paper maps have been issued for platoon commanders. They should be marked in the same manner as those issued with D.O. 213.

6. The success signal is a "R.G. White White White"; this should be fired at some point about 200 yards to the flank of the place which it is intended to hold.

7. An "international post" will be formed with the 18th Division in the trench at X.20.a.7.7.

8. Information has just been received that the advance of our troops to the North has been so successful that their objective is now BAPAUME.

   The following instructions apply to all operations of the near future :-

9. In consequence of the two severe defeats which the enemy has recently suffered and the repeated and successful attacks which we have been and are now delivering the situation now admits of much greater risks being taken than would previously have been justified.

   Therefore any objective which is laid down should be taken as being approximate only and advance to more distant if better ground should be made as opportunity offers. Attacks will be delivered with the greatest boldness. At the same time defensive precautions should never be neglected provided that they do not unduly hamper preparations for the offensive.

10. Machine guns must be used with boldness and pushed well forward.

11./

11. The importance of depth in both attack and defence must not be overlooked.
Stokes Mortars should follow the attacking troops and be brought into action as early as possible. These may be specially valuable in mopping up large areas and with their ammunition can be carried on pack animals.

12. The importance of reporting the situation must be impressed on all ranks, many delays and mistakes have happened hitherto due solely to want of information which the troops in front were able to supply, the same will continue to happen unless everyone remembers that there is someone behind him who must be informed as to how he is getting on. Negative information is often just as valuable as positive information.
Messages must be cut down as short as possible unless they are to be transmitted by runner.
The first means of communication to be established are visual and wireless; wires can be laid later.
When a Brigade Headquarters moves it must ensure that communication to its new Headquarters are in working order before it leaves the old ones.
Battalion Headquarters should be selected before an advance begins.
Pigeons must never be forgotten, and should be issued to officers in the leading waves.
During active operations B.A.B. Code should be used on wireless in preference to Field Cypher in order to shorten messages.

13. Flares <u>must</u> be lit when called for by aeroplanes.

14. Tools will always be required and men must be definitely/told off to carry them as part of their equipment. No attempt should be made to dig a continuous trench line; instead shell holes etc. must be made defensible.

15. All officers must carry compasses and must use them; the attack by the IV Corps in the mist yesterday would have miscarried if they had not been used. Compass "forward" bearings should frequently be checked by "back" bearings.

16. The following must always be carried (in limited numbers) - rifle grenades - hand grenades - flares - S.O.S. Signals - "success signals" - wire cutters.

17. ACKNOWLEDGE.

J. S. Munby
Lieut. Colonel,
General Staff, 38th (Welsh) Division.

Copies to - All units, 38th Division.
    V Corps.
    V Corps R.A.
    V Corps H.A.
    17th Division.
    18th Division.
    21st Division.
    'E' Squadron, V Corps Cyclists.
    15 Squadron R.A.F.

S E C R E T.   COPY.

                                           38th Division No.G__ __/18.

38TH (WELSH) DIVISION.

WARNING ORDER.

Probable attack by 18th, 38th, 17th and 21st Divisions tomorrow night 23r/24th instant.

1. <u>Right Attack.</u>   113th and 115th Brigades, the latter also be responsible for mopping up triangle between Right and Right Centre attacks.

   <u>Right Centre Attack.</u>   114th Brigade.

2. On right of Right Attack. - 18th Division.
   Left Centre Attack. -   17th Division.

3. 1st Objective BROWN LINE to be reached at Zero plus 40'
   10' halt on BROWN LINE. Advance from BROWN LINE at Zero plus 50'.
   Subsidiary 2nd Objective. GREEN LINE (Right Attack) to be reached at Zero plus 90'. 10' halt on GREEN LINE. Advance from GREEN LINE Zero plus 100'
   2nd Objective. RED LINE to be reached by Right Attack at Zero plus 140' and by centre and left attacks at Zero plus 90'.
   BROWN LINE & RED LINE to be consolidated.
   Advanced troops, to exploit success and cover consolidation to be pushed out to the general line shewn on RED & BLUE.

4. 21st Division attack BLUE LINE on the morning of the 24th.

5. Machine Guns partly barrage partly accompanying Brigades in attack and to cover final consolidation.

6. Bridges to be constructed during attack and ~~to cover final consolidation.~~ two capable of carrying guns.

7. Flares to be carried.

8. Pigeons and Visual by advanced troops.

9. Artillery programme to be issued.

10. 113th Brigade Right Divisional Boundary in touch with 18th Division. Left Boundary W.18.d.6.5. - RUMMAGE Trench - X.8.c.4.2. - X.8.b.8.0. - in touch with 115th Brigade. 115th Brigade right boundary as above. Left Boundary as shewn on map and responsible for mopping up of triangle between Right and Centre attacks.

11. 115th and 114th Brigades to leave posts as defensive flanks facing the triangle.

                                           T. ASTLEY CUBITT,
                                              Major General,
23.8.18.   Commanding, 115th Infantry Brigade.

S E C R E T.
XXXXXXXXXX
Copy No........

23rd August 1918.

38th DIVISIONAL ARTILLERY OPERATION ORDER No.80.

1. On night 23/24th August 38th Division is to attack. 18th Div. is attacking simultaneously on our right and 17th Division on our left.

2. (a) The attack of 38th Division is to be made in two converging lines as shown on attached Map "X".
   (b) RIGHT ATTACK is to be made by 113th Inf. Bde. on the right and 115th Inf. Bde. on the left.
   (c) RIGHT CENTRE ATTACK is to be made by 114th Inf. Bde.
   (d) Boundaries and objectives are shown on Map "X".

3. RIGHT ATTACK.
   (a) Forming up place will be dependent on the progress made by patrols during the day.
   (b) 1st Objective is the BROWN LINE - to be reached at Zero + 40. After a halt of 10 mins. the Infantry advance at Zero + 50 to the 2nd objective, GREEN LINE, to be reached at Zero + 90. After another halt of 10 mins. the advance is continued to the RED LINE to be reached at Zero + 140.
   (c) RED LINE is to be consolidated and patrols pushed out to the general line shown RED and BLUE.
   (d) Boundary between 113th and 115th Inf. Bdes:-
       X.13.a.3.5. - OVILLERS (inclusive to 115) - X.8.b.9.3.
   (e) 115th Inf. Bde. is to be responsible for mopping up the triangle between RIGHT and RIGHT CENTRE attacks.

4. RIGHT CENTRE ATTACK.
   (a) Forming up place - CHICKWEED RESERVE.
   (b) First objective is the BROWN LINE - to be reached at Zero + 40. After a halt of 10 mins. the infantry advance to the 2nd. objective, RED LINE, to be reached at Zero + 90.
   (c) RED LINE is to be consolidated and patrols pushed out to the general line shown RED and BLUE.

5. ARTILLERY SUPPORT.
   (a) RIGHT ATTACK.
       121 Brigade and 1 18-pdr. battery 122nd Bde. 1 18-pdr. battery 18th D.A.
       8 6" Hows.
       8 60-pdrs.
   (b) RIGHT CENTRE ATTACK.
       122 Brigade (less 1 18-pdr. battery).
       6 6" Hows.   1 18-pdr. Bty. 17th D.A.
       6 60-pdrs.

6. BARRAGE.
   (a) All the above mentioned artillery will be employed on a creeping barrage organized in depth.
   (b) The opening line of the barrage will depend upon the progress of patrols and position of the Infantry at Zero.
       Barrage lines are timed.
       A wire will be sent from R.A.H.Q. in the following form "KICK OFF" line plus 20 to plus 24".

This will/

-2-

This will mean that the 18-pdrs. will open on the line marked plus 20 to + 24 and will lift off at Zero + 24.
  4.5" Hows. and 60-pdrs. will open on a line 200 yards beyond that ordered for the 18-pdrs. and will keep their fire 200 yards beyond the 18-pdrs. throughout.
  6" Hows. will open on a line 400 yards beyond the 18-pdrs. and will keep their fire 400 yards beyond the 18-pdrs. throughout.
  (d) On arrival at the respective final protective lines fire will be maintained for 20 mins.

7. RATES OF FIRE AND AMMUNITION.

	CREEPING BARRAGE. r.p.g.p.m.		PROTECTIVE BARRAGE. r.p.g.p.m.	
18-pdrs.	2	"A"	½	
4.5" Hows.	1½	"BX"	½	H.E. DX.
60-pdrs.) 6" Hows.)		As ordered by Corps H.A.		

  One tenth of all ammunition fired by 18-pdrs. and 4.5" Hows. during the Creeping Barrage will be SMOKE.

8. LIAISON.
  121st.Brigade will detail Liaison Officers to be with 113th. and 115th.Inf.Bdes.
  122nd.Brigade a Liaison Officer to be with 114th.Inf.Bde.
  H.Q's are to be :-

    113th.Inf.Bde.   -   W.25.b.0.7.
    114th.Inf.Bde.   -   Q.28.a.9.4.
    115th.Inf.Bde.   -   W.3.d.8.5.

9. ZONES.
  After   completion of the operation Zones for fire purposes will be :-

	RIGHT BOUNDARY.	LEFT BOUNDARY.
RIGHT GROUP.	E. and W. grid line dividing squares X.16 and X.22.	E. and W. grid line dividing squares X.4. and X.10.
LEFT GROUP.	E. and W. grid line dividing squares X.4. and X.10.	E. and W. grid line dividing squares R.28 and R.34.

10. HARASSING FIRE AND S.O.S.
  (a) When the 20 mins. protective barrage is finished all guns will search forward to limit of range. Subsequently vigourous harassing fire will be carried out but there will be no fire within 500 yards of the RED and BLUE line.
  (b) "S.O.S" lines after the completion of the operation will be arranged by Group Commanders with   Infantry Brigadiers concerned.
  (c) To give freedom to patrols of flank Divisions harassing fire and S.O.S. lines will be kept 100 yards within the N. and S. Divisional Boundaries.

11. 310th. and 312th.Brigades R.F.A. (62nd.D.A.) are coming into action to-night and will be attached for orders to 121 and 122 Brigades respectively. Should these batteries arrive in time to take part in the operation, they will fire throughout on the 6" How.lines i.e. 400 yards in advance of the 38th.D.A. 18-pdr.lines (Vide Map "X".)

12/

- 3 -

12. **F.O.O's.**
    Previous orders re establishing O.P's on the high ground East of the ANCRE hold good.

13. Watches will be synchronised by an Officer from R.A.H.Q. who will visit Group Headquarters.

14. Zero hour will be 1 a.m.

15. ACKNOWLEDGE. (121, 122, 310, 312 Bdes., V Corps H.A. by wire)

J.E. Marston
Major R.A.
Brigade Major 38th. Divisional Artillery.

Issued at

Copy No.		
1 - 5	121st Bde R.F.A.	
6 - 10	122nd Bde R.F.A.	
11	D.T.M.O.	
12	D.A.C.	
13	S.C.R.A.	
14	R.A.Sig.Offr.	
15 - 19	310th Bde R.F.A.	
20 - 24	312th Bde R.F.A.	
25	38th Divn "G"	
26	113 Inf. Bde.	
27	114 Inf. Bde	
28	115 Inf. Bde.	
29	38th Div. Signals	
30 - 32	17th D.A.	
33	21st D.A.	
34 - 36	18th D.A.	
37	V Corps R.A.	
38 - 49	V Corps H.A.	
50 - 51	War Diary	
52	File.	

On His Majesty's Service.

SECRET

3rd Echelon

WAR DIARY of GENERAL STAFF 38th)WELSH) Division

INTELLIGENCE SUMMARY. VOLUME XXXIII.

Army Form C. 2118.

Instructions regarding War Diaries and Intelligence Summaries are contained in F. S. Regs., Part II. and the Staff Manual respectively. Title pages will be prepared in manuscript.

(Erase heading not required.)

Place	Date	Hour	Summary of Events and Information	Remarks and references to Appendices
West of HIGH WOOD.	SEPTEMBER 1918. 1st.		At 7.40 a.m. 114th Bde had taken MORVAL and held line East of it. 115th Bde reach 1st objective but had some trouble from hostile M.G's on left flank. 113th Bde relieved 114th Bde East of MORVAL and latter withdrew West of MORVAL as arranged. 115th Bde reached line of road running from point 1000 yds East of MORVAL to SAILLY SAILLISEL but were held up by M.G. fire. Heavy casualties were suffered by 2nd R.W.Fus. on left flank. Verbal orders issued by G.O.C., to 113th Bde to attack and capture SAILLY SAILLISEL, attack to commence at 6 p.m. in conjunction with 18th Division on right. At 11 p.m. 113th Bde reported SAILLY SAILLISEL captured and their troops holding line just E. of SAILLY SAILLISEL – BAPAUME ROAD. Prisoners taken during day – 3 Officers, 293 O.R. During the afternoon attack heavy M.G. fire held up 115th Bde but eventually they got through on left of 113th Bde.	APP.No.1 D.O.222.
	2nd.		Div.Order No.222 issued. 115th Bde to reform behind 113th Bde and advance to high ground E. of MESNIL EN ARROUAISE. 113th Bde to follow in rear of 115th Bde 500 yds distance. 114th Bde to move up to position just W. of SAILLY SAILLISEL. Attack to commence at 5 p.m., but was immediately held up by M.G. fire from M.G.Nests between our troops and the barrage: Line remained unchanged for the night. Order No.223 issued for new dispositions of Brigades as follows – 115th Bde to relieve troops	APP.No.2. D.O.223. APP.No.3. G.B.205.
	3rd.		of 18th Division in SAILLISEL. 113th Bde to advance N.E. and make touch with 17th Division on left. 114th Bde to be in Divisional Reserve. At 8.a.m. Patrols were pushed out and found no sign of the enemy, who had apparently withdrawn during the night to line E. of CANAL DU NORD and River TORTILLE. G.B. 205 issued. 113th Bde and 115th Bde advanced at once and gained line of trenches immediately E. of MESNIL EN ARROUAISE. Advance Guard was formed consisting of 114th Bde, 122nd Bde R.F.A. 123rd Field Coy R.E., 1 bearer sub division R.A.M.C. and 1 troop Carbineers and Cyclists Squadron, 1 Section 60 pdrs. At 2.15 p.m. Adv.Guard Bde passed through 113th and 115th Bdes who held trench line between MARTIN WOOD and MESNIL EN ARROUAISE and pushed battle-patrols along the high ground running down to the W. bank of CANAL DU NORD between MANANCOURT and ETRICOURT. Objectives for Adv.Guard shewn in telegram G.35. Division H.Q. moved from HIGH WOOD to LES BOEUFS opening there at 3.35.p.m. There was heavy hostile shelling of the area which the enemy had evacuated throughout the day, including gas shell. Line remained W. side of Canal throughout night. Our troops held ETRICOURT. Div.Order No.224 issued, 114th Bde to cross CANAL and reach line NURLU – EQUANCOURT, when this is done 115th Bde to pass through as Adv.Guard Bde.	APP.No.4 G.35. APP.No.5 D.O.224.

Army Form C. 2118.

WAR DIARY
or
INTELLIGENCE SUMMARY.
(Erase heading not required.)

Page 2.

Place	Date	Hour	Summary of Events and Information	Remarks and references to Appendices
LES BOEUFS.	September 1918.			
	4th.		Two Coy's of Adv.Guard Bde crossed Canal at 11.30 a.m. Troops being pushed along/support to the outposts. Prisoners of 6th Cavalry Division captured. Enemy counter attacked 17th Div. on our left at about 7 p.m. but were repulsed. Warning Order for relief by 21st Div.issued.	APP.No.6 G.54.G.58.
	5th.		Div.Order No.225 issued. Relief by 21st Division. During the day our battle patrols were active, but were unable to advance owing to heavy M.G. fire from line of trenches running just W. of NURLU and EQUANCOURT. During the afternoon some headway was made owing to flank Divisions advancing and easing the situation on our front. 113th and 115th Bdes were relieved by day and returned to bivouac areas as under:-	APP.No.7 D.O.225
			113th Bde - DELVILLE WOOD. 115th Bde - LES BOEUFS MORVAL area. Brigadier General de PREE C.B. C.M.G. assumed command 115th Infantry Brigade vice Lieut.Colonel Norman D.S.O.	
	6th.		Night was quiet. 114th Bde relieved in line. Relief complete bu 3.30 a.m. Command passed to G.O.C. 21st Division. 114th Bde returned to Camp in LE TRANSLOY. Total prisoners 29 officers 1886 O.R.	
	7th.		G.S.O.3 reconnoitred area in vicinity of ETRICOURT and MANACOURT and MARTIN with view to moving up Brigades closer to water supply (CANAL DU NORD). Notes on experiences gained in the recent fighting issued.	APP.No.8 S.G.25.
	8th.		G.O.C. and A.A.& Q.M.G. visited G.H.Q. 114th Bde and Coy M.G.Bn at one hours notice from 3.30 a.m. 8th/9th to support 17th Division or 21st Division on Corps front.	
	9th.		G.S.O.3 and D.A.Q.M.G. further reconnoitred ETRICOURT Area. Div.Order No.226 G.S.O.3 and D.A.A.G. reconnoitred are MESNIL EN ARROUAISE and LECHELLE. G.O.C. visited G.O.C's 17th and 21st Divisions. G.S.O.1 visited 113th Brigade H.Q. Relief of 17th Division by 38th Division.	APP.No.9 D.O.226.
	10th.		113th Bde proceeded from DELVILLE WOOD Area by march route to LECHELLE Area. 115th Bde proceeded from LES BOEUFS - MORVAL Area by march route to LECHELLE. Moves complete by 7 p.m. 114th Bde remained at LE TRANSLOY. G.O.C. visited G.O.C. 17th Div. G.S.O.1 reconnoitred new area. G.S.O.2 reconnoitred new forward Bde H.Q. D.O.227 issued.	APP.No10 D.O.227.
	11th.		G.O.C. accompanied by G.S.O.2. visited G.O.C. New Zealand Division. 113th Bde relieved 51st Bde (17th Div.) as Support Bde. Relief complete at 10 p.m. 114th Bde relieved 52nd Bde (17th Div.) as Reserve Bde. Relief complete at 5 p.m. 115th Bde relieved 53rd Bde (17th Div.) as Adv.Guard Bde. Relief complete at 12 midnight. Div.H.Q. closed at LES BOEUFS at 3 p.m. and opened at ETRICOURT at same hour. G.S.O.1 visited New Zealand Division, 17th Division and all Bde H.Q. Division Order No.228 issued.	APP.No11 D.O.228.

Army Form C. 2118.

WAR DIARY
or
INTELLIGENCE SUMMARY.
(Erase heading not required.)

Page. 3.

Place	Date	Hour	Summary of Events and Information	Remarks and references to Appendices
ETRICOURT.	September 1918.			
	12th.		New Zealand Division on our left attacked at 5.25 a.m. and obtained the line AFRICAN TRENCH. A Company of 10th S.Wales Bord. endeavoured to advance their line in order to keep touch. They reached their objective but were counter attacked and driven out. Further attempts met with no success, but liaison was established with the right flank of the N.Z. Division. G.O.C. visited 113th and 115th Bdes and 2nd and 17th R.W.Fus. and the 10th S.Wales Bord.	
	13th.		During the morning the enemy attacked our positions in HEATHER SUPPORT but was driven off with loss, many enemy dead being left in our trenches and in No Mans Land. G.S.O.1 and G.S.O.2 during the afternoon visited Bdes and the line. There was considerable hostile bombing activity in the early part of the night, but about 4 enemy planes were brought down in flames.	
	14th.		The night was generally quiet, but there was considerable gas shelling of support Bde area. G.O.C., G.S.O.1., and C.R.A. attended Corps Commanders Conference at 11.30 a.m. at H.Q. 21st Div. Reconnaissance was made in vicinity of GOUZEAUCOURT WOOD and on the FINS - GOUZEAUCOURT Road for a suitable place for Adv.Div.H.Q. G.SO.3. visited Reserve Bde. 5th Div.Commenced relief of the N.Z. Division on our left. G.O.C. held conference at 5.30 p.m. at Div.H.Q. following attended G.O.C. 113th and 114th Bdes., O.C's 13th, 14th, 16th R.W.Fus., 13th, 14th, 15th Welsh Regt., B.M's 113th and 114th Bdes, G.S.O.1 and 2., A.A.& Q.M.G., A.D.M.S., C.R.E., and C.R.A., O.C. Signals. During the day our aerial activity was very noticeable and 4 hostile balloons and 1 aeroplane were brought down in flames. D.O. 230 issued.	APP.No.12 D.O.230
	15th.		Apart from Gas Shelling hostile artillery was not active on the forward area during the night, but H.V. guns were active on the banks of the CANAL DU NORD in the vicinity of Div.H.Q. The day was fairly quiet and our line remained unchanged. During the evening from 8 p.m. to 11 p.m. there was considerable shelling of our back areas by H.V. Guns, also some gas shelling. Many hostile bombing planes passed over at night flying and one was brought down in flames by one of our night flying planes. Div.Order 231 issued. At 4.a.m. hostile H.V.Guns were again active on E. bank of CANAL DU NORD. At 11 a.m. G.O.C. held conference at H.Q. 113th Inf.Bde. Following reliefs took place on night 16/17th. 113th and 114th Bdes relieved the 115th Bde in the line. 114th Bde on the	(APP.No.13 (D.O.231. (G.S.S.1/22.
	16th.		right and 113th Bde on the left. 52nd Bde (17th Div.) prior to this relief took over a portion of 5th Division on our left. 52nd Bde (17th Div.) prior to this relief took over a portion of the southern front held by 115th Bde. Relief complete at 11.45 p.m. On relief the 115th Bde became Bde in Corps Reserve.	

Army Form C. 2118.

WAR DIARY
or
INTELLIGENCE SUMMARY.

(Erase heading not required.)

Page 4.

Instructions regarding War Diaries and Intelligence Summaries are contained in F. S. Regs., Part II. and the Staff Manual respectively. Title pages will be prepared in manuscript.

Place	Date	Hour	Summary of Events and Information	Remarks and references to Appendices
ETRICOURT.	September 1918.			
	17th.		During the night 16/17th the vicinity of Div.H.Q. and the banks of the CANAL DU NORD were persistently shelled by hostile H.V.Guns. Many bombs were also dropped. The shelling continued up to 10 a.m. The day was fairly quiet, but our aircraft were active. G.O.C. visited all Bdes and R.A., H.Q.	
	18th.		The night was quiet apart from some gas shelling N. of FINS – GOUZEAUCOURT Road. At 5.20 a.m. 113th and 114th Bdes attacked in conjunction with remainder of V Corps and 5th Div. (III Corps) on the left. 114th Bde reached there objectives after overcoming stubborn opposition and suffering many casualties. 113th Bde were held up but the Right Battalion managed to reach the second objective (green line) and on their left the line gradually receded back to the original front line. The 5th Div. did not advance on our left. Efforts were made during the day to clear up the situation, but no progress was made till the evening when 113th Bde extended their gains slightly taking 8 prisoners and 5 M.G's. At 9 p.m. the 113th Bde attacked in conjunction with 17th Div. with the intention of joining hands with them S. of GOUZEAUCOURT.	APP.No.14. D.O.232.
	19th.		News was received during the night that the effort to advance our line had not met with success. The enemy during the night counter attacked our troops in AFRICAN TRENCH and drove them out of the northern portion of it. The 113th Bde ejected the enemy and had completely restored the situation by 12 noon, taking a few prisoners. The line remained unchanged during the day, but during the evening some of the enemy got into a portion of the Right Bde (114) front line, but were eventually turned out. D.O. 232 issued. 17th Div. took over front of	APP.No.15. D.O.233.
	20th.		114th Bde during the night and 115th Bde relieved 113th Bde. Reliefs were complete by 5 a.m. The night was fairly quiet but there was some gas shelling. D.O. 233 issued.	
	21st.		The enemy's artillery was quiet during the morning, but was lively during the evening from 6 p.m. to 7 p.m. The 17th Div. further extended their front and relieved the 115th Bde. Relief complete at 4 a.m. On relief the 38th Division became Left Supporting Division V Corps and was disposed as under :- 113th Bde – ROCQUIGNY Area. 115th Bde – LE TRANSLOY Area. 114th Bde Trench System N. of EQUANCOURT. G.O.C. saw 113th Bde on their march out of the trenches. Div.H.Q. at ETRICOURT was continually shelled by hostile H.V.Gun from 9 a.m. till 11.45 a.m. Div.H.Q. opened near LECHELLE at 3 p.m.	

WAR DIARY or **INTELLIGENCE SUMMARY.**

(Erase heading not required.)

Army Form C. 2118. Page 5.

Place	Date	Hour	Summary of Events and Information	Remarks and references to Appendices
LECHELLE.	September 1918.			
	22nd.		114th Bde from N. of EQUANCOURT to the LECHELLE Area. Corps Commander held a conference at H.Q. 21st Division MESNIL EN ARROUAISE. G.O.C., G.S.O.1, and C.R.A. attended.	
	23rd.		Army Commander visited G.O.C. at Division H.Q. Brigades proceeded with training and reorganization. G.S.O.1 visited all Brigades and all Battalions of 114th Bde.	
	24th.		G.O.C. as President of Board in selection for N.C.O's for Commissions went to VIth Corps H.Q. to examine candidates. G.S.O.2 visited 113th and 114th Bdes and distributed target material.	
	25th.		Corps Commander and B.G., G.S. visited Div.H.Q. with a view to discussing future operations. All Bdes at training (chiefly musketry).	
	26th.		Corps Conference. G.O.C., G.S.O.1 and A.A.&Q.M.G. attended. C.R.A. and G.O.C. 114th Bde visited Div.Commander. future operations issued S.S.143. Divisional Instructions for	APP.No.16. S.S. 143
	27th.		Conference at Div.H.Q. attended by Brigadiers, C.R.A., C.R.E., A.D.M.S., O.C., M.G.Bn., O.C., Signals and Q. G.S.O.3 reconnoitred area round SOREL LE GRAND with a view to bivouacing Division on night 28/29th. IV, VI and XVII Corps attack. D.O.234 issued. Division moved to V.18.c.1.9. with Bdes on FINS RIDGE. G.O.C. visited American Division. G.S.O.2 returned from Tank Course. G.O.C's 113th and 115th Brigades reconnoitred ST EMELIE Area. Div.Order No.235 issued.	APP.No.17. D.O.234.
	28th.			APP.No.18. D.O.235.
	29th.		Division at one hours notice to move and fulfill one of the following roles – A. Relieve 105th American Regt. East of CANAL D'L'ESCAUT. B. Take up assembly positions between VENDHUILE and HEUDECOURT. C. Relieve 18th Division in Bridge Heads at VENDHUILE.	
V.18.c.1.9. 57 C.	30th.		The attack of the III Corps checked 3000 yards N.E. of LEMPIRE. American attack reported to have gained objective. LE CATELET – GOUY – Australians troops followed to go through, they were checked by pockets of enemy, over run by Americans and took up positions on line with III (British) Corps. Reconnaissance carried out for Bde H.Q. in the event of move forward. Situation unchanged. G.O.C. visited all Brigades during the afternoon.	

September 1918.

General Staff.38th.(Welsh) Division.

Captain,

SECRET
Copy No. 14

38TH (WELSH) DIVISION ORDER NO. 228.

Ref: Map 1/40,000.   11th Septr. 1918.
Sheet 57.C.

1. The IV Corps is attacking TRESCAULT Spur tomorrow and the New Zealand Division is attacking with objective the continuation of AFRICAN TRENCH Q.29. and Q.23.d.

2. In order to maintain connection with the N.Z. Division the 115th Brigade will seize and hold the trench line Q.35.a.2.5.- - Q.35.a.6.5. - Q.29.d.0.2. connecting with the N.Z. Division at the latter point.

3. The Artillery barrage is being arranged by the C.R.A. 17th Division in conjunction with the C.R.A. 38th Division and will coincide in time and lifts with that of the N.Z.Divn.

4. Zero for all the above attacks is 5-40.a.m. [5-25]

5. A Staff Officer 38th Division will call at the N.Z. Divn., 17th Div:Arty. and 115th Brigade (P.35.d.) between 2-30. and 4.p.m. today for the purpose of synchronising watches.

ACKNOWLEDGE.

Done

F.J. Harington Captain
for Lieut. Colonel,
General Staff, 38th (Welsh) Division.

Issued thro' Signals at 1.15 .p.m.

Copies to :-

    All Units, 38th Divn.
    V Corps.
    V Corps R.A.
    V Corps H.A.
    17th Bde.R.G.A.
    17th Divn.
    21st Divn.
    N.Z.Divn.
    17th Div:Arty.
    15th Sqdn. R.A.F.
    "E" Sqdn. 5th Cyclist Bn.
    Att. Troop, 6th D.Gds. (c/o 17th Divn.)

SECRET.   3RD NEW ZEALAND (RIFLE) BRIGADE.   NO. 10...

OPERATION ORDER, NO.180.

REFERENCE MAP: (SHEET 57c. S.E.
                (1/20,000.
                                            Headquarters,
                                            September 11th, 1918.

1. The Brigade will continue the attack, to-morrow, 12th September. The 37th Division on the Right, and the 111th Brigade on the Left, will attack at the same time and capture TRESCAULT SPUR.

2. Objectives, Brigade and Battalion boundaries and Opening Line of Barrage are as shown on attached map "A". The area between the Northern Boundary for the operation and the Dotted Blue Line is allotted to the 111th Brigade for assembly prior to the attack. Details as to handing over will be arranged between the O.C. 4th Battalion and the 13th Rifle Battalion.

3. The attack will be carried out by three Battalions - 2nd Battalion on the Right, 1st Battalion in the Centre and the 4th Battalion on the Left. The 1st and 4th Battalions will each attack on a Two-Company frontage, each Company detailing two Platoons for the first objective and two Platoons for the 2nd objective. The 2nd Battalion will attack with four Platoons. On the capture of the second objective each Battalion will send forward Reconnoitring Patrols to keep contact with the enemy. The ground gained will be consolidated in depth. Sentry Groups will be established approximately as shown on Map "A". In the event of a heavy counter-attack by the enemy Sentry Groups will give warning of the attack and retire fighting to the second objective.

4.   (a). The attack will be carried out under a barrage from six Field Artillery Brigades on the Brigade front. At ZERO the 18 pdrs, will open on the line shown on Map "A", advancing at the rate of 100 yards in three minutes (1st lift - ZERO PLUS THREE MINUTES).

     (b). There will be a pause of 10 minutes on the line 200 yards east of the first objective, and there will be a pause of 15 minutes on reaching the S.O.S. Line, 300 yards east of the second objective, on completion of which it will advance eastward and die away.

     (c). The 4.5. Howitzers will open on the first objective, north of Q.23.d.30.30, lifting to the second objective when the 18 pdr. barrage approaches to 200 yards, then lifting again on to selected targets. South of Q.23.d. 30.00 the 4.5-inch Howitzers will put a stationary barrage on selected targets beyond the objectives.

     (d). The attack will also be covered by three Batteries of 6-inch Howitzers which will bombard selected targets beyond the objectives.

     (e). The Otago and Wellington Machine Gun Companies, plus one Section of the Auckland Machine Gun Coy. will, at ZERO, place a barrage on the first objective north of Q.23.d.3.3. and south of that point will place a barrage beyond the first objective, the whole barrage lifting at a time to be arranged by the O.C. Machine Gun Battalion, to search the areas beyond our objectives.
          One Section of the Auckland Machine Gun Coy is placed at the disposal of each attacking Battalion for the purpose of holding the first and second objectives during and after consolidation.

- 2 -

(f). Two Medium Trench Mortars will bombard DEAD MAN'S CORNER,Q.23.c.7.3., from ZERO to ZERO,plus three minutes. Two Medium Trench Mortars will bombard the CROSS-ROADS and TRENCHES in Q.23.a.85.25. from ZERO to ZERO,plus six minutes.

(g). Four Light Trench Mortars will bombard the TRENCH from Q.22.b.05.15. to Q.22.b.10.90. from ZERO to ZERO,plus three,and two Light Trench Mortars will bombard DEAD MAN'S CORNER,Q.23.c.7.3. from ZERO to ZERO,plus three,then lifting 100 yards in advance of the Artillery barrage along the SUNKEN ROAD towards Q.23.a.85.25.

5. The attacking troops will assemble in position as follows:-

2nd Battalion in Trench from Q.29.c.10.00 to Q.29.a.35.65
1st Battalion:Right Company,in WOOD,Q.28.b.50.90 to Q.29.a.30.70.
Left Company,in SUNKEN ROAD and BANK,Q.22.a.
4th Battalion in SUNKEN ROAD,Q.16.c.

The assembly will be completed one hour before ZERO or DAWN, whichever is the earlier,and will be notified to Brigade Headquarters by the code word: "FACTORY". The assembly will be carried out in silence;no smoking or lights will be permitted. Protection against Machine Gun fire will be provided.

6. The 2nd and 4th Battalions will continue to hold the line until the time of attack but will ensure that the attacking Companies are entirely freed from all trench duties. The 3rd Battalion will continue to hold the Centre Sector until ZERO when the 1st Battalion will advance through the 2nd Battalion under arrangements to be made direct by the O's C. concerned. The 2nd Battalion will then be withdrawn into Brigade Support,occupying the Trench system in Q.15.c.,Q.21 and Q.27.
One Company of the 3rd Battalion will be placed at the disposal of the 1st Battalion and one Company at the disposal of the 2nd Battalion as Battalion Reserves.

7. All Battalion Headquarters will be established before ZERO. Immediately after the capture of the first objective each Battalion will establish an Advanced Report Centre,connected by telephone with Battalion Headquarters.
Each Company in the attack will fire one GREEN FLARE on capturing the first objective,and one RED FLARE on capturing the second objective.
Each Battalion will,in addition,arrange Code Words to be sent by Visual to Battalion Headquarters notifying the capture of the objectives.

8. Prisoners of War will be sent to Brigade Headquarters.

9. A Brigade Dump is established at P.18.d.40.00. Forward Brigade Dumps will be established before ZERO at Q.21.b.80.30. and Q.27.a.60.70.

10. ZERO hour will be notified separately.

11. An Officer from each Brigade Unit will report at Brigade Headquarters at 5.30 p.m. to-day to synchronise watches.

12. An Advanced Brigade Report Centre will open at Q.20.b.40.70. at 10 p.m. to-night.

- 3 -

13. Headquarters of Units will be as follows:-

    1ST BATTALION   Q.22.a.40.15.
    2ND BATTALION   Q.26.b.7.7.
    3RD BATTALION   Q.20.d.30.20
    4TH BATTALION   Q.16.c.30.20.
    3RD L.T.M.BATTERY   Q.13.d.6.8.
    AUCKLAND MACHINE GUN COY.   P.18.c.6.6.
    OTAGO & WELLINGTON M.G.COYS.   Q.13.d.7.8.
    BRIGADE HEADQUARTERS.   P.18.d.4.0.

14. A Contact aeroplane will call for flares at ZERO plus one hour and ZERO plus three hours, and a counter-attack machine will be in the air during the day.

15. ACKNOWLEDGE.

                 Major,
                BRIGADE MAJOR.

Issued at 1.30/pm

Copies to:

  1. G.O.C.
  2. 1st Battalion,
  3. 2nd Battalion,
  4. 3rd Battalion,
  5. 4th Battalion,
  6. 3rd L.T.M.Battery,
  7. Auckland Machine Gun Coy.
  8. Otago   "   "   "
  9. Wellington "   "   "
 10. 38th Division,
 11. 111th Brigade,
 12. New Zealand Division,
13 & 14. C.R.A.
 15. C.R.E.
 16. A.D.M.S.
 17. Staff Captain,
 18. Brigade Signal Officer,
 19. File.
20 - 22. War Diary.

Appendix No. I to 3rd N.Z. (Rifle) Bde. Order No. 180.

LINES:

Every Battalion will have one direct line to Advanced Brigade Headquarters Report Centre and alternative lines will be laid as wire is available under arrangements to be made by Brigade Signal Officer.

Battalions should confine themselves to one main line forward to a Battalion Report Centre, and to the use of Visual and Runner. Existing Company lines should be reeled up wherever possible.

POWER BUZZERS:

Power Buzzers will be established at Brigade Headquarters at P.18.d.40.00. and will work to power buzzer at Advanced Brigade Headquarters at Q.20.b.2.8. who will work to power buzzer at Left (4th) Battalion Headquarters at QUARRY in Q.16.c. and power buzzer at 3rd Battalion Headquarters at Q.20.d.2.3.

These will be established by 8 p.m. and tested out. B.A.B. Code will be used but messages may be sent in clear after ZERO at the discretion of C.O's Battalions.

VISUAL:

T.S. station established at P.24.b.4.3. and will signal to A.T.S. station which moves from Q.25.c. to Q.20.b.50.50. (approx).

A.T.S. will receive from Battalion Headquarters at BATTERY POST, Q.22.c.4.2. and 2 Battalion Headquarters at Sunken Road at Q.26.b.8.8. Lines have been reconnoitred and Battalions will arrange to test out at 6 p.m. to-night, 11th/12th September.

Battalions will man their ends permanently.

Messages from Battalions to A.T.S. will be D D till after ZERO HOUR.

The Visual Stn. at A.T.S. can see the whole of the ridge in 22 and 28 c and d, and is on the look-out for Companies calling them.

RUNNERS:

The most forward Brigade Runner Post will be at the Advanced Brigade Report Centre at Q.20.b.2.8. Indicating signs will be put out and a candle in a tin with indicating letters will be set up after dark.

SECRET
Copy No. 13

38TH (WELSH) DIVISION ORDER NO. 229.

Ref: Map 1/40,000.
Sheet 57.C.

13th September 1918.

1. From the 16th instant inclusive Brigades will be disposed as follows :-

    Front Brigade .. .. 113th Bde.
    Support Brigade. .. 114th Bde.
    Reserve Brigade. .. 115th Bde.

2. The necessary reliefs will take place on the night 15th/16th September.

3. Dispositions within Brigades will be taken over as they stand at present.

4. 'A' Coy. 38th Bn.M.G.C. will come under command of 113th Bde. from completion of relief.

    'E' Sqdn. 5th Cyclist Regt. will detail one troop for duty under the orders of the Front Brigade in future. This troop will be relieved as often as desired by the O.C. Squadron. The remainder of the squadron will rejoin their Regimental Headquarters.

    The attached troop Carabineers will cease to be under the orders of the Front Brigade from tomorrow inclusive and will report for orders to Divisional Headquarters.

    ACKNOWLEDGE.

J.S. Munby
Lieut. Colonel,
General Staff, 38th (Welsh) Division.

Issued thro' Signals at 11.30 pm.

Copies to :-

All Units, 38th Division.
V Corps.
V Corps R.A.
V Corps H.A.
17th Bde. R.G.A.
17th Division.
21st Division.
N.Z. Division.
H.Q. 5th Cyclist Regt.
'E' Sqdn. 5th Cyclist Regt. c/o 115 Bde
6th Dgn. Gds.
Attd. Troop 6th D.Gds. c/o 115 Bde.

SECRET.

Copy No. 15

38TH (WELSH) DIVISION ORDER NO. 230.

Ref: Map 1/40,000.
Sheet 57.C.

15th Septr. 1918.

1. 38th Division Order No. 229 is cancelled.

2. On the night 16th/17th Septr. the 115th Brigade will be relieved as follows -
    By 17th Divn. (52nd Bde.) as far North as W.5.c.4.5.
    By 114th Bde. from W.5.c.4.5. to C.T.- Q.35.c.1.8. inclusive.
    By 113th Bde. from C.T.- Q.35.c.1.8. exclusive to present left Divisional boundary.

3. On the same night 113th Bde. will take over from 5th Division (13th Bde.) as far North as Q.28.d.9.5.

4. Details of relief will be arranged between Brigades direct.
    52nd Bde.H.Q. are at LE TRANSLOY O.31.b.3.2.
    13th Bde.H.Q. are at LE TRANSLOY P.18.d.5.0.

5. On completion of relief the Division will be disposed as follows -
    113th Bde. H.Q. .. P.35.d.
        One Battalion . Front Line.
        Two Battalions. East of the EQUANCOURT Trench line.
    114th Bde. H.Q. .. P.35.d.
        One Battalion . Front Line.
        Two Battalions. East of the EQUANCOURT Trench line in accommodation to be allotted by 113th Brigade. One of these Battns will occupy trenches in W.3.
    115th Bde. H.Q. .. FOUR WINDS FARM.
        Battalions. .. EQUANCOURT Trench Line.

6. On completion of relief boundaries will be as follows -
    Between 17th Divn. & 38th Divn. a line East and West through W.5.c.0.5.
    Between 38th Divn. & 5th Divn. a line East and West through Q.28.d.0.5.

ACKNOWLEDGE.

Lieut. Colonel,
General Staff, 38th (Welsh) Division.

Issued thro' Sigs. at 1-50.a.m.

Copies to :-
    All Units, 38th Divn.   21st Divn.
    V Corps   33rd Divn.
    V Corps R.A.   5th Divn.
    V Corps H.A.   13th Inf.Bde.
    17th Bde. H.A.   52nd Inf.Bde.
    17th Divn.   "E" Sqdn. 5th Cyc.Rgt. (c/o 115th Bde.)
                                 Attd. Troop Carabiniers, (P.32.b.)

SECRET
GSS.10/100.

ADDENDUM NO. 1 to 38TH (WELSH) DIVISION ORDER NO. 230.

1. 'A' Coy. 38th Bn.M.G.C. will be under the command of the Front Brigade until the commencement of relief on night 17th/18th Septr. when the company will revert to the command of O.C. 38th Bn.M.G.C.

2. The attached Troop Carabiniers ceased to be under the orders of the Front Brigade from yesterday and will be under the direct orders of Divisional Headquarters.

'E' Squadron 5th Cyclist Regt. will detail one troop to act under the orders of the Front Brigade until completion of relief on night 17th/18th Septr. and from completion of relief one troop to act under the orders of each of 113th and 114th Brigades. The remainder of the squadron will remain with regimental headquarters until required.

38th Bn.M.G.C., Attd.Troop Carabiniers and 'E' Sqdn 5th Cyclist Regt. to ACKNOWLEDGE.

J.E. Munby

15th September 1918.
Lieut. Colonel,
General Staff, 38th (Welsh) Division.

Copies to All recipients of D.O. 230.

MESSAGES AND SIGNALS. No. of Message.................

Prefix...... Code...... Words......	Received. From ХСt	Sent, or sent out. At................m.	Office Stamp.
£ s. d. Charges to Collect Service Instructions.	By M	To .... By.................	

Handed in at Y.C.H. ....Office 6.6p m. Received 12.12p m.

TO 11SBoc

*Sender's Number	Day of Month	In reply to Number	AAA
GA92	15		

Reference DO 230 care to be taken not to overstep southern boundary all space south of that boundary is required by 17 Div. aaa adv'nce Brigades upto 17 Div.

FROM 38 Div.
TIME & PLACE 11.50am

"C" FORM.
MESSAGES AND SIGNALS.

Army Form C, 2123.
(In books of 100.)

Prefix	Code	Words	Received	Sent, or sent out	Office Stamp
			From	At .... m.	
Charges to Collect			By	To	
Service Instructions				By	

Handed in at ......Y.H. Ladd...... Office 8.4 m. Received 8.28 m.

TO ~~115~~ 115

Sender's Number.	Day of Month.	In reply to Number.	AAA
G179	15		

Ref para 2 of Addendum one to order 230 line 6 for 17/18 read 16/17

FROM PLACE & TIME 38 Div

"C" FORM.
MESSAGES AND SIGNALS.

Army Form C. 2123.
(In books of 100.)

Prefix....Code....Words....	Received.	Sent, or sent out.	Office Stamp.
Charges to Collect	From.... At.......m.	
Service Instructions	aaa	To..... By..... 6.52p

Handed in at........ Office ....m. Received ....m.

TO   115 Bde

*Sender's Number	Day of Month.	In reply to Number.	AAA
G176	15		
Ref	para	1	of
Addendum	no	1	to
order	230	line	three
aaa	For	17/18	read
16/17			

FROM PLACE & TIME   3? Div

"A" Form
MESSAGES AND SIGNALS.

Army Form C. 2121
(In pads of 100.)

TO: GUNO VUKA

Sender's Number: BM 15 – 8

AAA

Serial 5 of Table accompanying OO 270 is cancelled # GUNO will come under orders of VUKA # BM11 GUNO rptd VUKA

From: VUTU
Time: 8.21 p

FRANCE MAP TO ACCOMPANY 38TH DIV. O. No 231. SECRET.

EDITION 6f (Local). SHEET 57c S.E.

5 DIV.

113 BDE

114 BDE

17 DIV.

PRESENT APPROX FRONT LINE

ENEMY ORGANISATION, 21-8-18

Scale 1:20,000

115th Infantry Brigade B.M.1088.

38th Division.

NOTES ON RECENT FIGHTING.

The following are some of the additional lessons learnt during the recent fighting.

1. The importance of attacks in depth has again been emphasised

The tactics of the enemy rearguards during the past month have invariably been the same. Generally speaking they consist of Machine Guns (varying from 6 to 24 in number) of both heavy and light types, sited usually on forward slopes, well concealed and with a clear field of fire up to ranges of not much less than about 800 yards. Machine Guns are generally accompanied by snipers. Every Machine Gun Group is covered by artillery, the co-operation between the two being very close. Infantry appears to be used principally to counter-attack.

To deal with these tactics successfully, I am of opinion that Infantry should be more in depth and should keep in depth. The longer the advance the greater should be the strength in depth and the narrower the front. Battalions moving on a very wide front find themselves not strong enough to break through the enemy rearguard everywhere, and then their front quickly becomes disorganized, and they are not strong enough in depth to restore both the situation in front and to meet or to re-counter-attack on a flank.

When moving with an exposed flank, as is so often the case in advance guard actions, supporting troops whether they be companies or battalions, should I think be moved well in echelon on that flank in order to attack or to threaten the flank of a hostile counter-attack.

A further advantage of moving on a narrow front is derived from the fact that a greater concentration of artillery can generally be put down as a barrage.

(By a "narrow" front is meant one of 500 yards or less. A "wide" front would be up to 1,000 yards per Battalion.)

2. The training in use of ground and scouting has been somewhat neglected up to this year in favour of Physical Training, Bayonet Fighting and similar work. The lack of it has been felt in all the more open fighting since March 21st. It should be given a more prominent place in the training in future.

3. Map reading and compass work leave great room for improvement.

Every Officer, N.C.O., Scout and runner should be taught map reading. Units should be encouraged to apply for a liberal distribution of maps.

If N.C.O's and men never see maps they are not likely to learn to use them. On the other hand if a man has a map the chances are that he will try to understand it. The lamentable ignorance and indifference of the average soldier with regard to where he is or what is going on around him is largely due to want of maps.

As regards Compass work a bearing should be worked out for every attack, and no Officer should go into one without a compass. Every Company or Platoon Commander should have men of his H.Q.

trained in marching by compass bearing, so that he may be left free to watch the tactical situation.

4. More use should be made of Rifle Grenades.

5. For Battle Order the half-empty pack has been found more convenient than the overfull haversack.

[signature]

26.9.18.

Brigadier General,
Commanding, 115th Infantry Brigade.

SECRET
Copy. No. 13

1 copy to SC   BM 1120

38TH (WELSH) DIVISION ORDER NO. 231.

Ref: Maps 1/40,000 Sheet 57.C.   15th Septr. 1918.
     1/20,000 Sheet 57.C., S.E.

ACTION OF NEIGHBOURING FORMATIONS.

1. At a date and hour to be notified later the 5th Corps is attacking along the whole Corps front in conjunction with the Fourth Army and the French Army on their right.
   The 5th Division is making a simultaneous attack with the object of maintaining connection with our left.

Objectives.

2. Objectives and boundaries are shown on the attached map.
   The red line shows the final objective (for the 17th and 21st Divisions only). The blue lines show areas of exploitation which will be mopped up but not held. 17 Div advances against Red line at + 147".

ACTION OF INFANTRY.

3. (a). The 38th Division will attack with two Brigades, 114 Brigade on the right, 113 Brigade on the left.

   (b). The leading waves will be detailed to take the farthest objective.

   (c). Troops detailed to mop up the first objective will not remain on that objective but will after mopping up move, in order to escape the hostile barrage which is certain to be put down on that line, to a position at least 300 yards in advance of the first objective where they will consolidate and reorganise preparatory to moving forward if ordered to exploit the situation.

   (d). The leading wave will form up for attack IN 100 yards West of our present front line.

   (e). Within an hour after reaching the final objective patrols (not more than two per Brigade) will be pushed forward to ascertain whether GOUZEAUCOURT is occupied by the enemy. The time at which these patrols will move forward will be arranged between Brigadiers and the C.R.A.

ACTION OF ARTILLERY.

4. (a). The attack will be made under artillery barrages as follows :-
   A creeping barrage by 3/5 of the available 18 pdrs. commencing at zero preceded at two to three hundred yards by a creeping barrage by the remaining 2/5 of the 18 pdrs. preceded again by a barrage formed by 40 6" howitzers and 24 60 pdrs. (along the Corps front), the whole making a beaten zone of about 800 yards in depth. The barrage will lift 100 yards every ~~three~~ four minutes. (A barrage map will be issued by the C.R.A.) ×exact rate of lifts which will be after three minutes each.

   (b). A protective barrage will be maintained for 10 ~~15~~ minutes after the final objective is reached after which time the heavy artillery will form a barrage along the trench line X.5., R.34., GONNELIEU.

   (c). A smoke screen will be formed by 4.5 howitzers along the line X.1. - R.31. from zero till zero + 30 and West of GONNELIEU from zero + 30 onwards.

(d)./

2.

4. Contd.
(d) 18-pdrs. after lifting off the protective barrage will keep GOUZEAUCOURT and its approaches under bursts of fire.

(e) All Heavy Artillery not employed as above will be engaged in counter-battery work.

(f) 18 Newton T.Ms and 8 German Mortars will fire on selected targets from position about 100 yards in rear of our present front line.

ACTION OF L.T.M. BATTERIES.
5. L.T.M.Batteries will be employed to cover the advance up to the limit of their range. Four Mortars per attacking Brigade will then be sent forward under Brigade orders to assist in the protection of the final objective. Time for commencing fire will be taken from the opening of the Field Artillery barrage.

ACTION OF MACHINE GUNS.
6. 'A' and 'C' Cos. under the orders of O.C.38thBn. M.G.C. will barrage the following targets :-

HEATHER TRENCH in W.5 from Zero till Zero plus 1.
GREEN LINE in W.6 and Q.36.a.) will lift 400 yds.
Locality in Q.35.b.   ) in advance of the
) leading wave.

[margin note: SUNKEN Rd in W.5.d + its continuation in W.6.a. Green line Locality Q.35.b. *]*

Guns of these Cos. will afterwards be laid on S.O.S. lines for the protection of the final objective in Q.36.
Time for commencing fire of all machine guns, whether under Divisional or Brigade Orders, will be taken from the opening of the Field Artillery barrage.

ATTACHED TROOPS.
7. The following troops are placed under the orders of Brigades for this operation :-
  To each of 113th and 114th Brigades -
    One Co. 38th Bn. M.G.C.
      These Cos. will be employed in depth for the consolidation of the positions gained; two sections should be sited to protect the final objectives, the other sections the position in rear, on each Brigade front. These latter sections will be previously employed in barrage work under the orders of Brigadiers.
    One Company 19th Welsh Rgt. (Glamorgan Pnrs.) to assist in consolidation.
  To 113th Brigade,
    115th L.T.M.Battery.
  To 114th Brigade,
    One L.T.M.Battery of 33rd Divn.

POSITIONS OF DIVISIONAL TROOPS.
8. Field Artillery Brigades and Machine Gun Companies will be in action as follows :-

  121st Bde.R.F.A. .. .. W.3.c.
  78th   ,, ,, ... W.2.a.
  79th   ,, ,, ... Q.33.c.
  93rd (Army) ,,,, ... W.2.a. & b.
  155th   ,, ,,,, ... W.3.a. & c.
  122nd Bde.R.F.A. will be under the orders of 17th Division.
  'A' Co. 38th Bn.M.G.C. . Q.34.c.3.3.
  'C' Co. ,, ,, ,,   . W.4.c.7.5.
  "B" & "D" Cos.,, ,, as directed by Brigades.

/9.

3.

HEADQUARTERS. 9. Headquarters will be established as under -

        O.R.A.   )
        113th Bde.   ) Dugouts in bank
        114th Bde.   ) W.3.a.3.1.
        O.C., M.G.Bn.)

        121st & 155th Bdes R.F.A. .. W.7.b.8.2.
        78th Brigade R.F.A.   .. Q.31.b.1.1.
        79th & 93rd Bdes. R.F.A.   .. Q.32.d.2.5.

TANKS. 10. One Supply Tank will act under the orders of each attacking Brigade for conveyance of stores of all descriptions from the advanced Divisional Dump in W.3.b. to the front line.

They must be employed also for the conveyance of wounded on their return journeys.

They will be located at EQUANCOURT till the night 17th/18th when they will move forward to the Advanced Divisional dump and be loaded under Divisional arrangements with any stores required by Brigades.

CAPTURED GUNS. 11. The positions of any captured guns which have ammunition dumped near by will be immediately reported to the Artillery so that T.M. personnel may be sent forward to serve them.

LIAISON. 12. (a) Contact aeroplanes will call for flares at the odd hours, i.e. 7.a.m., 9.a.m. etc. RED flares will be lit when called for and officers and nco's will display their maps.

Ground signal sheets and strips will be displayed by all Brigade and Battalion Headquarters.

The dropping of a RED smoke bomb by an aeroplane denotes the assembly of hostile troops for counter-attack.

(b) "International" posts of one platoon each will be formed with similar units of neighbouring Divisions at W.6.d.6.4., W.5.d.7.7., Q.30.a.4.5., Q.29.a.8.5.

(c) A direct wire to neighbouring Divisions is being laid from the Divisional Test Station at Q.31.b.1.1. and also from Divisional Headquarters.

SECRECY. 13. The strictest secrecy is to be observed concerning these operations.

It is highly probable that the enemy has installed listening sets.

SYNCHRONISATION. 14. Watches will be synchronised by an officer of the Divisional Staff on "Y" Day at the H.Q. in P.35.d. at 12-30.p.m. and at the Headquarters in W.3.a. at 6-30.pm.

CORPS RESERVE. 15. 115th Brigade will be in Corps Reserve (in addition to 33rd Division) and will be in position on FINS RIDGE by 8.a.m. The trenches on this ridge will not be vacated by 17th Division till 8.a.m..

Battalions of 115th Brigade will not move from their present position till 6.a.m. and will avoid roads.

H.Q. 115th Bde. will be established at the huts in P.35.d. by 6.p.m. on "Y" Day.

Para 16 →

ACKNOWLEDGE.

J.E. Munby
General Staff, 38th (Welsh) Division.
Lieut-Colonel,

Issued thro' Sigs. at 11.pm.
Copies to :-
    (P.T.O.)

4.

Copies to :-

    All Units, 38th Division.
    V Corps.
    V Corps R.A.
    V Corps H.A.
    17th Bde.R.G.A.
    5th Division.
    17th Division.
    21st Division.
    33rd Division.
    15th Sqdn. R.A.F.
    "E" Sqdn. 5th Cyclist Rgt.
    Attd. Troop of CARABINIERS.

(Ref; Para. 2 - Maps only enclosed for 3 Bdes.   )
                                              38th D.A.   )
                                              C.R.E.   )
                                              38th Bn.M.G.C.)
                                              19th Welsh Rgt.)
                                              "Q"   )
                                              A.D.M.S.   )
                                              "E" Sqdn.Cyclists)
                                              Attd.Troop of))
                                                  Carabiniers.))

SECRET

GSS.1/22/A.

AMENDMENT NO. 1 to 38th (WELSH) DIVISION ORDER NO.231.

Para.2.

Boundary shown on map between 113th Brigade and 5th Division will be amended to run from Q.28.d.9.5. to Q.30.c.4.5. and thence to Q.30.d.9.8.
17th Division is advancing from the GREEN LINE against the RED Line at Zero plus 147 minutes.

Para. 3 (d)

For "About 100 yds. West of" read "in"

Para. 4 (a)

Last line but two for "three minutes" read "four minutes except the first two lifts which will be after three minutes each".

Para. 4 (b)

Line two for "15" read "10".

Para. 6.

Cancel lines 3 to 6 inclusive and substitute -
"Sunken road in W.5.d. and its continuation in W.6.a.
"GREEN LINE.
"Locality Q.35.b.".

Add at the end of the para. -

"A & C Cos. will be prepared, on receipt of orders from Div: H.Q. through O.C.Bn., to move forward to near our present front line to positions from which they can efficiently protect the GREEN LINE. This move will probably be made by one company at a time as soon after the GREEN Line is reached as the situation will permit".

Para. 12 (b)

For "Q.30.a.4.0. and Q.29.a.8.0" read "Q.30.c.4.5 and Q.29.d.6.5".

Para. 15.

Line 3 for "9.a.m." read "8.a.m."
Line 6 for "7.a.m." read "6.a.m."

Add New Para. 16. -

The "Success" Signal will be the same as usual, i.e. A three white stars parachute Rifle Grenade Signal.

J.E. Munby

16th September 1918.   Lieut. Colonel,
General Staff, 38th (Welsh) Division.

Copies to all recipients of D.O. 231.

2 copies Bde 1153.
1 copy to S.C.

SECRET
GSS.1/22/A.

AMENDMENT NO. 2 to 38TH (WELSH) DIVISION ORDER NO. 231.

Para. 2.

The 5th Division will not now attack the GREEN LINE but will seize and hold the sunken road running through Q.29.d.

An "international" post composed of one platoon of 5th Divn. and one platoon of 113th Brigade will be formed about Q.29.d.6.5. This is the only obligatory "international" post to be formed on this flank.

5th Division have engaged to deal with any counter-attack which may be made against this sunken road.

The final objective for the 113th Brigade will be the GREEN LINE as shown on the map issued with D.O.231 as far North as the sunken road at Q.30.c.2.2. and thence along that road as far as the "International" post at Q.29.d.6.5.

113th Brigade and 5th Divn. to ACKNOWLEDGE.

J. E. Munby
Lieut. Colonel,
16th September 1918.   General Staff, 38th (Welsh) Division.

Copies to recipients of D.O.231.

B.M...... 1176
Date.... 17/9/18
B.G.C..........
B.M............
S.C............
B.I.O...........
B.G.O...........
B.T.O...........

Ref: Vth Corps letter No G.X. 6223
of 30.8.18.

1. (a) Training. Although "Artillery formation" appears to be understood generally by the men, there is room for improvement.

Men did not appear to know exactly where to go when the platoon splits up into sections. Continual practice is necessary in this so that men automatically get into their proper formation with all speed. In the fighting about SAILLY — SAILLISEL, the troops were constantly coming on top of isolated groups of Boche and it struck an observer at once how good it would be if men could shake out more quickly & every man to his appointed place.

(b) Further training in "Searching" of ground essential. On many occasions men walked right into nests without looking where they were going.

(c) Training in rendering accurate reports necessary. Several instances occurred where ground was reported clear when the reverse was the case, causing increase in casualties.

2. Organization. Nothing to suggest.

3. Equipment. In "fighting order" it would appear that a half empty pack is preferable to an overloaded haversack. The latter does not hold sufficient

with the result that men went into action carrying a sandbag with rations & other articles thus hampering their movements.

16/9/18.

P. Welton Major
17th R. W. Fusiliers.

SECRET

38th Division No. GSS. 1/22.

All recipients of D.O.231.
  (Less V Corps
      V Corps R.A.
      V Corps H.A.
      17th Bde. R.G.A.
      17th Divn.
      21st Divn.
      33rd Divn
      15th Sqdn. R.A.F.)

Reference 38th (Welsh) Division Order No. 231 dated 15th September, 1918.

Zero hour is _5.20_ a.m. on _18th_ September 1918.

ACKNOWLEDGE BY RETURN.

17th September 1918.

J. E. Munby
Lieut. Colonel,
General Staff, 38th (Welsh) Division.

B.N............ 467
Det O............ 17 9 18
B.C.C............
B.M............
S.C............
B.I.O............
B.C.O............
D.T.O............

....

SECRET.   38th Division No. GSS. 1/22/A.

113th Brigade.   38th Bn. M.G.C.   38th Div. Arty.
114th Brigade.   38th Div. "Q".
115th Brigade.   38th Div. Signals.

Reference D.O. 231.

115 Brigade will be in a position of readiness under cover in the trench system about FINS Ridge by 8 a.m. on Z day. This Brigade will be prepared after that hour to counter-attack should the enemy succeed in penetrating our attack on any portion of the Corps front.

The Brigade if required to counter counter-attack or to restore the situation will do so under the orders of the Divisional Commander in whose area it is required to act. The necessary order placing the Brigade under the orders of the Divisional Commander concerned will be issued by Corps H.Q. and will be repeated to G.O.C. 38th Division. 115 Brigade will report as soon as the Brigade is in position on the FINS Ridge.

The 3rd Brigade R.A.F. are co-operating in the attack on Z day as under :-

One Squadron low flying Bristol fighting planes are being detailed to co-operate in the Infantry attack forward from the GREEN Line.

These planes will time their flight so as to approach the GREEN Line from the West as the Infantry advance they will then keep our infantry in view and from low altitudes will engage any enemy who appear to be holding up our advance.

All ranks are to be informed.

                                          Lieut. Colonel,
17/9/18.   General Staff, 38th (Welsh) Division.

INSTRUCTIONS FOR SIGNAL COMMUNICATIONS.
in connection with Divisional Order..3..of...15/9/18

LINES. 1.(a) Divisional Cable Head DV will be established in the Eastern entrance of the East dugout in the Bank(W.3.a.2.0) by 1 p.m. 16th inst.
113th and 114th Brigades and C.R.A. intend to establish report centres at these points; and all leading battalions and artillery brigades will be connected thereto.
When all Divisional Cables are working, one will be available for each of the 113th and 114th Brigades and C.R.A's Headquarters; these will also be interconnected.
This Cable Head will be in charge of Lieut.RICHARDSON, R.E. from the time of arrival of Infantry Brigade Signals.
   (b) Lines will pass through test points at QA (Q.31.d.central), PV(P.35.d.3.3), and a test point at CP(P.33.c.2.5.).
Priority messages can be sent over the 'phone from above test points.
At PV a telephone exchange will be installed manned by Div. H.Q. operators in charge Capt. ROWE, ready to open any time after 2 p.m. 16th.
Lines available are shewn diagramatically as follows:-

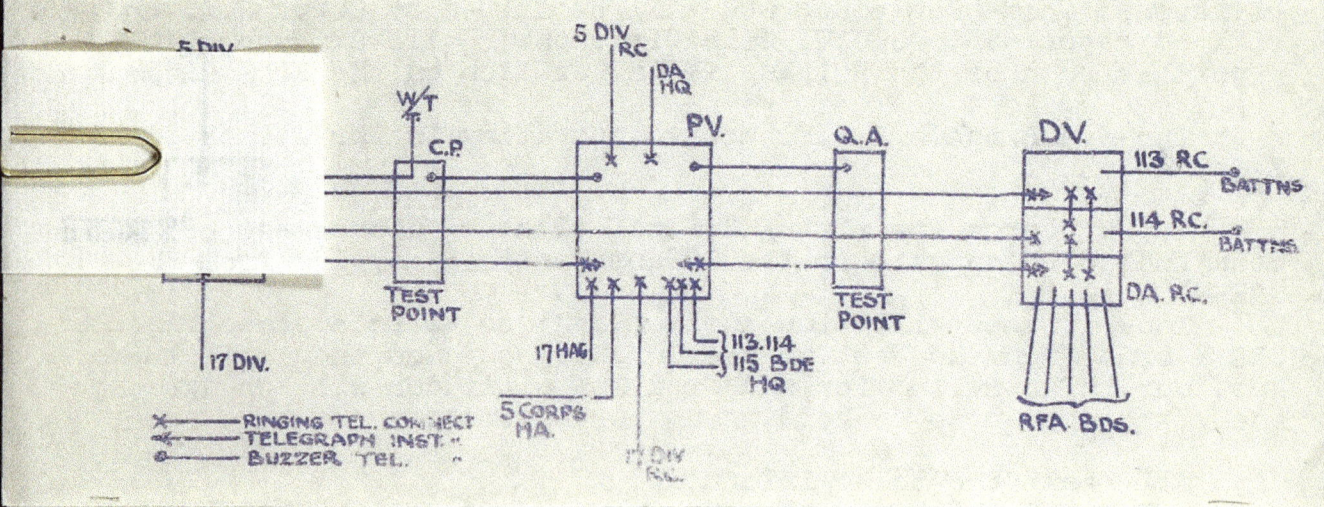

D.R's. Three M/C. D.R's will be available at DV from time of arrival of H.Q.
Two M/C. and 3 Mounted D.R's will be available at PV from 6 p.m. 17th.
Five M/C and 3 Mounted D.R's will be available at Div. H.Q.
Runner Posts at PV, QA, and DV will be manned by 113th and 114th Brigades combined.

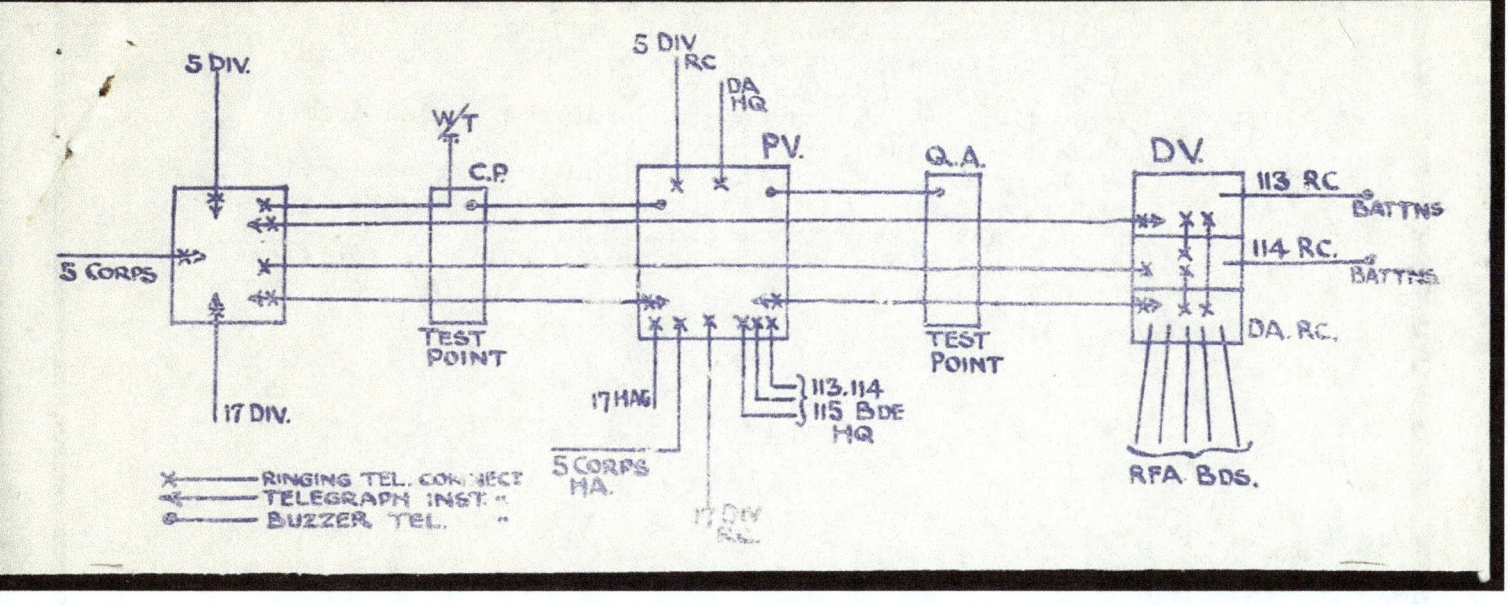

Bm 1123

INSTRUCTIONS FOR SIGNAL COMMUNICATIONS.
in connection with Divisional Order....3...of...15/9/18..

LINES.   1.(a) Divisional Cable Head DV will be established
         in the Eastern entrance of the East dugout in the
         Bank(W.3.a.2.0) by 1 p.m. 16th inst.
         113th and 114th Brigades and C.R.A. intend to
         establish report centres at these points; and all
         leading battalions and artillery brigades will be
         connected thereto.
         When all Divisional Cables are working, one will be
         available for each of the 113th and 114th Brigades
         and C.R.A's Headquarters; these will also be
         interconnected.
         This Cable Head will be in charge of Lieut.RICHARDSON,
         R.E. from the time of arrival of Infantry Brigade
         Signals.
            (b) Lines will pass through test points at QA
         (Q.31.d.central), PV(P.35.d.3.3), and a test point
         at CP(P.33.c.2.5.).
         Priority messages can be sent over the 'phone from
         above test points.
         At PV a telephone exchange will be installed manned
         by Div. H.Q. operators in charge Capt. ROWE, ready
         to open any time after 2 p.m. 16th.
         Lines available are shewn diagramatically as follows:-

                        see attached

D.R's.   Three M/C. D.R's will be available at DV from time
         of arrival of H.Q.
         Two M/C. and 3 Mounted D.R's will be available at
         PV from 6 p.m. 17th.
         Five M/C and 3 Mounted D.R's will be available at
         Div. H.Q.
         Runner Posts at PV, QA, and DV will be manned by
         113th and 114th Brigades combined.

(2).

VISUAL. Between Battalion Headquarters and Brigades a Forward Visual Post is being established in each Brigade Area for transmitting back information as to progress etc.
113th and 114th Brigades will notify locations of Receiving Stations to all concerned.

WIRELESS. From Combined Battalion Headquarters to Brigade Advanced Headquarters (W.3.a.S.O) by loop set.
From Brigade Advanced Headquarters to Rear Headquarters(P.35.d.S.4) and D.H.Q. by trench set.
From D.H.Q. to Flank Divisions and Corps by wilson set.
Between Battalion Headquarters of 113th and 114th Brigades by power buzzer.
A power buzzer will also be available for each of 113th and 114th Brigades for communicating information back to Brigade Headquarters.

Note. Information as to progress etc., is best signalled back in code to render it short and capable of being dealt with quickly

CONTACT AEROPLANES. 15th Squadron R.A.F. is being notified of locations of Battalion and Brigade Headquarters. Messages can be sent by these units to Divl. H.Q. Dropping Station at V.8.c.9.9 by means of Popham Panels.

PIGEONS. Owing to the distance of the loft, it is no use sending <u>urgent</u> messages by pigeons.

15/8/18.   O.C., 38th Divl. Signals.

SECRET.   A.D.M.S. No. M.56/45

Reference 38th Division Order No. 231.
MEDICAL ARRANGEMENTS.

1. O.C. No. 129 Field Ambulance will be responsible for clearing the line. His Headquarters will be at V.11.a.2.2.
On the evening of the 17th. instant he will open an A.D.S. at V.11.a.2.2. This A.D.S. will also be used by the 17th. and 21st. Divisions.
O.C. No. 130 Field Ambulance will place at the disposal of O.C. No. 129 Field Ambulance as many operating tents as possible and will detail Captain Melhuish, R.A.M.C. temporarily to his assistance.

2. CAR POSTS.
On the Left side at Q.31.c.2.2.
On the Right side at W.3.c.2.8. and W.8.a.1.9.
Cars will also be pushed up to W.4.a.central and beyond as far as practicable. Small scattered Car Posts will be established down the road between EQUANCOURT and ETRICOURT, only two or three cars being stationed in any one place. These cars will move up in rotation as others come down the line. Under arrangements with A.Ds.M.S. 17th and 21st Divisions, as many cars as possible will be placed at the disposal of O.C. No. 129 Field Ambulance for evacuating wounded from the A.D.S. to the combined M.D.S. at LECHELLE P.32.a.

3. EVACUATION.
On the left side. The R.A.P. will probably be at Q.33.b.2.2., whence wounded will be conveyed either to Q.32.d.2.4. and thence by the relay posts at Q.31.b.9.5. to the Car Post at Q.31.c.2.2., or, if circumstances permit, they will be brought down the tracks leading into the main FINS - GOUZEAUCOURT road at W.3.c.6.8. or W.3.b.10.5 whence they will be conveyed by car.
On the Right side.
The R.A.P. will be at W.4.a.central. Evacuation from there as far as possible by car.

4. WALKING WOUNDED COLLECTING POST.
O.C. No. 131 Field Ambulance will form a Walking Wounded Collecting Post at V.11.a.2.2. For this purpose he will have the assistance of two officers and 12 Nursing Orderlies from 17th. Division and one officer and 12 Nursing Orderlies from 21st Division. These should report to O.C. No. 131 Field Ambulance at V.11.a.2.2. at 7 p.m. on the 17th. instant.
The Walking Wounded Collecting Post will be used conjointly by the three Divisions concerned, and will, it is hoped, be cleared under Corps arrangements to the Corps Walking Wounded Post at V.2.central. Horse ambulances should also be used for this purpose, additional ones being obtained from Nos. 130 and 131 Field Ambulances., or from 17th. and 21st Divisions if required.

5. Under arrangements with 38th Division 'Q' it is hoped to establish a Canteen at the combined A.D.S. and W.W.C.P.

6. In forming the A.D.S. and W.W.C.P. Os.C. 129 and 131 Field Ambulances will make all their preparations tomorrow, but will, as far as possible, put up no canvas until after dusk.

7. A.T.S. will be given at the M.D.S. LECHELLE P.32.a. and Corps Walking Wounded Collecting Post at V.2.central

Please acknowledge.

                                                    Major
                                                    Colonel,
                                        A.D.M.S., 38th(Welsh)Division.
16.9.18
Fd.Ambs.   Brigades, 38 Div 'Q'
17 Div. 5th 21 Div. 38th " 'A'
D.D.M.S. V Corps

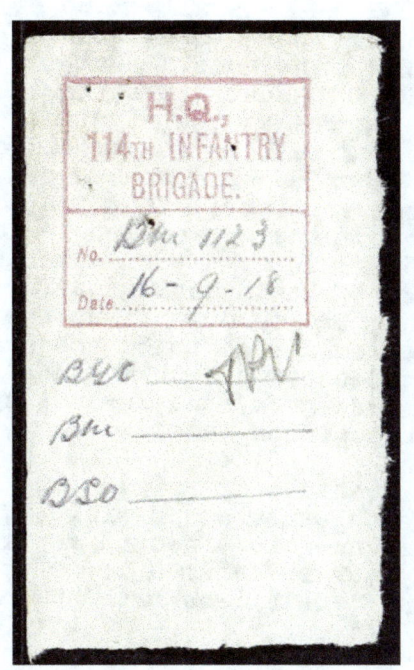

SECRET.   38th Division No. 1 B/54.

                                      HEADQUARTERS,
                                      INFANTRY BRIGADE.
113 Brigade.   38th Div. Arty.   No. BM/265
114 Brigade.   C. R. E.   Date 21.9.18.
115 Brigade.

H. DeP.

The following is a list of lessons learnt during the recent operations which it is intended to forward to the V Corps. Would you please send as soon as possible any amendments or additions which you can suggest.

1.   In order to prevent determined troops from crossing a river the defenders must occupy positions from which close rifle fire can be brought on to the water itself: to be able to fire at the banks is not sufficient: our troops were able to cross the CANAL DU NORD by finding a covered approach to the waters edge which was not under fire. The advance of the 113 Brigade across the ANCRE in ALBERT was accomplished with comparative ease once the enemy had been driven out of the town.

2.   The use of machine guns with the leading waves of infantry in the attack was found to be generally more of a moral than material value. Cases did occur where these machine guns were instrumental in silencing hostile machine guns. But the difficulty of ammunition supply made it necessary either to detail infantry carrying parties and so weaken the fighting strength of the infantry or to accept the risk of failure in ammunition supply.
        Moreover this use of machine guns necessitates companies working by independent sections; thus the control of the most experienced man, the company commander, is lost.
        But on the other hand the use of machine guns in companies well to the rear is not suitable to moving warfare; the enemy quickly gets out of range and also opportunities are missed.
        A medium course would seem to be the best i.e. the attachment of companies to Brigades for use during the advance as companies with the supports or reserves, and for use by sections or subsections in occupation of the position gained.

3.   It is a great advantage if Brigade and Battalion Headquarters can be kept as close together as possible. A great saving in cable and signal personnel is effected and liaison is simplified.
        Whether this system is adhered to or not it is necessary for the higher formation to detail beforehand the Headquarters to be occupied.
        Unless the command of the Artillery is completely decentralised, the C.R.A. should have his Headquarters with the leading brigades.
        Headquarters must never be allowed to close i.e. they must open at the new location before closing at the old one.

4.   The great wastage in signal personnel makes it necessary to maintain a large reserve, the number of signallers and runners required does not decrease in proportion to the decrease in fighting strength of units.
        Two remedies present themselves; one, the amalgamation of units which are considerably reduced in strength; the other, the retaining of a reserve of signal personnel above establishment away from the firing line i.e. deducting this reserve from the fighting strength.
        Neither of these remedies are at present permitted.

5.   The squared map is admittedly a great convenience but leads to a tendency to allot boundaries by means of grid lines instead of by tactical or natural features.

6./

6.   The failure of many regimental officers in map reading has been a severe handicap; map reading should be given special attention in cadet training.

7.   Where one formation is required to advance beyond the line held by an adjacent formation, the best boundary between the two is the top of a ridge. In other words the top of a ridge provides the best defensive flank; there should be no attempt to hold the outer slopes of this ridge, these slopes and indeed half the top of the ridge itself can be left to the enemy provided always that observation is denied to him.

8.   It has been found useless to attempt to "pinch out" high ground; such ground cannot be left in the hands of the enemy and passed by, it must be attacked and taken as early as possible.
     On the other hand it is often possible to "pinch out" stretches of low ground.

J.E. Manby
Lieut. Colonel,
21/9/1918.   General Staff, 38th (Welsh) Division.

H.Q. 115 Bde

Ref: your B.M. No 1088 of 12/9/18

1. The Tactics of the enemy rear-guards (met with by the battalion under my command) during the past month have (been) invariably been the same. Generally speaking they consist of groups of Machine Guns (varying from 6 to 24 in number) of both heavy and light types, sited usually on forward slopes, well concealed, and with a clear field of fire up to ranges of not much less than about 800 yards. Machine Guns are generally accompanied by snipers. Every Machine Gun Group was is covered by Artillery, the co-operation between the two being very close. A Infantry appear to be used principally to counter-attack. (They were found, on Sept 1st, in line with Machine Guns outside LES BOEUFS, but this was the only occasion and they were not in strength. Their counter-attack, later during the day, was in much greater strength, and was made from trenches passed by us on the left flank.)

To deal with these tactics successfully I am of opinion that infantry should be more in depth and should keep in depth. The longer the advance, the greater should be the strength in depth, and therefore the narrower the front. Battalions moving on a very wide front find themselves not strong enough to break through the enemy rear-guard everywhere and their front then quickly becomes disorganized, and they are not strong enough in depth to both restore the situation in front and to meet or to re-counter attack a hostile counter attack on a flank.

When moving with an exposed flank, as is so often the case in advance guard actions, supporting troops, whether they be companies, or battalions, should, I think, be moved well in echelon on that flank, in order to attack, or to threaten, the flank, of a hostile counter-attack.

A further advantage of moving on a narrow front is derived from the fact that a greater concentration of artillery can generally be put down as a barrage.

(By a "narrow" front is meant one of 500 yds or less. A "wide" front would be up to 1000 yds per battalion.)

Equipment. It is necessary that the men should be lightly equipped. The fatigue and strain of a long advance is very great and affects moral. Pack animals for carrying equipment not required for immediate use might have been more frequently employed.

Rifle Grenades have hardly ever been used by my battalion though there have been times when they might have been extremely useful. I think that a rifle-grenade party, organized from the support companies and handled in rear of the leading wave by an energetic officer with an independent rôle might be of great value. Stokes Mortars might with advantage work with them.

Map-reading. The lack of sufficient knowledge of map-reading by nearly all officers was most noticeable, and was more than once disastrous. The teaching of map-reading to young officers has not been sufficiently practical, while the teaching of the use of the compass & protractor has been bad. The importance of being able to give an accurate map-reference of the places they find themselves in cannot be exaggerated.

Young officers and N.C.O's do not realize, until they are told, that the stoutest Bosch in front of them (when they are on the defensive) is easily tamed by a thoroughly aggressive use of their Lewis Guns and Rifles.

C. Norman Lt Col
Comd 2/R.W.F.

23/9/18

SS.143/I

2nd American Corps
Orders + Instrns.

GERMAN TRENCHES IN BLUE.

FRANCE
Trenches revised from information received to 17-7-18

EDITION 5. e

SS.143/I

2nd American Corps
Orders + Instrns.

SECRET

2nd Corps MEMORANDUM G-3 NO. 1.

GENERAL STAFF,
38TH (WELSH)
DIVISION.
No. SS.143/I.   COPY NO.
Date 29.9.18

2nd American Corps,
FRANCE, 28th Sept., '18.

INSTRUCTIONS FOR OPERATIONS, SECTION NO. 14.

LIAISON.

1. Officers will be detailed as below for liaison work.

2. No officers will be detailed by divisions for liaison work with 2nd American Corps Headquarters.

3. Capt. R. S. Hall will be responsible for liaison between Headquarters of the 30th Division and the left flank Division of the IX British Corps.
Capt. T. B. Murray will be responsible for liaison between Headquarters of the 27th Division and the right flank Divisions of the III and later the V British Corps.
These officers are provided with motor cycle side cars.
Lt. Col. W. O. Boswell will be responsible for liaison between the 27th Division and Headquarters 2nd American Corps.
Major L. E. Hibbs will be responsible for liaison between the 30th Division and Headquarters 2nd American Corps. Two motor cycle dispatch riders will be furnished each of these officers and hourly situation reports will be made to Headquarters 2nd Corps.
Lt. Col. I. L. Hunt will be responsible for liaison between the IX British Corps and Headquarters 2nd American Corps.
Col. G. D. Moore will be responsible for liaison between Headquarters 2nd American Corps and III British Corps and later V British Corps.
Officers detailed for liaison with flank Divisions and Corps will report at Headquarters of those organizations not later than 6:00 p.m. "Y" day.

4. These officers must ensure that the Headquarters to which they are attached and the formation from which they are sent are kept fully informed at all times of all that is taking place.

5. Division Commanders of the 2nd American Corps are again reminded of the vital importance of transmitting promptly to Corps Headquarters full and accurate information of the situation of the units of their commands.
It is especially important that the above information be given at the following times:
  (1) 6:00 p.m. "Y" day.
  (2) At the time of the halt in the Artillery Barrage 500 yards east of the Canal Tunnel.
  (3) When the troops have reached the green line. At (1) and (3) it will be necessary to know the exact locations of Divisions down to and including Regiments.

The above object can be best accomplished by blocking out on a map the Areas occupied by the units.

6. All messages for 2nd American Corps will be sent to Advance Headquarters 2nd Corps at N.15.D.central.

By command of Major General Read:

G. S. SIMONDS,
Col., G. S., C. of S.

AWC/wrk

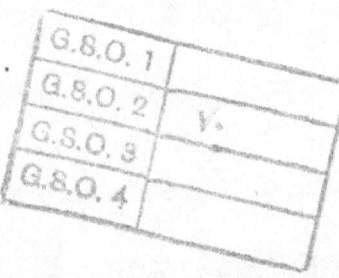

G.S.O. 1	
G.S.O. 2	Y
G.S.O. 3	
G.S.O. 4	

38th Div

War Diary.
G.S.
38th Division.
October 1918.

Index _____

SUBJECT.

No.	Contents.	Date.
	Work of Depots in early stages of the war	

Volume ~~III~~ IV

Comments on

Chapter ~~XIX~~ V

October 1918

V Corps

October.

ORIGINAL

WAR DIARY GENERAL STAFF 38TH (WELSH) DIVISION. Army Form C. 2118.

INTELLIGENCE SUMMARY

VOLUME XXXIV

Instructions regarding War Diaries and Intelligence Summaries are contained in F. S. Regs., Part II. and the Staff Manual respectively. Title pages will be prepared in manuscript.

Place	Date	Hour	Summary of Events and Information	Remarks and references to Appendices
	OCTOBER 1918.			
	1st.		Situation remained unchanged. Division now at two hours notice to move. Brigades carried out training in vicinity of bivouacs. G.O.C. visited Brigades during the afternoon.	
	2nd.		Corps Commander visited Divisional Headquarters during the morning. G.S.O.1. visited the Battle Surplus. G.S.O.2. reconnoitred sites for rifle ranges during the afternoon. Situation V Corps Front remained unchanged. Brigades spent the day training in the vicinity of bivouacs.	App 1
	3rd.		G.S.O.1. visited Battle Surplus, and lectured to Officers and senior N.C.Os on the subject of Patrols and Situation Reports, touching afterwards on Musketry discipline etc. XIII Corps(on Right) make a successful attack and capture LE CATELET, and GUOY. 113th and 115th Infantry Brigades and 2 companies Machine Gun Battn. ordered by wire to be ready at 1500 hours. to South of VENDHULE. G.25 issued. 113th Brigade move to trenches North east of EPEHY.	App 2
	4th.		115th Infantry Brigade and 151 Field Coy. R.E. to positions N.W. RONSSOY. 38th Bn. M.G.C. (less 2 companies) to positions west of PEIZIERES. Situation V Corps front not changed. G.53 issued 0120. 115th Infantry Brigade move to HINDENBURG LINE near BOMY. The moves of the Division dependant on the capture of the high ground immediately north of LE CATELET. 50th Division (XIII Corps) attack - their advance is checked by Machine Gun fire. When this is captured 38th Division is to relieve part of 50th Division front and attack the enemy on V Corps front in a N. and N.E. direction. Troops move accordingly - 113th Brigade to positions about 1000 yds east of LEMPIRE. 114th Brigade to positions about 1500 yards N.E. of LEMPIRE. Order No.236 issued. 115 Brigade take over positions obtained by 50th Division on the high ground N. of LE CATELET, from LA PANNERIE SOUTH to point about 500 yards S.E. of HARGIVAL FARM. The relief commenced about 1000 hours and was complete about 0600 hours 5th. Divisional Order	App 3
EPEHY.	5th.		H.Q. moved to EPEHY 0400 hours. Enemy retired from DELALERU - PUTNEY and HINDENBURG LINE opposite V Corps front. 113th and 115th Brigades move as ordered in Divisional Order No.237. 114th Brigade move to HINDENBURG LINE east of PUTNEY and OSSUS. Little opposition was met until the line VAUX HALL QUARRY, EASTERN edge AUBENCHEUL, Western edge MORTHO WOOD was reached.	App 4

Army Form C. 2118.

WAR DIARY
or
INTELLIGENCE SUMMARY.
(Erase heading not required.)

Page 2.

Instructions regarding War Diaries and Intelligence Summaries are contained in F. S. Regs., Part II. and the Staff Manual respectively. Title pages will be prepared in manuscript.

Place	Date	Hour	Summary of Events and Information	Remarks and references to Appendices
EPEHY.	OCTOBER 1918.			
	5th. (continued).		Order No.238 issued.	
	6th.		Line remained as above during the night. Patrols reported the MASNIERES BEAUREVOIR LINE to be strongly held by the enemy. Patrols were active during the day, and a line finally established SUNKEN ROAD S.E. AUBENCHEUL Eastern outskirts AUBENCHEUL midway through MORTHO WOOD. The enemy continued in force in the BEAUREVOIR LINE opposite the Corps front. G.O.C. attended Conference at V Corps H.Q. 1915 hours, with reference to the forthcoming operations. Three prisoners taken.	App. 5
	7th.		S.S.143/6 issued - Warning Order timed 0515 hours. G.O.C. attended Conference of XIII Corps at 1000 hours. Conference held at 115th Infantry Brigade H.Q. Brigadiers, M.G.Bn Commdr, C.R.A. attended. Situation unchanged - line as above. Some shelling of MORTHO WOOD and AUBENCHEUL during the afternoon.	App. 6
HINDENBURG LINE.	8th.		Divl. Order 239 issued - Divisional H.Q. moved to HINDENBURG LINE at 1100 hours. The attack commenced at 0100 hours. 115th and 113th Infantry Brigades (Right and Left respectively) met considerable resistance from trench line west of VILLERS &OUTREAUX but owing to the wire in front of this trench and the darkness, the attack was checked, and at dawn the Right Battalion 115th Infantry Brigade, who had formed up in the area of the 50th Division (XIII Corps) having gone well ahead into the barrage and meeting heavy M.G. fire from trench line running from S.E. side of VILLERS was somewhat scattered and the Left Battalion had been unable to enter the BEAUREVOIR trench line. Troops of 113th Brigade (on Left) were established in AUYGELUS ORCHARD and sunken road to the N.E. of it. 114th Brigade were ordered to postpone their move to assembly positions from which the second attack was to be made. It was found, however, impossible to stop the two Battalions of this Brigade which were to assemble N. of the village and they became involved in the battle with the 113th Brigade. By 1630 hours the situation had cleared; tanks having come up at dawn. The line of the Left Battalion was established due South from ANGLES CHATEAU whilst the Right Brigade commenced (Brigade) mopping up the village. It was decided to make the second attack at 1130 hours. 114th Brigade was ordered to be in their assembly positions by this time and the barrage arranged similar to that which should have been carried out at 0800 hours. 114th Brigade met considerable opposition and had to fight their way to their assembly positions N. and S. of the village on the road running N.W. and S.E. along the N.E. edge	App. 7

Army Form C. 2118.

WAR DIARY
or
INTELLIGENCE SUMMARY.

(Erase heading not required.)

Page 3.

Place	Date	Hour	Summary of Events and Information	Remarks and references to Appendices
HINDENBURG LINE.	OCTOBER 1918.			
	7th.		edge of VILLERS OUTREAUX. These positions were reached and the 114th Brigade moved off under the barrage at 1130 hours. Very little opposition was met until East of MACINCOURT Line finally taken up from the Southern corner of MILL WOOD to junction of MALINCOURT ELINCOURT and ELINCOURT WALINCOURT ROADS. Captures during these operations 7 officers 373 other ranks.	App. 8
	9th.		G.129 issued 2025 hours. 33rd Division passed through the Division 0520 hours. G.141 issued. 114th Brigade moved to CLARY. 33rd Division kept touch with enemy.outposts were established east of TROISVILLES.	
	10th.		G.152 issued 2035 hours. V Corps (33rd Division and 17th Division) in touch with enemy on West heights of valley of RIVER SELLE between MONTAY and NEUVILLY. 38th Division remained in support to 33rd Div. 115th Infantry Brigade moved to CLARY, (less 1 Battalion to BERTRY). Divisional H.Q. moved to VILLERS OUTREAUX 1600 hours.	
VILLERS OUTREAUX.	11th.		33rd and 17th Divisions attack 1700 hours to gain the crossings of RIVER SELLE. As a result of this attack some posts were established east of the river. Situation on the Corps front remained unchanged. 38th Division remained in the same positions, throughout the day less Divisional Headquarters to CLARY.	App. 9
CLARY.			1400 hours - Divisional Order 240 issued. 33rd and 17th Divisions attacked with a view to gaining high ground east of RIVER SELLE 0500 hours. The attack in the first place was only partially successful and finally it was decided to consolidate on the high ground west of the river. 113th Brigade moved to BERTRY 115th Brigade move to TROISVILLES and become Reserve and Support Brigades respectively under orders of 33rd Division. The move of 114th Brigade postponed to night 13/14th. Divisional Headquarters move to BERTRY 1600 hours.	
	13th.		Divisional Order 241 issued. 1930 hours. Situation on V Corps front unchanged. Relief of front Brigade 33rd Division by 115th Brigade commenced after dark being complete about 2320 hours.	App. 10
BERTRY.	14th.		Enemy shelled the road west of LA SELLE river and river valley heavily during the night. 115th Infantry Brigade in the line on two Battalions front. 114th Infantry Brigade in support. 113th Infantry Brigade in Reserve. Intermittent shelling RAMBOURLIEUX FARM -	

Army Form C. 2118.

WAR DIARY
or
INTELLIGENCE SUMMARY.   Page 4.

(Erase heading not required.)

Instructions regarding War Diaries and Intelligence Summaries are contained in F. S. Regs., Part II. and the Staff Manual respectively. Title pages will be prepared in manuscript.

Place	Date	Hour	Summary of Events and Information	Remarks and references to Appendices
BERTRY.	OCTOBER 1918.			
	14th (continued).		EAMBOURLEUX FARM - (Front Battalions H.Q.) during the day, otherwise quiet. Projectors installed by "N" Special Coy.R.E. on the Divisional front, which were to be fired at 0100 and 0200 hours 15th if conditions were favourable. Wind unfavourable for gas discharge.	
	15th.		Intermittent gas shelling (Blue Cross) of SELLE VALLEY during the night. Conference at Divisional H.Q. 1130 hours attended by Brigadiers, C.R.A., C.R.E., M.G.Bn. Commdr. etc, to discuss forthcoming operations. Day quiet.	
	16th.		Enemy fired several thousand gas shells on battery positions, chiefly Yellow Cross. Slight retaliation to a bombardment carried out by us of his positions on the Railway Cutting East of RIVER SELLE. R.E. working on maintenance of footbridges across the river. Except for some shelling of Battery positions and RAMBOURLIEUX FARM the day was quiet. Divisional Order 242 issued.	App. 1
	17th.		Situation on V Corps front unchanged. Attack by IV Army commenced at 0520 hours 66th Division being the left of the attack. In consequence of these operations hostile artillery was abnormally active on the Divisional front. The vicinity of RAMBOURLIEUX FARM was heavily shelled during the afternoon. Patrolling was carried out at night; an enemy post near the NEUVILLY - MONTAY ROAD was attacked and about 4 of the enemy killed. On our Right the 66th Division captured the line of the Railway East of LE CATEAU as far north as BAILLON FARM. Divisional Order No.244 issued.	App. 2
	18th.		The day passed more quietly on the Divisional Front. The attack on the front of the IV Army was resumed at 0530 hours. 66th Division cleared LE CATEAU and made progress on to the high ground between LE CATEAU and BAZUEL capturing the latter place. At dusk a strong patrol of the 115th Brigade endeavoured to establish a new post on the East bank of the river SELLE, but was unsuccessful. The enemy was encountered and fighting ensued in which both sides suffered casualties. Two machine guns were captured but had to be abandoned owing to our casualties. At night the Divisional front was extended Southwards so as to include the MONTAY - FOREST ROAD. The 115th Brigade and the 66th Division were relieved in the line on the new Divisional Front by the 114th Brigade on the left and 113th Brigade on the right, these Brigades taking over on their Battle fronts for forthcoming operations. 115th Brigade moved to TROISVILLES.	
	/19th.			

Army Form C. 2118.

WAR DIARY
or
INTELLIGENCE SUMMARY.
(Erase heading not required.)

Page 5.

Instructions regarding War Diaries and Intelligence Summaries are contained in F. S. Regs., Part II. and the Staff Manual respectively. Title pages will be prepared in manuscript.

Place	Date	Hour	Summary of Events and Information	Remarks and references to Appendices
BERTRY.	OCTOBER 1918.			
	19th.		The day passed quietly on the Divisional Front. No further attacks took place on the front of the 66th Division who consolidated the line previously captured. Preparations for forthcoming operations being completed.	
	20th.		At 0200 hours the British Third Army attacked. The attack by the V Corps was carried out by 17th Division on the left and 38th Division on the Right. 38th Division attacked with 114th Brigade on the Left and 113th Brigade on the Right, the objective being the high ground running S.E. from AMERVAL and overlooking FOREST. The assembly took place west and east of the river SELLE, over which upwards of 24 bridges had been constructed by the Divisional Royal Engineers; the assembly was carried out without incident. The advance was supported by acreeping barrage, which commenced on the line of the Railway. This was fired by the Divisional Artillery, the 33rd Divisional Artillery and the 13th Brigade R.G.A; all available and Light and Medium Trench Mortars co-operated in this barrage as well as the 38th Bn.M.G.Corps together with 2 Companies 33rd Battalion M.G.Corps. Two tanks also supported the advance, one assisting each Brigade; these successfully crossed the river by specially constructed bridges, but afterwards became ditched. 115th Infantry Brigade were in support, with one Battalion in Reserve to and under the orders of 113th Infantry Brigade. Another Battalion was moved at 0500 hours to a position in rear of 114th Inf.Brigade. The forming up of the 114th Infantry Brigade was carried out West of the RIVER SELLE. Hostile posts were known to exist very near the East bank of the River and an attempt to drive these in before ZERO proved unsuccessful. It was therefore deemed expedient to form up West of the River. Considerable opposition was met with along the line of the Railway, but this was overcome after some stubborn fighting. The advance continued successfully, and the 2nd Objectives were captured to time. On the Left touch was established with the 17th Division on the 2nd Objective. The advance of the Left Brigade to a third objective was held up at first, but was afterwards successfully accomplished. 17th Division continued fighting all day near AMERVAL which changed hands constantly and remained at evening in the hands of the enemy. Hostile shelling was heavy all day on the line of the Railway and on the crossings of the RIVER SELLE. At Zero it was raining heavily, though fine later in the day. /By evening	

WAR DIARY
or
INTELLIGENCE SUMMARY.
(Erase heading not required.)

Army Form C. 2118.

Page 6.

Place	Date	Hour	Summary of Events and Information	Remarks and references to Appendices
	OCTOBER 1918.			
	20th (continued).		By evening 1 officer and 211 other ranks had passed through the Divisional P.O.W. Cage and 225 enemy dead were counted. 4 Field guns 3 trench mortars and about 40 M.G's were captured. The objectives on capture were consolidated with the help of 2 companies of the Pioneers and were held without any serious enemy counter attack. Our casualties were about 18 officers and 400 other ranks.	app 13.
	21st.		Situation unchanged on the Divisional Front. During the night the 113th Inf.Brigade established a few advanced posts, which however proved untenable owing to enfilade T.M. and M.G. fire. On the left the 17th Division carried out a local attack at dawn and succeeded in capturing AMERVAL together with prisoners. For the remainder of the day passed without special incident and hostile activity was quiet. During the afternoon and evening the 115th Inf.Brigade relieved the 114th Brigade and 113th Brigade (less 1 Battalion), in the line. The two relieved Brigades moved back to BERTRY. o—o m/.	
	22nd.		Situation unchanged. Hostile artillery carried out counter preparation between 0100 and 0200 hours and from about 0430 to 0530 hours. Much Mustard Gas was also fired into the valley of the RIVER SELLE. In the evening the 98th Brigade (on the Right) and the 19th Brigade (on the Left) of the 33rd Division relieved the 115th Brigade in the line, and on relief the 115th Brigade moved to TROISVILLES.	
	23rd.		The British First, Third and Fourth Armies renewed the attack. The attack of the V Corps began at 0200 hours and was carried out by the 21st Division on the left and the 33rd Division on the right, with the 17th Division and 38th Division respectively in Support. The assembly was carried out on the line captured on the 21st instant, the final objective being a line running S.E. from POIX du NORD. The role of the 38th Division was to be prepared to assist the advance if held up, or to form defensive flanks if required. The attack progressed well and reached the general line VENDEGIES - VENDEGIES WOOD - BOUSIES. The Division did not come into action, but the following moves were carried out during the day. Advanced Divisional H.Q. moved to dugouts on the south side of the INCHY - LE CATEAU ROAD. 115th Brigade moved to positions N.W. of CROIX, with H.Q. in FOREST " " 113th Brigade " " " " " on AMERVAL RIDGE " " MONTAY.	
Dugouts on S. side of INCHY - LE CATEAU ROAD.				

Army Form C. 2118.

WAR DIARY
or
INTELLIGENCE SUMMARY.

(Erase heading not required.)

Page 7.

Place	Date	Hour	Summary of Events and Information	Remarks and references to Appendices
Dugouts on S. side of INCHY- LE CATEAU ROAD.	OCTOBER 1918. 23rd. 24th.		114th Brigade moved to TROISVILLES. At 0400 hours the 33rd Division continued the attack in conjunction with flanking Divisions. Progress was made, though at one time the situation on the right flank seemed insecure. 115th Brigade were, in immediate readiness to move to form a defensive flank, but their move was afterwards rendered unnecessary by the advance of the 18th Division. The general line gained was one running WEST of ENGLEFONTAINE to east of GHISSIGNIES (IV Corps Front.)	OP/14.
MONTAY.	25th.		No moves took place by Brigades of the Division. Advanced Divisional Headquarters moved to MONTAY. 33rd Division held a line running along the main road west of ENGLEFONTAINE. All preparations were made for the Division to relieve the 33rd Division but this relief was later cancelled. The 33rd Division wereordered to carry out an attack on ENGLEFONTAINE and to consolidate a line on the east side of the village. Brigades did not move. Divisional Headquarters moved to RICHEMONT.	
RICHEMONT.	26th.		At 0100 hours the 33rd Division carried out a highly successful attack North and South of ENGLEFONTAINE, capturing the village together with about 500 prisoners. During the day and early evening the 38th Division relieved the 33rd Division with 115th Infantry Brigade in the line, 113th Brigade in Support and 114th Brigade in Reserve. Relief was complete about 2230 hours.	
	27th.		An enemy counter attack was attempted at about 0600 hoirs. A heavy barrage was put down on our posts and on the neighbourhood of ENGLEFONTAINE, and an attack developed on a frontage of about 1000 yards. This was driven off with loss to the enemy, but at one point the enemy penetrated a gap between the posts and succeeded in capturing 12 of our men. No further action followed. Hostile artillery showed considerable activity at intervals during the day on the forward area.	
	28th.		The day passed quietly and without incident on the Divisional Front. In consequence of the shelling of forward villages and casualties to the civilian population, these villages were ordered to be evacuated and a great number of civilians were cleared during the day.	
	29th.		At 0800 hours the 17th Royal Welsh Fusiliers of the 115th Infantry Brigade carried out a successful raid east of ENGLEFONTAINE. The raid took place under a creeping barrage which drew heavy hostile retaliation. 25 prisoners were captured. /Hostile artillery	

Army Form C. 2118.

WAR DIARY
or
INTELLIGENCE SUMMARY.

(Erase heading not required.)

Page 8.

Place	Date	Hour	Summary of Events and Information	Remarks and references to Appendices
RICHEMONT.	OCTOBER 1918.			
	29th (continued).		Hostile artillery was active during the morning but quieter in the afternoon. 114th Infantry Brigade relieved 115th Infantry Brigade in the line during the evening, 115th Brigade withdrawing to FOREST on relief.	
	30th.		The day passed without special incident on the Divisional Front. The G.O.C. attended a Corps Conference held at OVILLERS at 1130 hours.	opp. 16 opp. M.
	31st.		Situation unchanged on the Divisional Front. Hostile Artillery shelled ENGLEFONTAINE and POIX DU NORD intermittently. These villages were at this date entirely clear of civilians.	

[signature]

Captain,
General Staff 38th (Welsh) Division.

October 1918.

War Diary

SECRET

38th Division No. GSS. 2/33.

SUMMARY OF OPERATIONS, OCTOBER 5th to 11th inclusive.

OPERATIONS.

5th October. On the morning of the 5th October the situation on the V Corps front was as under -

115th Brigade on line LA PANNERIE SOUTH (S.29.b.) to HARGIVAL FARM S.27.d. facing North, thus being astride the HINDENBURG LINE which faces West.
113th Brigade West of BONY.
114th Brigade East of EPEHY.

The intention had been to move the Division through VENDHUILLE and taking advantage of the fact that the HINDENBURG LINE had been turned to operate N.E. diagonally crossing the front of the 33rd Division who were along the line of the CANAL L'ESCAUT and the latter would then become supporting Division to 38th Division.

During the night 4th/5th the enemy retired from DE LA L'EAU and PUTNEY and HINDENBURG LINE.

115th Infantry Brigade Group moved directed on AUBENCHEUL.
113th Infantry Brigade Group passed through VENDHUILLE and operated on the left of 115th Brigade directed on MORTHO WOOD.
114th Infantry Brigade Group crossed the CANAL L'ESCAUT at OSSUS and moved to the HINDENBURG LINE.

The enemy rear guards were outfought and line at dusk was from VAUXHALL QUARRY - East edge of AUBONCHEUL - West edge of MORTHO. The Division was in touch with the 50th Division on the right and the 21st Division on the left.

Many enemy were killed in AUBONCHEUL.

38th Divisional Artillery crossed the L'ESCAUT on a temporary bridge at OSSUS at 1100 hrs. and came into action East of the HINDENBURG LINE. A Brigade of 18th Divnl. Artillery with 113th and 115th Infantry Brigades accompanied these Brigades and materially assisted their advance by rapid action on moving targets as opportunity offered.

6th October. The enemy held the BEAUREVOIR LINE West of VILLERS OUTREAUX with machine guns and infantry; enemy machine guns from VILLERS FARM T.21.a. being in an especially commanding position. Attempt was made during the day to force this line but it was found impossible to cut through the wire in daylight under the enemy M.G. fire.

7th October. Situation unchanged. Bridges were consolidated. Artillery and ammunition was brought up and all preparations made for a frontal attack on the 8th October along the whole Fourth and Third Army fronts.

/ 8th October.

2.

8th October.   The Division was ordered to make a preliminary night attack under a barrage. The 115th Brigade forming up in the 50th Divisional Area East of the BEAUREVOIR LINE and South of VILLERS OUTREAUX and the 113th Brigade forming up West of the BEAUREVOIR LINE and North of VILLERS OUTREAUX, with objectives North and South Line through the East edge of VILLERS OUTREAUX. The village itself was not to be attacked.

Subsequently at 8.a.m. the 114th Brigade was to pass through the 113th and 115th Brigades, in conjunction with attacks by right and left Divisions reach the high ground East of MALINCOURT.

The 115th Brigade reached their objective but at dawn the position was untenable owing to enemy M.G. fire from the village and the high ground to the S.E.

The 113th Brigade with heavy loss succeeded in getting elements through the wire and the BEAUREVOIR LINE.

The 114th Brigade moving up to pass through these Brigades became involved in the fighting but with the assistance of 6 tanks and a Battalion of the 115th Brigade mopping up VILLERS OUTREAUX were able to reach a forming up line East of the village at 1130 hrs. at which hour a creeping barrage had been arranged.

The resistance of a very strong rear guard having thus been overcome the 114th Brigade moved forward without opposition and at dusk were established East of MALINCOURT on their objective.

9th October.   33rd Division passed through the 114th Brigade and the 38th Division became Right Reserve Division V Corps.

15th October 1918.   Major General,
                              Commanding 38th (Welsh) Division.

(6339) Wt. W160/M3016 1,500,000 10/17 McA & W Ltd (E 1898) Forms W3091. Army Form W.3091.

G.145

Cover for Documents.

Nature of Enclosures.

Gas Operation 14/15 Octr

Notes, or Letters written.

"O" Form. MESSAGES AND SIGNALS.

Army Form C. 2122.
No. of Message ....

Prefix ...... Code ...... Words 58

Received. From CO By Cm

Sent, or sent out. At ...... m. To ...... By ......

Office Stamp.

Charges to Collect

Service Instructions: Urgent Ops

Handed in at E Co Office 19 37 Received 19 54 m.

TO: 38 Div (Deferred)

*Sender's Number.	Day of Month.	In reply to Number.	AAA
G16	12		
N	Spec	Co	RE
is	attached	forthwith	to
33	Div	and	to
38	Div	on	relief
aaa	K	Special	Co
RE	is	attached	forthwith
to	17	Div	aaa
OC	above	Cos	will
report	tonight	to	respective
div	hq	to	arrange
details	for	gas	discharge
on	both	divnl	sectors
night	13/14	inst	aaa
17	Div	hq	Montigny
33	Div	hq	S.
of	Montigny	O1865.2	aaa
ack	aaa	addsd	17

FROM: 33
PLACE & TIME: 38 Divs K and N Bkples RE Reptd 21 Div Q

5 Corps
19.30 hrs

33rd Division 'G'

Reference Operation GN/18.

Attached is map shewing area from which troops should be cleared and area in which Box Respirators should be worn. A copy of "Precautions to be taken during Projector Gas Attacks" is also enclosed, please.

[stamp: H.Q. 33rd Division "G" Branch — No. GS 3858 — Date 13/10/18]

[stamp: "N" SPECIAL COMPANY, R.E. No. SG 2 Date 13.10.18]

for O.C. 'N' Special Coy, R.E.

Precautions to be taken during Projector Gas Attack

All troops will be cleared from the area coloured blue on the attached map. If any part of the area cannot be cleared, the garrison should be reduced as much as possible.

All troops within the area coloured red will wear box-respirators from ZERO minus 2 minutes till orders for their removal are given by an officer. This will in no case be given till ZERO plus 30 minutes, and then only if the trench system is reported clear of gas.

All troops re-occupying trench systems after Projector attack will be preceded by Battalion or Company Gas N.C.O. who will advise the Officers concerned whether the trench is safe.

Battalion in the line will be notified by an officer of 'N' Special Coy., R.E. when discharge is complete.

38th Division 'G'

SECRET

Reference Operation GN/18

Herewith is map shewing zone which should be clear of troops and zone in which Box Respirators should be worn. Copy of "Precautions to be taken during Projector Gas Attacks" is also enclosed.

"Please".

SPECIAL COMPANY,
R.E.
No. S.G. 2
Date 13.10.18

Ivor P. Morris Capt M?
for O.C. 'N' Special Coy R.E.

Precautions to be taken during Projector Gas Attack.

All troops will be cleared from the area coloured green on the attached map. If any part of the area cannot be cleared the garrison should be reduced as much as possible.

All troops within the area coloured red will wear box-respirators from Zero minus 2 minutes till orders for their removal are given by an officer. This will in no case be given till Zero plus 30 minutes and then only if the trench system is reported clear of gas.

All troops re-occupying trench systems after Projector Attack will be preceded by Battalion or Company Gas NCO who will advise the officers concerned whether the trench is safe.

Battalions in the line will be notified by an officer of 'N' Special Coy. R.E when discharge is complete.

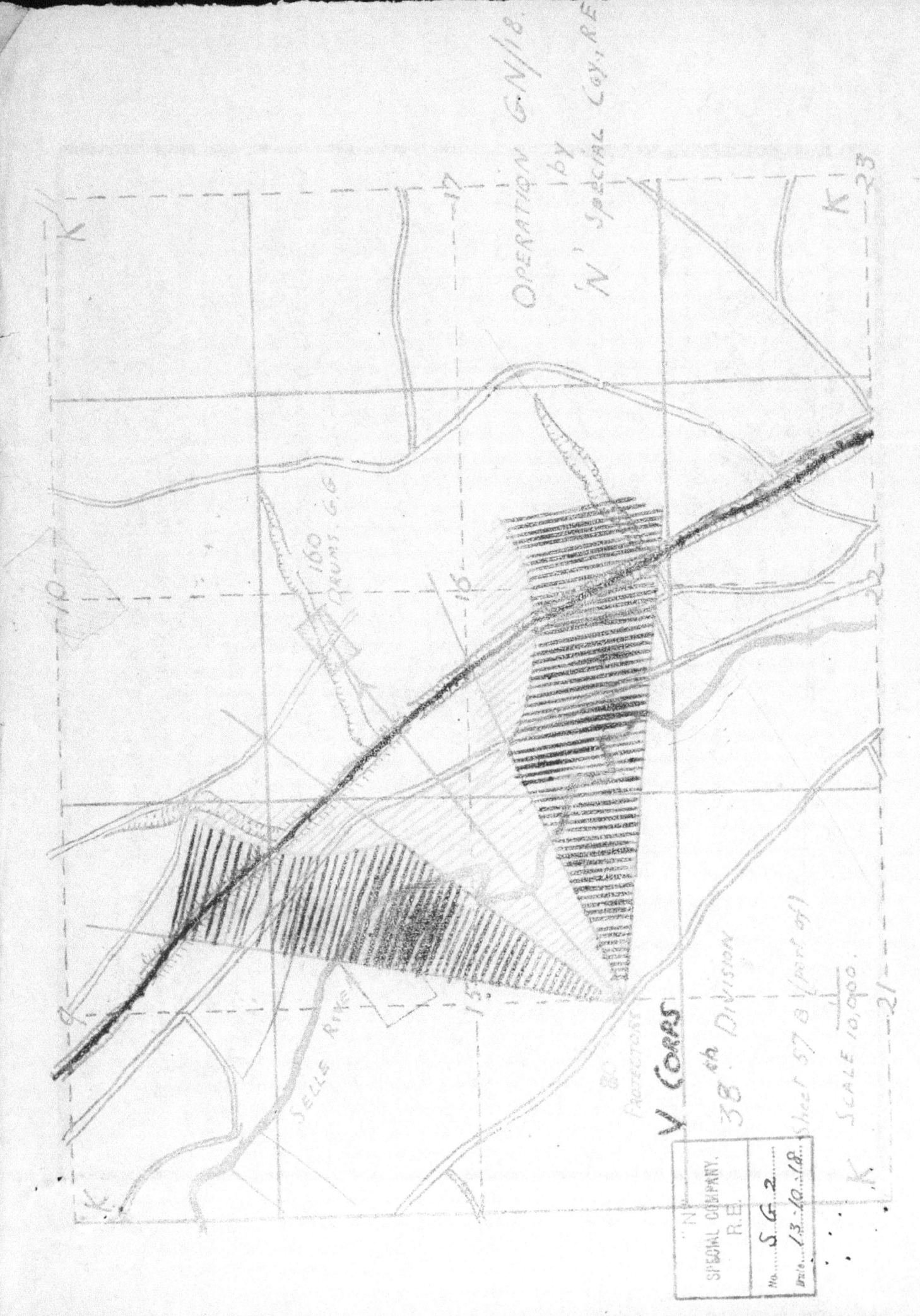

SECRET

38th Division No. S.S.145.

115th Brigade.
'N' Special Co. R.E.
38th Div: Arty.
38th Bn.M.G.C.
17th Division.
66th Division.
V Corps.

1.   'N' Special Coy. R.E. are installing projectors tonight 13th/14th at K.15.c.9.2.

2.   These projectors will, if conditions are favourable, be fired night 14th/15th.

3.   There will be two shoots - Zero hour for first shoot is provisionally fixed at 2200 hrs. The second shoot will take place exactly one after hour after Zero.

4.   Targets RAVINE K.16.a.

5.   B.G.R.A. will arrange for harassing fire to be brought to bear on K.10.c. and d. and (or) on K.16.b. at Zero plus 1 minute to Zero plus 10 minutes and Zero plus one hour and four minutes to Zero plus one hour 14 minutes. The majority of the fire being as far as practicable up wind.

6.   The above areas will be vigourously harassed by M.G.fire.

7.   O.C. 'N' Special Coy. will personally establish liaison with 115th Brigade, visiting their H.Q. at 1100 hrs. 14th Octr. and in consultation with Brigadier General Commanding 115th Inf.Brigade will advise Divisional Headquarters of the actual zero hour fixed, by wiring plus or minus the number of hours or minutes arranged for zero. No alteration of time of zero will be made later than zero minus 2 hours.

8   O.C. 'N' Special Co. R.E. will advise 115th Brigade of area to be cleared. No other Divisional area will be affected.

9.   Watches will be synchronised at 115th Brigade H.Q. at 1130 hrs. and 1700 hrs 14th October. Time will be given by 115th Brigade.

10.   Code word if no operation to take place will be F U T to be wired to Divisional Headquarters by 115th Brigade.

(sd) M.H.KING.   Major G.S. for
Lieut. Colonel,
General Staff, 38th (Welsh) Division.

13-10-1918.

SECRET.q   38th Division.No.S.S.145.
===========   ---------------------------

115th Brigade.
'N' Special Coy R.E.
38th Div.Arty.
38th Bn M.G.C.
17th Division.
66th Division.
5th Corps.
----

1.   'N' Special Coy R.E. are installing projectors tonight
13/14th at K.15.c.9.2.

2.   These projectors will, if conditions are favourable, be
fired, 14/15th. /night

3.   There will be two shoots - zero hour for first shoot is
provisionally fixed at 22.00 hours. The second shoot will take
place exactly one hour after zero.

4.   Target RAVINE K.16.a.

5.   B.G., R.A. will arrange for harassing fire to be brought to
bear on K.10.c and d, and/or on K.16.b. at zero plus 1 minute to
zero plus 10 minutes and zero plus one hour to zero plus one hour
14 minutes. The majority of the fire being as far as practicable
up wind.   /4 minutes

6.   The above areas will be vigourously harrased by M.G. fire.

7.   O.C., 'N' Special Coy will personnally establish liason
with 115th Brigade, visiting their H.Q. at 11.00 hours 14th Oct.
and in consultation with Brigadier General Commanding 115th Inf.
Brigade will advise Divisional Headquarters of the actual zero
hour fixed, by wiring plus or minus the number of hours or
minutes arranged for zero.
No alteration of time of zero will be made later than zero minus
2 hours.

8.   O.C., 'N' Special Coy R.E. will advise 115th Brigade of
area to be cleared.   No other Divisional area will be affected.

9.   Watches will be synchronized at 115th Brigade H.Q., at
11.30 hours and 17.00 hours 14th October.   Time will be
given by 115th Inf.Brigade.

10. Code word if no operation to take place will be F U T
to be wired to Divisional Headquarters by 115th Brigade.

                                              Lieut.Colonel.
13/10/1918.   General Staff.38th (Welsh) Division.

"C" Form
MESSAGES AND SIGNALS
Army Form C. 2123.
(In books of 100)
No. of Message 2

| Prefix | Code | Words 24 | Received From Eco By CC | Sent, or sent out At ___ m To ___ By ___ | Office Stamp |

Charges to Collect
Service Instructions

Handed in at YFE Office 1345 m. Received 00.23 m.

TO: 38 Div

*Sender's Number	Day of Month	In reply to Number	AAA
GR 50	12	—	

Reference your SS 145 of today can you please postpone times mentioned in para 3 by 4 hours

FROM / TIME & PLACE: 66 Div

"A" Form
MESSAGES AND SIGNALS.

Army Form C. 2121
(In pads of 100.)

TO 115 Bde

Sender's Number.	Day of Month.	In reply to Number.	AAA
G356	14		

Ref para 3 of SS 145 right Div no would much prefer # time mentioned to be postponed 4 hours + practicable to you

From 38 Div
Place
Time 0830

SECRET.

R.A., 38th.Div. No.G.S.309/28

14th.October 1918.

121 Brigade.
122 Brigade.
156 Brigade.
162 Brigade.
13 Brigade R.G.A.

1. (a) "N" Special Coy. R.E. is to fire Gas projectors to-night 14/15 from K.15.c.9.2.
   (b) Target RAVINE K.16.a.

2. There are to be two shoots: the first takes place at zero, the second at Zero + 1 hr.

3. (a) Brigades will arrange to place harassing fire on the areas K.10.c. and d. and K.16.b. at the following times :-

   Zero + 1 min. to + 10 mins.

   + 1 hr.4 min. to + 1 hr.14 mins.

   The majority of the fire should be placed up wind, if practicable.
   (b) Expenditure :-

   F.A.Brigades   - Average 1 rd. per gun per min.

   13 th.Bde.R.G.A. As ordered by O.C. Brigade.

4. Watches will be synchronised at H.Q.,115 Inf.Bde. at 17.00 hrs. 14th.October.

5. Code word if operation is to be postponed - FUT.
6. Zero hour will be 01.00 hrs. 15th.October.
7. <u>AC KNOWLEDGE.</u>

Major R.A.
Bde.Major 38th.Divl. Arty.

Issued at 14.00 hrs.

Copy to:- 38th.Div. "G".
          115 Inf.Bde.
          D.T.M.O.

G.S.O.1	
G.S.O.2	✓
G.S.O.3	
G.S.O.4	

"A" Form
MESSAGES AND SIGNALS.

Army Form C. 2121
(In pads of 100.)

TO: 115 Bde. N Special Coy
3 D(W) arty. 3 S MG Bde.
17 - 66 Div. v ?

Sender's Number	Day of Month	In reply to Number	AAA
GB92	15		

Ref SS145 - Projectors not fired last night will if practicable be fired tonight. aaa Zero plus three hours aaa all arrangements detailed in SS145 hold good aaa addsd all recipients of SS145

From 3 D W
Place
Time 12 15

38th Division

Passed to you
JR Lutridge Major
for G.O.C. 33rd Div
13/10/18

3 copies of
"precautions &
maps" fwd to
115 Bde
SS145/1
13/10/18

MESSAGES & SIGNALS.

TO

115th Brigade.	M. Special Coy.
38th Div. Arty.	38th Bn. M.G.C.
17th Div.	38th Div.	5th Corps.

G 232.   16.   AAA

Projectors not fired last night AAA G.B. 92 will be in force tonight and every night until projectors are fired AAA Added all recipients of S.S. 145.

38th Div.

10-40.

Captain., G.S.

G.S.O. 1	
G.S.O. 2	V.
G.S.O. 3	
G.S.O. 4	

Serial No. 22

SPECIAL COMPANIES, R.E., THIRD ARMY.

"N" SPECIAL COMPANY, R.E.

Zero Time: 01.00 hours / 02.00 "
Date 17.10.18

REPORT ON OPERATION No. GN/19   V CORPS.   38th DIVISION.

Purpose of Operation. To harass and to inflict casualties on the enemy in the ravine in K16a and on ridge at K10 central S of AMERVAL.

Targets, giving Map References.
a) Ravine at K16a 8.7.   Sheet 57B NE
b) Ridge at K10 central.   "   "   "

No. of projectors employed, or No. of Guns in Emplacements, with Spares*	a) 80 (2'.6") b) 50 (2'.9")	Map Reference of Emplacements.	a) K15d 0.3 Sheet 57B NE b) K15d 4.6 " " "
No. and Nature of Projectiles — Rounds Allotted.	130 C.G Drums for 1st shoot 130 " " " 2nd	No. and Nature of Projectiles — Rounds Fired.	1st shoot a) 80 } 115 b) 35 2nd shoot a) 76 } 125 b) 49

Reason for Discrepancy (if any).
1st shoot. 15 charges out of 25 in a battery failed to fire probably due to damp charges.
2nd shoot. 5 guns slightly damaged after 1st shoot could not be used.

Programme. Projectors to be fired at 01.00 hours, reset charged and fired at 02.00 hours. Harassing fire to be brought on K10 c and d and K16 b at zero plus one minute to zero plus ten minutes, and at zero plus one hour to zero plus one hour fourteen minutes. Same areas to be vigorously harassed by M.G. fire.

Direction and Velocity of Wind. 01.00 hours W-WSW 6 mph 02.00 " WSW 5 mph

Casualties:
Names of Officers. Nil wounded
Number of O.R. 2 O.R's (during preparation)

Name of Officer i/c Operation. Capt Ivor P Morris. Lieut P.W Waters. 2 Lieut G Stalker M.M

Sections Engaged. All sections of "N" Special Coy RE.

Remarks.
Artillery. After 1st shoot. there was but little response to calls by single red lights
M.G Fire   "   "   "   At first moderate but later became considerable.
Artillery After 2nd shoot. Heavy artillery retaliation after calls by several two red and
M.G.   "   "   "   Heavy M.G fire along the valley. two green rocket signals
The gas travelled up well along the direction of the ravine.

A copy of this Report has been forwarded to:—
  V Corps.
  38th Division. ✓
  C.S.C., R.E., Third Army (2).

Date 17.10.18   Ivor P. Morris Capt RE A. O.C. "N" Special Company, R.E.

* For Stokes Mortars.   † To include Artillery Co-operation.   ‡ By Targets.

"C" Form (Original).
MESSAGES AND SIGNALS.
Army Form C. 2123.
(In books of 50's in duplicate.)

Pm 1123 No. of Message 9

Prefix...... Code...... Words......	Received	Sent, or sent out	Office Stamp.
£ s. d.	From......	At 2.40 p.m.	
Charges to collect	By......	To......	
Service Instructions.		By......	

Handed in at VOTS Office 11 25 m. Received 11 44 m.

TO   38 Div

*Sender's Number	Day of Month	In reply to Number	A A A
Pm 14/6	14	OO 145	

Rin three hours and this
cancels Bm 14/4

9386

G.S.O. 1
G.S.O. 2
G. O. 3
G.S.O. 4

FROM   115 Bde
PLACE & TIME   11 15

"C" Form (Original).
MESSAGES AND SIGNALS.

Army Form C. 2123.
(In books of 50's in duplicate.)

No. of Message.... 14

Prefix	Code	Words 2	Received	Sent, or sent out	Office Stamp.
			From	At .... m.	
Charges to collect	£ s. d.		By	To	
Service Instructions.				By	

Handed in at ...... WTO ...... Office 1000 m. Received ...... m.

TO .... 38 Div

*Sender's Number: BM 14/4   Day of Month: 14   In reply to Number: 2886   AAA

Agree to alteration

Refer to gun Operation postponed
Zero
4 hours   MJ

FROM PLACE & TIME ...... 115 Bde 0955

* This line should be erased if not required.
Wt. 432—M437 500,000 Pads. H W V 5 16 Forms C.2123.

"A" Form
MESSAGES AND SIGNALS.

Army Form C. 2121
(In pads of 100.)

TO: 115 Bde   38 Div arty.   114 Bde
    38 MG Bn   17 - 66 Div
              5 Corps.

Sender's Number: SB7
Day of Month: 14

Ref SS 145 plus
three hours awa
add. 38 DA   38 MG Bn
       115 Bde   114 Bde
17 - 66 Divs   5 Corps

From: 38 DW
Time: 1159

"A" Form.
MESSAGES AND SIGNALS.

Army Form C. 2121
(In pads of 100.)

TO	V Corps.	33 DIV.

Sender's Number: 9B76
Day of Month: 13
AAA

Ref. your G.16 aaa strongly deprecate discharge tonight.

aaa addd 5 Corps
from 33 Div.

From 33 DW
Time 10-20

SECRET.   38th Division G.S. 2/23/1.

APPENDIX to REPORT ON OPERATIONS 23/10/18 to 30/10/18.
_____

   At 0800 hours 29th October the 17th Bn. R.W. Fus. raided
the enemy's positions in S.20.c., and mopped up the houses
on the main ENGLEFONTAINE - BAVAI Road, about S.26.a.9.9.

   The raid was carried out under a creeping barrage to
which M.G's co-operated; and Stokes Mortars fired on selected
points.

   The Raiders (strength 2 Coys.) formed up in our lines
between S.26.a.3.8. and S.19.d.9.5., and advanced and cleared
up the ground nearly as far as a line from S.20.d.1.5. to
S.20.a.2.3.

   Special parties detailed for the purpose then rushed the
hostile posts in the houses at S.26.a.9.9.   The Raiders
returned to our lines at Zero plus 60 minutes.

   Hostile M.G. fire was heavy especially on the right of
the Raiders and the thick hedges interlaced with barbed wire
proved a considerable obstacle, so much so that the right Coy.
failed to penetrate quite as far as their intended objective.
The enemy resisted stubbornly and heavy hand to hand fighting
ensued in which the enemy suffered considerable casualties
in killed and wounded.

   The enemy's counter barrage opened at about Zero plus
8 minutes and fell along the sunken road running N. in
S.26.a., and also in S.26.c.   The barrage consisted of
77 mms, 4.2. and 5.9.

   It is estimated that between 70 and 80 of the enemy
were killed.

   24 of the enemy were captured, 5 of whom were wounded.

   6 M.G's were taken and 2 destroyed.

31/10/18.
                                        Major General,
                              Commanding 38th (Welsh) Division.

SECRET.   38th Division No. GSS. 2/23/1.

V Corps.

REPORT ON OPERATIONS 23/10/18 to 30/10/18.

1.   38th Division was Right Supporting Division V Corps during the attack by 33rd Division and was disposed as under at 1500 hours on 23/10/18 :-

   Div. H.Q.   - S. side of INCHY – LE CATEAU Road (K.25.d.7.4.)
   113th Brigade – AMERVAL Ridge.
   114th Brigade – TROISVILLES.
   115th Brigade – N.W. of village of CROIX

   On 26th October and night 26th/27th October 38th Division relieved 33rd Division in the Right Sector V Corps front.

   At about 0600 hours on 27th October a hostile counter attack developed on a front of about 1000 yards against our posts N.E. of ENGLEFONTAINE. The attack was carried out under cover of a heavy barrage, but was driven off with loss to the enemy by rifle fire. At one point the enemy succeeded in penetrating between two of our posts and capturing 12 prisoners. Our line however remained unchanged and we secured identifications of the 57th I.R. 14th Division.

3.   For report on raid by 17th Bn. R.W. Fus. see ~~this action letter No. 237. 140/5 sent under separate cover~~. attached appendix.

4.   Hostile artillery has been active and many crashes have been fired on ENGLEFONTAINE. The main FOREST – ENGLEFONTAINE Road and the POIX DU NORD – ENGLEFONTAINE Road have been persistently harassed.

5.   Our artillery has been active throughout the period and has harassed the enemy's communications and fired gas concentrations on suspected battery areas by night.

CASUALTIES.

Officers.			Other ranks.		
K.	W.	M.	K.	W.	M.
1	10	1	52	238	29

31/10/1918.
                                              Major General,
                                    Commanding 38th (Welsh) Division.

            Copies to – 18th Division.
                        21st Division.
                        'A' & 'Q'.

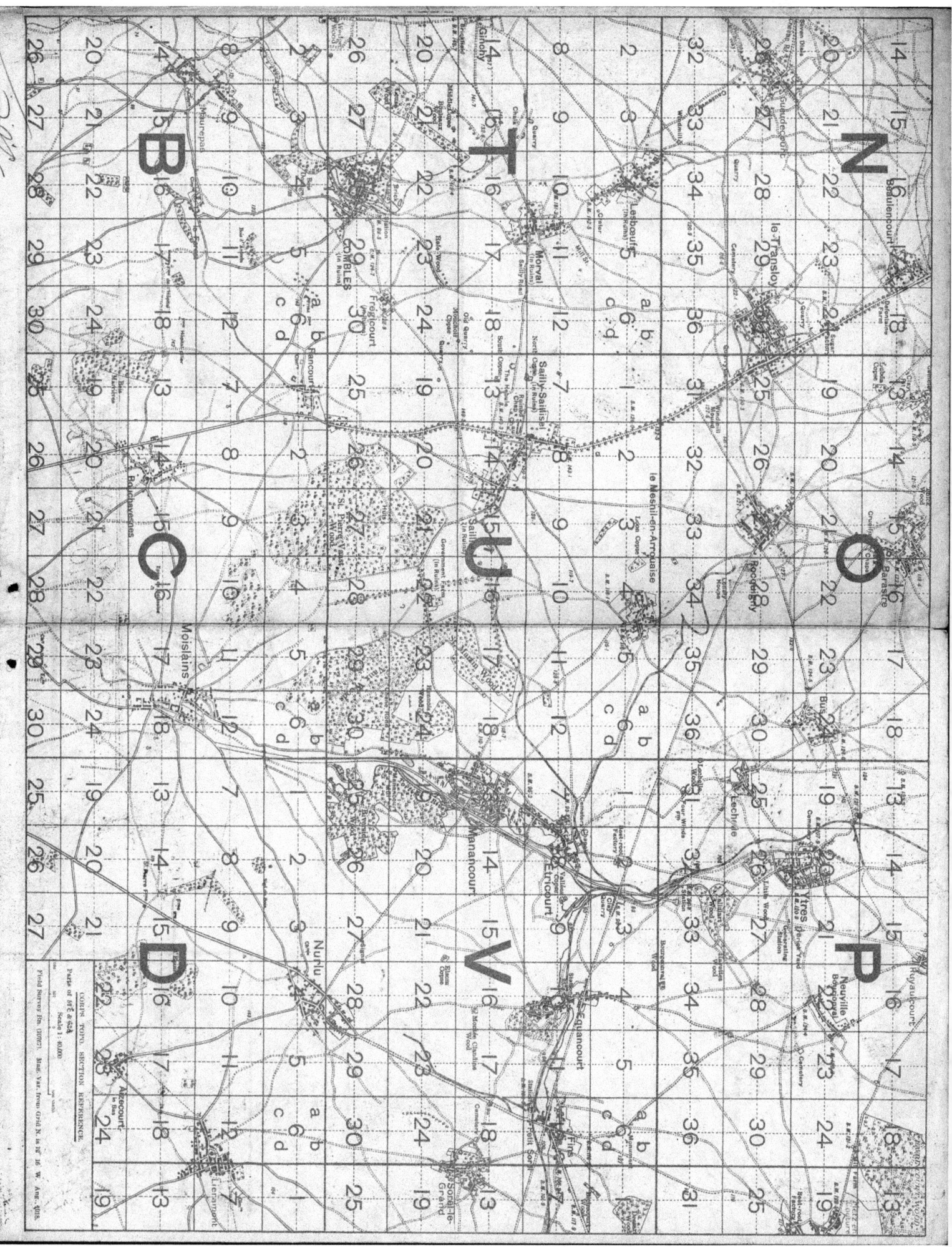

On His Majesty's Service.

The D.A.S. Echelon,
3rd. B.E. Force

Vol. 36.

General Staff.
38th Division.
November 1918.

Army Form W.3091.

Cover for Documents.

Nature of Enclosures.

~~GSS 1/22/J~~

~~38 B. M.G.C. Orders~~

Notes, or Letters written.

Army Form C. 2118

WAR DIARY of General Staff
38th (Welsh) Division.
or INTELLIGENCE SUMMARY   Volume XXXV.
(Erase heading not required.)

Instructions regarding War Diaries and Intelligence Summaries are contained in F. S. Regs., Part II and the Staff Manual respectively. Title Pages will be prepared in manuscript.

Place	Date	Hour	Summary of Events and Information	Remarks and references to Appendices
RICHEMONT.	NOVEMBER 1918.			
	1st.		38th Division held the Right Divisional Sector of the V Corps front. 114th Infantry Brigade were in the line holding positions East of the Village of ENGLEFONTAINE, with 113th Brigade in support, and 115th Brigade in Reserve. A patrol enterprise during the day resulted in establishing a post in a house on the HECQ road, which had been in NO MAN'S LAND. 34 civilians were rescued and brought back from this house. Hostile artillery was active at intervals on ENGLEFONTAINE, and very active during the afternoon on POIX DU NORD.	
	2nd.		Situation unchanged. Hostile artillery was active as on previous days. During the afternoon and evening 115th Infantry Brigade relieved 114th Infantry Brigade in the line, the latter Brigade withdrawing to the FOREST area. Divisional Order 250 issued.	oppd.
	3rd.		All preparations being made for forthcoming resumption of the attack. Situation unchanged. Hostile artillery was active on ENGLEFONTAINE and POIX DU NORD as on previous days. The G.O.C. visited most Battalions of the Division during the day.	
	4th.		At 0530 hours the attack was resumed by the British Third Army with other British and French Armies. The V Corps attacked with 38th Division on the Right and 17th Division on the Left; the direction of attack was due East, directly towards and through the FORET de MORMAL.
The attack of the 38th Division was launched at 0615 hours, with final objective the rides in the forest running N.E. and S.E. from LES GRANDES PATURES.
The Division attacked on a 1 Brigade frontage, each Brigade having an objective to capture and to hold until the Brigade in rear, leapfrogged through. 115th Brigade captured the first, 113th Brigade the second, and 114th Brigade the final objective. All these lines were reached according to time table and all resistance was overcome. The chief feature of the attack was that the movement forward took place in columns moving on small frontages and leaving considerable lateral gaps. The problem of keeping direction in the woodwas thus solved and many of the enemy were captured from behind. The final objective was reached before 1700 hours and was subsequently consolidated. At night the G.O.C. Division ordered patrols to be pushed out, to be followed by a few companies with orders to advance and hold the line east SABARAS - LA CROIX DANIEL. This line was reached during the night, though the darkness and /other	

WAR DIARY
or
INTELLIGENCE SUMMARY.

Army Form C. 2118.
Page 2.

Place	Date	Hour	Summary of Events and Information	Remarks and references to Appendices
RICHEMONT.	NOVEMBER 1918.			
	4th.		other conditions together with the men's fatigue, rendered this a most difficult task. The result was that at the end of the operations, the Division had reached beyond the line of the first objective for the subsequent day's operations and was 5000 yards ahead of troops on either flank. About 500 prisoners were captured during the day together with 23 guns. Our casualties were about 600. D.O. 251 issued, (battle to be continued). Divisional advanced H.Q. moved during the afternoon to ENGLEFONTAINE.	app 2 app 3
ENGLEFONTAINE.	5th.		At about 0600 hours the 33rd Division with the 100th Brigade leading passed through the leading troops and continued the advance towards the RIVER SAMBRE. The Brigades of 38th Division established themselves 113 and 114th Brigades in the FOREST, and 115th Brigade in ENGLEFONTAINE. Divisional H.Q. moved to LOCQUIGNOL. The Division was not involved in any fighting during the day. 33rd Division continued the advance and crossed the RIVER SAMBRE occupying PETIT MAUBEUGE and high ground N.E. of it. 38th Division Order G.60 issued. D.O.252 issued.	
LOCQUIGNOL.	6th.		113th Brigade moved to SARBARAS - RIBAUMET area. 115th Brigade moved to area vacated by 113th Brigade near LES GRANDES PATURES. 114th Brigade did not move. G.O.C. Third Army and G.O.C. V Corps visited G.O.C.	app 4 app 5.
	7th.		G.O.C. visited 114th Infantry Brigade H.Q. 38th Division Order 253 issued. 38th Division relieved 33rd Division in Right Divisional Sector V Corps - command passed 21 hours. (a) 113th Brigade in role of Advanced Brigade Group passed through leading Brigade 33rd Division on general North and South line DOURLERS - BOIS DU TEMPLE. (b) 114th Brigade moved into Support in vicinity of EQUELIN. (c) 115th Brigade moved into Reserve in POT DE VIN, area. Advanced Divisional H.Q. moved to LE BOUVIER. G.O.C. visited the 3 Brigade Commanders.	app 6.
	8th.		The Advanced Guard Group (113th Brigade) continued the advance during the night, and at dawn reached the AVESNES - MAUBEUGE ROAD. A minor operation at midday resulted in the capture of FERME DE LA BELLE HOTESSE. The attack was resumed in the afternoon, and our line was advanced 1500 yards to the general (north)	

Army Form C. 2118

WAR DIARY
or
INTELLIGENCE SUMMARY
(Erase heading not required.)

Page 3.

Instructions regarding War Diaries and Intelligence Summaries are contained in F. S. Regs., Part II. and the Staff Manual respectively. Title Pages will be prepared in manuscript.

Place	Date	Hour	Summary of Events and Information	Remarks and references to Appendices
LOCQUIGNOL.	NOVEMBER. 1918.			
	8th.		north and south line, FLOURSIES - BOIS LE ROY. The G.O.C. visited the 3 Brigade Command-ers. A.D.2.Su. arrived - 115 Bde to relieve 113 Bde.	app.7.
	9th.		The advance was continued during the day. The enemy withdrew his troops during the early hours of the morning and mounted troops were pushed to our outpost line to gain touch with him. WATTIGNIES - LA - VICTOIRE, DIMECHAUX, BOIS DU REUMONT, BOIS DE MADAME, HESTRUD, and BOIS DE BEAURIEUX were occupied. The enemy outpost line was encountered 500 yards East of HESTRUD and the last mentioned WOOD. The advanced Guard Brigade moved up to WATTIGNIES - LA - VICTOIRE during the day, and at dusk an outpost line was established covering the road leading east from DIMECHAUX, with Cavalry patrol protecting the line HESTRUD - BOIS DE BEAURIEUX. The G.O.C. attended Corps Commanders Conference.	
	10th.		The line remained unchanged and Cyclists patrolled the road and approaches in front of the outpost line. Brigades were disposed as follows :- Advanced Guard Brigade 113th Infy.Brigade. WATTIGNIES. 114th Brigade. ECUELIN. 115th Brigade. AULNOYE STATION. Squadron of Oxford Hussars was transferred from 38th Division to VICorps, and moved from 38th Division area to NEUF MESNIL, (near MAUBEUGE), at 1200 hours.	app.8
	11th.		G.O.C. visited 113th and 114th Infantry Brigades. Brigades carried out route marching. Hostilities ceased at 1100 hours, but Brigades remained in previous dispositions. G.O.C. visited all Brigades. Corps Commander visited Divisional H.Q. Brigades carried out training programmes, cleaning up and re-organising.	
	12th. to 13th. 16th. 17th.		Brigades continued to re-organise and training programmes were carried out. Recreational training carried out and football leagues formed. Armistice Thanksgiving Service for Divisional troops and 115th Infantry Brigade held at AULNOYE at 1100 hours.	
	18th. 19th.		Training and re-organising continued. 113th and 114th Brigades training. 2 squads of V Cyclist 115th Brigade Group/marched . Regiment (N.I.H.) left the Division and rejoined their Regimental H.Q. at POIX DU NORD. route /20 th.	

A.F.C.2113.

WAR DIARY.   Page 4.

Summary of events and information.

Place.	Date.	Hour.	
AULNOYE.	NOVEMBER 1918.		
	20th.		G.O.C. 113th Brigade (BRIGADIER GENERAL H.E. ap RHYS PRYCE, C.M.G., D.S.O.) left the Division to take up the appointment of Director General of Mobilization in INDIA. He was succeeded by BRIGADIER GENERAL CARTON DE WIART, V.C., C.M.G., D.S.O.
	21st.		G.O.C. presented medal ribbons to recipients of 113th Infantry Brigade at WATTIGNIES. All 3 Companies of R.E. moved to BERLIAMONT.
	22nd.		G.O.C. presented medal ribbons to recipients of 114th Infantry Brigade at ECUELIN.
	23rd.		113th Infantry Brigade moved from WATTIGNIES AREA to SARBARAS - RIBAUMET area. G.O.C. presented medal ribbons to recipients of 115th Infantry Brigade and 38th Bn. M.G.C.
	24th.		Church Parades - G.O.C. attended Non-Conformist parade. R.A. cross country run - Winners C Battery 122nd Brigade R.F.A.
	25th.		G.O.C. presented medal ribbons to recipients of 38th Div. Artillery and Royal Engineer Signal Company at PETIT MAUBEUGE. 115th Brigade route march. Other Brigades training.
	26th.		G.O.C. presented medal ribbons to recipients of R.E. Field Coys at BERLIAMONT. 113th Brigade Cross Country Run - Winners
	27th.		Brigades training. Further eliminating matches in Divisional Rugby Competition were played. 13th R.W.Fus. 10 points versus 16th R.W. Fus. 6 points. R.A.M.C. NIL versus 19th Welsh Regt. NIL.
	28th.		Brigades training. 115th Brigade Cross Country Run, Winners 10th S.W. Borderers., 2nd - 17th R.W.Fus, 3rd 2nd R.W.Fus. 10th S.W. Borderers winners of 115th Brigade Group Rugby and Association Competition.
	29th. 30th.		Owing to bad weather training consisted of indoor instruction and lectures. Training carried out by Brigades during morning and eliminating matches in Group Competitions during the afternoon. Rugby 13th Welsh Regt NIL, versus 14th Welsh Regt 6 points.

November.1918.

Captain, Major
General Staff 38th (Welsh) Division.

Vol 37.
N¹

General Staff,
HQ Division.
December 1918

On His Majesty's Service.

Registered

The Officer ic
A.G's Office
The Ba...

Army Form C. 2118

WAR DIARY of General Staff.
38th (Welsh) Division.
INTELLIGENCE SUMMARY
Volume XXXVI.

(Erase heading not required.)

Instructions regarding War Diaries and Intelligence Summaries are contained in F.S. Regs., Part II. and the Staff Manual respectively. Title Pages will be prepared in manuscript.

Vol 37

Place	Date	Hour	Summary of Events and Information	Remarks and references to Appendices
AULNOYE.	DECEMBER 1918.			
	1st.		Church Parade. Third Anniversary of the Divisions coming overseas.	
	2nd.		Brigades Training in the morning. Recreation in the afternoon.	
	3rd.		H.M. the King visited the Division and saw all troops on the AULNOYE – PETIT MAUBEUGE Road.	
	4th.		Brigades Training in Morning. Recreational training during the afternoon. Inter-group rugby match played R.E. (8pts) v 10th S.W.B. (nil).	
	5th.		Brigades Training. 114th Brigade Inter platoon competition. First 14th Welsh Regt. Second 15th Welsh Regt. Third 13th Welsh Regt. 115th Brigade route march AULNOYE, ECUELIN, LIMONT FONTAINE, BACHANT, AULNOYE. Inter group rugby, R.A.M.C. (14 pts) v 13th R.W.F. (nil).	
	6th.		Brigades training. Inter group semi-final rugby match played 14th Welsh (7 pts) v R.E. (3 pts).	
	7th.		Brigades training. G.S.O.1 went to new area.	
	8th.		Church Parades.	
	9th.		Brigades training. Inter group rugby final played. R.A.M.C. (nil) v 14th Welsh (nil).	
	10th.		19th Welsh (Pioneers) moved by march route from BERLAIMONT to ENGLEFONTAINE. Bdes training.	
	11th.		19th Welsh (Pioneers) march from ENGLEFONTAINE to SALESCHES and then entrained for the new area. Inter group rugby final replayed R.A.M.C. (nil) v 14th Welsh (nil).	
	12th.		Brigades Training.	
	13th.		Brigades Training. Inter group rugby final replayed and won by R.A.M.C. (5 pts) v 14th Welsh (nil).	
	14th.		Brigades Training.	
	15th.		Church Parades.	
	16th.		Brigades Training. Trial game for Divisional rugby team.	
	17th.		Brigades Training.	
	18th.		Brigades Training.	
	19th.		G.O.C. returned from leave. Trial game for Divisional rugby team.	
	20th.		113th and 114th Brigades Training. 115th Bde route march in afternoon.	
	21st.		Brigades Training.	
	22nd.		Church Parades. D.O. 256 issued. Move of Division to QUERRIEU Area.	(App.1. (D.O.256.
	23rd.		Brigades Training. Divnl rugby team played an Australian team. No score.	
	24th.		Brigades Training.	
	25th.		Xmas Day. G.O.C. visited all Units.	
	26th.		Final Soccer. R.F.A. v D.A.C. R.F.A. won 4 goals – 1 goal. Rugger match between 38th Div. and an Australian team ended in a draw, 6 pts each. Divl rugby team proceeded to Paris.	
	27th.		113th Inf.Bde Group moved to ENGLEFONTAINE Area.	

Army Form C. 2118

WAR DIARY
or
INTELLIGENCE SUMMARY
(Erase heading not required.)

Page 2.

Instructions regarding War Diaries and Intelligence Summaries are contained in F.S. Regs., Part II. and the Staff Manual respectively. Title Pages will be prepared in manuscript.

Place	Date	Hour	Summary of Events and Information	Remarks and references to Appendices
AULNOYE.	DECEMBER 1918.			
	28th.		113th Bde Group moved to INCHY. Divisional Artillery moved to NEUVILLY and MONTAY. G.S.O.1 went to see 113th Inf.Bde on the march and the Artillery at NEUVILLY.	
	29th.		113th Inf.Bde Group moved to CONTAY Area by busses. Artillery moved to MASNIERES and ENGLEFONTAINE.Area.	
INCHY.	30th.		115th Inf.Bde Group moved to INCHY Area. 114th Inf.Bde Group moved to BERLAIMONT. Artillery to MANANCOURT. Divisional H.Q. closed at AULNOYE 0930 hours and opened at INCHY 1200 hours. G.O.C. went to Paris to witness Rugby match between Div.Team and a.French Team.	
GLISY.	31st.		115th Inf.Bde Group moved to GLISY Area by motor busses. 114th I f.Bde Group moved to ENGLEFONTAINE. Artillery to ALBERT. Divisional H.Q. closed at INCHY at 0830 hours and re-opened GLISY 1500 hours.	

December 1918.

[signature]
Captain,
General Staff 38th (Welsh) Division.

General Staff, 38th.(Welsh) Division.

WAR DIARY
or
INTELLIGENCE SUMMARY
(Erase heading not required.)

Army Form C. 2118

Original N° E 538

Place	Date	Hour	Summary of Events and Information	Remarks and references to Appendices
	1/1/1919.		115th. Inf. Bde. Group moved to GLISY area. 114th. Inf. Brigade moved to ENGLEFONTAINE and VENDIGIES, Artillery to FRECHENCOURT area. Div. Rugby team played a French Team in Paris. French won 13 points to 6 points. G.O.C. witnessed the match.	
	2/1/1919.		114th. Inf. Brigade Group moved to St. Gratien Area. G.O.C. returned from Paris.	
	3 & 4/1/1919.		Brigades cleaning and improving accomodation for the comfort of troops.	
	5/1/1919.		Church Parade. Divisional Rugby Team played a Paris team in Paris and won 6 point to 3 pts.	
	6 - 8/1/1919.		Brigades Training, educational and recreational.	
	9/1/1919.		Two Companies 2nd. R.W.F. sent at 6500 hours to SAILLY LAURETTE to arrest outlaws. Two Australians arrested. Troops returned to Camp 13.00hours.	
	10-11/1/1919.		Brigades training.	
	12/1/1919.		Church Parade.	
	13/1/1919.		Brigades Training.	
	14/1/1919.		Divisional Headquarters closed at GLISY at 0900 hours and reopened QUERRIEU 1200hours.	
	15/1/1919.		Brigades Training.	
	16th.1/1919.		Presentation of Colours to all Battalions of the Division, Pioneers included (2nd. R.W.F. excluded) by G.O.C. Brigades and Divisional and Brigade Staffs attended. Colours consecrated by Rev. Leeks and Rev. Perry, 13th. and 15th. Welch marched past G.O.C. after Ceremony.	
	17/1/1919.		Brigades Training. Soccer match with 10th.S.W.B. and R.A.M.C. played at GLISY. Result R.A.M.C. 5 goals, 10th. S.W.B. 1 goal.	
	18/1/1919.		Soccer match R.E. v 15th. Welsh played at Allonville. R.E. won 1 goal to Nil.	
	19th.	Church Parade.		

Army Form C. 2118

WAR DIARY
or
INTELLIGENCE SUMMARY

General Staff, 38th. (Welsh) Division. (Erased.) (2).

Place	Date	Hour	Summary of Events and Information	Remarks and references to Appendices
	19/1/1919.		Church Parade.	
	20&21/1/1919.		Semi Final Ass. Football Competition R.A.M.C. v 16th. R.W.Fus. R.A.M.C. won 3 goals to 1 goal. Played at FRANVILLERS.	
	21/1/1919.		Brigades Training.	
	22/1/1919.		Rugby Match 38th. Division. v 17th. Division. at PICQUIGNY. 38th. Division won 56 points (2 goal 1 dropped goal. 14 tries) to NIL.	
	23/1/1919.		Final Association Football Match R.A.M.C. v R.E. played at Allonville. Result R.A.M.C. 2 goals R.E. 1.)	
	24/1/1919.		Tug-of-War at LAHOUSSOYE. 17th. R.W.F. beat M.G.C. 13th. R.W.F. beat 15th. Welsh Regt.	
	25/1/1919.		Tug-of-War at LAHOUSSOYE. 17th. R.W.F. beat 121 Bde.R.F.A.	
	26/1/1919.		Church Parade Bishop GWYNNE preached. G.O.C. attended.	
	27/1/1919.		Tug-of-War at LAHOUSSOYE. 17th. R.W.F. beat 13th. R.W.F.	
	28/1/1919.		Cross Country Race. 15th. Welsh Won. Capt Trafford R.F.A. winner.	
	29/12/1919.		Divisional Boxing Tournament. 2nd. R.W.F. v 13th. R.W.F.. 13th. R.W.F. won.	
	30/1/1919.		G.S.O. 2 Major KING MC. Left Division for Poland.	
	31/1/1919.		Brigades Training.	

Instructions regarding War Diaries and Intelligence Summaries are contained in F.S. Regs., Part II. and the Staff Manual respectively. Title Pages will be prepared in manuscript.

Army Form C. 2118.

38th. (Welsh) Division. "General Staff". WAR DIARY or INTELLIGENCE SUMMARY.

(Erase heading not required.)

Place	Date	Hour	Summary of Events and Information	Remarks and references to Appendices
	1919.		Throughout the month Demobilization was proceeding and drafts despatched to the Army of Occupation.	
	Feb. 2nd.		Corps Tug-of-War Competition at VIGNACOURT 38th. Division was beaten in the final by Corps Heavies 2 pulls to NIL. Corps Cross- Country Race at VIGNACOURT 21st. Division won 38th. Division second.	
	Feb. 4th.		Divisional Push Bicycle Race ALBERT TO PONT NOYELLES. M.G.C.Bn. Won. 15th. Welsh Second.	
	Feb. 5th.		Corps Boxing Tournament (Semi-finals) at VAUX 38th. Division was beaten by 17th. Division. H.R.H.Prince of Wales arrived at Divisional Headquarters on a Short Visit.	
	Feb. 8th.		Corps Boxing Tournament (Finals) Pte. WERNER 131st. Field Ambulance, fought Sgt. DULLER 21st. Division and won in a six-round contest.	
	Feb. 9th.		Semi-final Corps Association Football Competition. 38th. Div.(RAMC) v Corps Signals Coy. Score :- 38th.Div. 2 goals -- Corps Signals Coy. 0. H.R.H. Prince of Wales left for 19th. Division. Programme of visit is attached.	
	Feb. 12th.		Final Corps Association Competition at ALLONVILLE 38th. Div.(RAMC) v 21st. Div. Score 21st. Division 3 goals - 38th. Div. 0.	
	Feb. 19th.		Final Corps Rugby Competition at ALLONVILLE 38th. Div. (RAMC) v 21st. Div. Score 38th. Div. 32 points (2 goals and 8 tries) 21st. Div. NIL. Major SYKES and CAPT. PALMER proceeded to England to play in B.EF. Rugby Finals.	
	Feb. 20th.		G.O.C. 38th. Div. assumed command of the "V" CORPS during the absence of the Corps Commander on leave in the U.K.	

www.ingramcontent.com/pod-product-compliance
Lightning Source LLC
Chambersburg PA
CBHW081422300426
44108CB00016BA/2280